Frank Interlandi's July 23, 1976, *Below Olympus* editorial cartoon commemorated the July 20, 1976, *Viking* 1 Mars landing with an imaginary "first" photo: Ray Bradbury's mailbox, already placed on the Red Planet. *Reprinted by permission of Mia Interlandi-Ferreira. © 1976 by the* Los Angeles Times.

REMEMBRANCE

Selected Correspondence of Ray Bradbury

Edited by

JONATHAN R. ELLER

SIMON & SCHUSTER

New York   London   Toronto   Sydney   New Delhi

Simon & Schuster
1230 Avenue of the Americas
New York, NY 10020

First Simon & Schuster hardcover edition November 2023

SIMON & SCHUSTER and colophon are registered trademarks of Simon & Schuster, Inc.

For information about special discounts for bulk purchases, please contact Simon &
Schuster Special Sales at 1-866-506-1949 or business@simonandschuster.com.

The Simon & Schuster Speakers Bureau can bring authors to your live event. For
more information or to book an event, contact the Simon & Schuster Speakers
Bureau at 1-866-248-3049 or visit our website at www.simonspeakers.com.

Interior design by Ruth Lee-Mui

Manufactured in the United States of America

1   3   5   7   9   10   8   6   4   2

Library of Congress Cataloging-in-Publication Data has been applied for.

ISBN 978-1-6680-1697-8
ISBN 978-1-6680-1699-2 (ebook)

From "Remembrance"

. . . .

I came upon an oak where once when I was twelve
I had climbed up and screamed for Skip to get me down.
It was a thousand miles to earth. I shut my eyes and yelled.
My brother, richly compelled to mirth, gave shouts of laughter
And scaled up to rescue me.
"What were you doing there?" he said.
I did not tell. Rather drop me dead.
But I was there to place a note within a squirrel nest
On which I'd written some old secret thing now long forgot.
Now in the green ravine of middle years I stood
Beneath that tree. Why, why, I thought, my God,
It's not so high. Why did I shriek?
It can't be more than fifteen feet above. I'll climb it handily.
And did.
And squatted like an aging ape alone and thanking God
That no one saw this ancient man at antics
Clutched grotesquely to the bole.
But then, ah God, what awe.
The squirrel's hole and long-lost nest were there.

. . . .

I put my hand into the nest. I dug my fingers deep.
Nothing. And still more nothing. Yet digging further
I brought forth:
The note.
Like mothwings neatly powdered on themselves, and folded close
It had survived. No rains had touched, no sunlight bleached
Its stuff. It lay upon my palm. I knew its look:
Ruled paper from an old Sioux Indian Head scribble writing book.
What, what, oh, what had I put there in words
So many years ago?
I opened it. For now I had to know.
I opened it, and wept. I clung then to the tree
And let the tears flow out and down my chin.

Dear boy, strange child, who must have known the years
And reckoned time and smelled sweet death from flowers
In the far churchyard.
It was a message to the future, to myself.
Knowing one day I must arrive, come, seek, return.
From the young one to the old. From the me that was small
And fresh to the me that was large and no longer new.
What did it say that made me weep?
I remember you.
I *remember* you.

Contents

Introduction

THE GREAT WIDE WORLD
OF LETTERS

"The first words. They formed themselves slowly on the incredible paper."

One of the most heartbreaking tales that Ray Bradbury ever wrote was his 1952 story of Cora, a farm wife born and raised so far out in the Missouri hills that she and her husband had never learned to read or write. Now gray-haired and resigned to her circumscribed life, she lives for the summer days when her nephew Benjy will come from far away to visit. This year the boy has a wooden pencil balanced above one ear, a pad of paper, and his reading copy of a battered science fiction pulp magazine full of advertisements. He can write letters for her, and soon product catalogs, informational brochures, and then precious personal letters begin to arrive from the great wide world beyond the hills. Cora means to have Benjy teach her to write, but each day the enchantment of the strange marks he makes on the incredible paper, and the magic of touching and looking at the colorful letters that come in response, distracts her from this goal. Benjy reads her the mail, but soon he must leave and return home. The indecipherable catalogs and letters come less frequently, and finally they fail to come at all.

There is far more to this story than a summary paragraph can reveal, but Ray Bradbury's remarkable life in letters suggests that Cora's "The Great Wide World Over There" represents a reality that he could imagine with great power, but one that he could never have endured. *Remembrance: Selected Correspondence of Ray Bradbury* offers a first pass at the least-known aspect of Bradbury's wide-ranging writing passions. To his unusual gifts as a writer whose enduring fictions and life observations radiated out into stage, film, and television, a writer whose muse explored life through poetry, essays, and interviews, one must add his ability to express his hopes and his fears, his insights and his biases, and finally his great love of life through thousands of letters, almost always written for an audience of one.

Through these letters, we catch glimpses of his long life illuminated by intervals of sunlight in what has largely been darkness. Bradbury was one of the most popular authors of our time, and exemplars of his letters show up occasionally in publications and in the virtual world of online auctions; however, the selection of letters in this volume offers the first sustained look at his inner life from his late teens to his ninth decade. Bradbury's correspondence was far-reaching—he interacted with a rich cross section of twentieth-century cultural figures, writers, film directors, editors, and many people leading private lives who simply wanted insights or encouragement from a writer who had enriched them through his stories and books. The letters selected for this volume can only begin to show the broader tapestry of Ray Bradbury's complicated life, but the organization of the volume into categories of correspondents gives a sense of his progression through life as he knew it, and not necessarily as the public perceived him.

Letters to and from the mentors and influencers of his early decades constitute the first section of *Remembrance*. These correspondents include genre writers like Henry Kuttner, Robert A. Heinlein, Jack Williamson, Theodore Sturgeon, Leigh Brackett, and Edmond Hamilton—writers who sent him on, with blessings, to move into more prominent fields of writing than they themselves had wished to explore. But these mentors knew the broader range of art and literature, and Bradbury's letters occasionally reveal a naive but intense desire to discover the great masters and their influences.

His correspondence with these more experienced hands soon revealed that he cared nothing for genre labels and hated the concept of slanting his writing to maximize income from any of the genre markets. He did slant on occasion, for these markets held even the most experienced and popular writers captive by the limited pay scale that the genre pulps could offer. Bradbury started out making a half cent per word and soon settled in at a penny a word for *Weird Tales*, where he achieved his first success during and just after the war years. But even here he was at a disadvantage, for he never really gave his editors the traditional kind of weirds or formula fantasies that they desired.

Julius Schwartz, his New York pulp market agent during the early and mid-1940s, sometimes had to brace him up: "Where's your next *Weird* yarn—and don't forget horror, not arty or child stuff." But Schwartz was a good negotiator as well, and the editors at *Weird Tales* and the various detective pulps kept buying, sometimes against their better judgment, his off-trail stories, unconventional horror, and improbable child's fantasies. Success in the science fiction pulps soon followed, even though science fiction was often only an armature upon which he could build stories centered on the complexities of the human heart. Bradbury had a unique approach to storytelling, and during World War II, writing in a downtown Los Angeles tenement office by day and in his father's Venice Beach garage by night, he was slowly developing a poetic and metaphor-rich style. He was learning to write about what he knew best in life—the inner world of the child, and the way that world shapes the adult.

As he matured, he would often reveal more discerning discoveries and insights in his correspondence with new mentors—mainstream writers and cultural figures from a wider world. He often shared with them what he was learning about authorship and fame, and how he was beginning to blur the distinctions between popular art and fine art, and between genre fiction and mainstream literature. His letters became more and more insightful, but they never lost the spontaneous joy and sense of wonderment of the young writer who became Ray Bradbury. The second section, "Midcentury Mentors," focuses on such wide-ranging mentors as the Renaissance art historian Bernard Berenson, the British expatriate writer and philosopher Gerald Heard, and the Pulitzer Prize–winning poet Robert Hillyer.

The third section of letters, "Emerging Writers," illuminates significant moments with the younger writers he would influence or inspire in the same informal way that he had experienced during and after the war years. These younger writers include Charles Beaumont, Richard Matheson, Richard Bach, and Stephen King, who was already a prominent writer when he asked Bradbury to discuss the origins of *Something Wicked This*

Way Comes. In section four, "Literary Contemporaries," various mainstream writers and cultural figures respond to his work and his emerging place in postwar literature, including Gore Vidal, Jessamyn West, Somerset Maugham, Faith Baldwin, Anaïs Nin, Carl Sandburg, Graham Greene, poet Helen Bevington, and screenwriter Thomas Steinbeck, who penned one of Bradbury's most cherished letters—an account of the abiding appreciation that his father, Nobel laureate John Steinbeck, had felt for Bradbury's gift as a storyteller. The filmmakers that believed in him, yet who did not always agree with him, come next in section five; they include John Huston, François Truffaut, and Federico Fellini. Sections six and seven focus on Bradbury's interactions with the editors and publishing executives he encountered throughout his career, and literary agents like Don Congdon, whose sixty-year tenure guided Bradbury's negotiations with the fast-paced world of postwar entertainment and publishing in America and abroad.

Bradbury usually went his own way as a cultural visionary, at times antagonizing both the far left and the far right, and these encounters, great and small, are represented in the eighth section of letters, "War and Intolerance." It includes his personal views on the midcentury climate of fear in America, the nuclear brinksmanship of the Cuban Missile Crisis, and his heartfelt grief concerning President Kennedy's assassination. Section nine, "Recognition," recovers the accounts of leaders, including three United States presidents, who recognized his achievements. Sections ten and eleven of the *Selected Correspondence* showcase Bradbury's more personal interactions with friends he cherished, and the working-class Midwestern parents who loved the young writer far more than they ever understood his talents. The twelfth and final section, "Reflections," contains the most ephemeral correspondence of all—the reflective notes he wrote to himself, loose sheets buried here and there in his papers that capture rare interior monologues about himself and the world around him. Each section opens with a passage selected from his letters that provides a context and atmosphere for the correspondence gathered within.

Even his personal letters often focus on the creative projects of the moment, or the work of the younger writers he mentored. Where possible, Bradbury's letters are framed by letters from his correspondents that enrich our understanding of the dynamics at play across his personal and professional letter writing. In essence, though, *Selected Correspondence* reveals a writer who, for the most part, focused on the things he knew best—the hopes and fears, the dreams and nightmares, the loves and hates that rise from childhood and stay with us throughout our lives. He was a writer who felt that if you speak true things about ideas and emotions, you already have an innate style as a writer. Bradbury expressed that style through poetic prose illuminated by the metaphors that welled up from he knew not where. At their best, his letters trigger joy and fascination in the reading. At times his commentaries succumb to self-consciousness and even ego, but his letters almost always tell a story.

Many of these letters are spontaneous reflections of past memories or present experiences freshly felt, but others are veiled by the various masks that Bradbury occasionally pulled up when discussing his creations with editors and filmmakers involved in mediating his work for the reading or viewing public. He felt fiercely proud of his stories and books, and he was often at odds with those who wished to alter his stories and screen-plays. Some of his letters document the private side of his fight to break through the ever-present mainstream critical bias against science fiction and fantasy literature; others offer a counterbalancing sense of renewal that sprang from his firsthand encounters with art, architecture, and the giant machines of the Space Age.

Serious discussions of writer's block, tied to the larger but less tangi-ble terror of writing novel-length fiction, inform key letters to and from his agent Don Congdon and his longtime Doubleday editor, Walter Brad-bury. The short story was his true medium, and it was only natural for him to transform cycles of stories into two of his most enduring works—*The Martian Chronicles* and *Dandelion Wine*. The contents of the *Chronicles* were constantly shifting in his mind, leading him to eventually refashion this book into variant forms that remain in print today. The smoother structure of *Dandelion Wine*, torn from the larger problematic concept of his Illinois novel, would take more than a decade to emerge from that original novel. Letters in this volume also show an aging writer periodi-cally looking back at the young writer he once was, reliving the memories that had once channeled his creativity in mysterious and unpredictable ways.

In July 1976, as the *Viking 1* lander touched down on Mars, Frank

Interlandi's widely circulating newspaper cartoon offered an imagined image of *Viking*'s first photograph of the Martian surface—a bare horizon revealing a solitary mailbox with Ray Bradbury's name on it. Indeed, Bradbury's long and influential career as a storyteller and Space Age visionary ensured that many of his letters would survive. They exist in presidential libraries, in the deposits of major publishing houses, in institutional archives and private collections, and in the homes of countless individuals who wrote to tell him how much they loved his work, receiving a note of encouragement or wisdom in return. Many are known and documented, but the search will go on for decades.

In the end, we are spared the fate of Bradbury's Cora as she cries, "What's going on in that world out there, oh, I'll never know, I'll never know now":

> And at last the day came when the wind blew the mailbox over. In the mornings again, Cora would stand at the open door of her cabin, brushing her gray hair with a slow brush, not speaking, looking at the hills. And in all the years that followed she never passed the fallen mailbox without stooping aimlessly to fumble inside and take her hand out with nothing in it before she wandered on again into the fields.

The great wide world that Ray Bradbury discovered shaped his life and inspired the literature that forms his far-reaching cultural legacy in the twenty-first century. The letters selected for this volume—silent messengers from the past, preserved but largely unseen until now—allow us to witness his world through his eyes and the eyes of some who helped him shape it. Turn the pages and enter this world, reported with more fact than fiction, but unmistakably a Bradbury world of imagination, nonetheless.

—JONATHAN R. ELLER

A Note on Presentation

Ray Bradbury was a prolific correspondent. He prided himself on writing fiction (or adaptations of his fiction) nearly every day of his career, but the ever-increasing count of his known letters indicates that hardly a day passed where he was not deeply engaged in letter writing as well. The goal of this volume is to present as wide a range of his correspondence as possible in a single volume, and that endeavor at times required abridgement to capture the essential points of a letter unobscured by sidebar issues. Bradbury's growing maturity as a correspondent remains evident throughout the volume—there are moments of high and low humor, moments of strong emotion and quiet reflection, always presented here with the intention of illuminating his remarkable life without sensationalizing it.

Ellipsis points set in square brackets within the text of a letter represent points of abridgement for this volume; unbracketed ellipses are those of the author of the letter, made to indicate a pause or transition without the elimination of any text.

Bradbury only rarely indented paragraphs in his letters, but this distinction is a purely physical aspect of his writing and conveys no meaning. All running text paragraphs in the present volume are indented for clarity of presentation.

To avoid confusion, Bradbury's habit of placing titles in all capital letters is modified to reflect standard practice (quotation marks for poetry, essays, and short stories; italics for novels, published plays, and book-length poetry). Titles are also regularized where needed for his correspondents. Distracting spelling errors, such as those caused by typewriter misstrikes, are corrected, but care has been taken to preserve the author's stylistic preferences and eccentricities.

Dates are presented without modification, with one exception: missing dates, or missing portions of a date, are supplied within square brackets.

Heading information, such as addresses, are retained in the letters. Printed letterhead descriptions appear within the calendar entry for the letter at the end of the volume. The calendar entry for each letter provides a basic physical description of the letter and its source or repository.

I have just read two books by an American "scientifiction" author called Ray Bradbury. Most of that *genre* is abysmally bad, a mere transference of ordinary gangster or pirate fiction to the sidereal stage, and a transference which does harm not good. Bigness in itself is of no imaginative value: the defence of a "galactic" empire is *less* interesting than the defence of a little walled town like Troy. But Bradbury has real invention and even knows something about prose. I recommend his *Silver Locusts*.[1]

—C. S. Lewis to Nathan Comfort Starr, February 3, 1953

1

MENTORS AND INFLUENCERS

The Early Years

I sort of miss the old pulp days, to be perfectly
honest. I wasn't making anything, but I was learning
and times were a bit more adventurous.
—*Bradbury to Leigh Brackett and Edmond Hamilton, June 25, 1951*

EDGAR RICE BURROUGHS

The creator of Tarzan, Pellucidar, and John Carter of Mars was not a direct Bradbury mentor, but the adventure novels of Edgar Rice Burroughs (1875–1950) were a great inspiration for a young boy in Waukegan who roller-skated downtown to buy his father's weekend newspapers and their precious cargo of Tarzan comic strip adaptations. He continued to read Burroughs after his family moved to Los Angeles, and during his senior year in high school he began working on the publications of the local Science Fiction League chapter of fans and writers. Bradbury's letter inviting Burroughs to one of the league's bimonthly meetings survives, offering a sense of some of the writers the chapter had managed to bring in from time to time. Burroughs declined, citing a reluctance to speak in front of audiences, but Bradbury never lost his appreciation of the possibilities that Burroughs opened up to his own emerging imagination: "You must close part of your mature mind," he later observed, "to appreciate his wonders."

[November 1937]

Edgar Rice Burroughs
c/ of E. R. Burroughs Inc.
Tarzana, Calif.

Dear Mr. Burroughs:

Here in Los Angeles is located what we think is one of the most active branches of the Science Fiction League in America. We have our own magazine that we put out monthly and we have a fine record of famous people attending our meetings. It is a highly informal affair and we usually have about twenty members present. Since you are the most famous fiction writer in your type of story we have often wished to have a chance to meet you and talk things over with you. We have had many great writers from *Astounding Stories* come up and visit, most recently, Dr. Keller,[1] writer of hundreds of stories.

We hope that it won't be asking too much of you that if at any time in the future you are in Los Angeles you could drop in and see us at the

Brown Room in Clifton's Cafeteria on the second floor some Thursday evening. We have our meetings every two weeks on Thursday and if you could write me ahead of time when you are coming I would be glad to fix up a special meeting to fit your plans.

> Hoping to find you well
> I remain
> Ray Bradbury
> 1619 So. St. Andrews Place.
> Los Angeles, Calif

November 15, 1937

Mr. Ray Bradbury,
1619 So. St. Andrews Place,
Los Angeles, California.

My dear Mr. Bradbury:

I have to acknowledge, with thanks, your invitation to meet with the Los Angeles Branch of the Science Fiction League some Thursday evening.

Unfortunately, Thursday is the one evening in the week upon which it is almost impossible for me to depend for outside engagements. However, if at any time in the future, I find that I shall be free on Thursday, I shall be glad to let you know.

Again thanking you for the invitation, I am,

> Very truly yours,
> Edgar Rice Burroughs

Bradbury often observed that one should never be afraid to ask for something, especially if the wish were close to the heart. He apparently wrote a more determined note to Burroughs offering a more flexible window of time for the proposed LASFL visit. This led Burroughs to be candid with Bradbury while maintaining the appreciative tone that he felt toward his seventeen-year-old correspondent and the fans of the LASFL chapter.

November 22, 1937

Mr. Ray Bradbury,
1619 So. St. Andrews Place,
Los Angeles, California.

My dear Mr. Bradbury:

Now you have really put me on a spot and compelled me to explain to you that I never appear or speak in public, if there is any possible way in which it can be avoided.

I hope that you understand that it is not due to any lack of desire to co-operate with you and that I fully appreciate, and am grateful for having been honored by the invitation.

With all good wishes, I am,

Very sincerely yours,
Edgar Rice Burroughs

———————————————

ROBERT A. HEINLEIN

Twenty-year-old Ray Bradbury already knew Robert Anson Heinlein (1907–1988) from Los Angeles Science Fantasy Society meetings, and in 1940 Heinlein helped Bradbury place his first unpaid professional stories (little more than humorous anecdotes) in the pages of Rob Wagner's Script *magazine. Heinlein's Naval Academy education and experiences had informed his rise to prominence in the pages of* Astounding; *following his wartime work in naval research and development on the East Coast, Heinlein would return to full-time writing and become a major force in defining postwar science fiction in America.*

During the summer of 1940 Heinlein was in Chicago, and Bradbury wrote to continue some of the discussions begun in the "bull sessions" at Heinlein's home "on the hill" at Laurel Canyon. This letter remains unlocated, but Heinlein's answer has survived in Bradbury's papers, and it provides a sense of their relationship before the war years interrupted Heinlein's influence on his younger friend.

6104 Woodlawn
Chicago, Ill.

August 9, 1940

Dear Ray,

I am afraid that this will be a pretty skeletonized answer to your long and delightful letter. I let mail accumulate while completing a long (46,000 word) item, and am now too far behind to catch up properly. Let's look forward to another long, leisurely bull session on the hill sometime in September.

I don't know whether we will be at the convention or not. Reinsberg[2] tells me that you are coming—I hope so—but I may be forced by other matters to leave here sooner.

I have every intention of enclosing the dime for FuFa.[3] Look and see if I did it.

I'm not going to say anything about the war or politics. Those are matters more suited to a bull session. The whole business is depressing any way you look at it.

I hope that you are still keeping at your writing, and that you will have some more manuscripts that I can read when we get back. You are on the right track, I am sure.

We are leaving here for a few days (mail address unchanged) to visit Doctor Smith and his wife in Michigan.[4] After that, probably very soon after that, we will be trekking for good ol' Southern California, God's Country, hooray—and I can lick the guy who says I don't mean it, at least I can with my brother's help.

Till then, best,

Bob

Bob Heinlein

JACK WILLIAMSON

John Stewart (Jack) Williamson (1908–2006) moved to Los Angeles in 1940, and Bradbury was amazed that this well-known writer from the New Mexico highlands was willing to read and critique his stories. Williamson had broken into the genre pulps in 1928 and would continue to be a significant influence in genre fiction for the rest of his long life, winning Hugo and Nebula awards well past the age of ninety. In 1976, Williamson would become the second Grand Master named by the Science Fiction Writers of America; a dozen years later, Bradbury himself would become the tenth. When Williamson went home to New Mexico for a time in the spring of 1941, Bradbury wrote with updates on his writing fortunes just months before selling his first science fiction tale.

April 23, 1941

3054½ W. 12th Street
Los Angeles, Cal.

Dear Jack:

During a lull between stories I looked about myself and muttered, "Undeniably, there is something askew." [. . .]

Williamson was gone and had been gone for weeks. The niche which he filled in the hodge-podge whirlpool of life in L.A. was vacuumed clean and Jack had hied himself off to squat over a steaming typewriter in lonely N.M.

This state of affairs is fast becoming unendurable. What can Bradbury do on afternoons when he has finished a story and wishes friendly banter, a bit of criticism, an understanding ear [. . .] What are the Heinleins to do without that tall, easy-walking New Mexican. What will we all do? [. . .]

My detective story "On the Nose," the yarn about the criminal and the garbage truck, has been rejected by Munsey, *Thrilling*, Street and Smith and is now under submission at Popular's *Black Mask*. Nuts![5]

Sent my dinosaur story to Pohl. No report. Tremaine rejected "The

Hunt" and I sent it to Wollheim. *Story* rejected my story "The Well" and I sent it to *Harper's*. Wollheim rejected my story "Levers," I chopped four thousand words out of it and submitted it to Pohl, along with "Double Talk." Hornig rejected "Double Talk" because it was too good for his mag. Honest. Said I was writing over the heads of his public, which is puerile. Wollheim didn't like "Double Talk" at all, he has no sense of humor. But Horning almost split a gut laffing at it.[6] Ah, well, these editors. [. . .]

I just rifled my files and took one million words out and burned them up. I checked thru them all carefully, to make sure I didn't destroy anything valuable. Most of it was inane description, no plot, no idea. It hampered me, so I destroyed it. Still have another million words lying here staring me in the face. [. . .]

Not much other news. I stay home so much it isn't funny. Never go anywhere in the morning, always home typing, which is good. I manage to turn out at least a thousand words a day. I'm not saying this is finished copy, but at least I make that many marks on paper.

Don't get to shows at all anymore. And, if I do, I patronize the dime shows. Money, money, money. Olympic Blvd. still looks like a disgruntled potato patch, damn it! They'll *never* get it done.[7]

Guess it's time for me to buzz off, Jack.

Gosh, fella, you better come back to L.A. soon or we'll come down there and *get* you!

Sincerely,
Still an amateur hack,
Your friend,
Ray

HENRY HASSE

Bradbury's ability to sell off-trail but successful weird fantasies and detective fiction developed during the war years, while he was still finding his own science-fictional voice and original storylines. For a time, he collaborated with Henry Hasse (1913–1977), whose 1935 novella He Who Shrank *became a historical marker for pre–Golden Age science fiction.*

By 1939 the Seattle-based Hasse was corresponding with Bradbury and contributing to issues of Bradbury's Futuria Fantasia *fanzine. Hasse came to Los Angeles in December 1940 and began to work on five of Bradbury's science fiction stories that were in need of narrative refinement. Three eventually reached print, including a rewrite of Bradbury's amateur tale "Pendulum" (*Super Science Stories, *November 1941), his first paid professional sale. Bradbury's subsequent letters to Hasse reflected an author in the making, focused as much on comic adventures with their mutual fan-friends as on the world of science fiction publishing. Wartime delays in publication masked the fact that their collaborations were relatively short-lived; by late 1941, Bradbury was already making his own way as a maturing writer.*

August 2nd [1942]

3054½ W. 12th Street.
Los Angeles. Calif.

Dear Hank:

Nice to hear from you again; your position seems to be agreeing with you in Washington[8]—how does one get such a position and what does one have to do???????

How do you find time to write? And if you do write, where do you find room? I thot that conditions in Wash. were supposedly impossible. Rumor says that the neatest thing procurable is an upholstered sewer with hot and cold running politicians. Anyway, I'm certainly pleased you and Reiss[9] are getting along so lovey-dovey.

Firstly, allow me to get my good news off my chest. During the month of July I made three sales. First, I sold "The Candle" to *Weird Tales*, it will probably be out in September or November, don't know which issue.[10] Then, two weeks later, Campbell sent me a check for my short-short "Eat, Drink, and Be Wary" which appeared in the *Astounding* with the American flag on the cover . . . twenty bucks for three hours work, yah man!! (as I recall, you once predicted I would sell junior[11] before you would . . . here's hoping you can nick him soon) . . .

Lastly, a week ago, I sold a five thousand worder to *Thrilling Wonder*, which makes my third sale there, including "Gabriel's Horn," "The Piper" and this new one "Promotion to Satellite," which is a honey. Julie thot it my best.[12]

I'm working on a twenty thousand worder slanted for *Astounding* and it is the damnedest job I've ever tackled.[13] But it certainly will pay off if it hits. I've done a few love stories and I have a contact in New York now with a woman agent who handles stories to the slicks. I am being referred to her by Virginia Perdue who writes mystery novels for the Doubleday Doran Crime Club series, friend of the Heinleins I met last fall.[14]

Now, as to your requests.

If you had kept in contact with Julie you would know by now that Ray Palmer wants "Final Victim" for *Amazing*. He has instructed Julie to resubmit the story in the autumn, which isn't far off, explaining that he won't be given his fall budget allowance until then, and therefore he can't buy it now. He has also told Rocklin and Charlie Tanner[15] to resubmit material for sale, and I think it looks legitimate and almost certain. For further information, I suggest you contact Julie . . . I think it would pay to sell to Palmer and get ourselves in his good graces . . . it would mean a new market for both of us . . . and possibly future sales . . . even for such a story as "City of Intangibles" if Reiss doesn't take it.

Anyway, I'm sending you "City of Intangibles." I always have liked the basic idea of this one.

Rewrite it on the sixty-forty basis (60-40) we discussed earlier this year . . . if you make *remarkable* changes. But if the changes are really infinitesimal, which they probably won't be, now that I look at this piece of cheese, I shall expect the regular split. Anyway, make the changes, sixty-forty, and give me a by-line and I'll be happy . . .

OH, YES—one more thing ** in case they have too many of your stories on hand at Reiss and want to change your name, this action, of course, won't affect my by-line at all . . . the by-lines will read, for instance:

"The City of Intangibles"		"The City of Intangibles"
by		by
Hatzell Glinkh	or	R. Finkle Smootze
and		and
Ray Bradbury		(guess who?)

We'll keep "Final Victim" on ice until Palmer buys it, or rejects it. Then, if he bounces it, which is doubtful, I'll whip it to you and you can sixty-forty it to Reiss. I'm certainly glad you wrote, I've been wanting to do something about "City of Intangibles" for a long time.

I've been ushering at the Bowl this summer and just concluded seeing the Ballet Russe . . . one of the most entrancing experiences in my remembrances. Particularly liked *Rouge et Noir* and *Gaîté Parisienne*.

Who do I see at the Biltmore about ushering???[16] *Arsenic and Old Lace* is showing . . .

Does Julie handle any of your stuff any more? Or is your love for him dormant.

Belated congrats on your marriage, I hope it helps you in your writing.

Drop me a card and tell me where in hell to get in contact with Hannes.[17] Also all the other news.

Write soon, telling me what you think of all this.

Pleasant thoughts,
Ray

New address: 670 Venice Blvd.,
Venice, California.

Dec. 1942[18]

Dear Henry:

A bit late, perhaps, but still—a Happy new year to you and the wife.
I've talked with Mrs. Finn[19] lately and she says you two are happy,
and I'm glad to hear it. I hope you have time to write stories with
your Washington job, but as I recall from your last letter you were
quite in love with your work and not over-taxed for strength. You
and Reiss certainly get along fine. Brackett, Rocklynne and Hasse
seem to be the steadiest contributors Reiss has. Almost sold him a
yarn myself a few weeks back: Peacock[20] okayed it, but Reiss put the
squelch on the deal because the yarn was a little too off-trail. Hell.
Well, try again.

Briefly, my luck has turned up in the last few months. Two stories in
Weird already, one in the current issue which I think you'll enjoy—"The
Wind." And a third one coming up soon.[21] Outside of that I have placed
a yarn with Norton and several new stories with Margulies.[22] Wonder
when "Gab's Horn" comes out? Indications are that I'll sell to Campbell
again soon, and Palmer is supposed to kick through in a few days with a
check or two.[23] So things don't look too badly.

L.A. is beginning to resemble a haunted city. Only science-fictioneers
around town are women and 4-F's like Freehafer, Yerke and Bradbury,
not to count Joquel and a few others.[24] Nice to see Finn back. Haven't
been to many meetings lately.

The latest *Planet Stories* brings back dear memories to me. DePina
and Hasse. God, it was a long time ago you two were hopping on that
story together. And that ending: "a deep, singing quiet, too deep for
tears" that you've used in several stories.[25] Bless you, Henry. The
good old days, walking in Westlake Park, talking. We used to talk and
walk a helluva lot and I still remember it pleasantly. Walk until two
in the morning, and get picked up by the cops who thought we were
burglars. Remember the night in Pershing Square when we were eating

crackers, and the two plain clothes men stopped us and searched us and we answered questions, meanwhile cramming our mouths with soda wafers and spluttering crumbs in their faces, and finally wound up offering them some crackers? I laugh every time I think about it.[26] We had a lot of fun before the World and Fate and a lot of other things got around to splitting us and shoving us to the furthest ends of a continent.

What ever happened to "City of Intangibles"?[27] I talked to Finn about it, and she said you were just getting around to rewriting it when she left Washington. True? Or have you already had it rejected by Reiss? I'd like to know how it turned out. I'd enjoy hitting *Planet* very much.

Brackett and Kuttner have been a great help to me of late. Kuttner sent me an eight page critique on a story slanted for Campbell which I hope to have finished in a few weeks, and Brackett has been teaching me how to put "guts" in my story.[28] She's a wonder.

How is your housing problem? Do you have to sleep in a closet with the war correspondents, or do you have a bath-tub all to yourself? Washington sounds dazedly hectic to me. I'd like to come back that way next year, oops—I mean this year—if money, draft board and such permit.

My draft board has deferred me until June or July. After that—I'm praying. With guys like Ackerman and Hoffman going, I can't last long.

Have you read *Rocket to the Morgue*?[29] They say the murdered man might be Yerke? Who knows?

What's new from Hannes? Haven't written him in sooooo long. His *Unknown* novel was fair; too much description and not a damned mite of story.[30] I got tired about page forty and quit. His short stories are good, and I looked forward eagerly to the novel, but it disappointed me. Well, he'll learn. I look to see his next novel five times as good. It certainly was luck his selling that yarn. I bet it paid his board and room for the next year and a half.

I saw the Ballet this year. First time in my life. Saw every single performance. Favorites? *Rodeo, Gaîté Parisienne, The Snow Maiden, Rouge et Noir*, and, though trite, *Scheherazade*. And the others of course, in varying shades of approval and delight. The new Ballet Theatre arrives here in February for ten days and it's a sure bet for good entertainment.

Well—time to go. Have a heavy job of writing to do. Best of luck to you in your writing this year, and will you please write soon, Henry. I'd like to know what's been going on back there. Thanks.

Until next time, then,

Your friend,
Ray

P.S. Just got a letter from Julie and I have placed a third story with Norton![31]

HENRY KUTTNER

The versatile and prolific genre author Henry Kuttner (1915–1958) was perhaps Bradbury's most influential mentor during the World War II period. Kuttner's initial success in Weird Tales *rapidly expanded into the science fiction and fantasy pulps prior to World War II. He was well-read, apolitical, and evenhanded in his dealings with writers across these genres, and he had a solid understanding of both the genre and mainstream publishing worlds. In 1940, his marriage to the gifted writer C. L. Moore (1911–1987) led to a seamless collaborative dynamic in much of his subsequent work, veiled effectively by the Kuttner-Moore use of many individual and joint pseudonyms. Moore's views also surface in very subtle ways through Kuttner's letters to Bradbury.*

December 21, 1944

15 Pinecrest Dr.
Hastings-on-Hudson, N. Y.

Dear Ray:

Your letter, and the tequila, arrived together, yesterday. I was delighted to see that the tequila wasn't the ersatz rotgut from Cuba, but the genuine Mexican mescal. There's all the difference in the world between the two, but I stupidly forgot to qualify the matter previously. Your liquor dealer apparently knows what good tequila is. I have purchased lemons, and your health will be drunk. You may be in jail by now, of course, if the postal authorities have caught up with you, but I'll smuggle a file to you in a chocolate cake. *My* liquor dealer said that alcoholic stuff could be sent by express, and I cannot help but feel that something is wrong with this country. You have done halcyon service, however, and I feel slightly guilty about letting you in for such a hell of a job. Not too guilty, though, for the exercise is undoubtedly good for your fat little figure. If you should want a few Rockettes, or some cocaine, from New York, just let me know. I am especially pleased with the fact that the stuff masqueraded as bubble bath cologne. That has a mad, eerie note that puts the finishing touch on the whole fantastic affair. I confess that I was tempted yesterday to send you a wire saying, "I have just gone on the wagon," but I was sure it would drive you mad, so I didn't. I am at present recuperating from a binge in Rochester; Virgil Finlay got a pre-embarkation furlough, and we spent several days with him and his wife in Rochester—getting snowed in in the worst snowfall in 38 years.

I ain't read none of your stories lately.

Interested in what you say about DePina. I'd noticed a similarity in one of his recent *Planet* tales to Kat's "Judgment Night," and I am glad you confirm my judgment. Some day when I feel nasty I'll drop in on Peacock[32] and ask him what the hell that bastard DePina means by plagiarizing Kat's material. I'll let you know what happens. Guys who write letters praising themselves and decrying other writers deserve a kick in the groin, anyway. It is the hall-mark of the amateur—and the bastard. Me—I will never decry another writer's story to an editor, though I can and do praise 'em. I remember once De Camp sent a post-card to me, via Leo, pointing out an error in history I'd made in a *Startling* novel.[33] It was the post-card business that griped me. But I do not like De Camp anyway, so . . . . .

Murray Leinster (Will Jenkins) is, I gather, putting together a book of imaginative, fantastic and off-trail stories gathered entirely from the pulps. I forget the publisher, but it's a good one. An anthology, of course. Dunno whose stories he'll pick, but you might cross your fingers. Mine are crossed already. Incidentally, I rather gather that if Derleth publishes one's work in an Arkham House collection, he takes 50% of all future reprint rights. Don't quote me, as I didn't get it directly from Derleth—but it is certainly something I'm going to investigate before I close any deal with him. [. . .]

Kat says thanks and she's glad you liked "No Woman Born." She says she read a book on ballet. We are not as yet balletomaniacs, but are considering it. Got tickets tomorrow night for Dali's surrealistic ballet, *The Mad Tristram*. The reviews sounded fascinating. Tristram dying on a mad brain with white worms crooning lullabies. We shall see.

I shall look up the Chandler *Atlantic* article.[34] I do not like Huxley, though. Thought *Time Must Have a Stop* was awful. But *Forever Amber* was worse. Still, the worst book of all time was *The Robe*. And *The Love Letters* disappointed me. But I picked up Virgil Partch's little book of cartoons, and it's very fine. A little troubling, however.

Heigh-ho. Why don't you tackle a detective novel? I hear the markets are very, very wide open. I'm still trying to get at my various novels, but buying a house involves entirely unexpected expenses, and I must knock out a batch of pulp first. A couple of months at most should see me clear, however. As for trips west, I doubt if it'll be until spring. I finally discovered why the furnace wasn't heating the house. It seems that the radiators should be filled with hot water, and it's necessary to twist a tiny valve and let the air out, so the water can come in. Once I'd done that, the temperature rose sharply from 30 to 80. Science, bah.

It will be a white Christmas here, It snew [*sic*] a great deal. Pleasant. It's stimulating weather. . . . Just picked up a Rousseau reproduction. *Sleeping Gypsy*, for four bucks. Do you know Rousseau's work? American primitive, like Max Ernst—exotic jungle nightmare stuff.[35] . . . New movies that look good, but that haven't hit town yet, are *Farewell, My Lovely*, and *The House on Half-Moon Street* (?), with Nils Asther.[36]

And that seems to be all, pro tem.

Merry Christmas. *meu rapaz*,
Hank

Christmas Day, 1944—

Dear Hank,

The check received, and you are entirely welcome. The file in the
chocolate cake will not be necessary. In the future I'll be warned
concerning types of tequila; Cuban or Mexican I haven't acquired a taste
for it, but perhaps as I grow mellower . . . ?

Thinking back, I realize that I didn't say half enough about my real
feelings concerning "No Woman Born." I particularly want to point out
one scene which I believe is the damndest nicest bit of drama I've read
in any of Cat's yarns, bar none.[37] It's the scene of Deirdre's introduction
to the American public, in which the curtains part mistily one by one,
she descends the steps, she dances, she goes back up the steps, and
then—God Allmighty!—she laughs! *That laughter.* That's what got me.
I think it was wonderful! Only Cat would have thought of that. It was a
priceless touch. I still get chills up my spine when I think of it. And as
for the rest of the story, I honestly believe there's plenty of room ahead
for a sequel. I don't know, of course, whether Cat contemplates one.
In some ways, it might be best, leaving the yarn with its present, fine
ending. But in other ways my curiosity is aroused to a high, interested
pitch. Deirdre is really a character unto herself. I was surprised to
hear that Cat had "read a book" on the ballet. Her descriptions of the
dance were far better than stuff I've read on the dance by accomplished
balletomaniacs.[38] Incidentally, that Dali ballet sounds fascinating, I hope
it gets out here next year. Which group was it, The Ballet Theatre or the
Russe Covey?[39]

I've just finished reading Huxley's *Time Must Have a Stop* and
I am heartened to hear that you acclaim it awful. I was frankly
nonplussed with the thing. I got a snort out of your mentioning *The
Robe. The Robe* was given to me for my birthday in August. I made a
face, hastened down to the book store a number of weeks later, when
nobody was looking, and traded in the book for *Time Must Have a Stop,*
which, it turns out, was simply jumping from the frying pan into the
Gaseous Vertebrate.[40] In reading the Huxley blurb on the frontispiece
I wondered how in hell he could accomplish the transition from

Sebastian the boy into Sebastian the man in three hundred pages. He
didn't. The abrupt transition in the last chapter, from boy to man,
was quite a jolt for me, anyway, and the book did not convince me of
a darn thing. At first I attributed the failure to myself and my way of
thinking. Recalling Fadiman's article and his saying that it had taken
him sometimes as much as twenty years to read and appreciate certain
books, I immediately wondered if perhaps I shouldn't wait a year or
so and try *Time Must Have a Stop* again. But now that you make unkind
remarks concerning it, my doubts are confirmed. I'd like your opinion
on the metaphysical aspects of the book. I couldn't get head nor tail
from them, though here or there there were certain remarks made
which I could nod my head over and silently affirm. But, on the whole,
I found nothing in the book to clutch or believe in, because, like most
guys who try writing, I'm honestly looking for some philosophy which
correlates the old religiosity with the newer precepts of science. Perhaps
this is impossible. But I've grown out of my atheism (age fifteen to
twenty) and I've yet to find a religion that measures up to what I think
a religion should be. Perhaps you or Cat have evolved some philosophy
that might be of interest to me, or you may have read some good books
on the subject you might recommend.

"Before I Wake," by Henry Kuttner, was, I might say at this point, a
very pleasant little yarn.[41] I detect a reaction in the yarn to the idealistic
brats of Bradbury. Such sentences as the following: "—Pete might have
let his father crush the toad, but somehow he didn't, though he was
no kinder than the average boy—" were read thoughtfully. I shall learn
from Papa Kuttner and be far wickeder in the future . . .

If you read the *Saturday Review of Lit.*, you probably glimpsed the
article recently which tromped all over Franz Werfel for his recent
metaphysical journeys.[42] At a time when the world needs straight,
clean, hard thinking, Werfel insists upon stomping around, muddying
up the waters with a lot of poppycock. The article observed how
"Religiosity" like a disease, seems to attack middle-aged authors, even
Somerset Maugham, whose mind has generally been pretty lucid. The
advent of so many books on religion is disturbing at this time because
it leads man away from his real, factual, scientific problems. A picture
like *The Song of Bernadette*, for instance, which harps on miracles and

encourages superstition at a time when a lot of it should be junked, is really dangerous, I believe. There's too much lazy thinking in the world now. Faith isn't enough to solve our problems, though it may help. Naturally it'll help to *Believe* in peace, but as Dewey points out (I've read one chapter of Dewey, so I can afford to toss him in here to impress you) the trouble with our civilization is separation of means from end.[43] We talk a hell of a lot about peace, but when a problem arises which we can handle objectively, our beautiful ideas are not set in operation. [. . .]

I've had a helluva swell time during the past year discovering all kinds of art forms in my relaxation periods.[44] I've worked up a good liking for Van Gogh's paintings. I used to detest them. I've come to understand some of, but not all, Picasso's work, though I think his latest work (in *Life* magazine) stinks. I've done some water colors, sculptured some strange little modernistic men and women in clay, designed some interesting plates and painted their motifs in underglaze, my interest in ballet has increased, naturally, I get a kick out of Rachmaninoff (listen to his *Variations on a Theme of Paganini*, played by himself) or Prokofiev or Shostakovich. All in all, I'm trying to give myself a liberal education in politics, psychology and art. I've often wondered whether attending college would help my writing, but, from what I read, more good talent is broken in short story classes, than is ever made. Don't know if I ever asked you or not, but have you read Lajos Egri's book *How to Write a Play*? I don't mind confessing that its simple, basic, resilient rules of dramatic and dynamic law have helped me many times in the past. He only points a direction and seems not to constrict one with irrational diagrams and rules and numbers and charts. He points out the simple realities of character, conflict and theme very successfully. I'd like to know your opinion of him. This is Christmas day and I've been given *Brave New World* (by the way, do you dislike *all* of Huxley, or did you like this book?) and *Cluny Brown* by Margery Sharp, which should be a nice change from the super-morbid fare I've been at recently. Your comment on *Forever Amber* was correct. I read the first three pages and put it back on the shelf. Virgil Partch is quite a nice genius. His drawings are inspiring, especially that one of the guy in the bathtub with the tidal wave. [. . .]

I'm not familiar with Rousseau, but I'll look him up. Any other good classics you might suggest would be welcome. I'm not at all familiar with most of the writers before 1920, so you see I have a helluva lot to catch up on.

[. . .] Interested, *very* interested, though, in hearing about Leinster's anthology.[45] I wish there were some way for an author to (subtly) suggest his stories for such a book. I'm crossing my fingers. I hope he reads *Weird Tales* and all the rest. If you hear anything more concerning it, will you please drop me the news?

I was surprised to hear about Derleth taking fifty percent of all future reprint rights on stories used in the Arkham books. When you find out more about it, I'd like to know about it, too. [. . .]

Oh, yeah, next time you're in a record store, ask to hear *The Lonesome Train*. Norman Corwin produced it. Earl Robinson wrote it. Decca Records. Burl Ives singing, full chorus, orchestra. Wonderful! You'll want to own it.

Yours for fewer DePinas,
Happy New Year!
Ray

P.S. Okay, so I can't stop, but it occurred to me the other p.m. that it was pretty interesting that at the beginning of this century a remarkable thing was happening; the writers of the U.S. were getting away from romanticism into realism, but, simultaneously, the painters of the world were getting away from realism into impressionism, surrealism and such. Two art forms moving in divergent orbits. Or perhaps moving in the same direction, but one slower than the other, art started first toward impressionism, and the impressionistic writers followed at a much later date. Sorta interestin', huh? I wonder if anything has been written correlating the two?

'Bye.

March 5, 1945.

Dear Ray:

Things have been screwed up here as usual. Your travelogue letter was
safely received, read with much interest, and the suggestions acted
upon.[46] [. . .] Spring and autumn are the pleasant times in the east, and
therefore we'll postpone the Mexican trip either till hot summer or
cold winter—depending on how hot it gets around July. Since we are
back in the groove as far as writing goes, we don't want to interrupt the
program, though a vacation would be pleasant now. Still and all, this *is*
the country—the Hudson River flows broadly below, with only a few
ice-cakes on it, the melting snow reveals a horrible-looking yard full of
tattered brown leaves, through which green stuff peeps shyly; and I have
got the furnace's shoulders to the mat at last. Not that I don't have my
worries. A squirrel comes and sits on the windowsill and criticizes my
work, and blinding headaches have resulted in the welcome news that I
need new glasses—my old ones were from an army prescription, written
by an army doctor who was a great fool. However, my new lenses should
be ready tomorrow. I'm going to find out about contact lenses. If I
can get 'em, I can paint 'em blue and commit murder with impunity.
Impunity (Lester L.) is a homicidal philologist who lives in Squalor,
New Jersey, and a fine, good man he is, too. Where the hell was I?
      I have had quite an arduous program—had to watch my health, buy
this house, furnish it, and make dough at the same time. Not too easy.
I think I have it licked now, though. Finished a *Startling* last week—but
it took me a month to write. Am starting on a *Planet* yarn I promised
Peacock months ago. Peacock's a pleasant chap, I think he was once a
fan; anyhow, he's still a bit wide-eyed. Oh—you'll be interested in this.
Remember your remarks that DePina was—shall we say?—influenced
by Kat's work? I'd noticed that too, notably a re-written lift from the
Cyrille sequences of "Judgment Night." I talked it over with Peacock,
and learn that DePina, a western boy, is very much of a screwball, if
not actively psychopathic. He has delusions of grandeur, curses editors
when they reject his stuff, and (I believe) is pretty old. Ah, well. Did W.
Scott take the collab you did with Leigh? I'd be surprised if he didn't.[47]

Well. As for the Arkham House books—I have more information
now. August W. (for William) tells me that his contract is the usual
one, approved by the Author's Guild; it's true that he requires 50% of
reprint rights; but on radio, movie, etc., rights, he takes no cut unless
he's agented the stuff. In that case, 10%. Aside from that 50% reprint
business, the contract is, I think, fair. And that 50% angle is for the
writer to decide. I'm still undecided. It would depend, I think, on
what material I gave him. The old *WT* Gothic stuff—okay. The Padgett
stuff—I doubt it, for I think I might sell it as a collection to some
other house. Our contract with Messner's demands a percentage of
pocketbook rights, movie rights, etc., so Arkham House isn't chiseling
without precedent. Your idea about withholding material for *Child's
Garden of Terror* sounds practical.[48] My experience seems to indicate
that such an anthology—for either Bradbury or Kuttner—would be
damned hard to sell unless we'd a book out first—a novel. That guy who
wrote *The Great Fog and Others*. Previously he'd done *A Taste for Honey*
and a couple of other whodunits.[49]

Henry Holt published de Camp's books; I know they like fantasy. Try
them? But I do think getting a novel out first is a desideratum. (Good
word that. I'll use it again. Desideratum. There.) Have you any ideas
on tackling novels? Incidentally, I got another letter from *Collier's* last
week asking for stuff; why not try a kid story—a non-weird—with them?
They're unusually wide open. As for the Jenkins anthology, I've heard
nothing. As for Gillings, it takes months for letters to go to and from him.

Here's a possibility: you might write a number of publishers, stating
that you have had published in magazines a group of fantasies and weird
stories, with the child angle—and also some mystery-detective tales
from that angle, like that lovely about the gal in the attic trunk—and
would they be interested in taking a look at them for consideration as a
collection. *The Author and Journalist* runs a list of book publishers twice
a year; the library has it. Or look over the book sections of the papers
and see what publishers are advertising largely. From the response
you get, you'll be able to see how the wind blows. When I was with
D'Orsay,[50] I know we used to do that—query publishers and/or editors
when we had something unusual on hand. We seldom did, though.

You might try it that way. I doubt if Ann Watkins or any non-fee agent would want to handle the material unless you already had a nibble. A novel would be another matter, of course.

Julie told me you had a yarn up with Campbell; did he take it? Curious: Campbell is extremely sentimental, but he prides himself on not being sentimental; on having no emotions whatsoever. Whenever I do a Padgett story, I put on a Van Dyke, pince-nez, and look like Woodrow Wilson. I think Padgett resembles Wilson; a pedantic, sneering bastard, who teaches psychology at N.Y.U. We hate him. Lawrence O'Donnell, on the other hand, is a frowsy-headed Irishman—a professional Irishman—who seldom gets a haircut and who gets drunk and blathers loudly. Keith Hammond is a dreamy-eyed, thin person, much underweight; Paul Edmonds is an ex-reporter who looks like Pat O'Brien. Pseudonyms fascinate me. . . . As for selling to Campbell, however, I think it's partly bluff, partly underwriting. Ever notice that the general policy of his stories is, "See how smart I am? If you don't understand what I'm talking about, you're a great fool." There is also the matter of gadgets; but I will not write about gadgets, like most of his writers—partly because I'm no scientist, partly because I hate gadgets. I think Campbell believes I'm an expert psychologist. I use long words like empathy and deistic. Though what they mean I shall never know. One disadvantage of writing much for Campbell is that it's apt to spoil you for other markets; you specialize too much. Luckily I can write about what I want for him—no gadgets, by God!—but if he tried to make me follow a formula, I'd quit. If I want to write formula, I can do it for Leo, and get praise too. . . . My eyes are paining me. I must rest 'em.

Thanks again for the Mexico dope,[51] which we are saving for later use. Kat says hi; I say

Pff-f-f-t!

Hank

Kuttner's advice on how to approach the major market publishing houses and magazines was a big factor in Bradbury's submission and sale of four main-stream magazine stories during the spring and summer of 1945. As these stories began to reach print in 1945 and early 1946, Kuttner sensed that Bradbury no

longer needed the close attention of a mentor. When Bradbury sent him tear
sheets from the November 1945 issue of Mademoiselle *for his story "Invisible*
Boy," Kuttner used this milestone as an opportunity to bless his work and his
future in the gruff tones that Bradbury had come to appreciate over the years.

Jan 15 1946

Dear Ray

"Invisible Boy" is chiefly interesting to me as part of a pattern rather than
for itself. You haven't settled down as yet, and are experimenting, which I
think is fine. You've broken away from formula, while still using parts of it
when you need it, and you're putting in effective emotional stuff too. One
criticism I could make is that you're playing around too much with weird/
tricky dialect and unusual ways of saying what you mean, but I won't
make that criticism because I don't think it's a valid one, especially at
this point. A whole novel told in an over-elaborated style might easily go
haywire—for my chips, Jesse Stuart's long stuff stinks—but Dos Passos,
Steinbeck, etc., use a variety of styles in a novel, depending on what fits
into the sequence. Right now I think you're smart in varying far away
from the norm, while you make like a pendulum in your search for the
right medium. Remember that it's easy to criticize formula but it is not
easy to criticize the intangibles of distinctive writing. But "Invisible Boy"
certainly confirms my idea that you will be a damned good writer, if you
don't fall into the yawning pitfalls. You'll have recognized some of them
already. In your search for distinctive style, you may get so precious that
you'll obscure the sense and leave out the guts of the story. That hasn't
come yet, and I trust won't. A good novelist should have something to
say, and he should say it in the best possible manner for him. "Invisible
Boy" doesn't have enough to say, I suppose, but it does not pretend to be
a novel. It says enough for its length and treatment. It is a competent job,
and most interesting to me, as I say, as a straw in the wind.

I still don't know if you have anything to say. The only way to find
out is to try. I'm anxious to see a novel of yours. You're using the tools
well. Now, damn it, use them on something worthwhile. Don't wait too
long about it. A writer should keep moving on to harder and harder

jobs; he has got to work on jobs that make him work to the limit of his
capabilities, or he's not a good writer.

I've told you often before to take criticism selectively. Anyway, I have
no specific criticism this time. Just a pat on the back and the hope that
you're working on something harder now. Nice going. I'm mailing the tear
sheets back to you; you may want an extra file copy. They're useful.

Am lining up the schedule so I can get into town for a week.
Can't tell when yet. I'm still not back to my regular writing level, but
California is giving us what we need. Especially mental relaxation. God,
yes! That's something apparently non-existent in the east—especially
for a Californian.

Remember about that book. Write it.

Hank

---

*Henry Kuttner's sudden death in early 1958 stunned Bradbury, less because
it was unexpected than because he had to come to terms with losing his most
intense and enigmatic mentor from the early years of his career. Quiet, apolitical, and a great observer of human nature, Kuttner and his wife, author C. L.
Moore, had slowly withdrawn into a contented world of literary collaboration
and a midlife pursuit of college degrees. Bradbury, unable to decipher the friendship that peeked out between the lines of Kuttner's mentoring wartime letters,
was never sure if Kuttner even liked him, and this long note to Don Congdon
begins the process of working through his impressions of a writer's life.*

Bradbury
10750 Clarkson Rd.
Los Angeles 64, Cal.

February 7, 1958

Dear Don,

I heard from Chuck Beaumont and Bill Nolan the other day that
someone had already wired you about Henry Kuttner's death. If

someone hadn't telephoned me last Tuesday night I wouldn't have known of the death or the funeral Wednesday. There was nothing, absolutely nothing, in any newspaper here, all week long. Henry has vanished without a trace; a terrible and ironic thing to happen to one of the most talented and one of the most considerate people I have ever known.

I went to the funeral Wednesday remembering twenty years of meetings, on and off, with Hank. I met him in my last year at high-school. We had both had the same short story teacher at L.A. High, Hank about four years previously.[52] When I met Hank, he was already established in *Weird Tales* and *Wonder Stories* and he encouraged me steadily, at the science-fiction meetings held every Thursday night in Clifton's Cafeteria in downtown L.A. The encouragement continued for four years, until I sold my first story to *Super Science*.[53] After that, he re-doubled his interest in my stories, and often came by the house, on his way across town, to give me criticism. He was my best and most consistent teacher. He laid down the law to me, told me that if I ever wrote a purple passage again he'd throw me downstairs (I stopped writing purple that very day, he was so brutal, in a nice way, about a high-Renaissance story I had done). Hank put me on a schedule and made me read the worst pulp magazines, to digest the bare bones of plot, narrative hook, pace, etc. He shoved my nose into *Amazing* month after month, a terrible magazine. But I learned more from that experience than from reading *Harper's Monthly*. Later on, in 1943 and 1944, when I did a story titled "Chrysalis," and couldn't get it right, Hank went to John Campbell at *Astounding* with it and asked John to give his advice. Hank also said that he would collaborate with me on it if, finally, I couldn't bring the story off. He made me rewrite it at least ten times. I finally sold it to *Amazing*.

My story "The Candle," the first I ever published, in *Weird Tales*, was the result of help from Hank. The last page of that story still stands the way Hank wrote it back when I was 21.

Well, I could go on and on. I have a file of letters a foot high here in the garage to show his kindness and consideration down the years. I never really understood Hank, for he was a very quiet and reticent man, rarely social. Our meetings, over the years, save for a few times, were those of student and teacher. He was one of the most thoughtful people I have ever known, and by this I mean a thinking man.

So of course you can understand how I felt when I saw that none of the newspapers noticed that he had gone.

There's only one thing I'd want now for Hank and his stories, which I have always admired. I wish you would talk to Brad at Doubleday, or to Ian at Ballantine about getting all of Hank's things into one volume.[54] His stories have been strewn about, through the years, to various publishers. Now more than ever, Hank's things should appear from one publisher in one uniform edition. Perhaps a huge one volume edition of his stories, to be followed, later, by books containing his best novels, perhaps as trios under one cover. There isn't an SF writer in the field who wouldn't be proud to write an introduction to one or all of these. I've always considered Hank among the top three or four writing in the field. Leigh Brackett, for one, I'm sure, would be glad to do such an introduction, she was a pupil of Hank's, too. It goes without saying I'd do the job for free and be happy doing so. Think it over, talk it over with Brad or Ian. Someone should do it, someone must do it. At least the stories should be got together now. Later on, something can be done about the novels.

It's a shame Hank didn't live to use the ideas he often discussed that came from his years spent in college. He had primed himself for an exciting future. We would have had some wonderful books from all that. Perhaps Kat, from having lived an incredibly close life with Hank, will give us some small part of what he wanted. They were an astounding marriage; one I've often admired, in my own ego and selfishness. They held hands and worked the same typewriter, something I could never do.

Well, I guess that's it. I wanted to tell someone about these last twenty years and Hank. If there's anything I can do now to pay back an old old debt, all that you, or Doubleday, or Ballantine, have to do is tell me what it should be.

Yours, as ever,

Ray

THEODORE STURGEON

Arthur C. Clarke once observed that Ray Bradbury and Theodore Sturgeon (1918–1985) were two of the most emotionally powerful science fiction writers of their day. Sturgeon's rapid rise to prominence in John Campbell's Astounding *and* Unknown *during the early 1940s caught Bradbury's attention, but he was not aware that his own breakthrough stories in* Weird Tales *had drawn the attention and admiration of Sturgeon himself. Sturgeon reached out first, and Bradbury's responses mirror Sturgeon's ironic, offbeat, and humorous style of correspondence.*

Oct 22, 1946.

Mr. Ray Bradbury,
c/o *Weird Tales*,
Radio City, N. Y.

Dear Ray Bradbury,

I can't say this is the first letter of its kind I have ever written—I just got one off to Cliff Simak for the beautiful job he did with *Hobbies* in particular and the City series generally. That was my first; I never expected that I would get such a wallop again, so soon.

It isn't the same wallop. It's different in kind, rather than degree, and it's a kind rather closer to my own tastes. I wish I could do stuff *like Hobbies*. As much or more, I wish I could write horror *as well* as you.

"The Handler" was without exception the nastiest thing I've seen in print since Jane Rice's "Idol of the Flies" in the late lamented *Unknown Worlds*. But in your yarn, the touch was lighter, and the pacing beautifully consistent. Your characterization was as brilliant as Bradbury, and you have a genius for phrase. ". . . his hands like little biscuits before his stomach" for example, and ". . . A little dog trotted by with clever eyes . . ." and the many others. None seem to be too consciously clever, shouting "Looka *me!*"

I have enjoyed your copy increasingly, with emphasis on "The Lake" and "Let's Play 'Poison'!." I don't know how much longer you can go on topping your own stuff; but if you do, somebody better tell John Collier and Saki to get out of the way . . .

When you were in New York recently I was advised of the fact by Hank Kuttner, who gave me your hotel address. I called you repeatedly for four days, until they finally told me you had gone. I very much regret having missed you, and I hope that we may meet someday soon.

Sincerest thanks for "The Handler."

Cordially,
Theodore Sturgeon

Ray Bradbury
670 Venice Blvd.,
Venice, California.

October 30th, 1946

Dear Ted Sturgeon,

Five years ago I hadn't sold a darn thing; I was very busy reading and enjoying and envying two very swell writers in *Unknown*; namely Jane Rice and Theodore Sturgeon. I used to go through their stories with a red pencil and find out what made them tick. I hated their guts for being so goddam good; how could they do that? How could they dare to be so good? It was terribly unfair; my own stuff was so far from selling and so far from being good. I could hardly stand to read the Rice and Sturgeon stuff. One story, in particular . . . in the August 1940 *Unknown*—"It," was enough to make me a pitiful wreck of an egoist. If, some day, I told myself, I could do as fine a piece of writing as "It," I would take the rest of the year off and get drunk.

And now here it is, a bright California October morning and I have a letter from one T. Sturgeon. It is certainly the nicest fan letter I've ever had. It means a very great deal to me, since I have looked upon you with such mixed emotions of admiration and professional jealousy for so many years. It seems a bit weird that you should be writing me instead of my writing you. I had planned to write to you many times in the passage of years, but each time I failed to do so because I thought you might think me just another fan with just another letter of praise. I considered writing you at the time the latest Derleth book came out with "It" and "The Lake" in it. I was particularly intrigued by the fact that you were living at the time in the Virgin Islands, and more than amazed to discover that you were only two years older than myself. It was good to discover someone near my own age who has had similar luck in writing at least fairly successfully while one is young enough to enjoy parts of it.

I assure you I do not engage in log-rolling with authors. Ed Hamilton is a very near dear friend of mine, but I tell him frankly I think most of his stuff is odorous. Once in a while Ed will clank out something quite terrific, but mostly he's in the business for money, and enjoys life. Therefore, any of the above things I have said about Sturgeon need not be looked upon as the mouthings of an author who has been flattered because another author likes his stuff. If you were L. Joe Fohn or Fletcher Pratt I wouldn't be as nice. If you were Ray Cummings I don't know if I would be civil. But I still have fond memories of "Shottle Bop," "Cargo" and "It"—and also the Scrambler stories in *Astounding*. Seriously, at that time, 1940–41, I used to read and re-read your stories two or three times. I went through a Sturgeon period even as I went through a Rice period—the two coincided roughly. I remember particularly reading again and again a story called "Artnan Process"; I'll be damned if I can remember what it was about now, I believe I was more interested in the construction of your sentences than the story on that one. I worked a bit on "Butyl and the Breather," also.

I liked your work, and still do like it, because of its originality and freshness of thought. I hope we can get together for a bit of gabbing if I come to New York again next summer. I'm certainly sorry we missed connections.

Your letter perked me up no end; I was feeling sorry for myself, having just received a rejection in the mail from the *Atlantic Monthly*.[55] Thanks very much for your kind words; it'll make me keep on trying, by God.

I see you have the lead story this issue in *Astounding*. Haven't read it yet. I rarely read *Astounding* any more. Do you agree with me that it just is *not* the good old mag it used to be? I hate people who always look back to the golden days; but I think the 1939 to 1941 period was the peak for *Astounding* and *Unknown*.

Just checking through my files; I liked "Medusa" and "The Brat" very much. And I am very much in favor of "The Hag Seleen" . . . it was a corker.

Strange that you mentioned Jane Rice in your letter. She was so consistently good. I notice she's been writing for quality mags recently. She deserved to. Have you ever met up with her? I'd like to shake her hand.

Well, enough. Again, thanks for your fine letter. Let me hear from you again in the next month or so, when you have the time.

Oh, yeah . . . one other thing.

Dear Mr. Sturgeon: Where do you get your ideas?

Cordially,
Ray

P.S. I envy you your time in the Islands; I imagine you breathed in enough detail to supply you with several novels and a great host of short stories . . . eh? Have you anything weird to report on witch cults thereabouts?[56] Would like to hear if you'd like to tell. Best,

R.

---

670 Venice Blvd.,
Venice, Calif.

February 3rd, 1947

Ted, I hate you![57]

Having just read your story "Maturity," I have every reason to hate you. It is a damned nice story. Your sense of humor, sir, is incredible. I don't believe you've written a bad story yet; I don't think you ever will. This is not log-rolling, by God; I only speak the truth. I predict you'll be selling at least six stories a year to *Collier's* and *The Post* before long. You have the touch. "Maturity" was good.

I rarely read *Astounding* these days, save for the Padgett[58] or Sturgeon yarns. But next month I'm getting a copy to read dear old Jack Williamson's first story in years. You'd like Jack; he's a big, lean, wind-whipped, slow, drawling, easy-going fellow from New Mexico; lives out on the lonely prairie, has a lank lock of dark hair that falls over his brow, wears horn-rims, has a slow, friendly smile; best darn friend a guy could have. *Astounding* seems to be getting back in the groove again. Now if they could get Ron Hubbard, Heinlein, Cartmill and some of the other old timers to do some yarns, there'd be something to look forward to.

Glad you liked "The Meadow." I was pretty pleased, myself. I can see certain flaws now, with time, but still, for a first radio script, it came out pretty well.[59] There was a matter of rushing time at the end of the play. They ran out of time and had to finish up the conclusion in a rush. I was sorry. The fade-out, the footsteps, the clicking of the gate, the rising music, should have had full value, gradually and dramatically built to a peak.

Your taste in music is far superior to mine. I'm afraid I've been rather feeble-minded about it all. Maggie is trying to shame me into getting ahead somewhat. She's been taking me to concerts of harpsichord music played by Alice Ehlers, one of Landowska's pupils; we heard the *Goldberg Variations* some time ago, and I must say I enjoyed them immensely. Got around to hearing the Roth String Quartet, and the Budapest String Quartet; and my education, heretofore purposely neglected, in chamber music, is rapidly shaping up. Your mention of the Decca Album on authentic jungle drums and African chants sounds amazing; I'd like to grab onto that one, myself! Your remarks concerning Lombardo and Sammy Kaye are so true, dear friend. I just latched on to the *Fancy Free* album put out by Decca, conducted by Bernstein; I think it is some of the most original and stimulating American music since Gershwin sat down at the piano; better in some ways. The pressings are not very good, but the music comes through nevertheless. [. . .]

You and Derleth[60] would get on well. He has an immense collection of good jazz. Several thousand records, I estimate. I visited him last September, on my way to New York. I hope to make it back there again this year. Will look forward to meeting you, by God.

Sold a new story to *Charm*.[61] Otherwise, the week has been one long mass of rejection slips. [. . .]

I do not know how I have the intelligence or sense to write you today. This is one of my bad days, you know how they are, when you feel like melting down your typewriter and sticking it up the editor's nostrils. Got two of my very favorite stories bounced today, with weird reasons.[62] I am not appreciated. I am being persecuted. Evidently they do not know my middle name is Christ. Me and Kafka, kiddo. Stick around and you'll learn somethin'.

The editor of *Planet* has been a swell egg, as I may have mentioned. Two of my stories, which I submitted of late, have gone to *Planet*, but instead of taking them, he turned around and sent them on to *Collier's*, saying they were too good for *Planet*. Give that Paul Payne a pat on the cheek for me, if you ever meet him, Ted.[63] [. . .]

Let me hear from you, in between your manic-depressive phases. I trust you do fluctuate? If not, do not reply. I only correspond with neurotics. I shall think of you tonight as I shatter a Guy Lombardo record.

Luff,

Ray

New Castle, Pa.,
(But use the New York address)

Feb 18, 1947

Thass okay. I hate you too. Did I got a network program? Do I got a collection of my stories coming out? Did I ever have Simon and Schuster beg *me* for a novel? Did I ever create anything as compellingly disgusting as your beautiful little "Handler"?

And now we're on the subject of me, leave us stay there a while. (Didn't I handle that cleverly, tho?) I am a poor lost mixed-up s.o.b., a condition which has always been generally true, but particularly for the past three years.

So I woke up with a start a few weeks ago and took stock. What am I and what have I got? Two million words in print, a bunch of anthologizations, a lot of overseas reprints, some right pert special mentions in the highbrow press for "It" and "Killdozer." Also I got a reasonable structure of insolvency. And still writing for nothing but the pulps. What's wrong? I can write. I have the highest sales-to-production ratio of anyone I know—around 87%.

Well, two things are wrong. My production is low—very. I do not write my best stuff slowly, but there are sometimes weeks of interval between paragraphs. I walk around and chew on the characters and situations and stuff. I sit over the mill[64] for hours without touching it. Then comes one of those thirty or forty-hour non-stop stretches, three decks of cigarettes and a couple dozen cups of coffee, and it all comes out, finished copy, ready to go. Which is all very well, but you can't live well writing pulp with a low overall production. That's the second thing that's wrong—the word rates. I now get as high as can be expected in my pet fields, but 'taint enough. [. . .]

You mention ASF's groove.[65] I second same. But as for Heinlein, I dunno. I happen to know that he sold a short novel to Startling Stories. I don't know if JCjr[66] knows of that yet, but can predict he will blow his top when he finds it out. And don't tell me you missed the Feb 8th Satevepost with the Heinlein story and the fantasy by Vida Jameson, Malcolm's daughter[67] who is at present living with the Heinleins. (A very slick chick, by the way.) The difficulty with Heinlein and ASF is that John, though he does not really have to, insists on "all rights." Leo Margulies buys first NAS and English pub., and that's all, at the same or slightly higher word rates for a top author. Bob just got a little sick of arguing.

I envy you those Ehlers concerts. Did you know that the Roth outfit has recorded the entire Art of the Fugue? Quite a production: about 27 sides. The hell (said with all reverence) with Maggie's "shaming" you into music. Music is, in my opinion, worth a damn only if it can be listened to with the ductless glands. It's good if it gives you goose-pimples, and great if your goose-pimples get goose-pimples—it's as simple as that. By me, Wagner stinks on this basis; and the only thing you have to be to like Tchaikowsky, to quote my room-mate, is honest.

Balls on composers who avoid harmonies because they are writing
atonal stuff, when a natural progression would bring in an accidental
sonance. Nuts to conductors who transcribe for orchestra from organ or
quartet, and purposely quell some brilliance just because it was thought
of before by some other transcriber. [. . .] The enclosed check is for
Columbia album X (or MX) 216.[68] Eat that, dammit. You love words.
You couldn't write the way you do if you didn't love 'em. Well, there's a
word for this. It's a perfectly legitimate word. Too. It's "architectonic."
And I shall personally piss on you if you buy back. That isn't what this
is for. I am only doing it because I like to talk to you, and I'd take it as a
high compliment if you regarded this album as Sturgeon talking to you.
    [. . .]
So Derleth's a cat, hm? I didn't know. Wonder how much Django
Reinhardt he has. Know him? An illiterate French gypsy with two fingers
on his left hand, and the kind of guitarist that makes a three-chord man
like me wish he was dead—Hot Club of France. Dig him some time.
He's in the States now. . . . I don't think at this stage of the game, that I
need comment on your question on my neuroticism and the periodicity
thereof . . . write soon, but for God's sake don't wait until you can match
this length. Write a short one quick, or I'll never hear from you again,
and I want to.

As ever ever,
T.H.S.

March 18, 1947

Dear Ted:

Here's the letter I promised you on your apartment plans.[69] I trust you
received my other letter thanking you for the Bach album, which I play
every day, by God, and six times on Sundays! I'm still muchly indebted
to you for the fine thought that prompted your surprising me with said
album. This album should keep Stokowski out of hell when his time comes.
    Are you William Tenn?[70] There is something very Sturgeonish about

the guy's writing. I like his "Build a Man" story, "Child's Play," in the current *Astounding*. It's right up Sturgeon's alley? Well, son, is you is or is you ain't Tenn?[71] His name is highly suspicious, to begin with. Much too close to Tennessee Williams to suit my paranoid id. The grill room for you, Sturge! Come on, confess! *You* did it! Thumb-screws, Joe! Okay, Theodore, sweat!

My *Dark Carnival* will be out May 2nd, (it says here in small eensy-weensy print), that is what Derleth says anyhow. We shall see.

Interesting, you turning up in New Castle, as I may have said. That's Ed Hamilton's home town. He, on the other hand, in order to escape from New Castle, is now in California. Ah well. Green grass and other trite truisms, unya?

[. . .]

Anyhow, I really approve of your plans. I wish I had time to work on my studio. I've been fiddling with oil paints lately, have just executed two studies of clowns, in sombre blacks and shocking whites, my first stab at being an artist, old bean, and already I'm better than Rouault,[72] he kept insisting as they squeezed him back into the burnt sienna tube.

I've been correcting proofs all week on *Dark Carnival* and I'm sick of the damned thing. It's a swell book, but, Christ, the ennui, the vertigo, the inertia that overcomes one after hours of reading stuff you don't want to read anymore.

I shall leave you now, [. . .] so be a good chappie, eh, and write me as to what cooks, and how many stories you've sold this month so I can properly sneer at you, call you commercial, read you the riot act, and disclaim all knowledge of our friendship. Since my sale to *Harper's* I'm not speaking to anybody. Especially my grocer, my cleaner, my clothier, my radio man; to all of whom I owe money—you don't get much from *Harper's*, by God. Art, she is wonderful. Reputation, she is beautiful. [. . .] Enough paranoia for enow,

Luff,
Ray

March 18 [1947]

D' ré,

Hi and thanks for the knocked-out letter so promptly after the Bach. I was eagerly awaiting a reply, and hoped that the C mi job[73] would hit you that way, and I am with happitude.

You must be too over that splendid and very nasty little *Harper's* job. Don't *you* go ohing and ahing over *my* mind! You're downright nasty, son. I should be that nasty! Tell me, Mr. B.: where do you get your ideas? (Next letter, I'll ask you "You a writer? You want a story? Let me tell you the story of my life . . ." Jesus! If I hear that again . . .) "The Man Upstairs" was delightfully grisly, and you are to be complimented from here to there. The business of the colored windows was particularly fine, and you've been peeking into my childhood memories. I had a strong but uncrystallized and inexpressible idea of contiguous worlds at the age of eight, gained just that way. Of course, I chipped no rubbery cubes out of the paying guests . . . oh, but nasty.

I do like what you say about music. I'm only sorry that you let these quasi-intellectuals browbeat you for so long. Music is for the ductless glands. If it makes you jump, it's good. If it doesn't, it ain't good. If it sounds as if it might, it's worth playing over and over again to find out. As a matter of fact, by me the same attitude goes for many more things. Food, for example. I *love* to eat. In food, as with other aesthetic fields, I want subtlety, but I want it by the bucketful. My prime eating ambition at the moment is a beerstein full of creamed oyster-crabs.

Was talking to Paul Payne today.[74] He has the *Harper's* but hasn't read the story yet. Said he read the Heinlein opus[75] in the *Post* and had a Bradbury story[76] that was infinitely better. [. . .]

Hurry up and come east, will you hurry up and? Hey—you're ready for Villa-Lobos' Bachiana Brasileiros No. 5.[77] One 12″ platter. Eat that, and then let the pseudo's know what a ductless-gland listener has to say about music most of 'em have never heard of . . . get the Sayo recording, with the composer conducting. I think it's a Columbia Blue-seal. I don't have one. I've given six away already. Next one I get's going to stay here, by God. 'Bye now. Next time I write (please remind me—I always

answer with my correspondent's letter beside me) I'll have something
to say about "Equalizer."

Regards to all.
T.H. Sturgeon

During the winter of 1947–48, Sturgeon asked Bradbury to write an introduction to Without Sorcery, *his first story collection. Privately, Bradbury lacked confidence in his ability to eliminate self-conscious anxiety from nonfiction prose—a form of writing that still seemed unnatural to him. Instead of celebrating Sturgeon's creative power and range, Bradbury's first draft became a polemic against the relative weakness of contemporary horror and fantasy fiction and the shadow of intolerance that was rising against nonconformist literature in postwar America. Bradbury's cover letter conveys this sense of unease.*

Feb 22, '48

Dear Ted:

Here's the introduction, if you like it—fine. If not, be frank with me. You
needn't use it if you don't wish to, understand.

I meant to be a little more factual in my criticism of your preface
when I sent it back to you, but lacked the time and energy. I simply
meant that I thought your preface only fair because I expected more
from you, more about your background, your life, your travels, how
you "got your ideas," et cetera. I thought you took a helluva long time
to make your point, which was not very tremendous. I, as a reader,
would be far more interested in Sturgeon the writer, ya get me? Okay.

Sorry I'm a few days late with the enclosed, but hope it meets
your need. Let me know, eh? And when the royalties start rolling in,
remember, I only want 89% royalties; sound fair to you? All my good
wishes to you, Ted.

Luff,
Ray

P.S. You have my permission to correct any errors you may find in this last, incoherently typed copy. Forgive my mistakes. Thanks. I really enjoyed writing this; I had a lot of fun getting my wildly mercurial thoughts on paper.

R.B.

Sturgeon felt that Bradbury's initial draft introduction for Without Sorcery *was completely off target and off-putting for readers. On March 1, 1948, Sturgeon wrote a frank and levelheaded appeal to Bradbury to consider writing a completely new introduction: ". . . is there anything about my stuff which tickles you, or makes you laugh, or moves you, or thrills you a little? One couldn't tell from your intro. You said only what you thought about science fiction—and most of that's negative [. . .] Where, in that introduction, is the Bradbury who listens so sensually to music, whose letters laugh so readily and so deeply, who is so articulately childlike (childlike, not childish), so impulsive and genuine and simple in simplicity's most clean-cut form?" Bradbury agreed to write a new introduction, prompting Sturgeon to write again with thanks, and with a mentor's encouraging admonition to guard the spontaneity that made Bradbury a most original and emotionally truthful writer.*

one seventy three monroe street new york two new York

March 5, 1948

Dear dear Ray,

The Kinsey Report aside, I *love* you!

When you answered my fan letter a year or so ago, you did it with one of the nicest missives I have ever received from anybody. And here you've topped it. Youse is a *good* boy.

You topped that; you match something else. There is a quality in my beloved Mary Mair[78] which I thought was unique. It's a sort of built-in judge and jury, complete with bailiff, turnkeys, and a penitentiary, which latter has the Rack and a coupla knouts . . . when Mary does something unfair, which isn't often—just wait a minute. If you can wait, if you can hold out, hold off for a little while, you will suddenly hear the rap of that imaginary gavel; the prisoner goes before the bar; justice is done and the debt is paid.

You seem to have the same thing. I know you only from your work and your letters—I think you put a great deal of you into both of them. I am firmly convinced that if I had said nothing about this whole matter it would have descended upon you one night and caused you no end of self-castigation, which you would have poured me-wards. And then I'd have been in the position in which I frequently find myself with Mary— that of attorney for the defense!

In that role, I say now and with harshness to stop saying dirty nasty things about my good, good friends. Forgive this dutch-uncle tone, but lissen: there is only one Bradbury, and like a few—Gerard Manley Hopkins, P.G. Wodehouse, James Branch Cabell, and a coupla more from widely separated fields—you can't be imitated; you're an original. (This is unlike Hemingway, Saroyan, Herman Wouk, Farrell, Steinbeck, and yards and yards of others—particularly Damon Runyon—originators perhaps, but quite imitable.) One characteristic of the true original is that he does his work his way. (Alec Wilder[79] is one in music; Emily Dickinson was one in poetry.) . . . You are the only writer of whom I have been jealous; my jealousy, like all jealousies, had its basis in a sense of inadequacy, not necessarily in talent, but in principle. I let myself be forced into markets for which I didn't care particularly; I forced my styles into preformed molds. As far as I know you have never done this. Some of your stuff shows as not quite successful because it's formative and experimental. Some is unsuccessful because it's not quite suitable to an established market's accepted forms. But God damn it, it's all Bradbury, every last little bit of it. That is a quality that no other writer can get into his stuff; none ever has; none ever will. Think of that next time somebody takes you aside with patience and with kindness and explains to you carefully that you really have something, and it's a great pity that your work appears between these lurid covers on this porous paper. Ray, these people are, whether they recognize it or not, motivated by a strange and even force which looks like a monumental trowel, which travels ponderously back and forth over the unset concrete of humanity, driving down any peak or height to the level of the rest of the mass. Bear in mind that the trowel and its work are *superficial* in their function. . . . there is no plane surface in nature, except for liquids when they're *frozen* and no longer in flux. . . . snobs . . . this one can speak French and that one knows the calculus; the other laughs at whoever likes Ellington and talks knowingly about Scriabin and Pugnani[80] . . . all these things are good things, admirable things, but they're *acquired* things, and the only true credit due the snob who's snobbish in this way is due him for his acquisitiveness and for nothing else. Not one of them, not one single snob anywhere in the whole wide world can be Bradbury. Not one.

Puff-puff . . . .

[. . .]

When in God's name are we going to stick our heads into the same suds-bucket? Do you like beer, by the way? . . . I don't know what you think, but *I* think you rate a honeymoon—the kind that will bring you to New York.

Thanks, thanks, thanks, *thanks*,
T.H.S.

LEIGH BRACKETT AND EDMOND HAMILTON

Genre fiction legends Leigh Brackett (1915–1978) and Ed Hamilton (1904–1977) were two of Bradbury's closest friends and mentors during the war years. Hamilton's ability to plot effective stories had reached Bradbury since childhood through Weird Tales *and the science fiction and fantasy pulps, and the two men became friends during Hamilton's occasional stays in Los Angeles during the early 1940s. Leigh Brackett became a friend and encourager through the same concentration of LA Science Fantasy Society writers and fans that had attracted Hamilton; from 1942 through much of 1944, she would meet Bradbury Sunday afternoons on the beach at Santa Monica, where he would read her various works in progress as she critiqued his early circulating stories. She was in large part responsible for his break into* Planet Stories, *a reliable second-tier science fiction venue where she was regularly featured. He also learned mystery-detective writing through her example, while Hamilton introduced him to a wider range of English and American fiction and poetry than he had yet managed to discover through the libraries and bookstores. The naive overeagerness seen in his early letters was tempered by an enduring friendship that time and distance never diminished.*

Ray Bradbury
670 Venice Blvd.,
Venice, California

October 7, 1943

Dear Ed:

I've just been gabbing with Brackett over the phone and the name of the great master (Hamilton, naturally) has been mentioned. With quickened pulse and heated brow I hurry to my machine, unveil its glittering keys and begin my annual letter, long past due, stimulated by the mention of the fact that Hamilton is considering going either to Louisiana or to Los Angeles. This is damn silly. The only place to come, of course, is Los Angeles. Do you realize how long it is since you were here? God All Mighty, there are several million defense jobs to be had. You just close your eyes and poke your hand out, thus punching some harried personnel advisor in the eye. Brackett and I will probably crack you in the jaw if you don't come out to Los Angeles. It would be somewhat of a personal slight to us. We would realize, with bitter thoughts, that you no longer care.

All of that to one side momentarily, I hope this finds you in good health, typing among a litter of discarded beer-cans. Your trip to Mexico, from Brackett's report, sounds Utopian, what with balconies and beer and Captain Future to be written when you weren't imbibing Plato.[81]

I am in fine fettle. I'm still 4-F[82] and still enabled to sit at my typewriter many hours a day and try to pound out something halfway decent. My average is one sale out of every three stories, at present, though this may take a sharp decline due to the fact that I'm at present trying to switch over into the detective field. The s.f. field is so microscopic these days that it hardly pays to write the stuff. The stories are not transferable enough. I write a story slanted for Campbell, it's rejected and then there's no other market for the damn thing. It's a heck of a gamble.

I have two agents now. Julie, like always, for the s.f. and detective fields, and Ed Bodin[83] for the slick and literary (ha) markets. No good news from Bodin yet, but he's trying one of my things with *Vogue*, *Harper's*, *Charm*, etc. Meanwhile my detective things are a little bit too off-trail, according to Norton, and I must try to keep my sympathies on the side of the law . . .

Just got word from Campbell that I won first prize in the *Astounding* Probability Zero contest. That's the second time I won first.[84] I got bulges in the head for the moment.

[. . .]

Knowing how much you love good books, I venture to suggest one of my favorite novels, Christopher Morley's *Thunder on the Left*. You've probably read it already. It's one of the neatest human documents, interspersed with fantasy, I've ever read. Morley has a fine sympathetic ability for psychiatric detail, he portrays the human frailties so well, I'm certain you'll remember the yarn long after you've read it.

It's just about time for me to sign off. I'm going to write another story and cut in on a little of that dough Hamilton's been casually pulling down for so many years. *Weird Tales*, so far, has been my godmother, with Norton running a close second for sympathetic encouragement and criticism. Campbell, as always, remains a bit aloof. Anyway, it all goes back to a certain summer when Schwartz and Hamilton encouraged a certain bespectacled jerk to keep on with the making words.

Drop me a letter soon, huh, Ed? And when you decide to come to Los Angeles, which you most certainly will, just notify Brackett and me ahead of time so we can find a bass drum somewhere to pound.

Until then.

Agnostical blessings,

Ray

During the war years, Brackett's many weekly postcards, generally addressed to "Dear Genius" from "Muscles," culminated in the two notes below, telling Bradbury of her unexpected chance to script the Humphrey Bogart film The Big Sleep *for Howard Hawks, and her need for Bradbury to step in and write the second half of what would become the highly regarded Brackett-Bradbury collaboration on the novella* Lorelei of the Red Mist.

[August 31, 1944]

Dear Ray:

Some mad mix-up on the phone—I keep getting the Bureau of Power and Light.[85] Anyway, the job came through, I'm working and I still can't believe it. Bill Faulkner—*the* William Faulkner—is my teammate, and come next month we'll be working on the set with Bogey. My God—all this, and Republic too![86] Incidentally, I had a very nice lunch Tuesday, and there *is* one quiet spot in North Hollywood. I found it. Quiet, but warm. *Very* warm. —Seems this *Big Sleep* thing is supposed to be under the hat, so keep it to yourself, huh? I don't know why, but them's orders from the Boss. You should see my office—there's even a big, soft, rose-colored couch in it. H'm! Give me a ring sometime—call Warner Bros. and ask for extension 707. Meantime, no cracks in postcards, please, for I won't be home to grab them first. As to Sunday, I hope so, but I ain't sure. Mitt luff,

Muscles

[ca. September 1944]

Dear Ray—

Here it is—with my blessings & best wishes.

All you have to do is get the sea-beasts on our side, get 'em back to Crom Dhu in time to save Beudag & defeat—or should I say, destroy—Rann's fleet—& of course Starke will have to take care of

Rann. —Your carbon will follow. I couldn't find it this a.m. & I was
late anyway.

Thine,
Muscles

---

*The need to care for his elderly parents while continuing to write for the New
York pulp editors had kept Hamilton in his hometown of New Castle, Pennsylvania, during the later war years. A brief fall 1944 note from Bradbury (opening
with "Gosh, guy, whyncha drop a fellow a line once in awhile?") soon prompted
Hamilton to respond with a long letter that included a blessing on Bradbury's
future. Only the first page has been located, but the end of that page offered a
half-serious prediction of the future that would prove to be prophetic.*

1611 Pennsylvania Avenue,
New Castle, Penna.

Dec. 31, 1944

Dear Ray:

I guess I have safely established my record as the world's worst
correspondent. God knows how long since I have got off any letters. The
rumor that Hamilton was buried eight months ago is a foul slander.

The fact is that this year has been such a stinker for me in some
respects that I have not had much inclination to write letters. Critical
illness of my parents, the impossibility of hiring help or even nurses,
gave me quite a time. However, things have cleared up to a great extent,
I hasten to report with my fingers well crossed.

First, want to congratulate you on your fine yarns this year. You
always did have the "knack" of writing—I don't know just what to call
it but a person either has it or doesn't, and you do. Jack does, too. I
don't and wish to God I did, but have been able to compensate for it
by a strong faculty of plotting and a certain amount of craftsmanship

gained from experience. But you've added to the ability to pour it out, the ability to shape a story and make it flow smoothly to a satisfying conclusion, and that's what you needed most, so you are all set now.

The little yarn recently about the chap who destroyed things by writing poems about them is the one I liked best, I think.[87] The child-stories were probably better, and certainly came closer to being something unique. But they found an unsympathetic reader in me more than most, as I have no great liking for children. They can be amusing, and at times their innocence can be tremendously appealing, but still they are little savages, which fact is not altered by the fact that I was once one myself. All over this land there are large, elaborate buildings employing many people, and this tremendous plant is for the sole purpose of "educating" children—i.e., for the purpose of beating the elements of civilization into their barbaric minds. Boy, do I feel like old Scrooge, eh? Don't take me too seriously. Ever read Hughes' *High Wind in Jamaica*?[88]

Leigh Brackett's yarns have been unbelievably good this year. I thought her detective novel extremely good, and understand it won her a place in the stratospheric levels of movie writing, but I don't really like detec stories very well, so it's her s-f yarns I refer to. You know, that's the reason why old guys like me can make a comfortable living year after year out of the s-f mags without work—whenever any of you youngsters come along with enough talent to eclipse us completely, you write yourselves right up into the higher realms and deliver us from your ruinous competition in the pulps.

By the way, Jack Williamson was here on a furlough a couple of weeks ago and we had a pretty good time. [. . .]

Edmond Hamilton's occasional trips to Mexico prompted Bradbury to write for travel tips on the eve of his own fall 1945 Mexican journey to gather native masks for the Los Angeles County Museum. This letter also gave Bradbury an opportunity to tell his mentor about the series of major market sales that marked a major turning point in Bradbury's career as a writer.

Ray Bradbury
670 Venice Blvd.,
Venice, Calif.

[September 1945]

Dear Ed:

Well, it looks like our semi-annual letter is getting to be quite a habit,
only, in this case, I hope you'll reply before a week has passed. I hope
this finds you tip-top and full of information on Mexico. Because I'm
going down to Mexico on October first, with a friend of mine, driving,
and your name came to mind immediately. I know you've spent long
periods down there and speak the language, so perhaps you can
make some suggestions about traveling, the natives, places to see,
vaccinations, ruins, and so on. We hope to get on over to Oachamilco,
Oaxaca, Paricutín and other places (spelling not guaranteed) and I
thought you may know of some interesting off the beaten track places
we might want to see.[89] We're spending six weeks, which gives us plenty
of time to see quite a bit. We even plan to take a boat from Vera Cruz, if
such is obtainable, and go on down to Yucatan to see the ruins there. So
if you have any ideas, heave them at me!

About writing. Julie told me you had some difficulty getting a
manuscript out of Mexico. Do you think if I take my typewriter and bang
out some stuff on it, it might be wiser and safer to mail it out of the
country instead of trying to carry the completed script across the border
later?[90]

Julie writes and says he's coming to California next year or die
trying. Does this also mean Hamilton will come?[91] I am a firm believer
in Hamilton for California by 1946, so you had better start stirring your
bones and packing your bottles of bourbon and looking around for
transportation. It's been a hellishly long time since we gabbed.

As for me, everything seems to be happening at once. In the
last nine weeks I've sold stories to *American Mercury*, *Collier's*, and
Mademoiselle.[92] It's all very unbelievable and I'm still gasping and
holding a vial of smelling salts to my nostrils. How long this goes on

I don't know. I hope it'll last, but I'm writing some pulp yarns, on the side, just to be safe. After all those years of obscurity and editorial neglect it is a bit bewildering to get pleasant letters. I have been prostrate most of the time as a result.

Did you see Jack's yarn in *Blue Book*?[93] A darn swell yarn. I wouldn't doubt that when Jack returns he'll write a couple of good articles on meteorology and sell them to big markets, he's assimilated enough now to make for a good job.

Just bought the new *Weird Tales*. I'm a sucker for mythologies, and "Lost Elysium" was right up my alley.[94] I'll have to tell Leigh about it, you know how she dotes on Celtic characters. Anyhow, I think your Cullan yarns are the best this year! A change from the usual crap *Weird* prints![95] I guess I've gabbed enough. Let me hear from you as soon as possible, hunh, concerning Mexico? Wish you were out here so you could prowl on down with us. It'd be great fun, but *muy terrifico!*

Mitt luff to you,

Ray

In the late 1940s, Cold War concerns and a need for solitude had led Brackett and Hamilton to move to rural eastern Ohio, and the politically polarizing climate of fear during this period occasionally overshadowed Bradbury's expressed memories of earlier times. The letters exchanged during the late 1940s and early 1950s also document Bradbury's attempts to use his rising career successes to secure broader market publishing and film opportunities for his former mentors, little realizing that rural life and the chance to write in this setting meant more than the opportunities that Los Angeles offered. Hollywood and a milder climate would eventually lure his two friends back to Southern California, but only after the respite described in these exchanges of letters.

The first offers a creative thanks to Hamilton for a story read long ago in Bradbury's youth, a story that fueled Bradbury's keen sense for settings of wonder and strange otherness in his own tales.

[ca. 1949]

Dear Ed and Leigh:

Thanks for your nice card. Glad you are doing so well. Here's a nice
story: when I was ten years old I read a story that affected me for years
. . . science fiction . . . world of spiders that lived on floating metal isles
in the air . . . web between the islands over which the spiders bore
our heroes . . . also revolving pulleys with hand and footholds which
went down into metal cities . . . I drew pictures of this for years and
years . . . still have the pictures I drew . . . completely forgot the author
until yesterday, while browsing through book store came upon the
Spring, '29 *Amazing Quarterly* . . . the story, "Locked Worlds" . . . the
author—Edmond Hamilton! Ed, I love you! All these years remembering
a story I didn't even know was written by you! What a wonderful feeling
to see it again.

Love,

Ray

---

33 South Venice Blvd.
Venice, Calif.

January 13, 1950

Dear Ed and Leigh:

Well, here's a new year started, and I hope you are both producing great
reams of saleable stuff. And I also hope that things are beginning to
clarify, and that you'll soon be coming West again. In any event, by God,
I'll see you when I come East on May 1st! I won't have much time, but
it'd be nice just to see you guys again for a few hours. Maybe I'll hit you
both on the head and drag you West with me again!

Anyway, my first novel will be published May 4th, and I'm supposed
to be in New York for that, plus other business considerations.[96]

Maggie is fine, and the baby is persimmony and weighs 11 pounds and looks more like me, so say people, every day.[97] This is a rather poor way to start life, if you ask me, and perhaps she should go back and start over.

We've really started the year zooming. On Monday, this week, I sold an off-trail science-fiction story to *The Saturday Evening Post* for one thousand beautiful dollars, received a check from the *Philadelphia Inquirer* for $600 and had 2 of my stories picked for the *Best SF Stories of 1950*. Mag and I went to bed for an hour with cold compresses on our fevered brows. Jesus! Ironic thing is I haven't read the *Post* in fifteen years, and the story I sold them tells of 2 little kids in the future who destroy their parents with a super-invention and get away with it, somewhat like "Zero Hour"![98] Very off trail for the *Post*, I'd say, but . . .

I went to the Science Fantasy League Xmas party . . . or was it their Hallowe'en Party? . . . it's hard to tell 'em apart. Everybody looks just about the same. Aegh!

How are you doing with your detective novel, Leigh? My best to Bat-Man! Write soon. I got a couple of good hamburger steaks waiting in the ice-box for you guys to show up. They may be a little mossy by the time you finally arrive, but hell! Mag and Susan send their love.

Me, too,

Yours,

Ray

Bradbury's fall 1950 letter is notable because of its allusion to "Child of the Winds" (Weird Tales, May 1936), yet another old Hamilton tale of odd wonder and eerie otherness that inspired Bradbury, and the account of Bradbury's meeting with film director Fritz Lang, who became a good friend and served as the inspiration for a main character in Bradbury's novel of murder in a Hollywood studio, Graveyard for Lunatics *(1989).*

Bradbury
10750 Clarkson Rd.
L.A. 64, Calif.

October 8, 1950

Dear Ed:

In going over my boxes of material brought from the old house the other
day, I came across this tear-sheet of yours which you lent me two years
ago when I was planning that Harper's anthology. I have several other of
your tear-sheets here somewhere, and as soon as I dig them out, they'll be
coming your way. Thanks for the loan of this enclosed yarn; as you know,
I have a great liking for it; it is a strange thing to consider that perhaps
this yarn caused me to write "The Wind" years later; I'll be damned if I
know. My memory is conveniently faulty; but I wouldn't doubt that my
subconscious is guilty somewhere along the line.

Nothing much new here, except that I have made the acquaintance
of Fritz Lang, the director, and he had some fascinating things to say
about Germany 1920 to 1932, when Goebbels offered him the job of
heading the German Film Industry, and Lang got the hell out the next
afternoon, coming to America. Seems Hitler confiscated all prints of *The
Girl in the Moon* because it had the secret of the V-2 rocket in it, which
Willy Ley and Oberth worked on in 1923, and part of which was used,
in model form, for the rocket in the moon film. Ah, fantasy! Lang is a
fascinating gentleman; though I hear he is a heller on the set; certainly it
doesn't show in private life.

Enough. Hope you are both pouring out the work. Leigh's new
novelette in *TWS* is a beaut;[99] it's too long between Brackett stories, by
God. Mag and Susan send their best, as do I.

Yours,
Ray

Mar. 30, 1951

Dear Ed and Leigh:

Jesus, you guys seem to be on some sort of Conga line of illness. If
there's any justice in this world (and I haven't seen any lately) things
will clear up for all of you this year. [. . .]

It is bad news to hear of Leigh's novel being shelved, but
compensating to hear that *Shadow Over Mars* has gone to an English
publisher.[100] England is a great market; I've had a story in practically
every issue of British *Argosy* for two years now, at about 100 dollars a
throw for reprint rights. It's a market you two should look into. My two
latest books will be reprinted over there, too, one this year, one next.

As I believe I mentioned, I saw copies of *City at World's End* on sale
awhile back, latched onto a copy, and have enjoyed it immensely. There
is no one who can get his characters around like you, Ed, God bless you.

I'm glad Leigh will do a book a year for some publisher; you didn't
say which one? Leigh, you still haven't milked the Red Sea dry?[101] How
about more of that? I was going over some old Brackett tear-sheets the
other night and all of a sudden I was on the Santa Monica sands in the
hot sun, watching Brackett plunge about on the court, laughing, hitting
the volley ball, a copy of her Blue Behemoth or a Red Sea tale in my
hands. Jesus, I miss that very much; I miss you both very much, and I'm
sorry I won't be seeing you this year, but another year will give you the
time necessary to settling in, and if we're all not atomized, perhaps we'll
have those beers in '52.

Things are certainly getting terrible with the Communist smear
thing. Perhaps you are wise to pull in your heads and turtle it where
you are. I was supposed to lecture at LA City College awhile back, but
the English dept. talked it over and decided they wouldn't invite me,
because I'm a friend of Norman Corwin. I've known Corwin for three
years now and he's one of the most decent nice guys in the world,
certainly not a Communist, with many of the sensible ideas you hold,
Ed, but lately they've been after him, and now, by implication, I'm
verboten, and, of course, the fact you get mail from me ruins your
reputation, too. We're really going to hell on a roller-coaster.

The year has started well with a total of 31 sales in the past eleven weeks, new sales to the *Post*, *Collier's*, and a TV deal on my yarn "Zero Hour."[102] I'm taking the manuscript of a book of short stories and another manuscript of a novel I've worked on for five years with me to New York; hope to make a deal on both with Doubleday while I'm there.[103] My new book *The Illustrated Man* had three printings before publication; if you see it in your local book store, note the jacket, which I designed myself.[104]

My Bantam anthology contract has just been signed and the book will hit the stands in October;[105] it is a collection based on the following idea "to collect as many fantasy stories as can be found into one book, by authors who rarely if ever write fantasy in their careers." So I've got a fantasy by Steinbeck, one by Christopher Isherwood, John Cheever, Walter Van Tilberg Clark, Robert Coates, etc., all unusual stories by writers who ordinarily don't come within a million miles of the field. Bantam is paying me $1250 for an introduction to same; a really nice price, for getting the anthology together was no job at all, it was fun browsing through old book shops. The big task would be getting the permissions, but, I find now, Bantam will handle this for me, thank God. Bantam will also publish *The Martian Chronicles* in May, probably with several blue Martian tits on the cover, to help it sell.

Lippert Productions, makers of that terrible *Rocket Ship XM* made a bid for "Mars Is Heaven!" about two months ago, but you know the sort of money they would offer, very cheap indeed, considering they've cleared a million on their first film. So we have held off and are waiting for John Huston to come back from Europe; I heard from Huston in London the other day. I don't know if I told you, but I had supper with him before he headed East to make *The African Queen* with Bogart and Hepburn. He took all three of my books with him and read them on the trip and wrote back saying he would like to make a film with me.[106] So keep your fingers crossed. He's a really nice guy. Attended the preview of his new film *The Red Badge of Courage* and found it very moving, but certainly not a film that the average Joe is going to like, since it's approach to war is oblique and subtle.

[. . .]

Okay, guys, fish, sail, build, write, loll, ride horseback, float lightly down the golden afternoons to come. I envy you it all, and miss you very much, so write on occasion, will you? Mag, Susan and Gumpox[107] (that's what we call the unborn) send you their love, as do I.

Yours,

Ray

P.S. Incidentally, Gerald Heard was over to see us a few months ago. What a fascinating man, what a fascinating evening. You'd get a real bang out of talking to him, Ed; he reminds me of you in many ways, a fascinating erudition, a knowledge of everything, with the Hamiltonian grace of modesty and good cheer.

10750 Clarkson Rd.
Los Angeles 64, Calif.

June 25, 1951

Dear Ed and Leigh:

Been home from New York about a week now and thought it time to write and tell you that we have another baby girl on hand. The new one was born on May 17th and weighed 7 pds, 14 oz. Name: Ramona. A very quiet, unassuming, thoughtful lass who looks like Maggie. Now we have split up sides, Susan and I look alike, so we're the Plum-Pudding-Swedish half, and Mag and Ramona are the official representatives of the Cherokee-Slavic tribes,[108] so it's quite a family. [. . .] Mag had a very good time of the recent delivery [. . .] After I settled her in with our nurse here I headed for New York and stayed ten days and then was only too glad to get out of that damn town. Every year I can take less and less of it. It's not so much the town itself, but what the town seems to do to its inhabitants, that throws my trolley. [. . .]

It was a good trip, however, and I sold two more books to Doubleday and went into some talks with Bantam which resulted in the conclusion of a three book deal with them, so I've no kicks.[109] Had a nice chat with Clifton Fadiman and he turns out to be quite a s-f reader and a very nice gentleman indeed.

Went up and had lunch with Julie and he is the same lovable guy as always.[110] I sort of miss the old pulp days, to be perfectly honest. I wasn't making anything, but I was learning and times were a bit more adventurous. Of course I'm still learning, but the older you get the slower the process becomes and you aren't learning obvious things and making tremendous strides all at once. Now the concentration is on detail and characterization and subtler things, which, in its own way, is fun, but not quite as exciting as having Kuttner or Brackett jump on me with both feet and put my ego through a ringer.

I've been mightily pleased to see the reviews your new book is getting, Ed. Congratulations![111]

How are things coming at your country house? Getting things installed ready for the summer? Any thoughts of coming West any time this year, perhaps for the winter?

Once, a few months ago, I went walking down along the beach in Venice, and passed your nice comfortable old house there and remembered with much happy detail our many good talks there and wished that I might rap at the door and see your good faces. Going to Long Beach to the book store isn't quite the same without you.

I sincerely hope this letter finds you guys in wonderful health, along with all of your kinfolk, especially Betty and your mother, Ed.

I enclose some junk that appeared in the latest issue of Max Ascoli's *The Reporter*. Also a yarn of mine from the latest *Post* sent on because I believe I owe Leigh a debt for having, indirectly, suggested the story. In one of her stories, a detective yarn, years ago, laid in Venice, she described the ruins of the roller-coaster as being something like a prehistoric skeleton lying there in the night. This suggestion, plus the Fog Horn blowing out in the bay at night while I lived in Venice, a year ago, gave me the full-blown idea for the enclosed yarn which the *Post* generously re-titled "The Beast From 20,000 Fathoms." God help us all, said Tiny Tim.

Kuttner has sold a book to Harper's. Some sort of psychological-suspense story, I believe. Haven't had time to read Jack's new book, hope it's good.[112]

I guess this is all for now. Write when you have time and tell me all the latest. Julie said you were still writing for comics, which sounds very profitable indeed if somewhat miraculous. Where *do* you get your ideas?

Love to you both from Maggie, Susan, Ramona, and me!

Yours as always,
Ray

10750 Clarkson Rd.
L.A. 64, Calif.

[ca. early November, 1951]

Dear Ed and Leigh:

It's been quite awhile since I wrote, I'll be damned if I can remember when the last time was. Things roll along pretty much as usual here. The town could still stand a good dose of Brackett-Hamilton anytime you feel up to it. The family waxes healthily, Susan is now two years old, and Ramona six months, and both quite wonderful. I have taken refuge in the garage, where I do my writing now, oblivious to wails, screams and childish ululations.

There have been a lot of screen nibbles lately, some of which I could have taken, all of which I let drop for various reasons. One producer offered me $200.00 down on "Mars Is Heaven," with a total payment of 1500 bucks en toto. Quite a generous guy. Another producer went as high as $2500 on the same story, but I'll be damned if it isn't worth more than that.[113] I might be wrong and lose my shirt, but I don't think I'm wrong.

Gee, I had a chance to write the TV show *Tom Corbett, Space Cadet*. Maybe my head needs examining . . .

One deal that has been simmering awhile concerns a story laid on Venus which 20th owns.[114] We did some wangling on the deal two months ago and I let it lapse. Now they are interested again and I was thinking that if I decide against taking the assignment at any time in the coming 8 weeks that I might suggest you, Leigh, for the job. You've got plenty of film experience under the belt (my God, you worked with Faulkner!) and Venus is your meat rather than mine. So if you feel you'd like a whack at a film again some time this winter, drop me a line by return mail and when I go over to 20th for the talks it might be very well that with my work on my new Doubleday book and all, it would be better for someone with more know-how, like yourself, to be under their consideration. And anyhow, Eastern winters are *cold*.

Another deal cooking is a TV offer to film a series of my yarns here on the Coast; more on that later.[115] Think you might be interested in doing a TV science-fiction adaptation series, Leigh? Your name comes to mind over and over, for you are the only writer I know, outside of Heinlein, who knows films and film-writing; though Heinlein, come to think of it, had very little to do with *Destination Moon* in its final form.

In any event, let me know what you think of the above, and I'll keep my eye peeled for interesting jobs in the science-fiction TV or motion-picture field. I recall that one producer, at Columbia, is looking for a good Venusian story; why don't you have your Coast agent (who are you with now? I'm with Famous Artists) send some of your stories around . . . ?

The above applies to you, too, Ed. If any TV things arise here that I think might interest either of you, I'll whip you a line.

The other news is about the same, a couple of sales to *The Post*, *McCall's*, and *Mademoiselle*,[116] foreign rights to France on the *Chronicles*; ditto Denmark. Under separate cover I'm sending on a copy of the British edition of the *Chronicles* titled *The Silver Locusts*. Good reviews in London on it so far; including one in *Punch*.

What's new on your various books, both of you? Leigh, what about your novel?

I was glancing through my old magazines about five minutes ago and came upon the "Sorcerer of Rhiannon" which you had in a 1942 *Astounding*, Leigh. And it was with a shock of discovery that I found I owed you a story-debt on this one. Unconscious, of course. But, nevertheless, a bit stunning. My subconscious must have remembered your "Rhiannon" story for, years later, it came up with "Asleep in Armageddon." I suppose the resemblance is superficial, but it is there. Which only goes to prove that all the good stories and ideas were done first by Brackett and Hamilton.

Well, enough of this. Give me an answer on how you feel about movies and TV at this time, eh? Mag, the girls, and I send our love. Hope you have had a tremendously profitable year!

Yours, as ever,
Ray

RD 2,
Kinsman, Ohio

Nov. 15, 1951

Dear Ray,

I don't think I ever did send our congratulations on the birth of Ramona. Your letter came just at the time of the death of my remaining brother-in-law, and everything went awry. Anyway, we're sure she's a wonderful baby, and accept our congratulations, though belated.

And our felicitations on how well you're doing. We see your name everywhere these days. I shall be glad to receive a copy of *Silver Locusts*. I did get *Martian Chronicles* and believe that a better title than the new English one.

Star Kings was also published in book form in England—and Gallimard is publishing it as a book in France, and even sent an advance bigger than Fell gave me![117] It's also had serial publication in Denmark, and an Australian deal coming up. But you know how disappointingly small book returns can be financially—still, it's all velvet and mighty welcome. *City at World's End* went over much better with the reviewers.

As to movie deals—I shall let Leigh answer that herself. My own somewhat pessimistic view is that movie money is wonderful but that many are called and few are chosen, and that the many waste time hanging around Hollywood. But then I know from nothing about the business, I admit. I haven't thought much of most of the s-f pictures so far, except for *The Thing* and *Five*, which we both liked very much.

As you can see from our new address, we moved not too long

ago into the house we've been restoring for a long time. We think it's
beautiful, a knockout, the most comfortable house we've ever lived in—
so I'll let it go at that. It is soul-satisfyingly quiet and peaceful, yet we
can be in a big town in an hour (Cleveland). I remain blackly pessimistic
about the inevitability of war, and think this place will cushion the
coming shock some little, at least. Of course, we don't intend to
vegetate here, but will wander afield as soon as we lick our financial
wounds. [. . .]

Yours,

Ed

[*Brackett Postscript:*]

Dear Ray:

All these movie and TV deals sound mighty interesting, and thanks for
thinking of me. But right now, I dunno. Having worked like a beaver for
over a year to get in here, I'm inclined to sit for a bit! Hollywood seems
to me too uncertain a proposition these days, and besides, I have a mess
of work lined up for this winter—an expansion of *Starmen of Llyrdis* for
spring publication by Gnome Press, a *Startling* novel, and various other
projects. More than enough to keep me busy! I figure to let Hollywood
wait until such time as we get back out to the Coast for a spell—and I
reckon Hollywood will stagger along!

Yes, the Eastern winters are cold, but Heaven help me, I like 'em.
For sheer beauty you can't beat this expanse of woods and fields with
the snow on them. Ah, wilderness![118]

My very best to you and Maggie, and the babes . . .

Leigh

August 23, 1953

Dear Ed:

You may recall that, over four years ago, one night in the Mirror Maze at Ocean Park you suggested a story idea about a Dwarf, without intending to, in my ear-shot. Now, all this time later, the story is finally finished, and here is a next to last draft which I thought I'd send on to you for curiosity's sake.[119] You needn't return this; as I have a carbon. Hope you like the end-product of your remark that evening in February, 1949 . . .

I was so pleased to see the three of us lined up together, cheek-by-jowl, Brackett, Bradbury and Hamilton, in the new book on s-f by L. Sprague de Camp just out on the market.[120] He placed our biographical notices together; an accident, of course, caused by the alphabetical arrangement, but one that delighted me.

We often think of you.

Best, as ever,
from,
Ray

RD 2
Kinsman, Ohio

Sept. 14, 1953

Dear Ray,

Thanks for letting me see "The Dwarf"—to tell the truth, I had
completely forgotten my passing suggestion down in the Mirror Maze,
until I read your story. And it's good! Especially the Dwarf's own self-
told fragment of autobiography.

As a trade-last—my yarn in the current *Startling* shows Bradbury
influence in the subject matter.[121] Though as a matter of fact, the
inspiration was an old yarn I once read about the extinction of the
passenger pigeon. As to the yarn mentioned in de Camp's "Handbook"
by me—that is a funny story. I wrote that story in 1933, and still have
the rejection letters in which everyone refused it as too gruesome, too
harrowing, etc. I streamlined it a bit and sent it out a year ago and it was
hailed as a "new" Hamilton![122]

We have not yet seen *It Came From Outer Space* as it hasn't yet
hit our local movie. We saw *Beast From 20,000 Fathoms* and enjoyed it
but it seemed to have little Bradbury in it. All the feeling was left out.
Animation was fine, but it seemed to me a mistake to pop the Beast out
at people the first few minutes. Would have been more effective to build
it up by reports of a sinister mystery in the north, then finally let us see
the Beast the first time it swims solemnly along that undersea canyon,
peering at the bones of its perished fellows, deep chords of solemn
music—*you* know how that would have been done years ago.

Leigh sends her best to all—as I do, indeed. She has just finished a
yarn that I think her most sophisticated product yet.[123] I have to knock
off before the rural mailman comes along—but again, my thanks for
letting me see the story, which of course had unique interest.

Yours,
Ed Hamilton

NELSON BOND

From the late 1930s to the mid-1950s, Nelson S. Bond (1908–2006) was a very popular writer of off-trail science fiction and fantasy stories for the genre pulps as well as the more widely read Blue Book *magazine. His stories usually carried a trademark tone of humor and improbability that strongly appealed to Bradbury's early love of unconventional plots with twist endings. Bond began writing to Bradbury toward the end of his own career, and in later years Bond revived the correspondence as a collector of midcentury genre books. Bradbury's initial response to Bond came as his own career was moving into the mainstream magazines; it offers a backward glance at the inspiration that the work of Bond and others provided at the very beginning of his own writing career.*

Ray Bradbury
33 South Venice Blvd.
Venice, Calif.

February 15, 1949

Dear Nelson Bond:

Your letter awaited me when I returned from Mexico a month ago; I should have answered it long before this, save for the complications of finishing a radio script, six short stories, and a book. Today, I am going through my files and doing all the letters I should have done an eon ago.

I don't suppose you remember me, really. But I met you at the New York Science Fiction Convention on July 4th, 1939. That was a very good day in my life, for on that day I met Ross Rocklynne, Jack Williamson, and—Nelson Bond. I assure you I am not buttering you in return for your kind letter to me. But at that time, and since, I was a Nelson Bond fiend. I used to pull your stories apart (even as I did Theodore Sturgeon's stories, a year or so later) to see what made them tick. I'm afraid I did a bit of Bond imitating. The stories never sold. Perhaps that's for the best. When I started doing my own stuff in my own way I was on safer ground. There are only two funny men in the business for my money, you and Sturgeon, and I'll keep the hell away. I think I read everything of yours there for about five years, including your articles in *Writer's Digest*.[124] I particularly recall one of your articles which used a golf game to illustrate your approach to writing. I think you did one on "planting" that helped me a great deal, also.

Anyway, you can imagine how happy your letter made me. I've had very few pulp idols in the last ten years, and it was certainly a kick to hear from one of my particular favorites. I certainly want to thank you for being thoughtful enough to write and tell me how you feel about *Dark Carnival*; you've made me very happy. I've just finished my second book, *The Illustrated Man*, containing 20 stories—no publisher as yet— but I hope that I can keep you entertained in it.

Mentioning your stories, brings to mind one of your yarns which has stayed with me all through the years, one of your *Blue Book* series, the title of which has long since strayed from my mind, about a book shop that sells copies of books that would have been written by innumerable authors if they had lived an extra year or so.[125] A beautiful idea.

It's a long way from 1939 to here, and I never thought I would meet you again in quite this way (it's quite a change from a plump, loud, 19 year old Bradbury to the selling one today), but it certainly has been an unexpected and happy reunion. By all means write again when you have time and tell me what you've been doing, especially in radio, where I hear you've been burning up the kilocycles. Again thanks, and my apologies for this long silence.

Yours,
Ray

Bradbury's next letter to Bond offers a quick summary of the succession of book and magazine publications that framed what would become his breakout year in mainstream publishing and readership. But this letter is even more signifi- cant for his detailed comments on the role of inspiration occasionally generated through his reading of other authors. He had read little genre fiction since the mid-1940s, but he continued to read mainstream novelists and story writers.

Ray Bradbury
33 S. Venice Blvd.
Venice, Calif.

April 2, 1950

Dear Nelson:

It was a pleasant surprise to hear from you after such a time. You're a thoughtful guy, and God bless you for mentioning the fact that you have some extra copies of British *Argosy* with my yarns in them. No, I haven't seen copies of these, dammit. I've been beating my agent over the head and writing to London, but nothing seems to help. If you could send on any extra copies of these you have, I'd certainly appreciate it and I enclose stamps to cover the cost of mailing and etc. . . . I was especially surprised to hear that they had changed the title of "Million Year Picnic" to "Long Weekend," which is a nice title. I look forward to seeing these.[126]

Thanks also for your good word on "Mars Is Heaven." I have had phenomenal luck with that story. It has been anthologized twice recently, it was purchased by both NBC and CBS during the past four weeks, it went to Britain, Sweden, and South Africa, and only a few days ago sold to *Esquire* as a reprint, and also to *Coronet*, which flabbergasts me![127]

I was reading over *The Other Side of the Moon* the other night and chanced upon "Conqueror's Isle" again, and found it, as I expected, just as enjoyable on the second reading as the first.[128] Otherwise, I have been shamefully behind in my reading, both of Bond and others. I have a stack of books here to the ceiling that has collected during the last year and a half. My trouble is, luckily, a productive one; I begin to read a book by some writer and, halfway through, get some idea of my own perhaps suggested or kicked-off by something said or done by a character in the story I'm reading, whereupon I immediately lay the book down and head for my typewriter. I'm lucky if I ever get back to finishing the original story. Sometimes it is a simple thing. The other night I was reading the new Hemingway novel[129] in *Cosmo* when somebody mentioned a crew of professional bomb-finders and detonators who go through the farmlands relieving farmers of the burden of walking around in fields full of hidden dynamite. This suggested a story to me about a family and a field full of bombs,[130] and, bang! I never did finish Hemingway . . .

Anyway, I'm certainly pleased to hear of your good fortune in selling Doubleday a book.[131] I'll look forward to it. I sold them two books last June. One of them, *The Martian Chronicles*, will be out in May. The second, *Frost and Fire*, much later. As for *The Illustrated Man*, that will be off in the future sometime, thanks for asking.[132] I have a great affection in my heart for Lancelot Biggs; I've read him with relish down the years—he should make up a fine book.

I note also that your *Thirty-First of February* seems to be vanishing steadily from book shops that I frequent;[133] since this could hardly mean that they are throwing them out the window, my congratulations to you. Do you agree that this year, of all years, Doubleday *really* has a list? Thanks for your kind words. My best to you, Nelson!

Yours,
Ray

2

MIDCENTURY MENTORS

The Breakout Years

Here, too, it seems to be a creative truth, that so often a
single person believing in us and telling us we *can* succeed,
helps us over barriers. We go on, with the strength of ten.
—*Bradbury to Bernard Berenson, March 23, 1956*

PAUL RHYMER

The broadcast magic of Paul Rhymer's (1905–1964) Vic and Sade *quickly became one of Bradbury's favorite radio shows during its 1934 to 1946 run on NBC, and Rhymer's ability to capture the essence of small-town America in these short fifteen-minute daily episodes was a leading inspiration for the stories that Bradbury would weave into* Dandelion Wine *(1957) and its source novel,* Farewell Summer *(2005). The setting of* Something Wicked This Way Comes *(1962) also derives in part from the same inspiration.*

December 1, 1949

Dear Mr. Rhymer:

I was in the office of NBC director Warren Lewis yesterday afternoon talking about the possibility of their adapting some of my stories to radio when it suddenly came to me to ask a question I've wanted to ask for years, but always when I was in no position to ask it. The question was: "How can I get some recordings of that wonderful program *Vic and Sade*?" No sooner said than done. Mr. Lewis contacted a few people and arranged to have the programs dubbed for me if and when I knew which ones I wanted. Well, of course, after so many years it is hard for me to put my hand into my memory and pull out the correct dates. The next best thing is to write to you and ask you if you could possibly list your ten favorite *Vic and Sade* broadcasts by date so that I have them dubbed via Mr. Lewis here, at my leisure.

At the same time, Mr. Lewis' secretary gave me your address, and I feel fortunate in being able to at last write and tell you what a good thing you did for the listeners in the long and fine years you wrote *Vic and Sade*. I cannot think of another program that so well represented what the real America is like. I am not one to pull the flag off the mast and drape myself in it, Lord forbid, and I heartily protest against one faction claiming it is more American than another these days, but I do not see how we can escape the fact that *Vic and Sade* was the best argument ever advanced for a way of life in which we all grew up with our courthouse squares and Bijou theatres and Thimble Clubs and

Sacred Knights of the Milky Way. [. . .] I don't know if anyone ever pinned a medal on you, but let me pin my own personal one on you at this time for having given back to all of us some certain portion of our lives, our childhoods, our adolescences, our fathers, our mothers, in a shape where we could recognize and be gently amused by them. [. . .]

I don't know if you are familiar with my work or not. I have had stories published in *The New Yorker*, *Harper's*, *Collier's*, *The American Mercury*, *Charm*, and *Mademoiselle*. My book of short stories *Dark Carnival* has been published not long ago, and I do occasional work for NBC on the *Radio City Playhouse* and CBS' *Suspense*.

I was born up in Waukegan, Illinois in 1920, and Waukegan is pretty much Vic and Sade's town. There are thousands like it all over the country. I've been out West for sixteen years, but not a day passed when your show did not recall the small green town I had left behind. [. . .]

With my best wishes, and the hope that *Vic and Sade* will return soon to the air, I remain,

> Yours *very* sincerely,
> Ray Bradbury
> 33 South Venice Blvd.
> Venice, California.

GERALD HEARD

Henry FitzGerald Heard (1889–1971), a philosopher, lecturer, and theological scholar, immigrated from England to the United States with Aldous Huxley and his family in the early 1930s. He was already known as the BBC's first science commentator, and in America he continued to be widely interviewed for his studies of parapsychology, world religions, and hallucinogenic drugs. Heard had known H. G. Wells, and after settling in Los Angeles he became friend and mentor to a British expatriate community that included Huxley and Christopher Isherwood. Bradbury's connection to this group began with Isherwood's discovery of The Martian Chronicles *in 1950, but the young writer became closer to*

Heard than to any of the others. Decades later, Bradbury's story "Last Laughs"
(2009) offered an imagined farewell "escape" to Heard, who had spent his final
years bedridden following a series of debilitating strokes.

Dear Mr. Bradbury,

Thank you indeed for *Dark Carnival* which I shall prize and *The Illustrated Man* which I have started already. As I was being wound up in its magic I heard the *Daily News* barge in with Antonina Vallentin's "H. G. Wells."[1] Of course they would want that stale stuff— belle lettrism the bugbear of contemporary art—and are afeared of books with no set publishing date. But we will circumvent them—we will have to start with Wells as our cover but we shall emerge and end with Bradbury. And it won't be a forced convergence for what HG did much to start but couldn't complete you are now, I am sure bringing to its full maturity. Don't then trouble your publisher who of course will probably object as much as Scott O'Dell[2] to a far too early bird-call-review of yours yet to be officially born. We'll get the advanced publicity advanced through old HG as the stalking horse. Again best wishes and much admiration. Kindest regards to Mrs. Bradbury and Junior.

Sincerely
Gerald Heard
4th Nov. 1950
545 Spoleto Drive, Santa Monica.

Dear Ray Bradbury

How kind of you to send me "The Fireman" which arrived yesterday & is already consumed, gutted. I know I shall always be a Bradburian. One day, you know, I hope you'll publish poems—it is not merely a truly original invention that carries your own writing into its own stratosphere—it is the rhetor's power of fusing an image with a phrase & in the natural flow of narrative. The metaphors (which are as Eastman[3] said) the essence of poetry, are valid but new associations, recognitions of likenesses unperceived before but fused for good after you have linked them. You could, I fancy, surpass Christopher Fry.[4]

Come over some day when you can spare time. You take off, I remember your saying, an occasional afternoon. I am nearly always free from 2 to 4:30. If you can, give me a call & we'll find a free day in common. My number is Exbrook 44803.

Congratulations & with best wishes to you both & the baby.

Cordially,
Gerald Heard
18.i.51.
545 Spoleto Drive
Santa Monica.

Ray Bradbury
10750 Clarkson Rd.
Los Angeles 64, Calif.

August 2, 1951

Dear Mr. Heard:

Just a brief note, and, I hope, not too much trouble for you. My British publisher, Rupert Hart-Davis, learning from me in one of my letters that I had met you and that you admired my work, wrote to enquire today if there would be any possibility of getting a quote from you to use in publicity on *The Martian Chronicles* when it appears in England on September 15th. I haven't the faintest idea whether it is cricket to ask you for a few kind words or not, and if I'm out of bounds, please declare me out and I shall retreat in all haste. But if, on the other hand, you feel that you could drop me a few lines that I in turn can air-mail on to Rupert Hart-Davis, then I would be very happy and very grateful indeed.

It might seem strategic to mention at this time that I thoroughly admired, and was entranced with, your sea monster in the current *Magazine of Fantasy and Science Fiction*, but I assure you that, all commercial strategy aside, it was a delightful tale.[5]

I hope to call you some day soon, with the possibility in mind that I might come to see you again for another of those wonderful dives into free space and thinking that you always seem able to promote for me when I come within your gravity. In the meantime, I include a new story of mine[6] which appeared about 4 weeks ago in *The Post* and which, in a way, seems to be a second or third cousin of the monster in your story. One never knows! May I hear from you about all the above, when you have time? My very best regards to you, and may this find you in good spirits and health.

Yours,
Ray

August 5, 1951

Dear Ray:

Delighted to hear from you and many thanks for the *Post* story. I agree in the tiny compass they gave you you have brought off your double aim, the tactic of holding the public with a fantasy monster and behind it the strategy theme of life at different levels with its hopeless or perhaps not hopeless but agonizing attempt to make contact across the abyss.

I am equally delighted to send for Rupert H-D an 'Encore' he wants.[7] It's a great honor to be asked to applaud a work that will last. I'm complimentarily delighted and honored by what you say about "The Collector." I am at present at work on three stories at once which I honestly believe are odder than anything I have so far done. I would much appreciate showing them to you when they are through. I have to leave in mid-September for three months in St. Louis, coming back I hope on the shortest day. If you can't get round before then, make that as a date at which again we can start trying to get together. I certainly found your visit most stimulating.

I hope everything goes right with the family as I know it's going with the work.

Yours,
Gerald
545 Spoleto Drive
Santa Monica, Calif.

BERNARD BERENSON

The internationally prominent Renaissance art critic and historian Bernard Berenson (1865–1959) was nearly eighty-eight years old when he invited Ray and Maggie Bradbury to his home in Florence and introduced them to the art treasures of the Western world. Berenson reached out first; after reading Bradbury's "The Day After Tomorrow: Why Science Fiction?" in the May 2, 1953, issue of The Nation, *Berenson penned what he called the first "fan letter" of his long life, noting that "it is the first time I have encountered the statement by an artist in any field, that to work creatively he must put flesh into it, & enjoy it as a lark, or fun, or fascinating adventure." Bradbury's spring 1954 travels through Rome, Florence, and Venice were a revelation; after he returned home to Los Angeles, his letters to Berenson became almost a diary of reflections on his renewed creativity and his broadening appreciation of art.*

December 12, 1954

Ray Bradbury
10750 Clarkson Rd.
Los Angeles 64, Calif.
U.S.A.

Dear B.B.:

[. . .] Last weekend, in a great burst of enthusiasm, and energy, completely at ease with my techniques and thus unaware of them, I wrote six short stories in a period of 40 hours. From Saturday night

until Monday morning I lived in a constant state of euphoria. All
of the stories that leapt from my typewriter were the result of my
experimenting with word-associations. I usually put down two words
like THE HARP or THE RAIN or THE DWARF, or THE MIRROR or
THE TWINS. I don't question why my subconscious has supplied these
words. For some reason, it has, and like a good father I accept the voice
of my child. I know that around and about those words, thus simply
offered, has collected a pool of sensations and ideas which need to be
tapped. Nine times out of ten, the tapping process is successful. This
weekend, especially, the most incredible stories jumped to life from
touching on a few key words. The stories were of all types and sizes,
moods and genres. I have written one about a man in a small town
who discovers that the local maker of tapestries, which are incredible
displays of forest coloring, grass-greens, flower whites and blues,
touches of water and white pebble and brown stone, like the floor of a
woods in spring and summer—that the maker of these tapestries, I say,
employs jeweled spiders which he takes from the meadowlands and
forests and trains and brings into his shop where the spiders re-create
the natural life they experienced outside the town. The tapestries these
spiders spin and weave are, of course, beyond belief.[8]

I have written a story about some old men lost in a desert town
for many many years, waiting for the one day each year when the rain
comes over the town.[9] And when the one day comes, this year, the rain
holds off, and the old men are held in the ruinous heat of the sun until
an old woman, a traveling musician, comes by in the hot twilight with
a great golden harp closeted in the back-seat of her antique car. When
she plays her harp, in the sun-blazed lobby of the deserted hotel, the old
men quicken. For here, at last, with a touch of the hands on the strings,
quickly, softly, is the sound of the rain. The cool sound of the harp moves
through the rooms of the hotel and the old men know that the long
season of drought is over and that the good years of the gentle rains have
begun.

Those are only two of the stories, in brief—much too brief, really.
[...]

The most important thing I want to say here, and which it has taken
me a God-awful time to get around to, is, once again, how you have

changed and shaped my life in the very short time of this one year. No day, not one single blessed day, passes that I haven't my hand on your soul through your books here in the house. [. . .] What a fine collection of hearts you must have from people who came by your way and left without knowing, immediately, that part of them would always remain at I Tatti.

At the close of the year, then, again thanks to you for your thumbprint on my forehead. May the holiday season be joyous and wonderful to you and Miss Mariano.[10] Write, when you have a moment.

Yours with affection,
Ray

Bradbury's steady stream of transatlantic updates to Bernard Berenson included this summary of a crucial point in the seventeen-year evolution of Something Wicked This Way Comes (1962). *In 1955 the various prose fragments in his files solidified into a sustained screenplay that circulated even as he moved ahead, just three years later, with a full-length novel version. Bradbury would continue to relate these intense bursts of creativity to Berenson in subsequent letters.*

Bradbury
10750 Clarkson Rd.
Los Angeles 64, Cal.

August 4, 1955

Dear B.B.

[. . .] I'm on the eve of attempting my first three-act play, a challenge that has fascinated me for years. Later, perhaps in January of next year, I hope to make another motion picture of a small book I recently finished in manuscript form about a Gothic carnival that arrives one October midnight in a small Illinois town; the carnival having traveled all about the earth, with its alchemists and sorcerers, for hundreds of years, posing the problem of good and evil, and tilting the scales in its own favor—that is, of course, toward evil. I was in a fever, doing the story, for many days, earlier this year, not unlike some I have run with a fine head and chest cold, but without any of the discomforts. After a number of days of absolutely glowing in the dark, and feeling somewhat drunk, the carnival let down its black velvet tents and stole away, leaving me exhausted but happy, at my typewriter [...]

Please be careful; don't trip and fall into a Tintoretto. By the looks of some of them, you would never hit bottom.

Yours, as ever,
Ray

Bradbury's coming to terms with creative disappointments showed most fully in his continuing correspondence with his mentor Bernard Berenson. In this letter, he looks back through the two-year interval between finishing his screenplay for Moby Dick *and the successful release of the film, trying to understand his complex relationship with director John Huston. He also describes how the disappointment of his failed attempt to dramatize* Fahrenheit 451 *for Academy Award–winning actor Charles Laughton turned to creative satisfaction as Laughton inspired him to try his hand at a science-fictional operetta.*

10750 Clarkson Road
Los Angeles 64, Cal.
U.S.A.

March 23, 1956

Dear B.B.

A wonderful thing happened to me last Monday night when I saw *Moby Dick* on the screen for the first time. In the interval of almost two years since I had last seen my director-producer, various things had occurred to undermine our friendship, I had done much work, gratis, and sent it to him, as he was working on the picture, and he had failed to acknowledge receipt of this work and had done a number of things to aggravate and anger me. Yet, on the night when I saw the film this week, when I saw how incredibly beautiful some parts of the film were, and when I realized that here and there, anyway, we had captured Melville on film, I was so happy and excited that a chemical change came over me. The chemical change remains. If Huston had been in the room after the film was over, I would have embraced him and kissed him on both cheeks. Suddenly my little prides and vanities, my irritations and angers, vanished. They are still gone. Here indeed is a remarkable example of the power of an artform, big or little it matters not, changing the shape of one's mind in a few hours. I felt ashamed for my petty irritations and unkind thoughts. Huston the man is one thing, I can still know him as a man and know him, unhappily for what he lacks there, but over that picture I must constantly super-impose the image of his creativity. He has electricity in his fingertips and an eye that sees more than the normal eye can ever hope to see. He is not a man of great ideas, but he handles the things of the world with magical ease and a loving touch. He helps you to see things anew, which is certainly the mark of an artist. Being reminded of this, my enmity for the man fell into dust. I only wish now that Huston the man could view the work of Huston the artist and be remade as I was remade, into a kinder and more tolerant and more human animal, by the process. So often, it seems, the artist is cut off from the very benefits he offers mankind, he strews riches on the earth and dies of hungers in so doing. Huston feeds the world and yet cannot feed himself, an unhappy, tormented, and in some ways, Ahab-type of man.

I have also tried, and succeeded, in doing the book and lyrics of a small half-hour operetta recently, which should play in New York this fall, produced and directed by Charles Laughton.[11] Here again was a delightful experience, where I was released from my inferiority complex by Mr. Laughton coming to me and telling me I had the ability to try and succeed at this form which I had never thought of in my life. To write a lyric! Impossible! And yet I have done it. I have much to learn here, too, but at least a friendship has broken my doubts for me and I am on my way. Here, too, it seems to be a creative truth, that so often a single person believing in us and telling us we *can* succeed, helps us over barriers. We go on, with the strength of ten. The power of friendship, the power of love, how rarely we consider it, how rarely we realize the interior mountains it can blast apart and shake to nothing. The one thing I try to do when I lecture classes in the short story, once or twice a year, is knock down the inferiority I find in student after student, the devil imps that tell them they cannot do what in their hearts they most wish to do. If I can leave the class knowing that I have turned them back on themselves and helped them to look at and be themselves and produce from their hearts and souls, I am always happy and know I have taught well. So often I hear people say, But what have I to offer? And the answer is so simple: themselves. But they always throw themselves on a scale and toss weights on the opposite side to find themselves wanting. They do not trust their eye, their ear, their nose, their tongue, to see, hear, smell, taste the world, and tell what it means to them, as individuals. Their originality lies for them to seize it, but often, they will not so much as nudge it with their toe. It seems almost an act of ridiculous egotism to them, if you tell them they are, each of them, original and fresh, and it is their focus they must give, and later, sell, to the world. The world does not go alone to the better builder of mousetraps, it goes also to the man who says, I am a prism, my prism differs from all the other two billion prisms in the world! See how the sun strikes through me! See the spectroscopic rainbow colors my prism spreads glowing on the wall! The world seeks refreshment of the senses, and how few know they have it to offer if they could find a way to speak it, paint it, shape it, with tongue, pen, brush, or clay.

Lecture over. I step down from the podium. [. . .]

Yours as ever,
Ray

During the winter of 1957–58, Bradbury had to come to terms with the realization that his British readers, who usually found his science fiction and some of his fantasies engaging, had little to say at all about the nostalgic American memories permeating Dandelion Wine. *In Berenson, he had a reader who could appreciate his need to understand the ebb and flow of literary popularity, and how Bradbury hoped to navigate the margins between popular culture and literary distinction.*

February 28th, 1958

Dear B.B.:

The months pass, but there isn't a day when we don't brush near you
in walking through our house. Your books are in every room (you can
imagine how neat our filing system is!) and we think of you as we find
you, now in our living room, now in Bettina's nursery! Berenson from
the cradle on, is most obviously our motto. Our eldest, Susan, came
from school the other day (she's eight) asking if we happened to have
a book around the house concerning Raphael! I was pleasantly shocked
and surprised at this—for my opinion of some of the things going on in
education here these days is not high—and immediately took her on a
brief tour through your *Italian Painters*, which she found great fun. This
girl is also the one we found, in London, curled up with *Moby Dick*! I was
unable to read Melville and digest him, skin and all, until I was 33. It was
somewhat disconcerting to find Susan on pretty comfortable terms with
him last summer! She does what most critics should learn to do with
old *Moby*, abandon herself to some judicious skipping! She has read,
and approved, my *Dandelion Wine*. What in God's name will she think
of my terror tales when she hits them, later? I don't know if I could face
my daughter's disdain! Poe did the wise thing and died young before
any offspring could cut paperdolls out of "The Cask of Amontillado"!
Can you imagine Poe playing with children? Or perhaps I am being
terribly wrong. Perhaps children may have been the one kind of strange
creature he would have been comfortable with. I don't know enough of
his personality, save through his stories, to imagine whether he might
not have been fascinated by these creatures of another race that scuttle
about our feet, prepare traps for our pride, and see straight through our
flimsy masks. Right now, with three daughters and another on the way
(yes, in August, by God!!) I feel like the proprietor of a marionette show
whose puppets act in cruel opposites—I pull the string to the left arm,
the right leg dances! right arm and the left leg kicks! pull the string for
the feet and the head bobs! It's no go and no show with children! They,
contrarily, pull the string on my left hand and my left hand waves, right
hand and my right hand waves, etc., etc.!

I've had a strange experience with *Dandelion Wine*. The reviews in the U.S. have been, with one exception, really excellent. The reviews in England, however, with few exceptions, have been downright bad. It's the first time in all my years of publishing that I've had such a terrible reaction to a book from any country anywhere. I was a bit depressed by this, but then fell back upon my favorite theory, or rationalization, if you will, which may please or pique you. It depends in many ways upon an almost literal use of the word Taste. When I look back upon my adolescence it can best be illustrated by the ravening appetite one had for certain books. It was really a process of devouring certain authors whole and entire. It was true of childhood, too. It was literary cannibalism at full-pitch. I ate Jules Verne, fingernails, top-hat, and all. I made meals of Poe, Tom Swift, H. G. Wells, and later, Thomas Wolfe, John Steinbeck, Willa Cather, and many others. The point is, it was a hunger over and above any immediately rational explanation. I simply needed to be fed, my taste ran wild, I ate the food that sustained me. Later, my taste, my hunger, was refined. But there is still in me the raw excitement and admiration for magicians, runaway balloons, fireworks, dragons, castles, monsters, that filled me in those days. This takes me the long way around to my predicament, if predicament it is, with England and *Dandelion Wine*. A writer grows up in an environment where he hungers for certain artforms, shaped by his society, and in turn his hungers shape and form other parts of that society. If that writer is fortunate, when he comes to maturity, his subconscious puts forth into the open such food as his society will make meals of. He doesn't do it cynically or with any plan for profit, other than that of the ego, for his art is, if true, a gift from his secret self anyway. When I write my stories, I am as overjoyed as anyone who reads them later, to see them shaping on the page and to hear the characters talking their delightful talk. I listen and am amazed, for this is not myself talking, it is the other one, the sly one, the boy I keep in the attic, talking of his balloons and fireworks and dead seas. But . . . back to my point . . . these gifts from my subconscious, the gifts from any artist's subconscious are then displayed to the world for breakfast, lunch and dinner. The world eats sparingly or eats well. If the artist is lucky, the world comes back for seconds. The gift given is the gift wanted. The gift offered to the U.S. in my *Dandelion Wine* seems

to have been the one most desired. The response, by letter alone, has
been immensely happy for me. But now we find ourselves in England, a
country where I did not grow up, where I was not born or shaped in any
way. They do not hunger for my book, they find me all sticky marmalade
and no bread. What can I do about this? Nothing, of course. In fact, if the
same response had been given in the U.S. I would have been as helpless.
One goes on bringing forth the gift, even if it is refused. I suppose what
I'm trying to get around to in this argument, is a kind of philosophy for
any artist so he can live comfortably in the world. Rejection is less bitter,
if one understands the needs of the world. If you can look straight in
the face of one who finds sustenance elsewhere, and accept it, you are
well on your way to a long and adjusted life. It may be, of course, that
my argument is specious because it comes from one who has been very
lucky. If I had been met with raw dislike and been turned down by the
readers in my own country years ago, before I was old enough to come
to any ideas such as those contained in this letter, perhaps I would have
been destroyed or turned aside into another activity. It's all very well to
talk about climbing Mt. Everest when you're on top of the damn thing.

How do I sum up this interminable argument of mine?

Well, it seems to me that while there is a small core of aesthetic and
critical inquiry in the world, toward which an artist may cast a glance
on occasion, the world itself is this almost blind eating and casting out,
devouring and moving on. I don't necessarily approve of this blindness
and this appetite, for it results in much that we all deplore. It can
also result in some exciting art that appeals to just about everybody
immediately. I don't pretend to know how the mass moves or how the
intellects within the mass keep elbow-room. But then I don't even know
how my own creativity works. Both seem somewhat groping, my need to
put on paper, and their need to reach out, here and there, for the original
or the unoriginal, whichever makes them most comfortable on a given
day. If I don't like a thing, I try to spell it out, hoping that others who
don't like that thing, may respond. If I love a thing, this too I try to put
down, hoping others may reach out their hands. We are then part of this
great earthworm (block that metaphor) that eats tonnages of swill every
day, and with it a few vitamins (I consider myself a vitamin) with which
to sustain the brain in its head as well as the one in its tail. (Right now

the race is on between the brain in the head and the one in the tail to see which wins first with the hydrogen bomb, I imagine you could say).

My God, I feel like the *Laocoön* in the midst of this letter.[12]

There is then, I presume, the great taste, the great feeding which goes on, whether we like it or not, in the world. And the little tasters who run along beside the monster and try to tell it what it *should* like. Occasionally a writer finds himself popular not only with the Big Maw but with the critics and reviewers who trot beside the Idiot Beast. It doesn't happen often. I've had a little taste of it. It has pleased me to hear from nine year old boys in Poughkeepsie who find me the love of their lives as the result of my *Martian Chronicles*, though they correct me harshly for my scientific inaccuracies. It is fun to hear myself described, as I did the other day, by a sixteen year old girl as "real cool!" which is current Americanese for "okay!" And it has been the most heartening experience of all to know that people like yourself and Nicky find something of interest in my books. So, you see, I jog along sometimes outside the Monster, the Devourer I describe, and sometimes look out through the glass wall of his stomach as he rolls and rushes toward eternity. I'm part of his digestive tract. I'll be damned if I know what to do about it. Nothing but go back and write another story.

I'm a child of my time, really, an old and a trite way to put it. I grew up in a rapidly changing society of machines, so I have iron pollen in my blood. I am a child of the motion-pictures, which, I am sure, changed my mind and life with their everchanging symbols flashed on the screen in the dark. I am certain I would not write the way I do today if I hadn't been subjected to literally thousands of motion pictures in the last 37 years. The motion picture is a bastard form, admittedly, and mainly because there have been so few who come to it with loving excitement to make it tell the best stories possible. But I can't rebel at what's in my blood. Films, machinery, and nature, all mix together with magicians and carnivals and all find a way to resolve the problems through my work. But I'm lucky, because having this iron in my blood, knowing my society from having sprung up within it, I can offer it tidbits of criticism and observation which it finds hard to resist. Now, since *Sputnik* went into the air, my telephone has been ringing steadily. I find myself accepted as an "expert" if I wish . . . but have resisted putting myself on too many platforms with too many predictions. Instead I have gone back to finish another book of stories and work on another novel.[13] I am still, of course, wonderfully excited about the coming years, and what space-travel will do to our artforms, to our laws, and religions. The upheavals, once started, will be tremendous. I would prefer that space-travel waited on the maturity of man. But since it is obvious that we children are going into space, regardless, I can only hope that it will eventually turn into a United Nations Project. The Idiot jumps at the stars. With myself half in that Body and half-out, and with others like myself, perhaps the whole thing won't come to complete ruin.

A last point. While the English reject *Dandelion Wine* as so much sorghum and honey, they like my science-fiction very much. There they have appetite. There I am food. [. . .]

I hope my views here haven't horrified you completely. Perhaps I am only trying to justify my own luck here. Have at me with cudgels!

Love to you both from Maggie and yours ever,

Ray

I Tatti
Via di Vincigliata
Florence

March 6, 1958

Dear Ray,

[. . .] I cannot understand why you have taken the British reception of *Dandelion Wine* so hard. There is always a time lag between what is liked in one country and what is liked in another. I know it well from my own experience. Of course I am casehardened, having lived through so many kinds and phases of taste and revulsions from them.

Now let me tell you that the rest of your letter expresses as well as I have ever read what happens to the real artist when he creates. I have thought for 75 years at least about it. Ultimately it is a matter of the spirit blowing where it listeth. There is no accounting for genius, least of all to oneself. Hundreds of times I found myself writing what I had no idea was in me. And being a better talker than writer, I am amazed to hear myself saying things utterly beyond my own expectation. But you say it all a hundred times better in this wonderful letter of yours.

You say you would prefer that space travel waited on the maturity of man, but is man capable of maturity? I wonder. Nothing seems to be able to stop his lust for experimentation and his hunger for what is beyond and beyond.

I should love to see you all but you must not delay too long. Do not forget that I am within weeks of 93.

Love to you all,
B.B.

ROBERT HILLYER

With the passing of Bernard Berenson in late 1959 and the rapid physical decline of Charles Laughton, Bradbury's need for mentors and auditors was waning. He was now nearly forty years old, but he continued to write to older authors he admired, including the Pulitzer Prize–winning poet Robert Hillyer (1895–1961).

September 10th, 1959

Dear Mr. Hillyer:

I should have done this many years ago, but always put it off. Now, in reading *The Relic and Other Poems*,[14] I simply can't excuse myself any longer.

Quite simply, for a long time now, you've made me happy, sad, and tremendously alert with your poems. For all this, I want to thank you.

I'm sending on a few of my own books, hoping that some of my stories may please you as much as your work has pleased me.

One of the stories in *A Medicine for Melancholy*, titled "The Shoreline at Sunset," is the result of my reading one of your poems, many years ago, about a mermaid. Therefore I have more than the usual reasons for thanking you.

Best wishes always from
Yours,
Ray Bradbury

---

29 September 1959

Dear Mr. Bradbury,

I've waited to write you until your books should arrive and I should have a chance to read them. Now I close the covers and come blinking from another world.

They are the most wonderful stories I've ever read—full of wonder. I thought wonder had gone out of stories after *The Sea Children* and other strange tales that enchanted my childhood. Now here it is all back again. I wonder by what magic you managed to free your imagination in these crabbed times.

The Martian Chronicles bites deep, though; I don't think *Gulliver* bit much deeper. I wonder if Sam Parkhill will read about himself, thinking he is merely reading science fiction. I am amazed and delighted. (By the way, I keep repeating the word "wonder" in all its aspects. You can see I'm still rubbing my eyes on emerging out of your worlds.)

I was glad to find my mermaid again along "The Shoreline at Sunset," and I think you have treated her beautifully. I'm proud to think that my poem started you off.

All you say of my poetry is like Miss Hillgood's harp notes after a rainless summer.[15] I must have a faithful if small audience, because Mr. Knopf continues to publish me, but it's not often I receive a letter comparable to yours. And I'm glad *The Relic* still keeps your good opinion, for the other poem you spoke of, "The Mermaid," came out in 1924, 35 years ago! So, at any rate, I'm still going strong.

Please let me know when next you publish a book. I want to keep up with you.

With a thousand thanks and best wishes always,

Yours,
Robert Hillyer

Reading this over, I'm ashamed to send you such wretched style. The fact is, I've given two lectures today and my verbal energies flag. But I'll send this along, for I don't want to wait longer to thank you.

————————————————————

28 December 1959

Dear Mr. Bradbury,

Dandelion Wine is a wonderful book, a land of happy and innocent enchantment where I lost myself completely for several radiant hours. It seems to me miraculous that you can create all this so convincingly without a single flaw. My wife was as delighted with it as I was, and asked me to tell you so. My warm thanks for this lovely Christmas present.

You remembered so many little things; the folding steps of the trolley cars, for instance. This I had totally forgotten.

My own boyhood symbol is the paddle-wheel steamer, with its splashing paddle-wheels and plunging walking beam. Something sailed away with those ships when America lost them, something very important and never to be recovered.

Did I send you a copy of my most recent book of verse, *The Relic*? If not, would you like to have it? I know I intended to send you one, but I can't remember whether or not I actually did.

I am busily at work on two books at once, one on *The Pursuit of Poetry* and also my *Complete Poems* (swan song) for Mr. Knopf in 1961. The Pursuit book is for McGraw-Hill—a real chore.

I shall be 65 in June, and that means retirement from my professorship here. I think I have a Fulbright for Aix-en-Provence for 1960–61. That ought to be pleasant.

Thanks again for your book. I can't begin to tell you how much I liked it.

Yours, as ever,
Robert Hillyer

I wonder if you know my old friend Gene Fowler in L. A.? I am very fond of him, but we have not met in many years. He dedicated one of his books to me, *A Solo in Tom-Toms*, that I think the best of all his books.

January 9, 1960

Dear Mr. Hillyer:

Thank you for your fine letter about *Dandelion Wine*. It only proves what I have always known . . . that we write for those we admire . . . and when they in turn admire us, we have the real stuff of life given back to us.

Yes, I was one of those in line to buy a copy of *The Relic*. Thank you for offering to send me a copy. It is a stimulating book, all through.

I've never met Gene Fowler, but his early books were much read and admired by me. I've known, very slightly, some of the people he has written about . . . here and there my life touched theirs . . . people like Barrymore, W. C. Fields, and John Decker, the artist . . . and I was always touched and saddened, reading Fowler's book about Barrymore, to realize that these were all children, fantastic, wild, irresponsible children, all hurrying to bed, all rushing headlong toward the eternal comforts of the grave . . . I was in John Decker's art gallery a few days after the death of Barrymore, and Decker, entering from his living quarters in another part of the building, somehow took me for a friend, or at the very least an acquaintance . . . it was early in the day but he was well into his third or fourth martini, I estimated . . . Decker took me by the arm and led me into a small room where he opened a double set of doors in the wall, behind which hung a sketch of Barrymore made within moments after his death. Standing there and looking at Barrymore's profile, and the profile of Decker next to me as he stared at his sketch, I realized that within a

short time Decker too would be dead, and dead in much the same way
Barrymore died . . . of being the strange and frantic child, panicking at life
and itching after darkness. I have rarely had such a huge irony acted out
for me . . . for Decker bore quite a physical resemblance to Barrymore. If I
recall correctly, Decker was dead about two years later.

Good God, I don't know why I've told you this. Talking of Fowler
set it off. He, of the whole troupe, I gather, had sense enough finally to
conserve his sanity, energy, and talent, and has survived . . . though I've
heard little of him recently.

I'll certainly look forward to your *Pursuit of Poetry* when it is
finished. Meantime, I enclose a new story of mine from the *Post*.[16]
Please, please, no answer is necessary to this letter, no comment is
needed on the story. You are a busy man, with the *Pursuit* ahead of you,
and Aix-en-Provence waiting for your arrival. Happy New Year!

Yours,
Ray Bradbury

---

1 April 1961

Dear Ray,

It must be over a year since you advised me to stop corresponding and
apply myself to my work. Well, I followed the advice and produced two
books. I think I was already at work on the first one when we were writing
back and forth. It came out last November, and is a prose book called *In
Pursuit of Poetry* and was published by McGraw-Hill, who made a beautiful
volume out of it. Have you seen it? Even more beautiful is my *Collected
Poems*, published by Alfred A. Knopf, which will officially appear in May.

I was moved to write you not only by my continued admiration
for your work and my frequent thoughts of you, but, specifically, by an
advertisement of the Bread Loaf Writer's Conference, in which you are
to take part.[17] Thirty years ago, when Theodore Morrison was running
it, and Bernard De Voto was alive,[18] I used to be a member of it and
taught verse to many. Now, I am sure, I should never be asked, for John

Ciardi has always, for no reason that I can see, been hostile to me and my work. But I shall have friends there this summer, as well: you, Robert Frost, Theodore Morrison, Dudley Fitts, William Sloane, and especially Howard Nemerov, who was one of my students and with whom I am in constant correspondence.

Have you been to Bread Loaf before? We used to have high old times when Benny De Voto was alive. That must have been 1930–32, for Prohibition was still on the land and we would drive over the Canadian border to drink Bass's Ale. Sometimes temperaments (never mine) flared. Julia Peterson made a scene in the dining room once, as I remember it, against Morrison. Then De Voto and Frost had a falling-out that was never mended. But I don't know or remember what it was all about. Ah me, how long ago it seems; how long ago, in fact, it is! I am old now. [. . .]

I hope that this letter does not find you amid a whirlwind of work and that I shall hear from you again.

Yours ever,
Robert Hillyer

───────────────

As Hillyer prepared for retirement from his academic career, he shared memories of the great writers and poets who had been his friends or students. He could not escape, however, the bittersweet realization that some of the new generation of poets and critics had little respect for his work, and he shared these observations with his younger friend. In the end, it was Bradbury's turn to offer encouragement and to pose, in the postscript, an unanswered question. This is the last known letter between them; Hillyer passed away on Christmas Eve, 1961.

May 17, 1961

Dear Mr. Hillyer:

Thank you for yours of April 25th. Yes, please first-name me, and forgive me if I wait awhile to first-name you. I was raised in such a way, and still live by the example, of addressing my elders with respect. After we have corresponded for a few more times I will evolve toward the comfortable "Robert" or "Bob." I knew Gerald Heard for three years before I finally addressed him as Gerald. I've known Aldous Huxley slightly for some years, but have yet to use his first name.

The copy of your collected poems arrived, and I thank you so very much for this thoughtfulness. It is on my night-table where every night before going to sleep I can dip in, go for a swim, which is the way I always think of poetry.

I have a very simple way of looking at our position in the world as writers. If I had to give it a preposterous label I would speak of it as the Aesthetics of Need. There is no way to argue with people's needs. Or tastes, if you want to use another word. So I have long since stopped worrying. If people need me they will read me. If they don't need me, they won't. If they need Tom Wolfe, well, by all means, let them devour old Tom. I loved him dearly when I was twenty. I still respect the need of the person I was then, though I no longer read Wolfe. The trouble with most people is they forget old needs, hungers, and therefore old obligations. I will not turn my back on old loves. It would be heartless to criticize Danilova for not dancing well this year, when the heart remembers how well she danced twenty years ago.[19] Continuity of memory and obligation is everything if one wants to become and stay human.

So we won't worry if Ciardi likes or loves us, or Oscar Williams[20] or any others. If we don't fulfill some need of theirs, others will come along hungry for us. Right now, as always, I need you and your work. What more can you ask? And there are many others like myself with a similar appetite for Hillyer. [. . .]

Until next time, happy traveling to the Virgin Islands. And the respectful and affectionate regard of

Yours
Ray B.

P.S. I have always called your kind of writing the higher realism. It is, isn't it?

3

EMERGING WRITERS

I am reminded of my own morbidities in certain *Dark Carnival*
stories . . . You'll grow out of this phase, as I did. It's good to
write these things out of your system . . . you've got better
and more wondrous things coming up in your imagination.
—*Bradbury to Charles Beaumont, September 28, 1954*

CHARLES BEAUMONT

Bradbury first encountered Charles Nutt in a bookstore in the late 1940s, just before his young friend embarked on a significant writing career as Charles Beaumont (1929–1967). During Beaumont's rapid rise to prominence in the early 1950s, he sent stories to Bradbury for advice. Beaumont's talent was immediately apparent to Bradbury, who sometimes chastised him when a story wandered into what he considered gratuitous horrors or ballooned into overly expansive narratives. In September 1953 Bradbury's sudden departure for Ireland, where he would spend many months working with the demanding director John Huston on scripting the Warner Brothers production of Moby Dick, *took him away from the young writers he had been mentoring. The challenges of his first European working venture, and the presence as well of his growing family, led Bradbury to turn down Beaumont's request for an introduction to his first story collection. Bradbury's longtime friend Forrest J Ackerman, who at the time represented Beaumont, had made the request by mail, and Bradbury now had to clarify his decision to Beaumont himself.*

October 21, 1953

Dear Chuck:

Your letter, coming while my letter is still in process of going to Forrie, somewhat unsettled me, for, above all, I *do* have such a distinct admiration for your work that this whole experience has been very unhappy to me. I have felt terribly guilty turning down the chance to write the introduction to your work.[1] But I must reiterate what I said to Ackerman, that I think your work will sell on its own, *must* sell on its own, and that when it is in proofs I'll be glad to read the proofs and give you a quote for an ad. That should be agreeable, I think, and it takes the burden of trying to be true to two loves, you and *Moby Dick*, off my shoulders at this time. I can't say how truly happy in every way I am that you are selling so many stories, especially to Boucher and *Esquire*. All along, as you say yourself, I have watched your work growing and growing. I have never forgotten you or your work. In fact I found myself, at times, being almost infernally irritated and dismayed, when I saw you, and your fine talent, going off on byways and down dark alleys. I was so afraid you would vanish down a drain into t.v. or some damn film-company.

But now I see my fears were for nothing, and I feel that you are well on the road to going where you must inevitably go; right on up to the top, to give everyone, including me, a good shove to one side.

Please write me and say that you understand everything about my attitude. If nothing is clear, ask me to clarify it to you. Above all, nothing in my opinion on this matter must be nebulous to you. I value friends too much to be wishy-washy with them.

I'll be glad to hear from you any time or from Ackerman, any time *he* wishes to write. Things go well here. I've already done 50 pages of *Moby Dick* in script form and am pleased with what I see.

Saw Laurel and Hardy, *in person*, last week. A wonderful time. Had to travel 8 thousand miles to see them, but I finally did. Really fine.

Please write. Please forgive me if I have in any way hurt you by my refusal at this time to give you a "boost-up" via an intro. Give my love to Forrie, your wife, Len, everyone.

> Yours, as ever,
> Ray

11550½ Friar Street
North Hollywood, Calif.

October 30, 1953

Dear Ray,

At the risk of seeming an insensitive gibbon exceedingly ill met, I'm going to be completely honest with you. Your letter to Forry, in response to the cable, sent me into a bit of a wing-ding. I was hurt, I was disappointed, I was sore. Mostly, I guess, I was hurt. I fell prey to a gamut of emotions of which I am now not a little ashamed, viz. (or i.e. or whatever it is) Yeahyeah, sure, I understand, all right.

Bradbury's gotten too big, too big for little (sob!) fry like me, for us
poor struggling scriveners. He's forgotten what it's like. He's too
busy roaming the goddam heath and basking in Riviera sun (*hold*—let
me out with it all!) and soaking up the good, to bother with his old
pals. Sure. And what's with "giving up" *Moby Dick*—when it'd take a
couple of hours of his time, at most! Also, what is with this ". . . first
books should not have introductions—that comes later. . ." pitch?
Just what *is* an introduction, anyway? Something that *introduces*.
Here, folks, here is a guy you don't know, but I know him and if you
respect me, then you'll respect my word when I promise you that
he won't belch and fall face forward in his soup or embarrass you
or make you waste your three bucks. If not for a first book, then
what for? Like saying, "I'll introduce you to the van Heusens, yes,
of course, but first you must get to know them—on your own . . ."
And—aw, I know. Ol' Ray's gone and made it in the big league and
he'll *always* be too busy for . . .

   Well, that sort of thinking didn't last long. Helen and Len, both of
whom considered me a horse's ass for not understanding your side,
almost stopped talking with me. And all of a sudden I realized what had
happened. My natural envy and jealousy of your position, your talent,
etc., which had previously had no outlet, was now rushing forth at this
small provocation. I just wouldn't *let* myself understand. Unconsciously,
I had been carrying a great big chip on my shoulder and you'd knocked
it off.

   I confess this for no other reason than that we are friends and
I've always tried to be honest with my friends. And all I'm saying is,
your first letter gave me a chance to let off a lot of steam as well as
to flush certain poisons out of my system. I behaved altogether like a
nincompoop, but it had a salubrious effect and, to tell the truth, I feel
considerably better for it.

   Needless to say, I *quite* understand the situation now. You have,
as usual, been amazingly kind and considerate. And I am forced to
bounce your own question back to you: Please forgive *me*. For not
understanding *at once* what a very important time this is for you, for
not realizing how serious and sincere you were in your letter to Forry.
Following the reverse idea, it may be said that, instead of *you* getting

too big for your britches, it has been one C. Beaumont the seat of whose trousers seems to have grown incommodious.

Anyway, even though I may go berserk, I come around to normalcy pretty fast. Now, more than ever, I am keenly aware of how much I owe to you. No mush here, but a simple statement in case *you* have forgotten my debt to you. It's a big one; and I'll never be able to make good on it. For, without the constant encouragement of Ray Bradbury, I am positive I would not be where I am today. I've worked hard, but I've been lucky too. Not counting the nine months my mother stayed with us (during which time I got nothing done), I've been writing just about two years, and have made almost twenty-six sales. As of now, I have nearly $1,500.00 due in—including anthologies, etc. (I've five anthology appearances scheduled for next year.) Birmingham sent me a letter this week advising that my story "The Crooked Man" will be given a "high, wide and handsome send-off in the May issue."[2] I have a commission from Winston Publishers to do a science fiction novel (I've done the first chapter & outline), there's the Doubleday deal, am finishing up my first mystery novel, *Run from the Hunter* and—well, lots and lots of short stories still at their first places.[3] Everything's popping—just as you once said it would—and I couldn't be much happier. Thanks (and I mean it) to you, Ray. Thanks to you.

My love goes to you and Maggie and the chillun. In every sense you deserve all this good fortune and, now that the biles & juices are out of me, you can believe me when I say that no one could be happier for you than I.

You're a pretty great guy—God damn it.

Please write,
Chuck

Dec. 4th, 1953

Dear Chuck,

Thanks for your letter of some 5 weeks ago. It was heartening to know
you understand my position. You flattered me by thinking I could read
your work and write an introduction to it in a few days. I only wish
this were true. However a good example of my inability to work fast is
the article that the *Nation* ordered from me in November, 1952; I did 8
drafts on it, and only finished it in April, 1953, a few short weeks before
its publication.[4] It took all those months of thinking and writing to do
justice to the article. I would want to give as much time to anything
of yours. It isn't so much the time at the typewriter, which, in the
aggregate, might amount to two weeks of typing, say, at four hours a
day. You yourself know that it is the time *away* from the typewriter that
counts most; idle thoughts at idle hours. Right now, *Moby* is taking all
my idle thoughts at idle hours. Which is only fair, considering the fact
that I am an employee of a company earning a good salary each week.
This, plus the fact that the only introduction I ever wrote was terribly
bad (look up my Sturgeon introduction;[5] it is embarrassingly gushy
now), plus the fact that your work doesn't need an introduction, plus
the fact that introductions are irritating to most critics, makes it far
from wise to pursue such a course at this time. I'm glad you wrote such
a frank and honest letter to me about your hurt feeling and natural
outrage; believe me, I sympathize with your sensations. Thanks again.
God bless you and your family in this holiday season. Write soon. Luck!

Yrs,
Ray

---

*The sincere and candid tone of the Bradbury and Beaumont exchanges would
continue after Bradbury's return from Ireland, while the role of mentorship
gradually shifted into a peer relationship. Even so, Bradbury sometimes had
to bring Beaumont up short and remind him from long experience about the
pitfalls that lay ahead in a rising writer's career.*

[c. 28 September 1954]

Chuck, this "Open House" is, to me, horrible and un-nerving. Good enough in its writing, but terrifying in its implications, and, en toto, purposeless and of no value. I am reminded of my own morbidities in certain *Dark Carnival* stories, and of my own horrible and tasteless abomination "The October Game." You'll grow out of this phase, as I did. It's good to write these things out of your system, and I'm glad *Esquire* bought it,[6] but—you've got better and more wondrous things coming up in your imagination. Write what you want to write, by all means. There should be no limits. But I'd be a fool, and no friend, if I said I was charmed by this story. It brings back too many of my own earlier memories and fears, which I had to rid myself of in *DC* and in *Weird Tales*. This story of yours turns into wholesale carnage and goes too far.

But, hell . . . don't mind me! Get back to your typewriter. Nothing, but nothing, can stop you from pushing on ahead!

Boucher spoke of you with real warmth and admiration last week, in S.F., both as a person and as a writer. He told me that he expected you would do very very great things, and I agreed!

Best,
R.

Will mail "Gentilbelle" tomorrow!

R.

Sept. 29, 1954

Dear Chuck:

Here is "Miss Gentilbelle." How long ago did I read it first . . . two, three years back? It's still an interesting story, but we've *both* learned a *lot* about writing since you did this. If you look this over with a really sharp eye now, you can see that it still needs a good job of cutting and clarifying, which I think was my initial criticism. I take it you did a *bit* of cutting, from the penciled deletions indicated here, but it needs far more tightening and reasoning out. The reader is still left dissatisfied by the "conditions that prevail." It all adds up to . . . what? Can't we know more of Miss Gentilbelle's history and relationship with Drake? It could be utilized, subtly. And your scenes with the killing of the animals go on much too long and agonizingly. Really, they are repellent. You can be as Gothic as you darn well please, and realistic, but do it with taste and know when to cut the scene. How much better if you ended the scene with the bird as the knife came down at it. Then, later you can show Robert's memories of the incident. I don't think you gain a thing by going into detail. After all, *which* is most important, Miss Gentilbelle's past and *why* she does the things she does, or the actions themselves? The actions are only symbols of her disease and do not need prolonging. We only need to know they happen. Far more interesting to spend time delineating this woman who is, I'm sorry to say, still too much of a mystery. Also, why not more on Drake . . . he's awfully ephemeral.

The writing in this is and was good, fine, excellent. But with the knowledge you've gained from working over these last 30 months or more, you certainly can see now the basic flaws in this. The story could stand an entire shaking up or shaking down. A complete rewrite with attention paid to one and all characters. Also, I feel your ending is not as strong as it could be. It says nothing that hasn't already been said in the previous scene. How you can get around this, I'll be damned if I know. Perhaps your subconscious will provide the answer as you rewrite, if you feel up to the job.

No matter *what* you do with this story, it will be a hard one to submit anywhere save to *Charm*, *Mademoiselle*, *Harper's*, *Atlantic*, and the small reviews. Luck might spot it somewhere else, but that's unpredictable.[7] My story, "The Veldt," hit the *Post*, luckily, but one of the contributing factors was my veering away from any sensational gruesomeness in detail. You've got to learn to walk the tightrope, Chuck. It *doesn't* mean you have to be un-literary, or slant; it only means you must develop your taste. "Gentilbelle" should be polished down to a gem, and cut to the core, and given "taste." Your chances for a *literary* sale to a *literary* magazine would be trebled by so doing.

See you some time in October. Good luck!

Ray

10/21/54

Dear Chuck:

I think you have, indeed, improved "Fair Lady" and I've sent it off, with a note, to *Collier's*. In the same mail, I sent off "Tears of the Madonna" to *Mademoiselle*. I'll keep you posted on their separate Fates.[8]

Congratulations on "Point of Honor"! Your sale of this story should make you doubt every word I say to you from now on! Whether or not it could have sold on up the line, to *Harper's* or *Mademoiselle* or the *Atlantic* is still, to me, extremely doubtful.[9] All I can say is how happy this new sale makes me. Nothing better than being proven wrong; especially when it means money in the bank for Beaumont, and a healthy boost to your ego.

I hate to put you off, but Walter Bradbury was in town last week and set me to work finishing my novel for Doubleday.[10] If you will bear with me while I do my work, I will be glad to see those new stories of yours on—December 1st. That is a helluva long way off, I realize; and yet I feel I can't possibly plunge into this book (which is so near to being finished, after seven years) and do justice to it and your work. Both would suffer. So, excuse me: send the stories on December 1st. In the meantime, will probably see you at the Anniversary Club meeting.

Congrats, too, on the new *Playboy* sale! You're doing fine!

See you,

Yours,

Ray

11550½ Friar St.
No. Hollywood, Calif.

Feb. 11, 1955

Dear Ray,

Got your message via 4e:[11] rest your mind—you're forgiven. We all
understand. We may from time to time shed a tear and murmur, "Gosh,
wonder what ever happened to old Ray!" but these are human things.
Who among us is altogether free from the weaknesses of the species? In
absolute teetotal truth, we *were* beginning to get curious about the lack
of word. However, your call was reassurance enow.

Thanks for the googolnth time, by the way, for plugging away on
my behalf. Perhaps "Fair Lady" will justify your enthusiasm; I hope so,
I really do. "Tears of the Madonna" arrived, and will probably appear in
Playboy a year from now, in somewhat rewritten form. Russell liked it,
but wants a year to pass for final okay. Don't know why. Anyway, he feels
they'll do it. And he's a man of his word.

On the news front there's loads, of course; too much to cram into
a letter. I'll save it for when we get together for another gab session.
Briefly: to stay out of an 8-hour job I'm continuing with the comic
strips, selling pretty well (several hundred pages of stuff due for
print); *Fortnight* is buying quite a bit of factual material (see the latest
Hi-Fi issue for a sample: Beaumont on the species "Audiophilus-High
Fidelitus"); and I'm collaborating with a *Collier's* writer on a group of
T-V dramas, the first of which was bought immediately & is scheduled
for shooting this month. All of this is time-consuming, and it takes
away from my serious work, but not nearly so much as a full-time job
(the only other alternative) would. Even so, I've turned out a lot of
new stories, many first-rate—or as close to first-rate as I can get, at this
stage. Anxious to get your reaction to "The Hunger," coming up next
issue of *Playboy*. . . . *Esquire* apparently considering a new yarn, called "A
Long Way from Capri" . . . Tony Boucher gave the go-ahead on a sequel
to "The Last Word," which will appear in the April *Fantasy & Science
Fiction* (a collab. with Chad),[12] and tentatively okayed (with revision)

a yarn titled "The Vanishing American" (one of my best, I think) . . .
Ladies' Home Journal's Anne Einselen said she was "yearning" to buy one
of my stories, and laid herself open for a rewrite on "The Magic Man"
(which I'll hear on any day—keep your fingers crossed!) . . . etc., etc.

When do we see one another?

Thanks again, for everything,
Chuck

Hi to Mag and the kids! Elia Kazan showed some interest in "Black
Country"—finally pooped out . . .

In early 1955 Bradbury published Switch on the Night, *his first children's picture book. In it he explored the universal childhood fear of the dark, offering the
bright and never-ending majesty of the night sky as a remedy.* Switch on the
Night *would become an enduring Bradbury classic for the youngest readers,
but for a moment it became a subtle pawn used half humorously by Charles
Beaumont to deflect Bradbury's unrelenting advice to cut as he revised his new
stories. Beaumont's letter, and Bradbury's more serious reply, follows.*

March 6, 1955

Dear Ray,

Switch on the Night is a perfectly lovely book, in just about every way.
The story is charming (I'd read it over at Forry's a few days ago) and
the illustrations are beautiful. In all a wonderful thing, for which, once
again, thanks.

I have only one criticism. It needs cutting, desperately. Say down to
eighty words . . . Then we'd have the very marrow, with no fretwork and
foolery, no excess verbiage. (I know we're always arguing this point, but
you know my obsession for cutting . . .)

The rejection slip you sent does, I suppose, give me heart—but
not much. These are the heart-breakers. I received a letter from
Anne Einselen of *Ladies' Home Journal* last month in which she stated

(quote!): "... I am physically *yearning* to purchase a story of Charles Beaumont's ..." She loved "The Magic Man," referred to it as "another Beaumont unforgettable" and sent it back for revision (happier ending, of all things). I revised away, managed it without damaging the story, fortunately, and shot it back. And have been waiting ever since. Waiting and waiting. It's a 10,000 worder, too, which would mean quite a bit of change, in need of which we are the most. Meanwhile, I've sold two more to Tony Boucher, and this—according to those in the know—means I've sold as many to him as anyone has. Dick Matheson ties me, Chad has six, and Poul Anderson has six. I don't know about the Gavagan's Bar atrocities.[13] (One of these *F&SF* yarns I definitely want to get your reaction to; it's called "The Vanishing American," all about a little man who has worked so long at his job he hates and lived so long the life he hates that he actually begins to disappear; but it makes no difference, because no one's seen him anyway for years ...)[14]

I reread (for the thousandth time) "The Next in Line" last night, and I'll say again, there, by God, is a great story.

I'll phone you in a few days and we'll all get together. Thanks again for the book, it's wonderful.

Bestest,
Chuck

Mar. 11, 1955

Dear Chuck:

"The Magic Man" is a wonderful story. I can best compliment you by saying I wish I had written it myself. Congratulations on your steady movement ahead.

I have one suggestion to make however. At its present length, 27 pages, the story simply is not saleable to the average market. The *Post*, *Collier's*, *McCall's* etc., use stories up to 5,000 words only. Which is to say: 20 pages at 250 words per page. I suggest you cut this story down to at least 21 pages. Not just to fit space limitations at a magazine, no.

If I felt the present length was right, literarily speaking, I'd say to hell with the magazines. But the present length isn't right—literarily. Your beginning is much too long, for what it has to say. The story begins to pick up once your Magic Man is in town and begins to perform for the people.

Go through, selectively, then, and find the words and phrases, the extraneous bits and pieces, that need cutting. For instance, the first scene, which ends on page 6, could, with judicious concentration and condensation, end on page 4. You would get a fuller richer more vibrant picture of Doctor Silk if you cut much extraneous material here. Take a long look; ask yourself, what does this sentence or this paragraph do to move the story along, show necessary character, add atmospheric detail. If the material is repetitive, it must go. The first scene is much too long for what it has to say, what it has to establish. Pages 7 to 13—seven pages in all—could probably be cut down to five pages. Here again, look for the telling detail. Cut the extraneous. Cut and blend.

Then from page 14 to page 27, another 3 pages must come out, to concentrate the intense fire you wish to show on your page.

All this must be done if you want to hone your story down to a sharp cutting, wonderful edge. A writer cannot afford to be sloppy. This story is absolutely great, but its edges are fuzzed. It can be cleaned up and made positively clean and sharp.

You have combatted me in the past on these things, Chuck. But either you believe I know what I'm talking about, or I'll stop talking. I've sold 200 stories which have been not only commercial successes but literary successes. I know what I'm talking about, goddammit, when I talk about cutting. It is one of the great arts of writing. It explains why Collier is so fine; he cuts down to the intense heart of things, through draft after draft. I do the same. I sold a story to the *Post* this week which had ten drafts. The final draft, I cut three or four words on a page. When I can no longer find one word on one page that needs cutting, I send the story out.

I make the flat statement now, and will brook no argument from you. Positively and absolutely, this story must be cut to make it perfect. As it stands now, you might sell it to *Playboy*. That wouldn't mean it was a perfect story. It would mean editorial toleration of sloppy habits. You are too close to this story to see how loose some parts of it are.[15]

Cut 7 pages out of the story then, during the coming week. And see if the entire thing doesn't leap to a sharper and more wondrous focus. Then, it'll be ready to go to the *Post, Collier's, Harper's, Atlantic,* everywhere, anywhere. A fine story is a fine story; it will sell to *McCall's* or *Antioch Review.* Any magazine that prints "The Magic Man" will be a luckier and more literate magazine.

If you don't feel like cutting this story, if you feel rebellious about cutting it, if you refuse to cut it, I don't want to see another story of yours again. You absolutely need someone to tell you where and when you're wrong. This time, I'll brook no rebellion from you. This length is damned wrong and you must stick your nose in it and realize how wrong it is. If I sound hardboiled and egotistical, damn right, I am. Why? I know more about writing than you do, let's get that straight. I'll give and take with you, any day, about the philosophy of writing, etc., but I certainly won't listen to you about cutting. Cutting is the one art where you're still an apprentice, Chuck. The sooner you realize it and unplug your ears, the better. For the sooner you do it, the sooner you'll be selling more stories. All of your stories, to date, have been too long. Look over my other letters from the past. You'll see this mentioned again and again. You have been incapable of judging the value of each scene; what the toleration point of each scene is. I now hereby pompously declare "The Magic Man" to be a beautiful work of art, smudged around the edges by a couple of extra handsful of words. Get to work, clean it up, and send it to New York with your Index, and your tear-sheets, and your other fine stories. You won't be sorry for the extra work now. You'll probably hate me; but, hell, teachers expect to be hated.

Congratulations on the story. Congratulations on the even finer story it will be next week this time.

Yours,
Ray

One by one, Bradbury's earliest mentors blessed him and released him during
the mid-1940s. The blessings he had received from Leigh Brackett, Edmond
Hamilton, and Henry Kuttner were now transferred on from Bradbury to
Charles Beaumont, as he realized that Beaumont had fully matured as a master
of supernatural fiction. Such moments would always prove to be emotional for
Bradbury, who looked back on a period of creative mentorship that could never
be revisited again.

Tuesday night
Aug 30, 1955

Dear Chuck:

This is a happy time as well as a sad time; happy because you are on
the threshold of even bigger things, now that you have these two sales
under your belt today. When I came home this afternoon and Mag told
me you had called with the news I felt the two distinct emotions at
once, the happiness and the sadness. The happiness for your new phase
and the sadness for the death of the old; those years when you were in
your cocoon stage, the hardest years, the years when you learned more
every week, every day, every hour, than you will ever learn again. From
here on, you will go deep, but the territory will be not so wide, nor will
you ever be quite so young again. I rejoice for the work you did and the
work you will now do. A happy day of happy news. Keep going. And call
again some evening—it's the best time to call!—so I can talk to you and
make plans for you and Bill and I to get together. Do you like football?
There's a night game at the Coliseum a week from next Friday. Any
chance you and Bill might want to see that?
    Happy happy day. Onward and upward, Beaumont!

Yrs,
Ray

By 1959, Bradbury's recommendation of Beaumont to Twilight Zone *creator*
Rod Serling led to Beaumont's multi-season role as writer for the series. In this

letter Beaumont discusses the production decision on Bradbury's "Here There Be Tygers," one of the three scripts that Bradbury had sent to Rod Serling and coproducer Buck Haughton for Twilight Zone *consideration (of the three, only "I Sing the Body Electric!" would be produced). "Here There Be Tygers," the story of a planet that protects itself against an exploratory survey team, required special effects beyond the capabilities of the program during its initial five-season run.*

10/18/59

Dear Ray:

I'm returning your teleplay, "Here There Be Producers." It is a lovely, poetic job but an incredible choice for your first *Twilight Zone* assignment. The fault is Rod's for not choosing instead one of your many eminently adaptable stories. I personally do not see any major production difficulties, except of course for the flying. I don't know how they'll do it, though perhaps there is a way. (They didn't seem to have any trouble with TV Superman.)

At the moment I'm swamped, and, quicksand or not, I've half a mind to struggle. Due within a short time: Adaptation of *Macbeth* for Alcoa-Goodyear, pilot film for new series (*Bulldog Drummond*), script for *Hitchcock*, short story & long profile on Charlie Chaplin, for *Playboy*. It makes a guy sad and glad.

Incidentally, Joan Harrison gave me your script "Special Delivery," for studying purposes. I haven't read it yet, but the first page looks very good.[16]

We're fellow pilgrims, Ray. Now *I'm* going the rounds with a series idea. Called *The Unknown*, it's a fantasy show. I hope to use the grand old stories by Jacobs and Harvey and Blackwood and, B. willing, Bradbury. Everyone's excited—which is par for the course, I guess.

Best,
Chuck

In the fall of 1962, Bradbury's second Life *magazine article, "Cry the Cosmos," drew Beaumont's unconditional praise for its poetic and emotionally powerful vision of humanity's place in the cosmos and the powerful rockets that would soon take humans to the moon. But Beaumont's adherence to traditional horror genre rules clashed with Bradbury's unconventional triumph over evil in* Something Wicked This Way Comes. *The two writers would have very few chances to continue such discussions before Beaumont's tragic decline and death in 1967, at the age of thirty-eight.*

5060 Bellaire Ave.
No. Hollywood, Calif.

Oct. 3, 1962

Dear Ray:

The fact is, I consumed "Cry the Cosmos" almost two weeks ago, in Don's office. I loved it then and, on second reading, I love it now. Despite the circumstances, related by you at the *Shoot the Piano Player* screening, the article has great consistency of thought and seems as smooth as a creek-washed pebble. Add to that your best and most lyrical writing form and you have something (sob!) close to a classic.

I honestly regret that I can't become nearly as enthusiastic about *Something Wicked This Way Comes.* It took a lot of work, I know very well, and a lot of thought, but for me it lacks substance. Your prose in this one is like a diamond cobweb, Ray: can't see beyond the dazzle. Every so often I got a glimpse, but I didn't really like what I saw. I don't think evil can be laughed out of the world, chuckled out of it, or smiled out of it, and if that is your point—which it might not be—then we have a disagreement.

Goddammit! Honesty is difficult. Particularly under the circumstances. I'm involved in what may be the most important book of my career, that novel I told you of, though not about; I'm scared of it; it could be great or it could be terrible. So I know the pain and joy you endured. But I can't lie to you, Ray. And when I send you *Where No Man*

Walks I know you won't be able to lie to me.[17] Which is the way it is with friendships.

Let us, for God's sake, have dinner together soon, and talk and talk and talk . . .

Old

Chuck

PS I'm sorry I couldn't get to *Icarus*;[18] it was my first day home and the kids would have been heartbroken.

RICHARD MATHESON

Bradbury's publication of The Martian Chronicles *and the novella-length work* "The Fireman" *prompted Richard Matheson (1926–2013) to make contact. By the mid-1950s* I Am Legend *and* The Shrinking Man *established Matheson as a major genre writer. Matheson's first letter to Bradbury, and his subsequent move to Los Angeles, sparked the beginning of an enduring friendship. In 1959 Bradbury would play a significant role in Matheson's joining Rod Serling's Twilight Zone *writing staff, and in 1980 Matheson would script the NBC* Martian Chronicles *miniseries.*

222 E. 7th Street
Brooklyn 18, N.Y.

September 8, 1950

Dear Mr. Bradbury,

I found your address in the August *Rhodomagnetic Digest*.[19] I hope you won't mind me taking advantage of it to send you this brief note.

I wish only to be added to the long list of your sincere admirers and to thank you for many hours of pleasant reading.

I enjoyed your *Martian Chronicles* immensely and have always been affected by your delicate sense of fantasy. Your general stories are invariably unique and interesting. Moreover, I have high respect for that quality in you which all too few writers in any medium possess, or if possessing, have not the talent to express absorbingly; namely a social conscience.

My best wishes to you for a long and profitable future in all respects.

Sincerely,
Richard Matheson

Ray Bradbury
10750 Clarkson Rd.
Los Angeles 64, Calif.

September 12, 1950

Dear Mr. Matheson,

This is one of the pleasant coincidences that happen all too rarely in life; two nights ago I read your story "Third From the Sun" and told my wife, "It's the sort of story I would like to have done." In fact, I have a story out with my agent now in which a man and wife and their children escape but into the past, and go through a similar rigamarole about whether they should "lock the front door or not."[20]

Coincidence all around. Needless to say, my wife and I, though we have read only two of your stories so far, including that wonderful little piece about the green child in the McComas-Boucher magazine, think that you have every reason to be proud of yourself and look forward to a good future for you.[21] I do not know how old you are or how long you've been writing, or if you've sold to other non-s-f markets. I only know that your style is simple, touching, effective and causes empathy in the reader.

I am pleased that you have liked my stories and my new book. I have always tried to write to entertain and instruct myself, and thus entertain and instruct others. If there is any advice I can give you—and

you haven't asked for any, and I am being damned pompous offering
some to you—I would advise you to continue as you have done so
far, writing well and writing off-trail, and staying away from formula.
If there is any justice in this world, and if these first two stories are
examples of your imagination and taste, then you have a straight path
ahead to a reputation. Thank you for your good wishes, which I return
to you doublefold.

Yours cordially,
Ray Bradbury

Sat. Jan. 13, 1951

Dear Ray,

Just a brief note to tell you how superb I think your novelette "The
Fireman" is. I just finished it. And, in putting it down I felt a desire that
I rarely feel when reading science-fiction, or any fiction for that matter;
a desire to sit quietly and just think about what I've read.

I just read your story in *Esquire* too about the last day in the world.[22]
I thought it was beautiful.

What a wonderful field science-fiction is if only tilled properly.
The freedom to say the things you do in your stories is so rare
today; just about suffocated under the massy weight of commercial
requirements.

I'm beginning to get the feeling that reading your work is more
of a privilege as time passes. And, though it will take more than years,
someday I hope to be on your team in ability as I have been for some
time in spirit.

Best,
Dick

Ray Bradbury
10750 Clarkson Rd.
Los Angeles 64, Calif.

January 22, 1951

Dear Dick:

I cannot say how pleased I was by your letter concerning "The
Fireman." It was particularly gratifying because this one novella
occupied so much of my time a year ago and it contains some of
my strongest convictions. There is so much yet to be said; there are
things I had to leave out of the story because I didn't want to hit the
reader on the head with too much preaching. One thing I would like
to re-emphasize and detail, if "The Fireman" ever goes into book
form,[23] is the fact that radio has contributed to our "growing lack of
attention" simply because we tune in, see five minutes of one thing,
ten minutes of other, half an hour of this, an hour of that. This sort of
hopscotching existence makes it almost impossible for people, myself
included, to sit down and get into a novel again. We have become a
short story reading people, or, worse than that, a *quick* reading people.
I have to force my way into novels. Once in, I am fine, but it is the
initial chapter that is the hardest going. This is frightening. Also, I
want to re-emphasize the fact that we haven't time to think anymore.
The great centrifuge of radio, television, pre-thought-out movies,
etc. gives us no time to "stop and stare." Our lives are getting more
scheduled all the time, there's no room for caprice, and caprice is the
core of man, or should be the tiny happy nucleus around which his
mundane tasks can be assembled.

But enough of this. I am glad my story made you stop and turn a few
of its ideas in your mind. If only a few people do this, I will be
really happy. I am glad, also, that you liked the *Esquire* story; it was
written nine months ago in a fit of despair at midnight one evening
after a particularly depressing journey through the newspaper and my
friends' minds.

As you say, s-f can be the most exciting form in the world today. It is the only remaining form where one can say what one really thinks of the world without being called a Communist. The spectacle of "witchery" in this country today is appalling and disgusting.

Have no doubts, Dick, you are on my team, and have *been* on my team since the publication of your first story. My wife and I elected you quarterback two minutes after putting aside that first story. (Don't we sound like Hemingway and his sport terms?) I hope you will continue to work and develop and remember that there are only two intelligent editors in the field today, or at least who use, or try to use, their intelligence; these people are H. L. Gold and Boucher-McComas who I lump as one person. The other pulp magazines will try, or at least they used to try to force me, to tell you what to write, how to write, to do formula, to stick to the familiar, etc. But you must find your own way, take your own time, and write well and good all of the time. It is better, as you know anyway, to write 10 good stories a year, than 36 bad ones. Too many writers in the field have no respect, no love, no cherishment for writing as art or writing as literature. These "one-draft" people are nothing but day-laborers and you must never be taken in by their glib talk of profits and quick sales. I know that this advice is un-needed by you, but I feel I must re-stress it because in the years from 1941 until 1947 I received letters from an old agent of mine, and the publishers of *TWS* and *Weird Tales* which read like this: "For God's sake stop doing such off-trail stuff. Give us some of the old razzle-dazzle formula. Give us some ghosts like the regular ghosts. You trying to kill yourself off?"[24] Needless to say I went right on having fun writing what pleased me most, what was dearest and deepest to my heart. Only when you do that are you an individual. Only in that way can you be happy. I hope you will always be happy and glad to live with yourself, Dick, for you have had a much better beginning in writing than I had ten years ago, if you bother to check my early stories which were quite unreadable. Remember that you have my thoughts with you and that the field needs original talent badly to compensate for all the second-hand slush that gets published month in and month out.

This started out as a brief thank you note and has turned into a History of The Conquest of Mexico.[25] Let me say again how much I appreciate your fine letter. I'll be watching for your work every month. My blessings.

Yours,

Ray

Jan. 28, 1951

Dear Ray:

My sincerest thanks for your letter. It couldn't have come at a more propitious moment. I am, at present, wandering about through the halls of depression and non-activity, mumbling short cantos which all add up to the theme: Oh What the Hell Did I Ever Become a Writer For? with various contrapuntal variations.

Your letter did a great deal toward pulling me out of it. I want very much to feel that you're a friend and that you're rooting for me as I do for you. At my stage, I sorely need someone to tell me the things you told me in your letter. Not that I don't believe them for I always will. But I get discouraged and I forget them and I think, well maybe I'll boot out a fast piece of junk and make a million and then go back to writing from my heart and mind again. Now whether I have the ability to turn out potboilers, I don't know. I *do* get tempted to try though. That's where words like yours assume the status of a needed gospel.

Up to the present I've tried very hard to write as I believe and think I've done so, whether the story has a message or not. But I don't know. I've sold three stories to *Amazing* or *Thrilling Wonder* or whatever the hell it is, they all sound the same. I'm hoping they (the stories) aren't bad because they've been bought by that mag. I can only hope that standards have risen or that they're so short of stories they have to buy off-trail stories to keep up their thick outputs.

As to our tastes in editors we might be Siamese twins. I gain more respect for Horace with each issue of his magazine.[26] I've been to see him and his charming wife Evelyn a number of times and enjoyed their company immensely. He's been extremely kind to me and has

encouraged me all the way to write as I believe, commercial or not. He's
a good man. Likewise with Tony and Mick. I met Mick last year when
he visited N.Y.C. He and I had a very nice talk over drinks. Needless to
say, those two magazines are easily my favorites. I don't think they have
any competitors at all. Incidentally I have a short clinker coming out in
Fantasy next month.[27] I don't know why they bought it as I re-read the
ms now.

Again, incidentally, I don't expect you to answer this unless you
have much time which I'm sure you don't. Your letter was a fine answer
to anything I'll say anyway.

Your points on radio are, alas, only too true. And on television.
Reading a book has become something you do after you've broken a
leg putting up your television aerial. I hadn't thought about it, but it
definitely could be that the reason I have trouble reading is the one you
mentioned, the growing inability of our times to concentrate because
all things are handed to us in pills of minutes. Hideous thought. I have
to, generally, read a book entirely through to get it done in less than a
week. Otherwise it stretches over weeks, months. I gave up Fort after
two months.[28] And all the novels I want to read are too long to be read
at a sitting.

Sometimes I wonder Ray, what good it does to write of these
things. Oh, I couldn't give up writing of them any more than I could
give up loving music or eating or anything that is a part of my idea of
living. Yet, it's no strange thing to wonder if any tangible good comes of
saying these things over and over, tearing shreds out of television and
movies and Joe McCarthy and the insidious rise of a materialism in this
country almost as bad as that in Russia; worse, in the sense that it isn't
even honest materialism but has the added warp of hypocrisy. Home
of the brave and the free oh my God I missed Milton Berle. I suppose
the good it does is so small that it can only be measured over centuries.
What a pity we don't live longer. Then again maybe not. Trying to get a
philosophical foothold today is like trying to butter the Super Chief[29] as
it plunges through a stygian tunnel at one hundred miles an hour.

Yet I guess we can't give up. And if I can reach the point where
I don't mind making money for another ten years, I'll do some real
work for "our team" (I'm for kicking Ernie H. off the team after that

last fumble of his).[30] Surely there's no lack of material. The trouble
I imagine is to make these things entertaining. Race prejudice,
chauvinism, blind capitalism, warped Christianity, impossible arrogance.
We could write about those things until the black one plucked us into ye
olde Earthe, but unless we make them interesting no one will care. Of
course I don't know why I should kick. I'm sure I wouldn't like s-f if it
was easy.

What this all adds up to is solid agreement with you that people
can only be happy if they are individuals and a promise, a vow, what
have you that I'll do my damnedest to keep working on that principle.
I hope to God that nothing turns me from it. And, again I'll say, that
I want to be your friend and share with you and those few others the
responsibility for making the world better. I hope you won't mind
me writing now and then in a sort of vampiric searching for spiritual
sustenance. And thank you.

My best,
Dick

In 1996, more than forty years after these early letters, Matheson offered Bradbury his own perspective on the 1980 Martian Chronicles television miniseries
that he had scripted for NBC. Bradbury had read the Matheson teleplay adaptation in advance and found it to be a good one, but he would later take NBC to
task for how they had translated the teleplay into a ponderous and uninspired
production. Matheson's 1996 letter reveals a rare screenwriter's sense of the factors contributing to their mutual disappointment with the Martian Chronicles
project, and concludes with an even stranger tale of Hollywood mischief.

5/17/96

Dear Ray:

Thanks for your letter. I'm glad that you don't hold me responsible
for the unfortunate way *The Martian Chronicles* turned out. Clearly, it
was direction. Then, too, they omitted the House of Usher section and

wrote one themselves about the man who had turned his family into robots—or, rather, replaced his lost family.[31] I was disappointed by many things in the film. It started out on the wrong key with the first story which completely lacked what was in the story—and, hopefully, in the script. Actually, there were only two scenes that I thought caught the mood as it should have been caught—the one between Jon Finch and Fritz Weaver and the one between Rock Hudson and the Martian "ghost" near the end of the piece. I was especially disappointed when they dropped the adaptation of "There Will Come Soft Rains," sticking the scene in their expensive—and not too interesting—space center rather than in the house which I had made his brother's house. Oh, well. Not the first—or last—time that Hollywood will debauch a good project.

Richard[32] and I sold a script some years ago which we called *Face Off*. It was our first attempt at collaboration so we chose the most obvious genre, the police drama with a serial killer and some sort of "buddy" situation. We chose to make the serial killer a hockey player like Wayne Gretzky. The team was a hardened police detective—we visualized Burt Reynolds—and a young man who, though brilliant as a criminologist, was still suffering from the post-traumatic effects of something that had been done to him. Consequently, he had a multiple-personality disorder and would, at key moments, mostly of peril, "flip out" into some insane character—Captain Kirk, Errol Flynn as Robin Hood, etc. We visualized Dana Carvey but he was not in films then so they put in Dan Ackroyd who was too clunky for the role. The other man was Gene Hackman, which was fine; great actor.

The main problem was the director. Bob Clark. At first, we were delighted by the idea, thinking of *A Christmas Story* and *Murder by Decree*. We should have thought, instead, of *Porky's*. Bob decided that our story just wasn't good enough. Consequently, he re-wrote it so much that we have difficulty finding a line or two of dialogue still extant. Where our plot had to do, as I said, with the search for a serial killer who turns out to be a hockey star, Bob decided to make a few alterations. As a result, the final story had to do with a search by a porno ring gang and a neo-Nazi group for a pornographic film starring Hitler! I submit that no story has ever been altered so radically in the history of films—but I'm probably wrong. Anyway, Bob loused it up royally. It

ended up as an atrocity called *Loose Cannons* and, deservedly, died a
rapid death.

So, anyway, while it in no way equals having a loved and classic book
abominated, I do know the feelings you have.

Hope all is well with you and Mag and your girls.

Best as always,
Richard

RICHARD BACH

*Richard Bach's (1936–) abiding determination to write about flight never
waned, but his breakout novel,* Jonathan Livingston Seagull *(1970), only
emerged after years in reserve and active-duty military aviation and a great
deal of nonfiction and autobiographical writing.* Illusions: The Adventures of
a Reluctant Messiah *(1977) was also a bestseller. He found sustained inspiration in Ray Bradbury's novels and stories, and in 1962 he opened a correspondence with Bradbury that would last for many years.*

4 February 1962

Mr. Ray Bradbury
c/o Bantam Books, Inc.
25 W. 45th St.
New York, 36, N.Y.

Dear Mr. Bradbury,

It has been about seven years. At first, in high school, I enjoyed enough
of your work to make mental note of your name and remember it. Then
I actively sought your writing and consumed it, thoughtfully.

Out of the Air Force, in June, 1959, I heard you speak at a writers'
conference in Long Beach, California. Before your talk, I was looking
forward also to hearing the things that Rod Serling would have to say in
his hour, following yours. But I did not hear Rod Serling. I left, abruptly,

after your talk, knowing that you had spoken directly to me and that for me the conference was complete.

I appreciated the advice that you offered: work, never falter, be true to myself. Hearing you speak was finding a religion. Here was a set of precepts in which I believed, spoken with driving conviction by a man whose work I admired. ". . . I admired." An understatement. But to avoid the uncomfortable mistake of words gushing admiration, I shall merely say that my idea of the best of all modern reading lies with a stack of Saint-Exupery volumes at the left hand and of Bradbury at the right.

But the highest praise: I followed your advice. I wrote that thousand words a day, occasionally more. I wrote articles and stories about the fascination closest to my heart, the flying of airplanes. The stories did not sell, the articles did. A year and a half after your talk in Long Beach, I accepted a position as associate editor of *Flying Magazine*. I began the book.

It lagged, it did not seem right. I read my notes from the conference, my notes of Ray Bradbury. I continued. I wrote. I flew airplanes. I read again my notes. I wrote. Fifty-five of those thousand-word segments went together to make the book. They were rearranged, they were rewritten. The book was rejected. Nice comments, but still the final one was, "No."

My Air National Guard squadron was called to France, and a greater meaning for the book appeared. It was rewritten. It is now in the hands of Prentice-Hall, who is "interested."[33]

So what has this to do with Ray Bradbury. This. On that June morning you gave me encouragement that has forcefully continued over the last three years. But I did not want to write now and say my goodness Mr. Bradbury I think your work is keen and please keep it up.

I want to acknowledge that I owe a very great debt to you.

"Write him when you have *accomplished* something," I have been telling myself over the last years. The book has not sold, my name is known only to a very small group of people who are interested in flying airplanes. I thought that the time to acknowledge my debt is when I am known, when I am Someone.

A friend flew his airplane into a clouded mountain peak three days ago. What if I had been in that cockpit, I thought, and among other things, I discovered that I had a debt outstanding, that would never be paid or even acknowledged unless I wrote now to you.

I plan, when we are returned to civilian life, to establish a western editorial office of the magazine in Los Angeles. I shall scan the notices of writers' conferences. I hope, one day, to see your name again as speaker. I shall attend, one of 400 to whom you speak, directly. I shall think, as you speak, of the many stories and of *Martian Chronicles* and *Illustrated Man* and *Golden Apples of the Sun* and *Fahrenheit 451* and *October Country* and *Medicine for Melancholy* and most of all, of *Dandelion Wine*; of *Dandelion Wine*.

And I hope that I will have the chance to say then, as I say at last, thank you very much. For your advice. For your example.

Highest regards,
Richard Bach

STEPHEN KING

Stephen King (1947–) was well established in his long career before he asked Ray Bradbury to discuss what King considered his best work, Something Wicked This Way Comes. *Bradbury's eerie "Mars Is Heaven!" had captivated King's sense of horror as a boy, and he would come to see Bradbury as pivotal to the mid-twentieth-century evolution of the American Gothic tradition. As King would say in* Danse Macabre, *his 1983 book-length study of this tradition,* "Something Wicked This Way Comes, *a darkly poetic tall tale set in the half-real, half-mythical community of Green Town, Illinois, is probably Bradbury's best work—a shadowy descendant from that tradition that has brought us stories about Paul Bunyan and his blue ox, Babe, Pecos Bill, and Davy Crockett." In* Danse Macabre, *King presented much of the letter that he received in return for his inquiry.*

November 8th, 1979

Mr. Ray Bradbury
10265 Cheviot Drive
Los Angeles, California 90064

Dear Mr. Bradbury,

First—before anything else—I've been a fan of yours for nearly twenty-five years (which is going a bit since I'm only thirty-two now, but I swear it's the truth), and I want to thank you for all the fine times, the good writing, the marvelous adventures. I don't want to gush, but you do good work . . . as I'm sure one or two other people have had occasion to tell you.

However, this isn't just a fan letter; it's also a request for information, if you'd care to give it. I've written several books which have been classified "horror novels" for want of a better term, and Bill Thompson at Everest House decided that this probably qualified me to write a book on horror as it has appeared in various media since 1950 or so. Foolishly, I agreed and scrawled my name on the contract. As a result, I'm now busily trying to write a book that probably cannot be written. What's coming out is a long, rambling, mostly good-humored essay about horror in film, in books, on TV, and in the mass culture (i.e., things like Kiss, the rock group, cereals such as Frankenberry and Count Chocula, God knows what else).

It would be impossible and unrewarding to try and cover all the books in the genre in a single chapter or two, so I've decided to single out a round dozen and talk about them and what they do. Among others, I want to discuss *Strange Wine, The Body Snatchers, The House Next Door, The Haunting, The Shrinking Man, Ghost Story*, and your novel *Something Wicked This Way Comes*.

I'm not in the business of asking other writers to help me earn my living, but I've already written letters to several of the above (Shirley Jackson has gone beyond the reach of both the U.S. mail and Ma Bell, unfortunately), asking them if they have anything they'd like to say about the book under discussion—*Something Wicked This Way Comes*, in your case. If you care to respond, I would quote you pretty much *verbatim* from your letter . . . which is to say, I promise not to quote out of context, or any of that bullshit . . .

I suppose I'd be most interested to know how you felt while you were writing the book . . . what you wanted from it and how much of what you wanted you feel that you got . . . what its particular pleasures were for you, and what it says to you now . . . any ways you feel the book may have failed in terms of expression or image or character. The only specific question I have (and it's the only one I've made to any of the writers I've written to for my book) is exactly what is going on in the Theater? Why is it there, and why do we never come back to it as the book goes on? I've always thought it was one of the most puzzling and interesting episodes in the novel.

If you are too busy to respond to this query—or even if you don't want to—I'll understand fully; but any help you could give would be mightily appreciated. And, of course, if I can do something for you, just let me know.

Be well,
Stephen King

BRADBURY TO KING
[AS CONDENSED IN *DANSE MACABRE*]

[ca. 1979–80]

[*Something Wicked This Way Comes*] sums up my entire life of loving Lon Chaney and the magicians and grotesques he played in the twenties films. My mom took me to see *Hunchback* in 1923 when I was three. It marked me forever. *Phantom* when I was six. Same thing. *West of Zanzibar* when I was about eight. Magician turns himself into a skeleton in front of black natives! Incredible! *The Unholy Three* ditto! Chaney took over my life. I was a raving film maniac long before I hit my eighth year. I became a full-time magician after seeing Blackstone on stage in Waukegan, my home town in upper Illinois, when I was nine. When I was twelve, Mr. Electrico and his traveling Electric Chair arrived with the Dill Brothers Sideshows and Carnival. That was his "real" name. I got to know him. Sat by the lakeshore and talked grand philosophies . . . he his small ones, me my grandiose supersized ones about futures and magic. We corresponded several times. He lived in Cairo, Illinois, and was, he said, a defrocked Presbyterian minister. I wish I could remember his Christian name. But his letters have long since been lost in the years, though small magic tricks he gave me I still have. Anyway, magic and magicians and Chaney and libraries have filled my life. Libraries are the real birthing places of the universe for me. I lived in my hometown library more than I did at home. I loved it at night, prowling in the stacks on my fat panther feet. All of that went into *Something Wicked*, which began as a short story in *Weird Tales* called "Black Ferris" in May, 1948, and just grew like *Topsy* . . .

["Black Ferris" became] a screenplay in 1958 the night I saw Gene Kelly's *Invitation to the Dance* and so much wanted to work for and with him [that] I rushed home, finished up an outline of *Dark Carnival* (its then title) and ran it over to his house.[34] Kelly flipped, said he would direct it, went off to Europe to find money, never found any, came back discouraged, gave me back my screen treatment, some eighty pages or more, and told me Good Luck. I said to hell with it and sat down and spent two years, off and on, finishing *Something Wicked*. Along the way,

I said all and everything, just about, that I would ever want to say about my younger self and how I felt about that terrifying thing: Life, and that other terror: Death, and the exhilaration of both.

But above all, I did a loving thing without knowing it. I wrote a paean to my father. I didn't realize it until one night in 1965, a few years after the novel had been published. Sleepless, I got up and prowled my library, found the novel, reread certain portions, burst into tears. My father was locked into the novel, forever, as the father in the book! I wish he had lived to read himself there and be proud of his bravery in behalf of his loving son.

Even writing this, I am touched again to remember with what a burst of joy and agony I found that my dad was there, forever, forever for me anyway, locked on paper, kept in print, and beautiful to behold.

I don't know what else to say. I loved every minute of writing it. I took six months off between drafts. I never tire myself. I just let my subconscious throw up when it feels like it.

I love the book best of all the things I have ever written. I will love it, and the people in it, Dad and Mr. Electrico, and Will and Jim, the two halves of myself sorely tried and tempted, until the end of my days.

DAN CHAON

Dan Chaon (1964–) was still in his late teens when he began to write to Ray Bradbury, but he had already developed a promising style in his supernatural fiction. Bradbury recognized this talent, and his responses worked more deeply into Chaon's stories than he would normally undertake with a beginning writer. The third letter, written on board a transcontinental train, echoes the kind of interrogative approach he had used thirty years earlier with such promising young writers as Richard Matheson, William F. Nolan, and Charles Beaumont. Chaon would travel a similar path to prominence, carrying Bradbury's influence into the new generation of early twenty-first-century horror writers. His novel Among the Missing *(2001) was a National Book Award finalist. Like Ray Bradbury, Chaon's stories have appeared in the* Best American Short Stories *and* O. Henry Prize Stories *annual anthologies.*

April 30 / May 1, 1982

Dear Dan Chaon,

This, written on the train crossing New Mexico on my way home from 3 weeks travel, to Washington D.C., Bowling Green, Ohio, New York, etc. Lecturing, and tending to business. I carried your "Bickerstaff" story along, hoping to have time to read it, and comment. So now's the time . . .

I enjoyed it, immensely. Your style, as ever, is on the nose . . . evocative, imaginative, clever.

The story is a small gem, and perhaps, as with your other stories, too small. I can see it in some quarterly review, but you *do* want to move out into that larger world of fantasy and sf magazines, don't you? Study the current issues. Read all of the back ones you can find, and, of course, read all the anthologies in your library, if they have a decent supply. You must find a way to write longer stories, with a broader framework. Who, for instance, is Mr. Bickerstaff? Where did he come from, where was he going, what was his life? Why is this happening to him. It seems to me your story should start earlier, before he arrives at the bus-stop, with premonitions of Doom, along the way. Had he done something to deserve his Fate, or, like most of us, at times, is he simply run down, like someone in the street? There are thousands of undeserved deaths every day in all countries . . . a man killed by cancer here, a man gored by a bull there, a woman decapitated when an iron beam thrusts through her car window—sheerest coincidence. I guess I'm asking you the point of your story? Are you sure you have clarified it for us? for *you*? Is it a comment, via metaphor, on life? Shouldn't you fill in on Mr. B's previous life a bit? You are working here a bit in the vein of Franz Kafka, whose work shouldn't be imitated, it's far too forceful and strange and, let's face it, if he were sending out his stories today, he would have as much trouble selling them as when he lived.

Anyway, take a look at your structure here. What magazine did the story appear in? If it was a small college mag., you could still, as a rewritten tale, send it to *Magazine of Fantasy & S.F.*

What does Mr. B. want from life? I guess you have left that out. My characters write my stories for me. They tell me what they want, then I tell them to go get it, and I follow as they run, working at my typing as they rush to their destiny. Montag, in *F.451* wanted to stop burning books. Go stop it! I said. He ran to do just that. I followed, typing. Ahab, in *Moby Dick*, wanted to chase and kill a whale. He rushed raving off to do so. Melville followed, writing the novel with a harpoon on the flesh of the damned whale! Thanks for the poems, too. Very nice. But poetry is hard to comment on, criticize. I would prefer to be helpful with fiction.

Why are you going to college? If you aren't careful, it will cut across your writing time, stop your writing stories. Is *that* what you want? *Think. Do* you want to be a writer for a lifetime? What will you take in college that will help you be a writer? You already have a full style. All you need now is practice at structure. Write back. Soon. Luck to you!

Ray B.

Dan Chaon did indeed go to college that fall, but not before Ray Bradbury sent him a copy of Dorothea Brande's 1930s classic instructional text, Becoming a Writer. *Her emphasis on recognizing the creative roles played by both the conscious mind and the subconscious had deeply influenced Bradbury in 1939, and he often recommended Brande's book to others starting out on a writer's*

life. Chaon's final letter to Bradbury before college reveals an honesty and spon-
taneity not unlike what we find in Bradbury's early letters to his own mentors.

August 29, 1982

Dear Mr. Bradbury:

How exciting it was to receive a package from you! Thank you for the
book. Ms. Brande's advice has helped me a great deal already. I read it
cover to cover the very first night I got it, and I find it very useful as a
reference. It's something that I'll read again and again.

I was also very excited to see *The Electric Grandmother* on NBC.[35]
We finally got it out here in the country about two weeks ago. I don't
know how you felt, but I thought it was very well done. You know, often
one will find a wicked mother or father or uncle, but in very few works
of fiction does one find a wicked grandma! It is very powerful imagery,
and I was glad to see the makers of the film understood that and
capitalized on it. I had a lump in my throat the whole way through.

I read about *Something Wicked* (the movie) in *Twilight Zone*
magazine. I'm pleased that you're happy about the film . . . I'm certainly
keeping my fingers crossed. Many of my favorite books have really been
ruined by the movies: Peter Straub's *Ghost Story* despite the wonderful
old actors in the thing was ruined! Ditto with *The Lord of the Rings*! And
the list goes on and on . . . *Something Wicked* is one of my favorite books,
and I'd hate to see it massacred. But why am I telling you this? I'm sure
you know it already quite well.

In any case, I hope everything goes great! An Oscar to you, or
whatever.

I'm writing more and more now. I feel like the more I write, the
more I improve, but then it also seems like my very best stories take
no effort at all, while the real dogs are the ones I work the hardest on.
Something I write will at times be very easy, and at other times be very
hard. But it seems like everything I write during the easy periods are
good and everything I write during the hard periods are bad. Some times
I get very depressed because I don't feel as if I'm moving fast enough. I
feel as if I should be getting published more.

Then I look at the letters I received from you, and I feel better.

Oh! Mr. Bradbury, I'm very happy to tell you that I won a $150 prize for the short story "Welcome Home, Mr. Ottermole"! I sent it to you, do you remember? Also, I won first place in the NE Poets Association's High School Poetry award. I was very thrilled. [. . .]

Well, I suppose that I should end this. Once again, thank you for the book! If you have time, write me before I go to college (Sept 19) and tell me about all the wonderful things that happened on the set of *SWTWC* . . . tell me what you thought of my story . . . tell me anything you like, it would just feel wonderful if I would get a letter from you.

Once more, thanks, thanks, thanks.

I am, as always,

Dan

Dan Chaon

PS If you get a chance too . . . you might scribble off a few lines (one or two paragraphs would be fine) for *Scrivener*, the literary magazine I help to edit, as an introduction to the magazine. I think I sent you a copy.

PPS I must seem awfully pushy. I honest-to-God don't mean to be!

PPPS I hope I didn't seem too gushy in this letter, either. I was just so excited, you see.

PPPPS (the last one) I'm sorry about the mistakes in typing. You can't use liquid paper on yellow paper!

JOSEPH ROBERTS

An aspiring young writer from Alabama wrote on February 9, 1963, to ask how Bradbury knew the right descriptive words at key points in his stories: "Do you ramble through the dictionary, memorizing it from cover to cover in that wonderful subconscious self of yours?" Three days later, Bradbury replied through a series of extended metaphors designed to move a young writer away from such self-conscious exercises entirely.

February 11, 1963

Dear Mr. Roberts:

Using the right word at the right time? Great gods and good griefs, an age old question, and what the answer? There is only one answer, of course: work. When I began to write I did not know the words, but I learned them. So must you. You must read one poem every night of your life. Are you listening? You must read one short story every night of your life. Do you hear me? You must read one essay every day of your life. Will you do it? And you must write every day of your life for a lifetime through on to the end. Are you up to it?

For writing is like learning to walk. First you lie there. Then you rock. Then you crawl and creep. Then you sit up. Then you stand. Then you fall down. Then you stand again and take a step, and fall down. And then at last you walk. And at last run.

Or learning to talk. First you must move your lips. Then your tongue. Then move air out of your throat over your tongue and lips. Slow. Slow. And one day, by God, the first word.

Don't worry about all the right words now, worry only about the right emotions. Live your stories, emote them, and the words will come, and as they come will grow better.

Best wishes to you always,
Ray Bradbury

TOM THOMAS

Throughout his career, students of all ages, often unpublished, wrote to Bradbury for advice and critique. For writers still in high school, Bradbury felt that the best service he could provide was to give them a sense of the dedication required to produce fiction worthy of review. Thomas Thurston Thomas was a high school junior when he wrote to Bradbury. He would go on to become an engineer and a professional science fiction writer who at times collaborated with David Drake, Frederik Pohl, and Roger Zelazny. At the age of seventeen, Thomas wanted a sense of his potential as a science fiction writer and asked if he could send excerpts of a science fiction novel in progress to see if the work was acceptable. Bradbury's lengthy reply follows Thomas's letter, offering guidance based on how he had discovered his own emerging talent as a young and inexperienced writer.

April 8, 1965

Dear Mr. Bradbury,

How does an aspiring young writer approach the master? I am a seventeen-year-old boy, a high school junior, who has begun his first novel in political science fiction. After two years of planning and rewriting, I am finally able to see my goal of finishing sometime this August. I spend, on the average, three or four hours a day at the typewriter in addition to my school work, which includes an honors course in English. I have had no formal instruction in the writing of fiction as an art.

It is at the suggestion of my father that I write to you. Anyone having seen portions of my manuscript has encouraged my efforts. But none of these are experts, and beginners have no critics. It would be very helpful, I feel, to have the honest criticisms of a professional author in my field. I cannot know if my work is acceptable, or if my time is wasted. It is my hope to publish as I think very seriously of becoming a writer.

My novel is not pure science fiction. I use that as but the vehicle for my plot. I write of an interstellar empire beset by external war, revolution, and bureaucratic jealousies. My protagonist leads the camp of the revolutionaries. To date I have finished a rough draft of the entire work, depicting the main plot, and have finished the first four chapters; the completed book will have approximately twelve chapters. I have worked my explanations of government, economics, and war into these four.

If it would not be inconvenient, would you let me send you a copy of a few chapters? I would greatly appreciate the criticisms of an expert.

Respectfully yours,
Thomas Thomas

May 5th, 1965

Dear Tom Thomas:

Thank you for your good letter of April 8th.

I want you to read and re-read this letter at your leisure, for I want to be as direct and honest with you as possible.

I began writing at the age of 12, kept steadily increasing my output at sixteen and seventeen and eighteen, on up to the age of twenty. Most of the material I wrote during those years was not good, to put it mildly. But it had to be done, in order to learn and grow. The important thing was I decided to *be* a writer! That important decision is now yours. Nobody can tell you if you are a writer, or if you can be a writer. Your mother, your father, your relatives, your friends, your teachers, none of these can guess your want, your need, your great desire. It is your lonely and proud decision to make. Let no one swerve you from it, once made.

Now, at your age, there is no way to judge if you can be a writer. All of the stories written by boys in their teens, including all the stories I wrote in my teens, are simply not good. Most of mine were dreadful. So if anyone had read them, they would have said, for God's sake, boy, give up, lie down, go away, stop it, don't be a writer, no!

So, I have made it a practice never to read stories by boys in their teens. I wouldn't want to judge them, criticise them, hurt them, in any way. They are not ready to be judged, criticised, or hurt. There is only one thing they should do. Write. Write every day of their life. Write and write again. It doesn't matter if it is good or not. What matters is wanting to write, wanting to live the life of a writer. Then, when you are twenty or twenty-one, you will have a lot of junk out of your system and will be ready to be criticized, and, most important, will have learned enough to judge and criticize yourself, without mercy.

Also, never let anyone judge a novel of yours by a few chapters. That would be fatal to your finishing the novel, for if they criticized out of ignorance they might depress you and cause you to stop short. Also, don't ever tell any of your ideas to anyone. Not to your parents, friends, or teachers. Bottle them up. Then, explode them out on paper.

Between now and your twentieth birthday I want you to write at least a thousand words, four pages, a day, or the equivalent of a short story a week.

Only with this kind of disciplined schedule can you learn enough, do enough, to be a writer. You must write and burn several hundred stories in order to be a writer. Is this too large an order for you? I wrote millions of words by the time I was 21. I have since published over 300 stories. And written over 1,000 stories in all, some of which will never be published, for they are bad.

Here is a list of books you must save up for and buy and keep in your library and read every year of your life so that you will know them by heart:

Lajos Egri: *The Art of Dramatic Writing*. Simon and Schuster, publishers.
Dorothea Brande: *Becoming a Writer*. Harcourt-Brace, publishers.
Somerset Maugham: *The Summing Up*. Doubleday and Co., publishers.
Maren Elwood: *Characters Make Your Story*.

Read these. Take a short story course in high school, if you can. Take short story for one year in a night school at college. Stay away from college, otherwise. College ruins more writers than it makes.[36] You must educate yourself at your typewriter, every day. Get a parttime job when you are out of high school, and write the rest of your time. Let no day pass you are not in a book store, browsing, or in a library. You must love books with all your heart and dive deep into them.

Follow your own taste, dream your own dreams, believe in yourself.
Work hard.

When you are twenty, and have written a million words at least,
send me a short story to criticize. You will be ready then to hear what I
will tell you without being hurt. You will have grown a good shell over
your tender skin.

Good luck, Tom, and let me hear from you in three years, if you
really decide you want to be a writer with all your heart.

Best,
Ray Bradbury

GREGORY MILLER

*Through much of the first decade of the twenty-first century, Pennsylvania high
school teacher Greg Miller became the last writer whom a rapidly aging Ray
Bradbury actively mentored. Bradbury passed Miller insights and critiqued his
writing on a regular basis through detailed exchanges of emails and frequent
cross-country visits by Miller. Although Bradbury had to dictate his responses,
many of them offer glimpses of the unknown worlds that can open out for a talented and passionate young writer.*

May 10, 2004

Dear Ray,

It's been a wonderful two weeks! I've been taking your advice on studying
poetic rhythm and rhyme very seriously, and have been immersing myself
in traditional poetry for fourteen days now. Although I've always loved
poetry, I've rarely read it with such intensity or purpose. . . And traditional
poetry isn't an area in which I've studied or read widely before.

I think the poems that have struck me the most forcefully, either for
their rhythmic qualities, their rhyming qualities, or both, are:

Poe's "Ulalume," "Anabelle Lee," "The Bells," and, of course, "The
Raven,"

Emily Dickinson's "I dwell in Possibility," "I know some lonely
houses off the road," and "I years had been from home,"

Wordsworth's "The Prelude" and Tennyson's "Ulysses,"

And, of course, *your* poems "Remembrance II," "I Die, So Dies the
World," and my long-held favorite, "This Attic Where the Meadow
Greens."

Anyway, I wanted to let you know how valuable your suggestion has
been to me, and will continue to be, for I know this is just the tip of a
very deep iceberg. By telling me to read poets of this type, you've sent
me off on a fine journey of emotional and literary discovery. And it's
broadening my horizons at an exciting pace.

I hope to talk to you soon, and look forward to seeing you in
October!

With much love,

Greg

May 11, 2004

Dear Greg:

Your reaction to my suggestions and my criticism brought tears to my
eyes because you are a super student. There's an eagerness about you
to learn which is incredible. This means you must certainly be a terrific
teacher too, because you recognize the needs of your students.

I've tried to live with the motto "I can hardly wait" in mind. In other
words, every day jump out of bed because you're curious to see what the
day holds, and what you can find, and what you can create, because it's
all so wonderfully exciting. Your letter is full of that excitement because
you're discovering things; you go through all the poets in history and
learn where you can learn. You then come back like a dog with a big
stick in his mouth, saying, "Look here, look what I found!" with that
incredible brightness in that dog's eyes, that love of the journey, and
the discovery, and bringing back that discovery, and then running out to
find more.

It's great when this information that you're seeking and finding goes into your subconscious and begins to reappear in your work without effort or thought; you put it away in your blood so it pops up with wonderful surprises. Sometimes in the middle of a line, an interior rhyme will suggest itself, maybe two or three words in, and suddenly a word you didn't know you had in you appears and you say, "My God, where did that come from?" That's what poetry really does; it surprises.

If you take a look at my long poem, "Christus Apollo," which is in my big book of poetry and also in my book of religious verse,[37] that was written in one afternoon in Palm Springs about 35 years ago, when I had no typewriter with me, only a pad and pen. I knew I had to write something to appear at Royce Hall, a cantata, with the music to be written by Jerry Goldsmith, with a full chorus. I knew I had a basic idea, but two hours later the whole thing had flowed out, unconscious, in great surprising lines.

There's a great invisible game out there, Greg, and you can hardly wait to run forth and get into that place where nobody loses and everyone wins. So, my dear young student, my eager friend, continue and stay in touch; I know you're going to do some great stuff.

I return your love, redoubled,

Ray

4

LITERARY CONTEMPORARIES

Death. Violence. Sex. Murder. I have seen it several times as it
brushed by over my hair-ends and fingertips in my life. Death
is a Lonely Business is the overall response one has to it.

—*Bradbury to Jim McKimmey, October 24, 1963*

GORE VIDAL

The postmodernist writer Gore Vidal (1925–2012) was best known for novels of political history (Burr, 1876, Empire, *and others*), *satirical novels* (Myra Breckenridge), *and political essays. Bradbury met Vidal in 1950 or 1951, during one of his periodic trips to see Don Congdon and various major market magazine editors in New York. In this letter, Vidal reacts to reading* The Martian Chronicles *shortly after Bradbury's trip.*

[ca. 1 July 1951]

Dear Ray,

What a wonderful book it is! You have that curious gift for verisimilitude in time: you create a world and give it a past, a present, a future and then indicate life on several levels . . . something Mr. Burroughs the master could never do. He was excellent at showing what went on in the King's throne room or in the scientist's laboratory but he gave you no feeling that a country existed to support the King, that there were Kings before him, that the scientist's science no matter how fantastic was based on some interior logic. In that sense he plays a Marlowe to your Shakespeare. Marlowe could deal with the thunders, could unleash his mighty line but he was not various . . . and never simple. Do keep on just as you are. It is very rare for any writer on any level to create a world and, having done it, stay with it. The miracle might not happen again.

I was pleased by the references to the Oz books[1] . . . I have read all thirty-odd of them and would far rather have written them than *Moby Dick.*

It was good to see you at Rita's. Keep in touch with me, and give Chris my love should you see him.[2]

Yrs
Gore
Barrytown, N.Y.

Ray Bradbury
10750 Clarkson Rd.
Los Angeles 64, Calif.

[July 5, 1951]

Dear Gore:

Your short letter was tremendously welcome. I'm pleased that you found
many things in the *Chronicles* to your liking. Yes, I certainly agree with you
that it would be worth everything to be the author of the Oz books rather
than *Moby Dick*. It has been a dream of mine that perhaps some day I can
wrangle a deal to write an Oz book; that would be very jolly indeed.

Chris called last week and will come to see us this week some time,
we hope, so I will pass on your regards to him. He seems to be doing
well with his new book-in-progress.[3] Things go well here; Doubleday
has definitely taken the 2nd of the two books I brought to New York
finished and in-embryo.[4] I enclose my latest *Post* fantasy.[5] The original
illustration came to me in the mail today, a vast thing, three feet by
three and a half, I'd say, and a real corker for my den walls. Hope you
like the tale. I look forward to reading more of your material soon. It
was nice meeting you; very nice indeed, and here are my best wishes to
you for a successful and happy summer.

Yours,

Ray

P.S. Dear Truman has done it again. "The Grass Harp" in the current
Bazaar has some nice atmospheric touches, but like always, (shades of
Welty!) nothing to say.[6] Are you happy?

*In his next (undated) July 1951 letter, Vidal described "The Beast from 20,000
Fathoms" as a "charming" tale, but he found the saurian illustration too sensa-*

tional; Vidal sent Bradbury his own short book A Search for the King, *which "also has a dragon in it, in a minor way," and spoke of the searing heat of the New York summer.*

Bradbury
10750 Clarkson Rd.
Los Angeles 64, Calif.

July 31st, 1951

Dear Gore:

Thanks for your note on "The Beast from 20,000 Fathoms" (My God, that title!) and for the copy of *A Search for the King*[7] which I look forward to reading as soon as I finish writing this book for Doubleday which should be done by Oct. 1st.

I don't envy you being in the East at the heart of summer. I hear that United States Steel instead of using their blast furnaces in July, closes them down and sends its metal to be tempered, instead, on the sidewalks of any Eastern town. So help me, I believe it.

Just sold another fantasy to the *Post*, which delights me, as it is a very off-trail story of an April Witch, a girl who can inhabit any other person's body and use them for her own pleasures, look out from their eyes, make their hands move, etc.[8] The *Post* sent on the original illustration from my sea monster story and, framed, it will hang in the nursery. All our children, needless to say, will grow up looking like dinosaurs.

You'll hear from me again, later. Thanks again for the book. Best wishes to you.

Yours,
Ray

JESSAMYN WEST

Bradbury's long friendship with Jessamyn West (1902–1984) began shortly after she sent him a carbon of her response to Doubleday for receiving a publisher's copy of Bradbury's The Golden Apples of the Sun. *They both found great success in crafting book-length fiction from evocative stories of earlier times. Bradbury had great admiration for her Indiana Quaker families of* The Friendly Persuasion, *and he deeply regretted that his own publishing deadlines forced him to decline director William Wyler's request to write the screenplay. The stories and books that emerged from his Illinois childhood struck a similar chord with West, but her letter shows that her regard for Bradbury extended across his entire creative landscape.*

Wellesley College

March 23, 1953

Dear Mr. Johnson,

Your letter and Ray Bradbury's stories followed me on from Napa to Wellesley where I'm being something called a "writer in residence." There's been more residency than writing so far, but I have hopes.

I very much appreciate your sending me *The Golden Apples of the Sun*. Bradbury not only writes well—he writes like Bradbury which makes him unique. I've heard him called "the Thoreau of the Chrome Age," "the Edgar Allan Poe of the Space Ship," etc. These efforts I sympathize with, because the only way to convey the quality of something unique to those ignorant of it *is* by comparisons. I just think these are the wrong comparisons. Bradbury is really the John Donne of this age, a writer of metaphysical prose as Donne was of metaphysical poetry, a man who, like Donne, thinks with his heart, feels with his head. He is the first writer to put men on Mars; before his time nothing recognizably human had landed there. That's why Bradbury is so effective a writer. What happens in his stories—and it's always plenty—is happening to a human being. It matters. It signifies something. And these significant exciting happenings in which real human beings are involved is put down in a nice clean exact prose. What else is there? In writing?

It's a new synthesis he's attempting: as Donne attempted a synthesis of thought and emotion, Bradbury is attempting a synthesis of man and science. He is perhaps the first really "modern" writer—and he is first in a good many other respects too. I am making myself read slowly so the stories will last.

Thank you once again for sending me the book.

Sincerely,
Jessamyn West

W. SOMERSET MAUGHAM

In early 1959 Bradbury sent a copy of his new story collection, A Medicine for Melancholy, *to the influential British novelist and playwright W. Somerset Maugham (1874–1965). Maugham, nearing ninety, gradually read all the volume's stories and offered the following comparison to another American writer who, like Bradbury, was sometimes called "The October Man."*

9th April, 1959.

Dear Mr. Bradbury,

I waited to thank you for sending me your book until I had read all your stories. I did that gradually because I don't think it is fair to an author to read his stories one after the other. I need not tell you that I enjoyed them. You have a very individual gift. I think I liked best "The Town Where No One Got Off"; I have an idea that it would have given Edgar Allan Poe a peculiar satisfaction to write it himself.

Yours sincerely,
W. S. Maugham

CARL SANDBURG

The Pulitzer Prize–winning poet and Lincoln biographer Carl Sandburg (1878–
1967) met Ray Bradbury in 1958, when Bradbury worked with Hollywood direc-
tor George Stevens Sr. on an eightieth birthday celebration for the iconic American
poet. In 1960, Bradbury declined to script Stevens's The Greatest Story Ever
Told, *but he joined Stevens in securing Sandburg the role of screen consultant*
for the film. While in California, Carl Sandburg finally saw John Huston's 1956
production of Moby Dick, *adapted to film by Bradbury; in March 1961 Sandburg*
wrote to congratulate Huston and sent his carbon copy to Ray Bradbury, with a
superimposed handwritten note of gratitude to his younger friend for bringing
Melville's powerful prose to a broader audience on screen.

March 21, 1961

Dear John Huston:

Saw *Moby Dick* last night. This is only to salute you on intelligence,
perception and true courage. In a sense it is better than the book
because children, to whom the book would be too heavy, can enjoy the
picture. Your father would have had pride about it.

Dear Ray: Above has gone to J. H. A great script you did so the above
goes in part for you.

Carl Sandburg

March 26th, 1961

Dear Carl:

It was a gift from the blue, on a day when I was depressed about my
work, to have your letter come through to me about *Moby Dick*. Your
words remind me again of the natural and correct pride we can take in
that film.

I hope to telephone you soon. We have a writers' group that has met every two weeks for 12 years now and it would be fun for all of us to have you sit in with us some night, if you wish.

Best, as ever, and thanks.

Yours,
Ray

Bradbury's response to Sandburg included an invitation to attend his writing group, which had been formed in 1948 to gather writers whose work had appeared in Doubleday's annual Best American Short Stories *volumes (Bradbury earned that honor four times). Sandburg's brevity and distinctive prairie-grown turn of phrase transformed a declined invitation into a note of optimism and encouragement.*

April 4, 1961

Dear Ray:

In the immediate future there are time pressures so I couldn't attend your writers' group. You may be sure I want acquaintance with them and that I want talk with you ere I leave this curious corner of America.

With salutations on the fine, original work you have done.

Carl

FAITH BALDWIN

A prolific author of novels centered on working women of influence that appealed to a vast audience of middle-class women, Faith Baldwin Cuthrell (1893–1978) was popular in both magazine serials and books from the 1930s through the 1950s. Like Bradbury, she was involved with television, hosting a fiction anthology series on ABC in 1951. She may not have met Bradbury, but she read much of his work, and appreciated the truths underlying the supernatural realism of Something Wicked This Way Comes.

Oct. 30 / 62

Dear Mr. Bradbury—

I've been reading you for quite a while, and am a pushover for fantasy and science fiction. Now I must write you about *Something Wicked This Way Comes*. It is fitting that I read it just before I go to a costume Halloween party as Lady Macbeth, which suits my mood on a raw, raining night.

I just want to say that, quite aside from fantasy, suspense or terror, you have written a beautiful, and basically true, book.

Gratefully yours,
Faith Baldwin

JIM McKIMMEY

Professional writers occasionally came to Bradbury for advice, including crime fiction writers like Jim McKimmey (1923–2011), an underrated pulp veteran who already had an established correspondence with Bradbury when he sent his recent novel Squeeze Play *(1962) for critique. Over time, McKimmey's noir legacy expanded beyond Bradbury's view of his work, and even in its day* Squeeze Play *was favorably reviewed. This letter is significant, however, because Bradbury's mid-1940s success as a writer of off-trail detective stories played into his advice, which included examples of tragedies he had observed in the downtown tenement where he kept a writing office during the war years.*

Bradbury

October 24, 1963

Dear Jim:

I thought you might enjoy having these tearsheets which I saved up after reading your stories over a period of time, and all of which I enjoyed.

I still would like to see more of McKimmey himself in your future stories and books. I read your new novel a week or so back and have hesitated to write you about it, because I have mixed feelings. I feel that the structure is there, the action, but without true philosophic asides, McKimmey asides, the richness we look for in novels is missing. The moments of truth are what make most novels, and these are generally the kind of "slow" thing that tv producers and film producers throw away because "nobody will be interested." But even in an Ian Fleming novel, the fun comes in the "gunk" the extra tidbits and canapes he throws in, along with an overall outlook toward life which, if we don't agree with it, is at least individual.

I think you are on your way to putting McKimmey on paper, what you really think about; life, death, love, sickness, misery, sanity, insanity, with large or small letters, but these are still too rarely encountered in your books. For an example of what I mean, wander through Montaigne's essays, or some of Voltaire's philosophical dictionary work. What do you, for instance, think of *being alone*? What does color mean to you? What day did you discover you were first alive? how old were you? at what hour did the discovery come, and in what fashion did the miracle shake you?[9] It came different to each of us, to me when I was ten, and I found I could really die, and was shaken, when I was fourteen. What is old age to Jim McKimmey? What is, truly, a woman, a man, a child? If your characters could become walking ideas, extensions of yourself, how extra rich your stories and books would be.

I hope I am making myself clear without hurting you. Jesus prevent that. But I want you to dig, excitedly, into yourself more as the years pass. I hate to illustrate from my own work, but it is at hand. If I took out all the scenes in *Something Wicked* where the father talks about night, three in the morning, old age, sickness, death, sex, the scene on the front steps in the night, the scene in the library, and left the skeleton of my book, it would still be a novel, right? But it would be less moving and less meaningful, again right? Only when the heart speaks clearly and with loving detail, can we begin to care much more for those we are watching in a novel or story.

Your novel is good as it stands, as are these stories. But the entirety could be more touching, moving, and wondrous, if you summoned forth your responses, as needed, on the meaning of Darkness, mirrors, light, high mountain air, cities, time, distance, illusion, etc. We read as much for philosophy as for plot. Behind every writer stands not a woman, but a soul, his soul. To bring that lamp out and light it in public, to allow it to issue forth through the seams of a story, is the great thing.

But now, really, what is Murder? What do you really think of it? Do you smell it? Do you hear it? Can you touch it for us so we thrill and recoil? I knew a man and wife once in a tenement downtown in LA, she shot him, he died crying in her arms, weeping for a priest, and she wept her tears down on him. This was murder, of a big dumb blundering slob human by his unkempt slutty dumb slob wife, but suddenly there they were, he had done bad things to her but he loved her, and she had done this thing to him but loved him and now he was dying, and her crying on him and kissing him and sorry for that awful moment she had fired the pistol, but it was too late and now he was dead, and her picture in the papers. Or one night a young man waited out front of the tenement in his car, I saw him there, and three hours later he was found, stark naked, in his big empty rich house a mile away, his head bashed in by someone never found. This was death and murder to me too, and I remember the far image of the young man who was to die, who didn't know it, a few hours later, how lonely my memory is of him, as if he were on a ship going out in a harbor on a trip and me not knowing and him not knowing, and him in the papers the next day.[10] Death. Violence. Sex. Murder. I have seen it several times as it brushed by over my hair-ends and fingertips in my life. Death is a Lonely Business[11] is the overall response one has to it.

Jim, look in the mirror. I want more of McKimmey's eternal soul in the next novel. This new one is good for starters. But the next one . . . wow! I want to be knocked on my pins!

Best from your friend,
Ray

ANAÏS NIN

Angela Anaïs Juana Antolina Rosa Edelmira Nin y Culmell (1903–1977) was a French-born Cuban by heritage and later an American novelist known best for her journals and erotica. Bradbury met Nin through his friend the architect Lloyd Wright. She often attended Bradbury's lectures, as well as the Los Angeles run of the three one-act science fiction plays The World of Ray Bradbury, *which opened at the Coronet Theatre on October 14, 1964.*

Nov. 30, 1964

Dear Ray:

I was in N.Y. when your theatre opened, but saw it later. I wanted to tell you my reaction to it. You know how much I enjoy your imagination and your explorations of future worlds. I thought the plays were presented with originality. I liked the abstract backgrounds, sounds, and particularly in the one about the children *suggesting* the televised spectacle was very strong. I am not sure that any theatre could do more than that. The question is whether your work, with its many dimensions might not be better filmed—For imagination the film can do more. I hope one day these plays will be filmed. For in your work the atmosphere around the words—worlds which words can almost not penetrate—is as important. Whatever you do, I'm one of your admirers—Someone who knows this sent me a quote from Shaw: "Living truth cannot be found by reason. Truth can only be caught in flight, when the passions detonate us and we surprise our true selves in the middle of an avalanche. After the uproar is over we can think about what we caught unaware rushing out of our subconscious note paper."

.I hope you read by Inner Space as well as I read your flight into the future.

Anaïs

RUSSELL KIRK

Bradbury's friendship with scholar and cultural critic Russell Kirk (1918–1994) began in the mid-1960s, when Kirk singled out Bradbury's mythmaking prose as part of the larger mythopoeic preservation of traditional literary values he found in the imaginary worlds of C. S. Lewis, J. R. R. Tolkien, Charles Williams, John Collier, and others. Although Kirk was an architect of postwar American compassionate conservatism, and Bradbury more a democrat in his origins, they were independent visionaries who criticized special interests of both the right and the left in American culture. Kirk considered Bradbury "a man who overthrows idols by the power of imagery"; their early correspondence set the foundation for sections of Kirk's influential book Enemies of the Permanent Things *(1969).*

September 12, 1967

Mr. Ray Bradbury
Los Angeles

Dear Ray,

What an interesting prospect—the Picasso film! And I do hope *Dandelion Wine* will appear and triumph in New York before long.[12]

Monica Rachel, our heiress, is seven weeks old now: an amiable child, eager to converse. She will be an Algonquin Indian, like her mother. I shall work away here at Mecosta until about October 5, when I have to commence speechifying.

At present, I am at work upon *you*. I am writing a piece, as yet untitled, about your work, which probably I will publish in the *Kenyon Review*.[13] Also it will be a chapter in my ethical book, which I am finishing now: *The Enemies of the Permanent Things: Reflections on*

Abnormality in Letters, Politics, and Schooling. (You are one of my chief exhibits of true normality, along with T. S. Eliot and Max Picard.)

I think I have collected everything of yours between book-covers (though you are a dreadful problem for any bibliographer) except *Dark Carnival, The Meadow,*[14] and *Switch on the Night.* I never have seen these. [. . .]

You are difficult to write about, in the sense that though the rising generation understands you, those "whose hearts are dry as summer dust" don't; and they form the dominant serious literary public. They are at once the victims and the predators of what, in my books, I have called "defecated rationality." What desiccated minds, as you know! A conscience may speak to a conscience only if the auditor-conscience still is alive. But it is most heartening (cheerfulness *will* keep breaking in!) that the hungry imagination of the rising generation senses what you mean. I find that my three nephews, who have spent most of their lives in Persia, swear by practically all your books.

Now for a few inquiries—not that I ask men of letters to explain themselves. (People are forever trying to do that to me.) First—what with the bewildering duplication of stories in your various collections— how many short stories have you published (not counting, if you wish, those that you don't think are worth reprinting)? How many book-length tales? How many plays? Second, have you been influenced at all by William Morris, George MacDonald, C. S. Lewis, and J. R. R. Tolkien? Third, is it possible for you to suggest, in a few words, and without much bother, any general literary and ethical assumptions that are the foundation of your writing?

I won't vex you further just now; as Samuel Johnson put it, "Questioning is not a mode of conversation among gentlemen."

In a few weeks, you'll be in my page in *National Review* again: a piece called "Librarians and *Fahrenheit 451*," touching upon the censorial matters I raised in my previous letter[15] to you. [. . .] Best wishes. If you have opportunity, let me hear from you about the small matters mentioned on the preceding page.

Cordially,
Russell

Sept. 16, 1967

Dear Russell:

Thanks for your latest good letter. I am pleased to hear you will be doing
the article on this hybrid animal Bradbury. I enclose a huge parcel of
material, many articles, from which I think you can glean my basic ideas.
After you read these you might wish to ask further questions.

Above all, at heart, the thing that drives me most often is an immense
gratitude that I was given this one chance to live, to be alive the one time
round in a miraculous experience that never ceases to be glorious and
dismaying. I accept the whole damn thing. It is neither all beautiful nor
all terrible, but a wash of multitudinous despairs and exhilarations about
which we know nothing. Our history is so small, our experience so limited,
our science so inadequate, our theologies crammed in mere matchboxes,
that we know we stand on the outer edge of a beginning and our greatest
history lies before us, frightening and lovely, much darkness and much light.

If I were to name the one man who comes back into my life
constantly, it would be Bernard Shaw. Every time a new play is
published, I re-read Shaw.

Under separate cover I am sending on *Switch on the Night* signed to
the new papoose.[16]

I must confess your considering me as an exhibit of true normality fills
me with secret amusement and delight, for, of course, each of us knows that
we are not normal, each of us is some kind of monster kept each in his own
tower, a private keep somewhere in the upper part of the head where, from
time to time, of midnights, the beast can be heard raving. To control that,
to the end of life, to stay contemplative, sane, good humored, is our entire
work, in the midst of cities that tempt us to inhumanity, and passions that
threaten to drive through the skin with invisible spikes.

I have published about 300 stories in all. I have published six plays,
and written, in all, about 12 plays. No, I have not been influenced by
Morris, MacDonald or Tolkien, though I have read and enjoyed Lewis'
Screwtape Letters; however he has not been an influence that I know

of. Shaw, Shakespeare, Robert Frost, Steinbeck, Hemingway, Faulkner, John Collier, Eudora Welty, the Restoration playwrights, are my most constant friends. I also admire the writing of Loren Eiseley very much.

Best and many thanks!

Ray

P.S. the stories in *Dark Carnival* were reprinted, with a few deletions in the later volume retitled *The October Country*, so you need not worry about reading *Dark Carnival* since all the *good* stories appear in *Country*.

R.

ARTHUR C. CLARKE

Bradbury first met Sir Arthur C. Clarke (1917–2008) in 1953, but science fiction readers as well as mainstream reading audiences had already identified both authors with Mars and its symbol as humanity's first step to the stars. Bradbury and Clarke were instrumental in bringing science fiction into the literary mainstream, and the geographical distance between them never diminished the easy friendship found in Clarke's letters. These two letters were prompted by Bradbury's 1968 film review of 2001: A Space Odyssey, *in which Bradbury praised Clarke's screenplay but criticized director Stanley Kubrick's changes, and the 1992 foreword that Bradbury wrote for Neil McAleer's biography of Clarke.*

Hotel Chelsea
222 W 23
N.Y. 11

24 May 68

Dear Ray,

Just seen your review—I still love you, tho' Stanley won't! (I'm—cattily—dying to see his reaction to your remark that he shouldn't have been allowed near the screenplay!).

I hope you've now seen the shortened version—but the enclosed shows one can't please everyone!

All the very best

Art

PS Try to get hold of the big article about *2001* in the *N.Y. Times*, Sunday 12 May.

August 11, 1992

Mr. Ray Bradbury
10265 Cheviot Drive
Los Angeles CA 90064

Dear Ray,

I'm writing to thank you for your much appreciated introduction to the biography.[17] I burst out laughing when I read the first page because— you won't believe this—*at that very moment* I was unpacking a marvelous new laptop computer, which I've just bought, and which must have been light years ahead of the one I showed you in Beverly Hills.[18] (For your information, it's the first laptop with good colour—the Compaq LTE Lite 25C). I've already fallen hopelessly in love with it, and even did some work on the flight back to Colombo, when I switched it on for the first time.

I'm delighted to know you've discovered the pleasures of flying— just when I'm trying to give them up! I can't decide whether the Concorde is better than a First-Class Jumbo, in which you can sleep, relax, and walk around.

I'm just recovering from a hectic, but enjoyable month in UK for the (slightly premature) celebrations of my 75th birthday (no way I'll go to UK in the winter!). I had time for just two engagements (1) turning the handle of the reconstructed Babbage calculator, finally completed a hundred and fifty years too late, (2) seeing the animated dinosaur display at the Natural History Museum, which is really quite scary. (I can't wait to see *Jurassic Park*!)

Now to get back to work—I have 55 projects on line, including, I'm afraid, two new novels (unless I can get out of it).

Still feel sad about Isaac.[19] It's getting lonely up here on Dinosaur Plateau; isn't it?

Love,

Art

GRAHAM GREENE

British novelist Graham Greene (1904–1991), a master of Cold War postcolonial fiction, was impressed with Bradbury's 1953 long story "And the Rock Cried Out" (originally "The Millionth Murder"). He commended the cinematic possibilities of the story to the independent British film director Sir Carol Reed, who had already filmed Greene's novel The Third Man *to high acclaim. Bradbury secured a Swedish publisher through Greene's unsolicited recommendation, but Greene never directly corresponded until Bradbury reached out in the late 1970s.*

Dear Graham Greene:

This is a letter that should have been written to you many years ago, because of an old debt I believe I owe you. Back in 1957, Carol Reed read a short story of mine called "The Rock Cried Out" and wanted to make a film of it for Hecht-Hill-Lancaster.[20] He flew to the States and came to visit me about the story. Later, I went to spend a fine summer with Carol in London. I finished the screenplay, but the film was never made. Years later I discovered that it was you who gave the story to Carol to read.

Now, for dozens of reasons, I suddenly think of you, and got your address from Barnaby Conrad III at *Horizon*[21] and simply wanted to thank you for improving my life by bringing Carol Reed into it. Beyond that, I am a huge admirer of *The Third Man*, have seen it 20 times or more, and think it should be shown to everyone who cares about films beautifully written and beautifully directed and acted. It is a sad, wise, moving film.

Also, on many days of my life in the past 30 years, when I have had a touch of dry spell, I get out the short stories of Graham Greene and re-read them and prime the pump and go back to my work with love and energy.

That's it. An old debt, on many levels. Thanks for being my companion in writing, my helper, and my introducer to Carol. What can you do for me right *now*? Another novel, please! or, God, more stories!

Yours,
Ray Bradbury
April 18, 1979

2nd May 1979

Dear Ray Bradbury,

Many thanks for your very nice letter. Yes, I do remember in those far off days suggesting that Carol should make a film of your story. I never knew it went as far as a screen play. In fact I never knew that he had taken the idea up. It was sad that Carol died as he did.[22] He wanted to make a film of a book of mine called *The Honorary Consul* and I was told that he was not financeable in America. Films are merciless, but it does seem appalling that the maker of *The Third Man* was not financeable. The last thing he was offered and I am glad that he refused it was the American-Russian production of *The Blue Bird* which Cukor took on when Carol turned it down. Being a revengeful man and hearing what a mess he had made of a book of mine I was glad that his version of *The Blue Bird* was a disaster.[23]

I am glad you like some of my stories as I like many of yours.

Yours ever
Graham Greene

June 22, 1979

Dear Graham Greene:

I'll keep this short. But I couldn't resist telling you something about Cukor and *Blue Bird*, once you had mentioned it in your letter, and having seen *Travels with My Aunt* on tv a few nights ago. Cukor called me about six years ago and wanted me to do the screenplay of *Blue Bird*. I read the novel and went to lunch at Cukor's where Katherine Hepburn was waiting for me, to try to convince me I should do the screenplay. I protested to both of them that time and science had passed Maeterlinck's play by. When *Blue Bird* was produced, in 1905, you went to the graveyards every Sunday to visit your families. Half your children were there by the time they were ten, and most of the grandparents. So the play made morbid sense. But starting in 1939 with penicillin and the sulfas, death went out of style for children, and one helluva lot of older folks. The auto has taken over much of the work once done by germs. Hepburn saw the sense of what I was saying. Cukor didn't. I warned him not to make the film unless he found a writer far cleverer than myself. The rest is history.

Hoping this tale gives you some sort of small vengeful satisfaction.

Absolutely no answer to this, please. Finish your next book and make me happy. Thanks for your kind letter of early May.

Cordially,
Ray Bradbury

15th December 1984

Dear Ray Bradbury,

Thank you so much for your Christmas greetings and I return them as New Year greetings as they will be too late for Christmas. You and

Ballard are the only Science Fiction writers whose books I welcome because neither of you are merely Science Fiction writers but artists.

Affectionately yours,
Graham Greene

Dear Graham Greene:

THANKS in turn for your New Year's wishes.

I enclose two stories to be read at your leisure, or never at all, for I realize you have as busy a schedule as mine.

One, "Banshee," is sent because we have all had strange experiences with film directors. Mine was with John Huston on *Moby Dick*, as you will soon recognize. About 80 percent of the dialogue in this is from remembrance of real scenes with that odd man. The Banshee, of course, never existed, but Huston did his best to convince me of same.

How different my experience with Carol Reed that dear man, all through the summer of 1957. And, of course, that good experience, as I told you a few years back, was because of your giving Carol one of my stories to read.

The other story, enclosed, "Bless Me, Father," I hope might appeal to a side of you I have seen in many of your novels and stories, and in "The Potting Shed," which I read always to be immensely touched and moved in the final scenes.[24] My story does not compare, of course, but it is a true one. I wrote it to forgive myself for sins committed when I was 13.

Please, do not feel obligated to read and certainly not to respond. But there are so few writers in the world these days that I give a damn about. You are one, and special. Please stay well in 1985, and give us more books!

Yours,
Ray B.
1/11/85

22nd January 1985

Dear Ray Bradbury,

Thank you very much for the two stories. I enjoyed "Banshee" whilst
I thought of you and John Huston. I enjoyed too "Bless Me, Father,"
and the only thing that worried me was why the priest was in bed at
midnight on Christmas night because surely he would have been in the
church anyway holding a midnight Mass. However I am sure the sins
were forgiven! When are we going to have another book from you.

Yours
Graham Greene

2/6/85

Dear Graham Greene:

Good grief, you are right!
　　My priest should have been up at Midnight Mass on Christmas Eve.
That's what comes from my Baptist background! The sad thing is, none
of the editors caught that, and no other reader. You're the only one!
Anyway, glad you enjoyed the stories. My first suspense mystery novel
Death Is a Lonely Business will be published by Knopf in October. You will
be among the first 5 to get copies. It's taken 20 years to finish, though
I didn't work on it all that while. Otherwise it would be a dreadful
overweight book. I simply had to wait for about 10 characters to step
forward, one by one, and ask to be let into the novel. When they were
all assembled and looked properly grotesque or unusual in some way, as
witness *The Third Man* or *The Maltese Falcon*, I could plunge ahead. [. . .]

Thanks!
Ray B.

HELEN BEVINGTON

*Bradbury had a high regard for poets like Phyllis McGinley and Helen Bev-
ington, who wrote light verse in the traditional and meditative traditions. He
regretted never corresponding with the Pulitzer Prize–winning McGinley before her passing in 1978, but he subsequently initiated a warm correspondence
with Pulitzer Prize finalist Helen Bevington (1906–2001) in the early 1980s.
Her reaction to Bradbury's autobiographical mystery novel* Death Is a Lonely
Business *triggered a revealing response from Bradbury about the novel and the
impact of popular and literary culture on his life.*

24 February 1986

My dear Ray,

I sit here trying to find words to say to my friend that don't sound too
wildly extravagant. How do you do it all, so much and so well? Contrary
to the usual way of reading a suspenseful novel to reach the end at one
sitting, I have been living with *Death Is a Lonely Business* in a word-for-
word relationship. I like your similes that are many and imaginative. I
like the young writer (yourself) who has a weird adventure a minute. It
is very heady business to accompany him. Even if it weren't a mystery,
and such a good one, I wouldn't be able to read it other than with
excitement. I like the time of it, the setting, the nostalgia—oh my, you
are wonderfully inventive and clever with language, and I am happy to
know you and be in your good graces. How is it that a man so obviously
in love with life, living it so aware, happy, should be concerned with
death? Well, I guess we have to be. I give you my loudest request to
write more mysteries, so long as you write poems too, please.

I sought and failed to see your dramas on HBO, which nobody
I know has acquired in this backward countryside. It was my loss,
a real loss. But I think with your success I shall be able to see them
later. My greatest pleasure is to hear you say you are the most
fortunate writer in the world. The writers I know make it their
hallmark to be unhappy. Somebody said that writing brings out the

worst in a man, but you have proved how hollow that claim is. You
thrive and succeed.

Somebody else said, "Nobody *asked* me to be a writer," and that is
my view. It is an addictive occupation that I cannot live without. Right
now I am wandering still in Tibet, each day vivid and real among the
yaks and lamas and a darling young man named Ke-ping who told me
about nirvana.

But my mind is on you in this letter, your good works, so let me
end with my gladness that you keep thus bountifully in touch. Bad rice
to you.

And with love, yours,
Helen

3/21/86

Dearest Helen:

Your letters are a treasure to me. I am happy that you like my mystery.
I absolutely love it. It is a special child to me, with a special face and
flavor (do faces have flavor? yep, especially mouths). I am enclosing
a poem which explains how I live with myself. This affair, lying in bed
with me, started long ago. Out of bedding myself, and listening to
voices, all my good stuff has arrived. I am sure much of your work has
arrived the same way, through that peculiar thing called intuition. I tell
my friends, step on a landmine every morning, clean up at noon. Or
throw up every morning, shower at noon. The novel wrote itself because
at seven each morning Crumley or Rattigan or Fannie or the blind man
started talking in tongues. I listened, stirred, got up, and ran to the
typewriter. I haven't had so much fun in years. Anyway, dear special
Helen, I go to Connecticut to the Eugene O'Neill theatre, in two weeks
for a run-through of my opera *F.451*.[25] Then on to London and Paris to
introduce my mystery overseas.

You ask me how I do what I do. I have answered it partially overleaf,
but the great thing is I have a list of loves, started when I was 3, and I

have stayed in love with all of them for a lifetime. Out of this fabulous trash, I have built my life. Quasimodo, dinosaurs, Buck Rogers, Tarzan, the Chicago World's Fair, the New York World's Fair, the history of architecture, H. G. Wells, Jules Verne, ten thousand motion pictures . . . *Prince Valiant* (I corresponded with Hal Foster who drew it, for 30 years!), oldtime radio, Burns and Allen, Fred Allen, Jack Benny, Bernard Shaw, Shakespeare, Melville, The Bible, Alexander Pope and . . . Helen Bevington . . . you all go with me everywhere. I have left none behind on the road. Good company, high, low, in between, lots of laughs, grand jokes, serious faces on occasion, but mostly the fun of being alive one time and knowing I will never come again, all of which prompts me, each morn to step on me, my own landmine, and watch my limbs fly off and around the room. You *had* to ask, didn't you? I send you love through the new spring and the great summer into autumn the sad/happy time. Say, didn't you use to sit across the room from me in school, 50 years ago and stare out the window at the weather, and write poems? Yes!

Love—

Ray

THOMAS STEINBECK

The elder son of Nobel laureate John Steinbeck, Thomas Steinbeck (1944–2016) was an accomplished photographer and documentary screenwriter who, later in his life, published short fiction and several novels. His early life experiences included extensive travels with his father and brother during the 1950s and 1960s that fed his innate love of literature and provided an exposure to the work of writers his father found significant—including Ray Bradbury. For half a century, Bradbury knew nothing of this interest; he was a great admirer of Steinbeck's novels, and had actually met him in 1945, when they both happened to stay at the same rooming house in Mexico City. But the young Bradbury was too self-conscious to speak of his own writing at that time, and he regretted the missed opportunity for decades. A late-life meeting with Thomas Steinbeck soon revealed all.

June 27, 2003

RE: Steinbeck's holiday reading

My Dear Mr. Bradbury,

It gives me great pleasure to write you in any format other than a simple
fan letter, though it now occurs to me that this indeed is a fan letter,
and possibly more insidious than most, since it represents sentiments
of sublime gratitude from two generations of Steinbecks. I feel it only
appropriate that I speak for my father on this occasion, since it was he
that first introduced me to the joys of your writing.

This is not to say that my father was a great fan of science fiction,
per se, but he was a great admirer and proponent of the short story; the
subject matter made little difference. He loved *The Martian Chronicles*,
for instance, because he found his way to it through "The Million-Year
Picnic" and "The Naming of Names." He too designed larger works from
shorter stories and truly appreciated the complexity of the process.

I distinctly remember the first Bradbury story my father ever gave
me to read. I should remember, I have read it in turn to hundreds of kids
over the years. The damn thing still works like a Swiss watch. It's called
"The Flying Machine," and I loved it from the first sentence. Perhaps
it was youth, but what the hell, I'm still deeply fond of *The Wind in the
Willows* and Fu Manchu. What can you do?

Before I begin, I feel obliged to preface the following narrative with
a thumbnail sketch of my father as it pertains to his love of reading and
holidays.

John Steinbeck was a lover of ceremony and tradition, especially if
he could invent them out of whole cloth and make them serve his own
purpose. In that context, he was the innovator of some of the silliest
family traditions ever conceived, but that's another story. Nonetheless,
these odd and charming customs were always extremely entertaining,
and only rarely life-threatening.

One of these quaint traditions always included a "holiday story."
Any holiday would do if my father were in the mood. Sometimes
he would just make one up for the hell of it. [. . .] For reasons we

have ceased to wonder about, my father liked telling ghost stories at Christmas. I think this was some kind of Dickensian holdover from his childhood. Coincidentally, Robertson Davies produced a new ghost story every year, which he told at High Table at Trinity University in Canada every Christmas Eve. The following year my father would serve it up to us with the holiday goose. Sometimes Jean Shepherd's *A Christmas Story* would make the cut. My father was a big fan of Shepherd's late-night radio show, and so were we.

But there were other tales, which by virtue of their universality, structure, and moral payload, became hard-core favorites. Among these well-worn standards was our "summer story," (always read on our vacation journeys to Nantucket or Sag Harbor). It was, in fact, your story, "The Lake."

There were also those holidays that existed on the verge of implied social chaos. The most important of these in my father's estimation was, of course, Saint Patrick's Day. On that holiest day for all rebels, John Steinbeck boldly disdained Yeats, Joyce and even John B. Keane in favor of "The Terrible Conflagration Up at the Place."[26] This tale seemed to augur, and "enable," bad behavior on the part of young and old alike. My father reveled in it.

Halloween was always the season of richest pickings. There was so much to choose from. Poe and H. P. Lovecraft were practically patron saints in our family. But when Halloween's harvest moon rose on the perfumed vapors of desiccating pumpkin guts, it was your story, "The Emissary" that took thumbs up every time. (My father loved dogs. He had also spent time bedridden with rheumatic fever as a child. His only companions were his little sister, Mary, and a curious and animated wirehair terrier named Mr. Pins.) Thanks to my persistent and annoying vote, however, your story, "The Scythe" came into favor every other year. I think it was secretly my father's favorite, but he would read "The Emissary" to appease his own beloved ghosts.

The last memorable choice always came at that time of year when "film folk" choose to celebrate their mutual genius. On the eve of this self-congratulatory bacchanal, John Steinbeck would read his sons "The Wonderful Death of Dudley Stone." I wonder why? [. . .]

Since those ever so distant and happy days, and because of my father's generous influence, I have read everything you have ever published. For that matter, and for the very same reason, I have also read everything Robertson Davies has ever published. The list is endless, and in that regard my life has proved itself a strange, right-brained, blessing. It has graced me with the privilege of growing up with an author-teacher who esteemed the craft and labors of other writers with sincere reverence. His enthusiasm lives on in me, but I somehow think that was his sinister intention all along. [. . .]

Vaya Con Dios,
Thomas M. Steinbeck

5

FILMMAKERS

Cyril Cusack turned out to be a beautiful choice simply
because he was *not* evil, and did not play his part like a
villain. Charm has always been one of the great cards
played by evil people in this world. They invite you in
with smiles and comraderie, and give you the poison with
your cake, and you die never knowing what happened.
—*Bradbury to François Truffaut on* Fahrenheit
451 *casting, September 18, 1966*

Moby Dick

JOHN HUSTON

Bradbury met John Huston (1906–1987) over a Hollywood dinner arranged by their mutual friend, agent and producer Ray Stark, in February 1951. Huston was in the early years of a decade of filmmaking outside the United States, basing his operations in England and occasionally Ireland, where he soon settled. Back in London, he read and commented on the three books that Bradbury had given him at dinner—Dark Carnival, The Martian Chronicles, and The Illustrated Man. Over the next two years, letters from Huston to Bradbury indicated a strong interest in collaboration.

[ca. late February 1951]

Dear Ray—

I just finished the three volumes & the novelette[1] you so generously gave me at dinner the other night. Impressed is hardly the word for my state of mind. I'm positively swinging. It would be hard to name favorites but if enormous things hung on it I'm sure "The Traveller" & "The Tombstone" & "The Other Foot" &—oh hell, I'll end up by putting down half of them & then taking up the challenge for the other half.

The M——— C———s I find most beautiful & wise & moving. There's nothing I'd rather do than work with you on a picture.

My sincerest thanks
John H.

Rome

1st February 1953

Dear Ray,

I was very happy to get word from you. Needless to say, your liking
Moulin pleases me immensely.[2] As for our doing a picture together, I feel
exactly as you do, because it seems to me yours is just about the most
striking and original talent in America today.

As a rule, short stories don't make very good full length pictures. I
do wish you would give some thought to a story in a form which would
call for greater length. Of course, we could do three or four short ones
that have something in common in the way of idea. However, to repeat
myself, I would infinitely prefer to do one long one with you.

Do let me know if you have any notions. I shall be in Italy for the
next six weeks; address me c/o Romulus Films, Albergo Palumbo,
Ravello.

As ever,
John

---

*Bradbury's March 23 response provided an interesting turn of mind toward
the challenges of spaceflight and the unimaginable stresses on a ship's crew. His
thinking was probably influenced by his emerging desire to adapt episodes of*
The Martian Chronicles *to film. Yet circumstances would soon shift the creative focus to another kind of voyage entirely—the letter casually notes Bradbury's intention to send Huston his latest collection,* The Golden Apples of the
Sun. *It opens with "The Fog Horn," a modern myth of the sea that successfully
carries overtones of Shakespeare and the Old Testament; by August, "The Fog
Horn" would prompt Huston to ask Bradbury to adapt a literary work of similar tone and magnitude for his next film project—Herman Melville's classic sea
novel,* Moby-Dick.

Ray Bradbury
10750 Clarkson Rd.
Los Angeles 64, Calif.

March 23, 1953

Dear John:

Your letter from Italy, some six weeks ago, was much appreciated,
believe me. I have you in mind much of the time, and if finally I should
come upon *the* idea which I think would please you for a film, I'll airmail an outline of it to you. In the meantime, I hope that next time you
hit L.A. we can have a few hours chat together. I have been thinking
in terms of an all-male cast (I remember very well how beautifully
you work with such a set-up, as in *Treasure of Sierra Madre*) and the
tremendous problems of acclimating to space-travel and exploration.
It's the sort of thing we might have a fine time chewing over
conversationally when again I see you, and you probably have some very
vital and lively ideas on men and space-travel yourself, which I would
like to hear. But letters take time, and you are damned busy, I know, and
right now, with my new book out, I'm running around in ever-widening
circles. Under separate cover I'm air-mailing on a copy of the new
collection; hope you like it. I'll write again if I should come on a really
solid framework idea for a Huston "day after tomorrow" film. I wish
you luck on your new picture, and hope to see you when circumstances
allow.

Yours, as ever,
Ray

Huston secured Bradbury for the Moby Dick *screenplay in late August 1953,*
setting in motion a nine-month odyssey in England, Ireland, and Europe for
the writer and his young family that included an intense seven-month stretch
working directly with his demanding director. Bradbury literally read the novel

for the first time as he led his family from Los Angeles to Europe by rail and sea,
but he nevertheless managed to rearrange the action scenes to create a successful
progression of rising action and climax that retained the spirit of the original
novel. The pressure was intensified by the fact that Bradbury was temperamen-
tally unable to sustain the pace of high living that Huston demanded, and a rift
in their working relationship led to an uneasy parting when Bradbury com-
pleted the script in April 1954. Bradbury had lived too close to the novel for too
long, however, and he spent part of the summer of 1954 making long-distance
revisions that he was not at all sure Huston would consider.

June 18, 1954

Bradbury
10750 Clarkson Road
Los Angeles 64, Calif.

Dear John:

You have probably been cursing me, mentally and aloud, for some time
now. Time gets by and I haven't sent you the rewritten Father Mapple
speech or the scene between Starbuck, Stubb, and Flask. There's no
excuse except complete exhaustion on my part. If you saw the letter
I wrote Lorry[3] from Rome, I think you know already how I must have
felt. I've never been so beat, fagged, and bushed in my life. If Jesus
Christ himself walked up to me this afternoon and said he'd produce
The Martian Chronicles on a screen two miles wide by one mile high, I'd
scream and run the other way. I don't want to do another screenplay for
two or three years. My decision, years ago, to do a few screenplays, was
based on some vague half-knowledge of how exacting the form could be.
Now that I've gone in one end of *Moby* and out the other, I have nothing
but awed respect for people like Peter, and yourself, who can stick to
that business year in and year out without getting stomach boils.[4] My
flight from the script, into Italy, was not unlike Jonah's flight before the
wrath of God.

   Well, now we're home. I'm beginning to touch my typewriter again.
I saw Paul Kohner[5] yesterday and talked to him about the script, briefly,

and I hope now, before many days have passed, to have the Father Mapple speech rewritten and off to you, plus the Starbuck-Stubb-Flask scene. You have probably said "goddam" to me and done the thing yourself by now, but maybe my version will be of some help. I hope so.

I got in touch with Clift, in New York, not knowing that he had already given a final refusal to you on the film.[6] I hoped I might be able to make a selling point or two with him. We had a pleasant talk one afternoon; he seems very nice indeed and he was explicit and concrete in his reasoning on not taking the job. I couldn't help but admire him; though I was disappointed, on your behalf, that the film would lack his work. I hope you have luck now in finding a proper Ishmael.

More from me, God willing, in about a week. I hope you will forgive this long silence. Believe me, I owe so much to you. I'm sorry I have delayed in paying some of it back, in the pages you need.

Thanks again, and love,

from

Ray

Bradbury spent much of June and early July reading scholarly book-length studies of Melville and Moby-Dick, *and these readings played into the script revisions that he continued to send to Huston throughout the summer of 1954. They also stimulated Bradbury's speculations on how Captain Ahab's character illuminated Huston's views of death, as well as his own. Bradbury's July 12 letter to Huston offers unexpected insights derived from these dark thoughts as he rewrote a pivotal discussion between Ahab's first mate Starbuck and the other officers, Stubb and Flask, who oppose Starbuck and remain supportive of Ahab's pursuit of the white whale.*

Ray Bradbury
10750 Clarkson Road
Los Angeles 64, Calif.

July 12, 1954

Dear John:

Here is the *Stubb-Flask-Starbuck* scene at last. Only now, many weeks
after leaving London, have I got a long fresh look at the script.[7] I
hope to go on from this rewrite to a few other scenes. I'm working
on the Starbuck-Ahab scene in the cabin, which I think can stand
intensifying. I am also trying to find logical places, later, to insert one
or two lines to remind the audience not only of the hatred of Ahab
for the White Whale, which certainly we show again and again, but of
the fact that the White Whale represents life and blind destruction
and the hidden horror of the universe to Ahab. I've been having a
fascinating time reading up on Melville now, particularly in Newton
Arvin's book *Melville* in the American Men of Letters Series published
by William Sloane Associates, New York, and in an even more detailed
accounting of Melville's struggle to adjust his religious education with
the reality of the world in a book titled *Melville's Quarrel with God* by
Lawrence Thompson, published by the Princeton University Press.
Walking with Hawthorne one afternoon, Melville said, "I have resigned
myself to annihilation."[8] He had *not*, of course, or he would not have
written *Moby*. Ahab speaks out against annihilation. Death is the whole
cornerstone of the book. Death is always ticking in man, and Ahab
hears it and looks upon death as the most "enormous indignity heaped
on man by a malicious God." God nuzzles man and touches man,
peripherally, each day; death is never far from each man's mind; the
loveliest days are somewhat tinged with sadness because they cannot
last. Melville was impressed with Hawthorne's ability and said this:
"You may be witched by his sunlight,—transported by the bright
gildings in the skies he builds over you; but there is the blackness
of darkness beyond."[9] And of Shakespeare: "his dark insinuations
which we feel to be so terrifically true, that it were all but madness

for any good man, in his own proper character, to utter, or even hint of them."[10]

In relation to which, my rewrite of the enclosed scene adds an extra element. Over and above the points we wish to make in this scene which are the following: a. to show Starbuck's doubts and fears; b. to show the crew's affection and belief in Ahab—and Stubb and Flask's opposition to Starbuck; c. to clarify a captain's position on his own ship as that of a tyrant . . . sure death will come to Stubb and Flask if they put in with Starbuck. Much better they take their chances with a tyrant any day; over and above these points, let me repeat, I have added the extra grain of tolerance of Ahab, in the crew, and in Stubb and Flask, because Ahab represents, to them, their own externalized protest against life, the sea, and the ever-hungry death that will some day devour them all. They keep their fears to themselves and accept death. Ahab speaks out against the final indignity, preceded by all the malicious nuzzlings and murmurs and rumors of darkness coming. Therefore, when Ahab moves, he moves for that dark spot in all of us which would like to find a convenient enemy to strike. Ahab finds it for us all. This is an additional, if subliminal in the men, reason for siding with the captain. We need not dwell on this, but in Stubb and Flask's speech, here, it is declared in their own language. I hope this strikes you as valid and of interest.

I recall you saying once, John, that you were not comfortable in any situation unless death was near. At this time, thinking of you as blood-brother to Ahab, even as I think myself to be, I would like to rewrite your comment this way: I, John Huston, am not comfortable unless I am over-riding and proving myself better than death. Death will *not* bully me, John Huston, so, by God, I'll get on my horse and ride the damn thing till it falls down. They won't keep me in the ditch, I'll climb out on my crutches and get on the damn horse again. This is not far from Melville, really; you take a different way of doing what Ahab does. Ahab finds a convenient big whale to strike with his fury. You find a horse and thumb your nose at Darkness. I run and hide. But Ahab's in me; Ahab's my boy. He speaks for me, too. You taunt death, you make fun of it by being near it, John; which is essentially little different than putting a spear into it, as Ahab does. I suppose I put my spear into it with my typewriter. I don't know. All of us, like Pip "see God's foot on the treadle of the loom." Each of us finds what adjustment he can. That's why I think this book, and this film, are so tremendously important.

Have you read *Melville's Quarrel with God*? If not, notify me by cable and I'll airmail you a copy. It's not too late in the day, in reading it, I think, for you to add a few minor details to your knowledge of Ahab. There was so *much* of Melville that came out in his Captain.

Needless to say, if you still want another rewrite on the enclosed scene, all you have to do is yell. I'm back in form now and very excited by the things I've been reading about Melville. Much hogwash, of course, but, here and there, you pick out things you can use.

I'm now going to work on the *Ahab-Starbuck* cabin scene and on other, later scenes.[11] If you'll keep me posted far enough ahead on all scenes you will be shooting, I'll try to give all of them final touchings-up.

All the best to you, Ricky, Lorry, Jeanie, and to Greg.[12]

Yours,

Ray

Fahrenheit 451

FRANÇOIS TRUFFAUT

French New Wave film critic and Academy Award–winning director François Truffaut (1932–1984) spent six years considering, developing, and filming his adaptation of Ray Bradbury's Fahrenheit 451. *His friend producer Raoul Lévy recommended the novel to Truffaut in the summer of 1960. Truffaut had little interest in science fiction, but he did have a passion for books, and made plans to move ahead when he had cleared his current commitments. The early 1962 release of his successful film* Jules and Jim *opened a window of time, and Truffaut wrote to Bradbury to see if they could meet in New York that spring. Bradbury came east by train for two April 1962 meetings, which left the impression with Bradbury and Don Congdon that Truffaut was interested in filming an omnibus of Bradbury stories as well as* Fahrenheit 451.

Mr. Ray Bradbury
10265 Cheviot Drive
Los Angeles 64, Calif.

Paris, April 27, 1962

Dear Mr. Bradbury,

I have delayed in answering you because my decision was hard to make, and once made it was difficult to convey without giving you the impression that I am a terribly indecisive man. In short here are the facts: I have renounced to shoot a movie based on your short stories and would ask you to shift our agreements on *Fahrenheit*, which would become my next feature. Here are my reasons:

1/ Upon returning to Paris it occurred to me that we were about to have a tidal wave of European sketch movies: famous love stories, renowned crimes, the great international swindles, Satan and the Ten Commandments, La Fontaine's Fables, etc, etc . . .

All these films are now being shot or about to be, but these days on Parisian screens we can see *The Seven Deadly Sins*, *Girl on the Road*, and I myself have collaborated on an international film titled *Love at Twenty*. A star-studded cast often ensures the success of these movies. But these same stars who agree to shoot three or four days in between greater pictures are often the cause of artistic failure. Even with short stories, one is forced to make many concessions to assemble them.

2/ Bringing a film based on a number of your short stories to fruition would necessitate intense preparation. There would need to be tremendous scouting efforts for futuristic locations as well as for ultra-modern costumes and accessories. In so doing I would risk being less inspired for the preparation of *Fahrenheit*, this is the most important point.

3/ I only shoot one major picture every 18 months. If I were to shoot a movie based on your stories it would postpone *Fahrenheit* to 1964. By that time, I think even producers will have understood that, since Gagarin, we cannot keep on making exactly the same movies. It is quite important that *Fahrenheit* be the first European science-fiction movie.

4/ During our conversation, Mr. Congdon insisted on the necessity that you retain the television rights for the stories that we would have put into film. However, for two years now, it has been impossible to sell a French film to foreign distributors without conceding the broadcasting rights for television as well. On that point we would be faced with almost unsurmountable difficulties.[13]

Thus, I think we should proceed with the rights to *Fahrenheit* with Mr. Congdon right away. We can then work together this summer at the planning of *Fahrenheit*, on the dates that best suit you, and start shooting at the end of the year.

I enclose a copy of this letter for Mr. Congdon.

I do not think it will be too hard for me to convince you, since we had initially met to discuss the making of *Fahrenheit*, but I ask you to forgive me for making you witness hesitations I usually keep to myself. I make my decisions rather slowly but when I do they are for good. I knew I was going to meet you in New York, so I read all your books in a hurry and did not take the time to weigh the pros and cons of all the options.

Fahrenheit is a *strong* subject that should yield a *strong* movie, and this is what I want to focus my efforts on.

My wife is currently in the south of France, to consider the issue of your accommodation during our joint labor, and I will naturally need additional details from you. It seems exceedingly difficult to find a suitable house at the seaside.

Do you like Saint-Paul-de-Vence? Do you know La Colombe d'Or? How many will you be?

I am asking Mister Berbert who manages my company, Les Films du Carosse, to get in contact with Mister Congdon, and let us continue to correspond until our next meeting.

I am very pleased to have met you and I believe we have many similar ideas about entertainment.

Sending you my admiring and friendly wishes,
François Truffaut

May 3rd, 1962

Dear Monsieur Truffaut:

I appreciate the facts you have stated concerning your not wishing to do the film based on 6 or 7 of my short stories at this time. And I am glad you wish to go ahead, instead, making a film of *Fahrenheit 451*.

However, this places a different situation before us: I have spent so much time, over the years, on various aspects of *Fahrenheit 451*, both as a novel, and as a stageplay, never produced, that I feel I would be the wrong person to try to adapt it for the screen. I am very tired, very exhausted, on this novel, and would do you a disservice if I accepted the commission to write it for you in screenplay form. Therefore I suggest you arrange to buy the rights from my agent Don Congdon, and hire another writer to do the screenplay.

I felt very happy and right about doing the short stories for you, for

I am fresh and intrigued with them. But the novel is another, harsher challenge. I wish I could adapt it for you, but there is no use fooling myself. I would hate to go on the job and do poor work for you. You would wind up hating me, and I would hate myself.

I hope this will not diminish your interest in the novel, for this same situation came up with Raoul Levy, and at the time he indicated he would buy the novel and get someone else to adapt it.

We are all disappointed, of course, insofar, also, as our visit to the South of France was concerned. We could not but have our hearts leap up at the thought of spending a summer in that lovely country. Perhaps, later, we shall make the trip, anyway, and visit you while you are busy preparing *Fahrenheit 451*.

Let me know how you feel on all this. I sincerely hope you go ahead and make the film, which would be tremendously fresh and exciting.

It was a pleasure, meeting you and your charming wife. My best to you both, from yours, cordially,

Ray Bradbury

Mr. Ray Bradbury
10265 Cheviot Drive
Los Angeles 64, Calif.

Paris, May 29, 1962

Dear Mr. Bradbury,

Please forgive me for only responding today to your May 3rd letter. I must tell you that I was watching six to eight hours of film per day at the Cannes festival, and usually came out too stunned to write a letter.

I am sorry that you cannot collaborate to the adaptation of *Fahrenheit*, but I understand your reasons completely.

I am enthused at the thought that this will be my next picture, and everyone around me found the novel wonderful.

Mr. Berbert and Mr. Congdon are corresponding, and I

believe they are close to reaching an agreement. For my part, I am considering collaborating with Marcel Moussy to adapt the text and the dialogues. We had written the screenplay for *The 400 Blows* together.

As I have mentioned, I am seriously considering Jean-Paul Belmondo for the lead role. The shooting would take place either at the end of this year, 1962, or at the beginning of the year 1963.

I am not giving up on the idea of adapting the short stories someday; maybe for television once France gets a second channel.

Jean-Louis Barrault has told me about his vision for the *Martian Chronicles*, and I truly think it will be very fine. He is considering a mix of real actors and life-size string puppets on stage.

I hope to see you during the shooting of *Fahrenheit 451*, but we will probably have the opportunity to meet before that, perhaps even in Los Angeles. I am thinking of going there with Helen Scott to have a prolonged interview with Alfred Hitchcock in preparation for a book.[14]

> With my best wishes,
> François Truffaut

June 11, 1962

Dear Monsieur Truffaut:

Thank you for your latest letter. I am happy to hear you are going ahead to get a contract on *F.451*, and hope everything is finalized soon. Your mention of Belmondo is exciting to me, and to many whom I have told of the possibility. I hope this, also, works out.

I still feel strongly about the short-story film, and if you could find someone to believe in it for us, it would be great fun for me to write the stories into scripts and perhaps deliver them to you when we come to France to visit during the filming of *F.451* and, concurrently, to see Barrault's staging of my novel. It is something to consider, and when you come to Los Angeles, perhaps we can talk more of it.

Meanwhile, I am happy to see the excellent reviews of *Jules and Jim*, especially in *Time Magazine*, which is so very hard to please, ever, with anything.

> Best wishes to you and your family,
> Ray Bradbury
> 10265 Cheviot Drive
> Los Angeles 64, Calif.

> August 12th, 1962

Dear François: (if you will permit me now, at last, please)

I write because we saw *Jules and Jim* last night.

I write to tell you what you already know but must be told again—you were born to make motion pictures.

Your body, your eye, is a camera. The camera does not exist separate from you. You and the camera are one looking at and finding the world and surprising us with it.

A beautiful film, of such texture and humanity, I simply am spelled by it.

I will stop now, before I say too much.

I only add, I look forward to *Fahrenheit 451* with intense excitement. How are things going with the screenplay? Have you thought any more about a film of my stories, for later, next year? I would very much like to write it for you, as you know.

I enclose a new story which I hope your wife will read to you with some pleasure.

> With great admiration, and thanks,
> Yours,
> Ray

Truffaut was able to schedule his planned interviews with Hitchcock for August in Los Angeles, allowing an opportunity to meet with Bradbury in a more relaxed context than the April visits in New York. Bradbury described these evenings in a letter to Don Congdon.

August 19th, 1962

Dear Don:

Just a brief report. Helen Scott and François Truffaut were here all week and I spent two evenings with them, both very friendly and enjoyable. Truffaut will really get down to work on the screenplay upon his return to Paris this week. I showed him around up in the hills, here, where you can get a fantastic view of the greatest City of Light in the world, 500 square miles of illumination![15] I also took him into our newest, biggest, freshest, loveliest, supermarket, and when we came out he said "What a shame I have to shoot *F.451* in France, with all *this* to work with!"[16]

It is a shame, of course. I wish he spoke English.

Truffaut was here to interview Hitchcock 9 hours a day, for five days in order to write a book on Hitch. Truffaut and Helen Scott are now looking for an agent to handle this book for them here. *Life* is already interested in the book, as would be many other magazines I'm sure. I told Helen Scott she should get the best agent in the world . . . so she's telephoning you tomorrow, Monday, to tell you their problems and ask for your services. [. . .]

Jesus God, this has been a fantastic year, and an even more fantastic month! If I knew where God was, I'd go thank him personally, but since I believe God is spread around through all of us, there is only one way to be grateful and that is by doing your work well, which benefits everyone and gives back the gift better than thanks or any mute gratitude.

That's enough from the old philosopher for today. [. . .]

Best, as ever,
Yours,
Ray

Truffaut's mid-August visit with Bradbury in Los Angeles, aided by Maggie Bradbury's fluency in French, moved their professional relationship into a true friendship. The Screen Writer's Film Society, which Bradbury had cofounded, showed Truffaut's new film, Jules and Jim, *shortly after Bradbury and Maggie had seen Truffaut's* Shoot the Piano Player *in a local theater. These events provided a chance for Bradbury to describe his emotional responses to Truffaut's films in more detail than ever before.*

August 31st, 1962

Dear François,

You asked me to write you about the audience reaction to the showing of *Shoot the Piano Player* at our Film Society, so here is my report.

There are those who think *Shoot the Piano Player* is better than *Jules and Jim.*

And there are those who think *Jules and Jim* is superior to *Shoot the Piano Player.*

Are you as amused at this as I am? You should be, for I learned long ago that people, all through my career, would be making these almost useless comparisons. The fact is, some people *need* some of our work more than other works that we do. Some people prefer my fantasy to my science fiction. Some people prefer my realistic romances to my fantasy, and so it goes.

So, too, I find it difficult to make any comparison between *Shoot the Piano Player* and *Jules and Jim.* Technically, I feel a more persuasive agility with the camera, a fluid motion in *Jules and Jim* and a sense of atmosphere that seems somewhat stronger. But otherwise, the films are similar in that they reveal your high vitality and your sense of fun, at the same time you see, beyond the window, the falling of the night. Your films can best be compared to a Fox Hunt wedding I attended in Ireland, a hilarious day in which horses, hounds, and foxes waited for a Unitarian minister to marry an old freeloading fox of a man to a miserable sniffling cold-ridden girl, and when the ceremony was over, all, instead of retiring decently to the bridal bed, went off to hunt the fox. I am writing the story now, and it is all high comedy based on fact, but, at any moment, the whole wild Keystone Kops day could have ended in tragedy if a horse had stumbled and killed any one of a hundred people on the hunt. Fact is, the Hunt Wedding was delayed for a week because of such a death. So, everything in your two films is of a piece. We laugh and . . . suddenly . . . stunned, we cry. You blend the two with great artistry.

So, there you are. Some love one of your films better, some another. Some love all. The general reaction was very favorable, in sum.

Jules and Jim, you'll be glad to know, has been held over at the theatre here. It was originally supposed to close the week after you left, but now has been playing a full month. I am happy about this.

Your visit here with Helen was very heartening, and I hope you will come back for a longer visit some day.

Meantime, I hope you are hard at work on *F.451*'s screenplay. I know you will do a magnificent job, and the two of us will be notorious everywhere because of your fine work.

My friendly wishes go to you, your wife and family, and to Helen.

> Best from your admirer,
> Ray
> Bradbury

Paris, 24 September 1962

Mr. Ray Bradbury
10265 Cheviot Drive
Los Angeles 64, Calif.

My dear Ray,

A belated thank you for your letter following the screening of *Shoot the Piano Player*.

I have conveyed to the newspaper *L'Express* the texts that you had entrusted me with. They kept one of them to publish in a body of texts about you (I believe it is a letter to the editors or something of the sort).[17]

I gave them your address and I think they will suggest an interview by mail.

Pierre Kast is a filmmaker friend of mine and a science-fiction enthusiast, we should definitely have him direct an episode when we adapt your short stories; currently though, he is compiling an anthology of science-fiction for Robert Laffont a great Parisian publisher. He is going to write to you to ask for an unpublished short story—or at the least unpublished in France.

Since my return I have been working on adapting *Fahrenheit 451* with *400 Blows* co-author Marcel Moussy. The work has proven more difficult than I expected but so exciting that this has been the most pleasant part of the year for me. I will naturally keep you updated with our work as it progresses.

Don Congdon has agreed to represent me in America for my book of interviews with Hitchcock, which pleases me to no end.

My dear Ray, I hope to see you again soon, and send you, your wife and your daughters—the one who was still awake on my visit as well as the one who was already asleep—all my best.

Yours,
François Truffaut

Working from England, American producer Lewis Allen eventually brought together an Anglo-European consortium to finance François Truffaut's adaptation of Fahrenheit 451. *Bradbury's working knowledge of Hollywood and his interactions with a wide range of actors, directors, and producers provided the background for his casting recommendations in the following letter to Allen. Although Bradbury and Truffaut had developed a long-distance friendship and enduring mutual respect, he was not contractually involved with the film venture. Despite Bradbury's recommendation, Rod Steiger and Claire Bloom were not cast in Truffaut's 1966 Universal release of* Fahrenheit 451 *(Oskar Werner and Julie Christie played the principal roles), but they would costar in Warner Brothers' 1969 production of Bradbury's* The Illustrated Man.

March 27, 1964

Dear Lewis:

This is a difficult letter to write, for one automatically feels like the usual egotistical, interfering Author. But write it, I must, for I have strong feelings about the Casting of *F.451*.

I am very upset to hear that Terence Stamp is set for Montag. I saw him in *Billy Budd*, in which he was well-cast, and I was impressed with him in that part. But he is far too young, too immature, and therefore would be, I think, unbelievable, as Montag. Is it too late to reconsider someone else for the role? It should be a man in his middle thirties, to whom the knowledge of his book-burning sins would come as a more stunning and dreadful blow.

As for the girls you mention, I, unlike many, have never been impressed with Jean Seberg, nor, from what I have seen, by Jane Fonda.

I realize Miss Seberg is catnip in Europe, to many, many people, but she is a neat zero to me.

Couldn't we use someone like Claire Bloom for the girl next door. This wonderful quality of moonlit but intellectual beauty would be right for the role.

Also, I have always thought Rod Steiger would be perfect for the role of the Fire Chief. *Would you consider him?* I have talked to both Steiger and his wife about the book, and both like it very much, and are back in Brooklyn Heights now, after a brief time on the coast. Will you please think about both of them very seriously?

For that matter, I would prefer Steiger for *Montag*! Please think of him for that role, also. Steiger as Montag, and Robert Ryan as the Fire Chief, wouldn't that make for powerful casting?????

Good luck in financing the film. Keep me posted. And I would appreciate hearing back from you and François, reacting to this letter. Am I indeed Mad? Am I a fool? I think not. I hope not.

But I do fear Stamp. Tell me what you think.

Best,
Ray

It took time for Lewis Allen to build the financial backing for Truffaut's adap-
tation of Fahrenheit 451, *and at one point, Truffaut made contingency plans to*
make another film while he raised alternate funding for Fahrenheit. *This led*
Bradbury to revive old hopes (both with Don Congdon and with his Hollywood
agent, Mal Stuart) that American producer Sam Spiegel might be persuaded to
produce for Truffaut; Spiegel had produced three films that Bradbury admired
greatly: The African Queen, On the Waterfront, *and* Lawrence of Arabia.
In the end, Lewis Allen brought together the production funding, and Truffaut
began production of Fahrenheit 451 *in the winter of 1965–66.*

August 4, 1965

Mr. Ray Bradbury
10265 Cheviot Drive,
Los Angeles 64, California

Dear Ray:

[. . .] Truffaut was in New York recently, to finish up his book about
Hitchcock, and I asked him about progress on *Fahrenheit 451*. He says
Lewis Allen now has until next March to start film production. If he does
not start production by then, the rights will revert to Truffaut. He did
not indicate to me that there was anything much to be expected from
Allen between now and next March. He did say, however, that he would
definitely shoot *Fahrenheit* himself, either in France or in England, in late
1966, should the rights revert to him. I asked him if he would have trouble
with financing, and he said "no." He thinks he may shoot a different film
this fall or early winter if Allen doesn't get *Fahrenheit* rolling.

Malcolm Stuart commented upon Spiegel's plans and interests, but
I think this is old stuff. I gather that Spiegel is no longer in the picture,
judging by my conversations with Truffaut. [. . .]

Not much else to report at the moment. We're all as busy as hell,
but I look forward to your being here the middle of next month.

Yours,

Don

As Fahrenheit 451 *production neared, Truffaut was able to study television ad-*
aptations of Bradbury's "The Jar" (broadcast February 14, 1964) and "The
Life Work of Juan Diaz" (October 26, 1964), which aired on the final season of
The Alfred Hitchcock Hour. *Bradbury always felt that the hour-long episodes*
had many of the production values of feature-length films, limited only by the
show's television budgets. Truffaut, whose interviews with Hitchcock were soon
to reach print, apparently found the Bradbury episodes useful to study as he
prepared to begin shooting Fahrenheit.

Paris, November 15, 1965

My dear Ray,

I do believe that ever since 1962 my New Year greetings have unfailingly
been followed by "This year will be the year of *Fahrenheit 451*."

This time though, it seems we are nearing our goal. We should be
starting at the Pinewood studios on the 10th of January with Oskar
Werner, and Julie Christie in the double role of Clarisse and Mildred.

Until then I will immerse myself in your work by rereading all your
short story collections.

The film is produced by MCA for Universal.

In the last few days I have attended two MCA screenings of
adaptations of your stories "The Jar" and "the Story of Diaz" by
Hitchcock.[18]

Both movies were very interesting, and their scores were
composed by Bernard Herrmann, who will be our composer for
Fahrenheit 451.

I will write to you again before shooting starts to give you more
indications about the film, and then my highest hope will be not to
disappoint you.

Fahrenheit 451 is a wondrous story. During all these years of waiting
I have tried not to reread the novel or the screenplay too often for
fear of growing tired of it; but every time I did my enthusiasm for this
powerful and superb story only grew stronger.

My dear Ray, the best and friendliest regards to you and your family from

François

Nov. 19, 1965

Dear François: The news is wonderful about Oskar Werner and Julie Christie. I am fascinated to think of her playing the double role of both Clarisse and Mildred. I think this is brave and challenging. I am pleased also to hear that you will use the admirable talent of Bernard Herrmann for the musical score. I have again suggested to Lew that perhaps Rod Steiger, or Alec Guinness, might be excellent for the Fire Chief! What do you think? Guinness, especially, since he has done few such roles on the screen, might well be worth consideration. I look forward to more word from you, later, when you have time. Good luck, my dear François! I wish I might be there! Yours with gratitude,

Ray
Bradbury
Nov. 19, 1965

January 16, 1966

Dear Ray,

As you undoubtedly remember, it took us no more than three and a half hours to reach agreement on *Fahrenheit*. Three and a half years later, I am at last able to report that the filming gets under way tomorrow.

We had a few days delay because Julie Christie was having some trouble with her teeth, but in actual fact, the shooting's already begun since we spent two days doing all the scenes that will be shown on the magnavision screen.

In the role of the Captain, we have cast an Irish actor, Cyril Cusack, whom you may know from his recent role in *The Spy Who Came in from the Cold*.

Without being a really large-scale production, our budget will enable us to do justice to the scenario: The props and costumes are good and the sets are excellent. We are shooting in color and all indications, so far, are extremely satisfactory. Within the next two weeks or so, Helen Scott will be sending you a first set of stills that will give you a visual concept of the picture.

On that point, I am writing to Don Congdon separately, to suggest an idea that may appeal to you, namely to prompt the various publishers of the many *Fahrenheit* editions throughout the world to issue a new edition that would be illustrated by 20 to 30 stills from the film—the photos to be selected from those scenes that are common to your book and my picture.

Needless to say, I shall be thinking of you often in the ten weeks ahead. But I trust, my dear Ray, that you will understand and forgive my silence until the shooting is over.

With best wishes to your wife and daughters and kindest regards to yourself, I am

Yours sincerely,
François Truffaut

Dear François,

Thank you for your letter in the middle of your incredibly busy schedule. I am overjoyed at your casting of *Fahrenheit 451*. Julie Christie dominates not only *Darling* but steals all of *Zhivago* intact. Oskar Werner is absolutely amazing in *Ship of Fools* and takes all the honors in *Spy Who Came in from the Cold*. I remember Cyril Cusack from dozens of pictures, and am especially fond of his performance in *Odd Man Out*. So you have a very happy man here, an Author who approves wholeheartedly and is very grateful. Please send my best wishes to your Cast. I know they will work their hearts out for you.

The addition of Technicolor is another fine thing. Bravo.

I will pass your suggestion about a new edition of the book, with pictures from your film, on to my publishers, hoping they may want to do just such a publication.[19] I have already sent them the initial advertisement, very handsome, which appeared in the trade papers last week.

Good luck through all the hours of each day in the coming months, my dear François. Everyone I tell about your Cast and your plans is excited to absolute admiration.

Yours,
Ray
January 24th, 1966

Dear François (*and* Helen)!

Thank you for the still photographs which have just arrived. These are wonderfully exciting to look at, and I have carried them around town to show to various friends who could not escape my clutches as I arrived, waving the photos! I shall treasure these pictures as part of a very important year in my life, which you have begun to enrich. Everyone I have talked to about you and the film, has become excited, knowing that you are working with such an incredible cast.

The best thing I find in glancing through the photographs is the sense that time has turned back 14 years and I am at my typewriter finishing the first draft of *F.451* as a novel, and the people and places are held inside my head waiting to be let out on paper. Now you have taken them off the paper again and brought them full out into the air. My "friends" are free at last to move in the real-unreal world of films. But they most certainly are the images I held and projected against the dark insides of my skull a long time back. I am deeply grateful.

Please, extend my affectionate best to Julie Christie, to Oskar Werner, to Mr. Cusack, and all the rest. I shall look forward to more photos from you, later, when you have a chance to pick some out.

Thank you, thank you,
Yours,
Ray
February 27, 1966

Truffaut experimented with his English in a handwritten letter to Bradbury dated June 24, announcing that he would be presenting Fahrenheit 451 *in September as the British entry in the Venice Film Festival. "You should come," he urged Bradbury, "maybe invited by Universal. Why not?" Truffaut's request prompted Bradbury's reluctant confessional below.*

Bradbury

July 20th, 1966

Dear François:

Thanks for your most recent letter and the wonderful news that *Fahrenheit 451* will be shown at the Venice Film Festival. How I wish I might be there with you! But, as you have guessed, it may well be years, or never, before I get over my fear of jet-travel. Balloons are more my speed; though I realize this is only ridiculous romanticism on my part. The day I go up in a balloon for the first time may well be the day lightning strikes the damn thing to pay me back for my rampant illogic.

François, please, do you have two or three additional photos of the final scenes of *F.451* in the falling snow? I have been interviewed by a local cinema magazine and when I told them of your good fortune in having snow fall during your last day of shooting, they asked if they might reproduce a still from that portion of the film. Can you possibly help me on this? Many thanks. I hope this finds you very busy and very happy, yours,

Ray

Fahrenheit 451 *was one of the most exhausting films that Truffaut ever made, requiring five years to develop and film. The underlying constant was his enduring friendship with Bradbury, and the mutual respect each had for the other's work. Bradbury's initial response to seeing an August 31, 1966, studio screening of the film was a telegram praising their shared vision of book and film: "My novel looks at your picture and sees itself. Your film looks at my novel and sees itself! How rare are such twins in the world of film." A few hours later, Bradbury composed the following letter summarizing his initial reactions in detail.*

My dear François:

This, written only a few hours after seeing *Fahrenheit 451* here at the studio. I think you have done a very fine job indeed, and I will probably know more about how fine it is as time passes and I see it again, next time among friends and some beloved relatives, perhaps. I was very nervous at the studio, for it was like having a baby. Yes, I know, *you* had the baby, you went through the great agonies . . . well, then my agony was sympathetic, I guess you could say. Anyway, almost without exception I thought you had put the essence of my novel on the screen, and now I am waiting to see how others react, for I fear, in sitting in the theatre, that my lack of objectivity might have painted more into the frame than was truly there. One comes from such a screening with so many emotions which one tries to juggle, turn over, examine, and re-examine. So if I am not coherent it is because I feel as if I had been hit by a truck and do not at this moment know the license number of the vehicle which ran off down away.

I have only one minor suggestion to make, and this, I realize, is made late in the day so that in all probability nothing can be done about it. I felt that the chase after Montag was too short. Not necessarily because it was long in my novel and so should be long here, but purely for cinematic reasons, it would be fun if you had any extra footage of the men flying in the air, rushing after Montag, and also any additional footage in which Montag watches his own pursuit on various screens as he crosses the city. Why do I say this? Because I feel we need a longer period of tension in the running chase before the lovely quiet period at the very end, which is just right. For contrast, then, I offer this suggestion. Again, I know I speak when the work is all finished, and perhaps should not speak at all. But you might consider the good fun, if you have the footage (if extra film *was* shot, that is), which might be cut into the pursuit. Beyond that, I have no suggestions. I feel that

Christie did beautifully in her double roles, as did Werner. The sets were absolutely right, imaginative without being overbearing, in just the proper taste and balance . . . as were the costumes.

Will you be making any further changes in the film between now and when it is released in the United States? I will see it again later this week, and if any further minor suggestions come to me, I will pass them on to you. *But . . . only* if they were of any real help this late in the game. I don't want to bother you with any irritating detail that cannot be acted on.

To sum up, now, I loved what I saw, and have been nervously exhausted the remainder of the afternoon. I hope that you have a huge reception for it in Venice, and that when it opens in Paris, the gods will smile.

Keep me posted from there as to reactions following the Festival screening, will you, please?

Good luck! And thank you, thank you, for this tremendous experience.

Yours,

Ray

August 31st, 1966

By mid-September, as he read Truffaut's published diary entries on the making of the film, Bradbury felt confident in offering Truffaut his more objective analysis of Fahrenheit 451, *including comments on cast performance and directorial strategies.*

Bradbury

Sept. 18, 1966

Dear François:

I hope this finds you in excellent spirits as a result of the Paris Premiere of *F.451*. I have as yet to hear any news of the Opening, but have high hopes for you and the film. Probably tomorrow, Monday, I'll get some reviews from Universal Pictures. They have been most prompt and courteous about keeping me informed.

I enclose a Spanish review you might not have seen as yet. It was sent to me by a fan in Madrid. And it is a very good review.

I have been reading, in English, provided by Universal, your Diary *re F.451* and the filming of same. I find it fascinating and, above all, educational. I feel like a student again, reading what you have to say, which is important. Though I am a great lover of films, and have been since I was a small child, I still have certain restraints to learn. I was especially pleased to hear you speak of casting against the script, and of photographing against the casting, and of editing against the photography, so that you do not build a monster layer-cake of emphasis and re-emphasis on the obvious. As you say, Cyril Cusack turned out to be a beautiful choice simply because he was *not* evil, and did not play his part like a villain. Charm has always been one of the great cards played by evil people in this world. They invite you in with smiles and comraderie, and give you the poison with your cake, and you die never knowing what happened. This was one item I protested against in *Sweet Smell of Success*, some years ago . . . Burt Lancaster played his villain much too villainous . . . if he had been all love and smiles and friendship, the impact of the film would have been twice as hard.

Anyway, I am glad now that I did not come to London in February. I would have got in your way. I would have wondered about this and that, and some other things, and we would have had some fights and it would have been entirely wrong. My greatest feeling from the start was to let you shape your future world in your own head. By working against my material often, you created my material. Done by another director, it would have been another Bond film. Not that the Bond films aren't fun, they are indeed. But I heartily approve of your keeping the tv-screen small, for instance, instead of filling up a wall with it. I might have induced you, had I been there, to over-gimmick the picture. You, by quietly cutting back on the mechanical foliage, have given me a lesson in taste and quietude.

Yes, I very much miss the Hound, but he isn't necessary. The airplane jets and the war are gone out of the sky over the city, and Good Riddance! Simplicity. Simplicity. And again Symplicity.

[. . .]

The ending of the film is one of the finest on any film in many, many years. It is a cliche, but must be repeated, if a brilliant film ends badly, people think you have only a good film. But if a good film ends brilliantly, with fine, sure strokes, people think you have a brilliant film all through. We carry from the theatre that end delivered into our hands, and savor it above all else. [. . .]

Enough. Dear François, thank you for an exciting month. Good luck in the months ahead with the various openings of *F.451*.

Yours,

Ray

Jan. 10, 1967

Dear François:

Thank you for your telegram. I doubt if I will be in Paris until late spring or early summer, depending on many things. I leave tomorrow for Houston, Texas, and Cape Kennedy, to interview the Astronauts who will be landing, we hope, on the Moon in the near future.[20]

I didn't tell you before, but the week I was supposed to meet you in New York my mother became ill. On the weekend of the New York Premiere of *Fahrenheit 451*, she died unexpectedly.[21] So life mixes its sadness with its elations. The Holiday Season has been a strange combination of feelings for me, but now the New Year challenges me to revive and work hard. Have you had any thoughts about *Something Wicked This Way Comes*? I repeat my question *only* because there is great interest here from many directions. If the book does not appeal to you, you know of course that I shall remain your understanding friend,

Ray Bradbury

February 6, 1967

My Dear Ray,

My problems in getting together with Helen[22] kept me from
responding sooner to your kind letters about *Fahrenheit* as well as
to the sad news of your mother's death. I hope you will forgive my
lapses.

I'm happy to have read *Something Wicked This Way Comes*; it's a
beautiful book and I was particularly impressed with the subtle handling
of the adolescence theme. Yet, as I mentioned in my cable, it does not
fit in with my current film projects.[23]

I am holding off for awhile, until I have some assurance that
Universal is happy with *Fahrenheit*'s box-office results, before going
back to our old and initial idea: an omnibus sketch film based on five or
six of your short stories, to be directed by myself and four or five of my
friends.

Naturally, we would have to determine the availability of those
stories that are of interest. And since it would, in all probability, be a
French picture, I imagine that each participating director would require
"carte blanche" on the adaptation.

[. . .]

Re: *Fahrenheit*, reports from Sweden, Denmark and Finland are
exceptionally favorable. The results in France are very good and I
believe they are satisfactory in the U.S., but you know far more about
that situation than I do.

At any rate, I can tell you that I breathe much easier, now that our
long, joint adventure on *Fahrenheit 451* is over with. While any adventure
is exciting, I must admit that I often felt that this particular undertaking
may have been too ambitious for me and I was constantly in fear that
my efforts might not live up to your work.

I am particularly pleased and proud that the Swedish edition of
Fahrenheit 451 joins your novel and my diary into one volume.[24]

My dear Ray, I hope you will bear with me until the day when I can finally express, in your own language, the value I attach to your many and concrete manifestations of our friendship.

Faithfully yours,
François Truffaut

The Martian Chronicles

As early as 1952, producer John Houseman (with the encouragement of director Vincente Minnelli) approached Bradbury with the idea of adapting The Martian Chronicles *for film. After promising but unsuccessful efforts by Kirk Douglas during the 1950s, Bradbury was able to work under successive agreements to write a screen treatment for Julian Blaustein at MGM and finally a full screenplay for Alan Pakula in the early 1960s. Subsequent scripts prepared in 1977 and 1997 also never reached production. The high and low points of these ultimately unproduced materials carry through in letters to his agent Don Congdon and his producer-director friend Roger Kay. The first two letters capture his emotions in finally working at MGM and refashioning his* Chronicles *characters during the summer of 1960.*

Monday July 18th 1960

Dear Don:

Just a note, for no reason at all, save one of pure sentiment . . .

26 years and 3 months ago, I arrived in L.A. with my brother, mom, and dad, at the heart of the Depression. Dad was looking for work out here in the west. I was not quite fourteen.

The first day after settling in, that April in 1934, I walked down to the nearest intersection and asked the news-seller there, "Which way is it to MGM?"

"That way." He pointed. I started off. The news-seller called after me, "Hey, where are you going?" "To MGM," I said. "You can't do that!" he cried. "It's twelve miles!"

I had no money for the streetcars, and none for food. I started walking, but it was one of the hottest days. I never made it.

Which is a long way around to saying, finally, it took me 26 years and some weeks, but an hour ago I came through the gate and am in my office at my desk at MGM.

It was a long walk, and the best thing about today is the boy who started out in this direction in 1934, is still somewhere inside me, mighty

pleased, and mighty excited. For his sake, as well as my own, I hope to
do the best job possible.

    End of sentiment. End of letter.

Best, as ever,
Yours,
Ray

July 29th, 1960

Dear Don,

Enclosed, signed, are two copies of the Doubleday severance letter. I've
kept one for my files, as you indicated.[25]

    Not too much to report. Fascinating thing about working on *The
Martian Chronicles*. Eleven years ago, whatever knowledge I had about
characterization was pretty intuitive, and hidden from myself. While a
great lot of my character knowledge is still pretty much touch and go,
play by ear, I can do more "thinking" about them now and going through
the book I've had to sit down and work out a real background for each
of the characters I did in sketch form so long ago. Most of the captains
in *Chronicles* have no real Past. Spender, also, when you come down
to it, was an Idea in motion.[26] It has been really fascinating to figure
out what I was up to, and also to let my current subconscious run free
with old subconscious devices and people. I am, in a way, riding happy
piggy-back on the younger writer who did the book. I now have 18 pages
of character analysis which will go back on file into my subconscious
against that day or hour in the coming months when I'll need it in the
screenplay. No sooner do I "know" a thing then I try to "forget" a thing,
a very important part of writing, I feel. To know a thing too obviously
can put you out of joint. But to recognize and put into shadow the
materials you need makes for a relaxed approach to coming problems.

    That does it for today. More next week.

Best, as ever,
Ray

At times, Hollywood agent Ben Benjamin joined Don Congdon in mediating Bradbury's complicated MGM situation. Over the years, Bradbury would send a retrospective end-of-year letter to Don Congdon, but in the late summer of 1960, his fortieth birthday milestone—combined with unforeseen contractual complications with his MGM adaptation of The Martian Chronicles*— prompted a reflection on his entire career and the childhood he had never left behind.*

August 22, 1960

Dear Don:

Just thought I'd drop you this note with the latest.

I was at MGM five weeks on Friday last. They were supposed to pay me $2500 the day I went in there 35 days ago. Three weeks ago I asked Ben to check on it for me, and he started checking, and they started, supposedly, doing something about it. This went on and on, and I waited patiently. Now, it seems, they want me to sign a letter saying I'll give the money back if the contracts don't work out. I received this news with something less than delight. It's the best of all possible worlds when you can get a writer to work for 5 weeks, plus additional weeks coming up, supposedly, and then take all the money back on your own terms. So I told Ben to tell them I was leaving the studio and would not be back until the money was forthcoming. Also, naturally, I would not sign that paper.[27]

[...]

Last week, MGM gave me a copy of the screenplay *Butterfield 8*.[28] My suggestion for a new title: *Pigs at Trough*. The whole project is so reprehensible I want to go out and campaign for the hydrogen bomb, one anyway, to drop on all the characters in the story.

I am forty years old today. Jesus God. The irony is, I still feel like the boy who woke up summer mornings in Illinois thirty years ago. Hell, it's a collaboration between him and me still, anyway, his early delights, and my later wisdoms knocking together and coming out in stories. It's not

a bad combination, and it has been a good life. I wouldn't mind a few
more years at it, God Willing, as the Irish say.

> More, later in the week,
> Yours, Ray

As Bradbury's work on his Martian Chronicles *screen treatment slowly came
to a standstill at MGM, the studio asked him to prepare the voice-over narration
for Nicholas Ray's* King of Kings, *which was entering the editing phase under
the guidance of legendary film editor Margaret Booth. Bradbury's narration
would have to be cut into the film and scored by the film's composer, Miklós
Rózsa. This experience represented Bradbury's best weeks with MGM, and he
would fictionalize aspects of it in his 1989 novel,* A Graveyard for Lunatics.

> November 3, 1960

Dear Don:

Just a note to report on the latest. Ben has already told you by now of
my newest employment at MGM, for two weeks, rewriting the narration
on *King of Kings*. It has been one of the most stimulating events of my
life. For one thing, I have always wanted to learn more about cutting and
editing films. Now I'm working with one of the finest editors in the world,
Margaret Booth, who has been at MGM for a lifetime, and has cut every
major film they've ever made. We get on fine, for I find that she thinks in
the same terms I do about creativity, spontaneity. She cuts her films as
I cut my stories. Too, I've enjoyed going back to the Bible after all these
years and discovering again the refreshing influence of its style. Above
all, with this exciting week in progress, it has caused a new spurt in my
Martian Chronicles screenplay-treatment, and when Blaustein returns
from Paris this week-end, I should have about 70 pages to show him![29]
    MGM has allowed me to have my way with the first reel of the film.
I can cut it and put it back together any way I want. I sit downstairs for
a few hours each day playing with a fabulous toy, sitting at the heart of
the projection room machinery, running the film forward, freezing it,

and running it back. I enjoy working the miracle of pulling spears out of dead men, healing their wounds, and putting them back on their feet. I love throwing people back *up* to the tops of cliffs, there to find them in good health again. All in all, you see what fun I'm having, and how good this is for my spirits and all my writing.

I will get a special narration credit on the film when it is released, incidentally. Most fun of all has been my experience yesterday. I went on a sound-stage and narrated a sound-track of my first reel material. Today they are fitting my voice into the film, putting an orchestra behind it, and this afternoon, accompanied by 100 fine musicians, I will hear and see my opening for *King of Kings*.[30] Who could ask for more, for an old hambone like me? [. . .]

More next week. I go now, to rewrite the Dead Sea Scrolls.

Yours,

Ray

In the late 1960s veteran television director Roger Kay (1921–2001) would direct a reading performance of Dandelion Wine *on the experimental stage of Lincoln Center, but in the late spring of 1961 he became one of the first friends to receive Bradbury's highly emotional response to the failure of his yearlong* Martian Chronicles *venture at MGM and the denial of official writing credits for preparing the voice-over narration to* King of Kings. *In this omission, Bradbury was not alone; Orson Welles was also not credited on-screen for reading Bradbury's narration.*

Dear Roger:

May 15, 1961

I have had six or seven experiences now, all of them winding up brutally or bitterly, with many groups of people. I know now I am not cut out to be moving through the world, the business world, or the artistic world, attempting to work with others. I should have faced this long ago, instead of smiling, agreeing, and hurting people with promises that could never be kept. . . . Call this weakness, call this even, if you wish, paranoia, but I flee the financial as well as the artistic marketplace of cinema, TV and stage. This seems sane to me.

I know my place is in hiding out, retreating, being a hermit, and writing short stories and novels, so I never have to see anyone or have any advice about my work. I know I am my own best advisor and can go on for the rest of my life being happy, working alone. The ten months at MGM have capped this, along with my name being taken off *King of Kings.*

I see the pattern now that I could not recognize in myself. And it was my creative intuition which threw monkey wrenches into the machinery again and again over the years, for I only thought I wanted to work with people. I was kidding myself. I have never needed anyone nor will I ever need anyone, as long as I stick where I belong, in the safe small quiet hidden world of short stories. [. . .]

In 1963 Bradbury began two years of work on a more fully developed Martian Chronicles *screenplay under the guidance of Alan Pakula, producer of the Academy Award–winning* To Kill a Mockingbird. *The following year, the* Chronicles *project came to full development under an agreement with Universal, the studio where Bradbury's original screen story,* It Came from Outer Space, *had been produced in 1953. In early May 1965 Universal rejected the project, ending this period of work on adapting* The Martian Chronicles *for film.*

May 5, 1965

Dear Don:

As I suspected some time ago, the Universal-International deal on *The Martian Chronicles,* has finally fallen through. Our first definite note was struck on last Friday, and yesterday, Tuesday, May 4th, UI finally rejected the whole project completely. Alan Pakula telephoned me to tell me that this was only a lost battle, not a lost war, and that he and

Bob Mulligan intended to move ahead to some other studio with my
script. They want me to come over tomorrow to talk for an hour or
so about our major strategy. I don't know all the reasons why UI (Ed
Muhl and Mr. Tucker) rejected the screenplay, but I believe it is because
of the nature of the screenplay itself. Perhaps they expected another
It Came From Outer Space, which, incidentally, would fail if it hit the
screens. Anyway, I have gone through several days of depression but,
you know me, I have bounced back. I have just interviewed Disney, had
a good lunch with him, walked around the lot with him, and gone to his
robot factory to see all the incredible machines he is building to fit into
Disneyland in the coming two years. Next time you are out here I hope
to show all this to you. I go out to Disneyland twice next week to see
behind the scenes! And, to think, I'm being paid for this Fun!

I am very curious now to know your reactions to my *Martian
Chronicles* screenplay. If you have any hard criticisms to offer me now,
they would be very welcome. What do you say?

[...]

Best, as ever, yours,

Ray

Bradbury's final full version of his far-traveling Martian Chronicles *screenplay resulted from a 1996 request by Universal Studios, which had rejected his
1965 script for Alan Pakula. Bradbury finished this version in 1997, but Universal again declined to take the project further, effectively ending a long relationship with the studio that had included the successful releases of* It Came from
Outer Space (1953) *and* Fahrenheit 451 (1966).

September 18, 1996

Dear Don:

I think you might expect a telephone call from Universal Studios today
about a possible contract for me to write a screenplay of *The Martian
Chronicles*. I've been meeting with various people there during the last

two weeks and they seem ready to negotiate. If you want to call me, later, so we can discuss a price for the screenplay, please do.

I'll believe it when the ink dries. Fond best,

Ray

———————————————————————

The Illustrated Man

CLAIRE BLOOM AND ROD STEIGER

There were disappointments for Bradbury in the Warner Brothers 1969 feature-length film adaptation of stories from The Illustrated Man, *but he found great pleasure in seeing his friends Claire Bloom (1931–) and Rod Steiger (1925–2002) in the principal roles. Producer Ted Mann brought in a business associate to script the three stories selected for the film, and director Jack Smight never really brought the Bradbury touch to balancing the three tales selected from the stories that, in the film's framing scenes, emerge from the tattoos on the body of the Illustrated Man himself ("The Veldt," "The Long Rain," and "The Last Night of the World"). Instead, the continuity and the quality of the film came through in the masterful performances of Steiger and Bloom, who at the time were in the final year of their ten-year marriage.*

Steiger's friendship with Bradbury went back to the mid-1950s, and he began work on Bradbury's film shortly after completing In the Heat of the Night—*a film that earned Steiger an Academy Award for Best Actor. Bradbury was delighted when Steiger agreed to take on the framing role of the Illustrated Man as well as the male leads in all three of the internal stories. Claire Bloom, who had performed with the great Shakespearean talents of the day, brought a distinguished film and stage career into her portrayal of the female leads in two of the stories as well as the overarching enchantress who creates both the art and the curse of the prophetic tattoos.*

[summer–fall 1968]

Dear Clara and Rod:

I have waited to write you until I had a chance to see the rough-cut of *Illustrated Man*. I saw it on Monday this past week and the film looks good. The trouble of seeing a rough-cut, of course, is that without music,[31] and with varying levels of sound, plus a few sound-effects, plus variations in color, one can misjudge what one sees. I will sit down with

Jack and Howard[32] next week and discuss any minor changes with them which I think might be of some help. I think "The Veldt" passes a bit too swiftly and should be paced out some. I believe they have certain shots which would help this, particularly in surveying the Room, The Veldt, itself, and allowing the audience to savor the experience. By this I mean the first encounter with The Veldt when you, Rod, the Father, come home. I am not worried about this, for I feel it is a minor problem which can be licked between Jack and his editor.

The film runs about an hour and 49 minutes and it is one of the few films I have seen in recent years that I wish were longer.[33] So many films, one feels one would like to chop with an ax. But *Illustrated Man* is different. It could use another five minutes or more of time, and if Jack has any out-takes that would slow down its sometimes headlong pace, I will encourage him to use them. A hard thing to describe in a letter, but it has to do with an audience perceiving and understanding what it watches. I would like to linger longer on the home in which you and Clara live, that big dental laboratory place, and the clean clean entrance to that wild and ferociously dirty Veldt. . . .

Anyway, how are you? How go things there? I was frustrated the final week of your being here, that we never had the chance for a last evening at our place. Only now, many weeks later, has Mag finally recovered from whatever in hell went wrong with her shoulder tendons. I guess it was one of the results of her car-demolishment. Mag guesses otherwise. In any event, she has had a lousy two months but is okay now.

Please write with all the news, when you have time. Susan leaves for London and Oxford on the 15th. It doesn't look as if we'll make it over, ourselves. God, how I wish we could.[34] My admiration, my affection, my friendship, remain constant to you both.

Love,
Ray

Something Wicked This Way Comes

JACK CLAYTON

Academy Award–winning director Jack Clayton (1921–1995), whom Bradbury had known and respected since his 1953–54 Moby Dick *screenwriting adventures with John Huston in Ireland and London, hired John Mortimer to make substantial changes to Bradbury's screenplay for* Something Wicked This Way Comes. *Clayton had worked effectively with Bradbury to revise earlier versions of the script, but as filming began, the final revised script greatly altered and in effect eliminated what Bradbury considered the pivotal motivational scene of the entire film. He conveyed his concern in a letter to Clayton and his longtime assistant, Jeanie Sims.*

Monday, August 31, 1981

Dear Jack & Jeanie:

You asked me to react to the screenplay, and here are my reactions. . . .
　　Overall, very good.
　　But, if you will permit me, not necessarily as the writer of the original screenplay, or the book, but as a dramatic critic, who has tried to help his friends, many of them, over the years—here are a few suggestions.
　　I enclose a Xerox of a basic scene, or scenes, a pivotal confrontation, at the center of my screenplay, even as it is central in the revision. I ask you to consider, to reconsider, the passionate and mysterious virtues of the original, as against the more familiar and less exciting human collisions in the revised new scenes.
　　In my version, when the two boys pursue Mr. Cooger, disguised in the flesh of the nephew Robert, back to the carnival, they inadvertently, via the carousel, age him to the point of death. Both panic at the thought of what the carnival will do to them as a result of this terrible deed. They bring the ambulance and the police. Will, of

course, simply wants to save Cooger, he feels responsible, and wants to get the carnival "off their backs." Jim has deeper motives. He wants to prove he is okay, a good guy, so that perhaps the carnival may invite him in for a "ride."

Both are dismayed when, arriving at the carnival, they find Mr. Electrico (Cooger, very old, very dead) propped up in the electric chair. The medics sense death here, but are shocked and fooled, when a switch is thrown, and Mr. Electrico comes to life! There ensues a marvelous scene, so I think, where Electrico questions and threatens the boys, all witnessed by the medics and the police, who misinterpret what they hear and see as a joke. Only the boys, and *we* know, this is utterly serious; deadly, in fact.

This is a delicious scene, and it is the dynamo at the center of our film, from which all else takes its impetus and drive.

The boys are now truly trapped, between carnival and law, between monsters and the innocent town. They know the truth, but cannot tell it. They have been threatened in front of everyone, yet it is considered a joke. The scene works on a variety of levels—suspense—human—and future danger.

For, you see, we have been waiting for a truly *Big Scene* now for almost half the film. We must finally deliver.

Not enough that Cooger gets on the carousel, goes backward, becomes a boy. That's good stuff, but it doesn't pay off yet. It finally pays off when Cooger, trapped on the machine, ages and appears to be dying or dead. That is a shocker, and the film needs that dramatic moment, not just for shock's sake, half way in, but to set up the ricochet board against which the final scenes play.

The carnival, in sum, must truly hate the boys for having destroyed Cooger, or semi-destroyed him, and half-ruined their plans for the town.

The carnival must now: repair the carousel, transport Cooger to it, age him backward to his former venomous self.

And meanwhile, seek out and find the boys. The scene, as I wrote it, gives them ten times the passion and motive. Dark and his friends are revenge incarnate now.

In the revision, much of the delicious fun has been lost. We find merely the Lightning Rod Salesman in the electric chair, a gratuitous guest you might say, with no special reason for his being there, and no threat to the boys. [...]

Please, please, reread my scene carefully, and see how the dynamo functions. Then reread the revision. Then, call me. I'll come in for a chat. Right now, I am fearful that the center of our film will fall like a pie in an oven when a door slams. [...]

All of this said with some trepidation, but much love for you and Jeanie, and in hopes ...

Yours,
Ray

P.S. [...] Fantasy must not just be fantasy, it must be rooted in metaphor. I have rooted my fantasy in machine metaphors. We see the machines at work, so therefore they must not be fantastic, after all, thinks the viewer, they must be *true*. The carousel machine kills Cooger (almost) we see it, know it, feel it, so it is *so*. The electric chair saves him. Two devices. Two machines. Two metaphors. The second metaphor, the second machine, saves him while the first, the carousel, is being repaired! So, by God, when Mr. Dark stalks through the town, it must be as avenger, not just with the knowledge that the BOYS *know*, but that they have DONE something awful: tampered with one machine, the carousel, so that the second machine must be brought into action to buy time until the carousel is fixed, Cooger restored, and the BOYS Demolished! R.

TOM WILHITE

The summer of 1982 proved crucial to the reshooting and final editing of Disney's 1982–83 feature film adaptation of Something Wicked This Way Comes. *After the initial screening, Bradbury, whose heavily mediated script still formed the core of the film, was actively involved in planning the new shots and editing adjustments with director Jack Clayton and others. Bradbury began by pinpointing the crucial sequence he felt needed no editing at all*

as the final effects were added. His letter to Disney vice president Tom Wilhite
(1952–) centers on this scene—the library confrontation between Dark and
Mr. Halloway.

[ca. July 1982]

Mr. Tom Wilhite
Disney Studios

Dear Tom,

I have brooded over the ideas we discussed yesterday *re* the library
scene in the film between Halloway and Dark. Some of the notions that
have come to the top of my mind since are as follows:

The scene, as it stands now, is a perfection of drama; riveting,
touching, suspenseful, beautiful.

There might well be a great danger, if it is tampered with, that any
extraneous matter injected at this late date, might cause the scene to
inadvertently fall over into comedy.

Drama is a strange business, as we know. Certain O'Neill plays
work on the stage but, on screen, run the risk, with the accumulation
of detail, of suddenly provoking laughter. That is because the screen
is a more intimate, closeup, form of drama. Which means you must be
careful not to overload.

In sum, since the library scene is the strongest scene in the film,
the great confrontation we have been waiting for, I should imagine
that, for the time being anyway, we turn our attention elsewhere in the
film to those scenes which we feel, by the merest touch of sound, or
the addition of one second or two seconds of old or new film, can
be heightened. Any area we feel can be clarified, etc. The arrival of
the train, the setting up of the carnival, where we feel that perhaps
something delicious can be added that won't in any way throw the film
out of balance, and increase our pleasure at the mystery. Debating the
two ends of the film, for instance; well worth thinking about amongst all
of us—you, Jack, the editor, myself, etc.

Anyway, there you have it. All of this offered gingerly and carefully, for I am not Lord God of the cinema (I wish I were), but only a small magician in the outer garden.

Thanks and best,
Ray
Bradbury

Copy to Jack Clayton.

————————————————————

Other Cinema Voices

FEDERICO FELLINI

Bradbury counted his long friendship with Federico Fellini (1920–1993) as one of the great inspirational blessings of his life. The Italian director won the Academy Award for Best Foreign Language Film for both La Strada *(1954) and* Nights of Cabiria *(1957), and he won two more Oscar nominations for* La Dolce Vita *and* 8½ *during the 1960s. Fellini was greatly appreciative of Bradbury's 1977* Los Angeles Times *book review of Christian Strich's influential study,* Fellini's Films. *Bradbury had met Fellini in Los Angeles in 1970, but it was Bradbury's 1977 book review that prompted Fellini to reach out and begin the friendship. As these letters show, Fellini's comments on life, the state of the world, and filmmaking were often candid; he found a kindred spirit in Bradbury, who was able to visit Fellini in Italy twice (1978 and 1991) before the director's death on Halloween 1993.*

———————————

January 26, 1978

Mr. Ray Bradbury
Book Reviews
c/o Los Angeles Times
Los Angeles, California
U.S.A.

My dear Bradbury,

I am sending this letter care of your newspaper because I do not have your personal address.

My Swiss editor sent me some American newspaper clippings.[35] Your review and comments of the book on my film was among them. I read everything you wrote and felt profoundly flattered and touched. I admire you very much, dear Bradbury. And knowing you like what I do and seeing it expressed with such fervor is one of those things that's good for the heart and makes one want to go back to work right away. Unfortunately, films cost a great deal of money and "right away" is always the day after tomorrow.

Will you ever come to Rome? I don't know when I'll come to America. I have insistent offers to come make a film there. Many offers, expressed in very flattering terms, many guarantees . . . but I don't think I could make a film in another language, in another country. I would feel lost, overwhelmed, confused and I wouldn't even remember how to do my work. And yet, for some time now, I have been thinking about attempting this very risky summersault because everything here in Italy has become very difficult. And there is the ghost of an unhappy, resigned ageing. Each day I hope the next week will bring changes and that life may once more have all its charms, surprise and the delight of days gone by. This holds me back but I don't want to bore you with this melancholia but thank you for all you have written on my work.

> With esteem and gratitude for what you have written . . .
> Federico

[February 1978]

Dear Federico Fellini:

I will keep this letter very short, for, at this time, I only want to thank you for your long and warm and really beautiful response to my article. I will write you a longer letter in a few days. For the time being, I want to enclose a play of mine which I believe contains the seeds of a possible Fellini/Bradbury collaboration. I feel that this play *The Wonderful Ice Cream Suit*, with a few changes, would fit Rome as easily as it once fit Los Angeles. I believe that its Latin temperament would travel. I sense that there is little difference between the dreams of six young Latins trying to own one suit in California, and six young Latins in Italy trying to do the same. I hope you agree. I will be sending on other stories or books in the next few weeks. I have always felt and hoped that one day we might work together. I feel that now might be the time. I think we need each other for many reasons.

Thank you for your letter. I shall treasure it always.

[Ray Bradbury]

Rome, 3 March, 1978

Ray Bradbury
10265 Cheviot Drive
Los Angeles, CA 90064
U.S.A.

Dear Ray:

I received your very affectionate letter and book.

My knowledge of English is rather terrible. Therefore, I am having it translated. As soon as it is ready I will greedily read it.

You're really simpatico, Ray.

Thank you again so much for your kind thought and enthusiasm.
a presto . . . . . : . . . . . buon lavoro . . . . . . e . . . buon fortuna . . .
Federico

Rome, Dec 28 1980

Dear Maggie and Dear Ray,

Your greetings, noted on the lovely poem (which I had translated by the splendid girl who is now translating this letter) pleased me immensely.[36]

What a pity that you don't live in Rome, or at least in a town a bit closer than Los Angeles, because you really inspire the idea that you are the ideal friends, those with whom one is well even in silence.

Dear Ray, of course I'd like to make a movie with you, and I would

do it right away! But you see how lazy I am, how unwilling and how
I give up before starting, and precociously aged, imagine that at only
sixty-one, I already look over forty. How often I've been offered to
make a movie in America, and I kept on saying no, pulling out heaps of
excuses which sounded even convincing, justified, actually, when I recite
them, I see that I put on a good show for myself, and I am looked upon
with esteem, I am approved of with great participation about the artist's
reasons, this artist who can only express himself in his own language,
who cannot de-root himself, etc. etc. . . .

The truth is I should try dropping everything and try to be reborn
somewhere else. Who knows if I'll manage to be convinced sooner or
later? I'd have plenty of motives, the way things are going over here, it
couldn't be worse, and the image of the immigrant is fully justified.

I don't know. In the meanwhile I'm preparing another movie. Will
I really start it? It's become so difficult to get a picture standing, and
when you do, you even feel slightly embarrassed to actually make it,
because in this life which is so dramatical and desperate, making a
movie seems a very frivolous thing to do. On the other hand, it's all
I know how to do. I should start shooting in March.[37] I'd like to tell
you the story and have your opinion, but the splendid girl is fretting,
it's getting dark and it's snowing outside, and she has to go to a party
somewhere. I must end here.

I embrace you, dear Ray, with brotherly love, and I truly hope to see
you soon. Best regards to Maggie as well.

With my warmest wishes for your work and for good luck, sincerely,

Yours
Federico

Love from Juliet[38]

FRANK DARABONT

One of Ray Bradbury's most ambitious yet short-lived Hollywood dreams centered on his plan to use a screenplay and visual displays to give "virtual" flight to the legendary ocean transport aircraft the Spruce Goose, the largest airplane of its day. It was the creation of millionaire businessman, aviator, and film producer Howard Hughes, but his wooden-framed Spruce Goose only flew once, for just over a minute, in 1947. Bradbury's interactive-museum concept began while Disney owned the Spruce Goose in the 1980s, and in 2007 he revived his idea one more time in a letter to his friend, Hollywood director Frank Darabont (1959–).

January 16, 2007

Dear Frank,

About twenty or so years ago the Long Beach City people called me in because I told them I'd like them to let me help "fly" the Spruce Goose. I went to the auditorium where they had it placed in a huge room that encompassed the entire plane, but there was really hardly any reason to go in and look at a dead air ship. I told them I wanted to write a script to help them bring it to life and that I'd make all the plans and tell them how to do it so that people could come in and witness, close-up, and get on board the ship and fly the Spruce Goose. I made some plans, including a screenplay and some technical equipment they needed, not to mention a couple of hundred thousand dollars, but they never followed up with me. Instead they sold it to the people in Seattle and moved it up there. It's on display somewhere up there, but it's dead in the water. I'd still like to present my plans to the people in Seattle and help them fly the Spruce Goose.

I'd like you to be affiliated with me, if that's something you might be interested in. If we got the job you'd be the director and technician who would figure out the way to make the illusion happen.

The thing you could do now, again, if you are interested, is try to locate the proper people in Seattle so that I can be in touch with them and tell them of our interest in flying the Spruce Goose.

I did have a chance, once, as I said before, but it didn't work out, but I've been looking at the fine film, *The Aviator*, many times in the past few months and I've been fascinated with Howard Hughes because I met him on two occasions when I was 19 and working with Laraine Day in her little theater group.[39]

Now, late in the day, I still want to fly the damned wonderful thing. Think about it and get back to me.

In the meantime, I wanted to let you know that come the first week of February I'll be opening a new play over in Pasadena. I hope that you'll be able to attend.

God bless and much love,

Ray

TENNY CHONIN (DISNEY)

For nearly four decades Ray Bradbury worked with the Disney Imagineers, collaborating in the evolution of such milestones as EPCOT's Spaceship Earth at Disney World and advising on projects for Euro Disney. He knew Walt Disney and shared Disney's conviction that "nothing has to die." Disney Studios also produced two feature-length Bradbury films, Something Wicked This Way Comes *and* The Wonderful Ice Cream Suit. *In 2007, Bradbury wrote to Disney's Tenny Chonin, then director of the artistic development division, in hopes that he could work with Disney one more time in his life. Chonin's offer of a series of Bradbury creative roundtables came too late in life to be realized, but the discussion prompted Bradbury to write a summary of his Disney memories to Tenny Chonin and Maggie Malone, Disney's director of creative development.*

February 23, 2007

Dear Tenny and Maggie,

I'm eager to get you to put me at the center of your creative activities. I've been a Disney fan since the age of nine, when I saw *Skeleton Dance*—I saw this eight times! And when I was eleven years old I became a member of the Mickey Mouse Club; I always wanted to be part of something having to do with Disney.

Back in 1964 when I was Christmas shopping at a store in Beverly Hills, I saw a man approaching me with an armload of gifts and his head poking over the top. I saw that it was Walt Disney and I cried out, "My God, how wonderful!" I ran up to him and said, "Mr. Disney?" He said, "Yes." I said, "I'm Ray Bradbury." He said, "I know your books." I said, "Oh, that's wonderful." He said, "Why?" I said, "Because I want to buy you lunch some day." His response: "Tomorrow." How incredible! When is the last time that someone said "tomorrow" and actually meant it? The next day I was in Disney's office, eating soup and sandwiches off a card table with Walt Disney and he took me on tour of the studio, even though he had other appointments.

When Disneyland opened there was criticism by the New York intellectual critics who didn't like Disneyland because it was too clean. I wrote an article defending Disneyland against these intellectuals saying that I went there for the first time with actor Charles Laughton. We flew over Big Ben in London on the Peter Pan ride—what a way to see Disneyland! [. . .]

You speak of creating from the interior of your group and I think you need someone like me in the interior. I would love to be with you and work with you because I love what you are doing and you've made some of the greatest films of all time.

Also, the Disney Studio made two of my finest films, *The Wonderful Ice Cream Suit*, which you can ask Roy Disney about this and his work with me. Disney also did *Something Wicked This Way Comes* in which I came in at the last minute and helped direct the film, edit, and get a new composer for the film.[40]

So you see, I'm a creative person and I'm there to be called upon and am good company. You should hire me and put me on a small salary and let me be part of the Disney organization.

I would be proud because when *Fantasia* appeared in 1939 in L.A. I was there the very first night to see it. I remember staggering out and saying to my friends, "That's one of the greatest films ever made."

When Disney did a new orchestral score for *Fantasia*, they knew how much I loved it, so the people at the studio called me and said,

"Will you come over to the studio tomorrow because we've got an orchestra and we're doing a new score for *Fantasia*."

I arrived at the studio and there, up on the screen, over the orchestra, were images of "Night on Bald Mountain" and I stood there, exhilarated that they'd asked me to come watch the thing being re-recorded.

When the recording was over, the conductor of the orchestra saw me standing to one side and grabbed and rushed me over to the podium and introduced me to the orchestra and the orchestra applauded me because they knew that I was a lover of what they were doing.

So you see what kind of a person you have here? I want to be with you. Hire me, pay me a small salary and let me work from the interior with *The Halloween Tree* and all my other projects and we can have fabulous meetings with Marty Sklar and Roy Disney, who both know me very well.[41]

God bless you,
Ray

6

EDITORS AND PUBLISHERS

I have taken my style to the edge, the very rim, of the precipice in this book. It was a risk, a gamble, I set for myself, knowing I could well fall off the edge into rhetorical nonsense. From here on, I will probably skirt back a few feet further from the edge.

—Bradbury to August Derleth, January 15, 1963,
on writing Something Wicked This Way Comes

DONALD A. WOLLHEIM

*The long and influential editorial career of Donald A. Wollheim (1914–1990)
began in the amateur and semiprofessional science fiction magazines of the
1930s, and by early 1941 Wollheim was editor of the extremely small-budget
professional pulps* Cosmic Stories *and* Stirring Science Stories. *Wollheim
was able to produce only three alternating monthly issues of each title with his
original publisher, but by that time he had attracted the attention of the twenty-
year-old Ray Bradbury. They had met at the 1939 first World Science Fiction
Convention in New York, and in the first half of 1941 Wollheim evaluated three
stories for Bradbury: the never-published "Double Talk" and "Levers," and
"The Piper," which had already appeared in the September 1940 fourth and
final issue of Bradbury's amateur fanzine,* Futuria Fantasia. *Bradbury had not
heard back from Wollheim about "The Piper" by July 1941, when he revised it
and found an opportunity to place it elsewhere through his new agent, Julius
Schwartz. Bradbury's rambling letter to Wollheim requesting return of "The
Piper" shows that he remained somewhat in awe of the professional editors he
was beginning to meet.*

3054½ West 12th Street
Los Angeles, Cal.
July–1941

Don Wollheim
New York City,
New York

Dear Don:

I have been considering the facets to my gem (?) "The Piper" recently
and I've hit upon a better plot construction for it. I would like to rewrite
the story entirely. A writer always wishes to do his best work and I do
not believe the story is perfect now. Therefore I wish to remould it
while the chance is still mine to take.

My agent has made several suggestions for changing it. Edmond
Hamilton, in fact, made several good comments which I wish to use.[1] I
have hopes, at some time, of making the story twice as good.

Could you return it to me? You never were *positive* that you
would use it—and I promise you that if and when *Astounding* rejects
it in its new form—which it probably will—I will skoot it right back
to you.

Am I being ethical or diplomatic? But you understand how I must
feel—having a chance to hit *Astounding*—because you've been there
yourself. *Unknown*, wasn't it? with "The Haters"? or a similar title?[2] A
good yarn, anyway.

Astonishing, under Norton, has accepted my "Pendulum" yarn,
rewritten by myself and Hasse.

I think you will like my *new* "The Piper" even better. And I don't
believe I am violating any publication or editorial rules by asking for the
return of a manuscript that has never really been accepted.

Have been talking many nights with Ed Hamilton and he is a
sincere, remarkably swell guy.

Wish I could have been in Denver to see you and the others.[3]
Heinlein took some color stereo shots of the bunch that came out
miraculously clear and pretty. All in all it must have been fun—one big
beer binge—Yerke has told me all about it—and how Yerke loves his
beer or rum—

Thanks for the trouble, Don. And, if you have already made
plans for running it in its present form and it's too late to change,
well go right ahead, but if this reaches you soon enough I would
like to have "The Piper" come home to mama for a change of
diapers.

Thanks,
Ray Bradbury

---

*By mid-August 1941 Julius Schwartz was about to head back to New York from
his summer stay in Los Angeles, and he urged Bradbury to write a stronger
letter to Wollheim requesting confirmation that "The Piper" remained free for
Schwartz to circulate elsewhere. Bradbury was still naive in the ways of editorial negotiations, and his second letter (August 10) contained a mix of pleas and*

legalisms that prompted Wollheim to declare his opinion that any of Bradbury's
amateur pieces were unsuitable for professional publication, even if rewritten
(Wollheim to Bradbury, August 14, 1941). Bradbury rebutted this contention in
his third letter, but he closed with an attempt to reconcile—a reconciliation that
also addressed Wollheim's observation that fans were sometimes ungrateful for
editorial favors.

Aug–18–1941

3054½ W. 12th Street
L. A. Calif.

Dear Don:

[. . .] I'm sorry if my second letter to you was harsh or inconsiderate.
But I had to have action. My agent leaves for New York in a few days
and I wanted to be sure everything was cleared up so he could take "The
Piper" with him.

The irony of this whole situation will probably be when my New
Version is bounced all over the place. I will then be very sheepish and
you will have a chance to laugh. I don't know. I *hope* the damned thing
sells, but who knows? I'm taking a chance.

To conclude, I hope this friction cools off quickly. We all need
friends and life is so damnably, tritely, short. I've always appreciated
your taking time to criticize the things I've sent you. A beginning writer
always appreciates such things. Please don't say fans have no gratitude
in their hearts and vocabularies.

Thanks for all the trouble. Hope to write you from time to time in
the future.

Sincerely,
Your friend (I hope)
Ray

Time (and Bradbury's unchallenged rise to market prominence) healed the breach with Wollheim, and by the early 1950s Wollheim had negotiated reprint rights to Bradbury stories in his Avon Fantasy Reader *and* Avon Science Fiction Reader *series of hybrid magazine-anthologies, as well as a reprint of "King of the Gray Spaces" in the 1951 anthology* Every Boy's Book of Science Fiction. *Bradbury's response reflects a level of maturity and success that he could not have commanded a decade earlier. The following letter replies to Wollheim's anthology request of March 28, 1950, just two years before Wollheim began his long and influential run as science fiction editor with Ace and, eventually, with his own DAW imprint of science fiction titles.*

March 31, 1950

Dear Don:

It's been quite a while since I last heard from you and it's nice to see your letterhead in the postal box again. Hope you are doing fine; it certainly sounds as if you are thriving with all of these book and magazine ventures you're amidst.

Thanks for asking to use "King of the Grey Spaces"[4] in your anthology of *Every Boy's Book of S-F*. Sounds like a fine idea. I have turned your letter over to my agent, Harold Matson, in New York, and he will be in touch with you sometime in the next few days about the details.[5] I'm sure everything'll work out well.

This year has been phenomenal so far; I've just sold 2 s-f yarns to *Collier's*, 1 to the *Post*, 3 to *Esquire*, 1 to *Coronet*, 1 to C.B.S., 2 to N.B.C.[6] In other fields, I've stories coming up in *Charm*, *Flair*, and the *Phila. Inquirer*. This, coupled with the new baby in our family, a little girl named Susan, born in November, makes me just about the happiest guy in the world.

I'll be in New York in May, and hope, in the midst of all the flurry, to at least have time to call you and perhaps see you for lunch for a long talk. It'd be nice. It's been—hmm—almost 11 years since we were up at Erisman's office, remember, and got all excited over a Paul cover he gave us.[7] Remember? My God, we've all come a long way since then, and have much to be thankful for. Again, Don, my thanks to you for asking to republish "King of the Grey Spaces." With all my best to you.

Yours,
Ray

P.S. If all of the above sales sound hideously prolific, I hasten to add that most of them were written during the last 2 years, and three of them (to *Esquire*) will be reprints from *T.W.S.*

R.

AUGUST DERLETH

Bradbury's correspondence with Arkham House founder August Derleth (1909–1971) began in the early 1940s; the apprentice tone of Bradbury's early letters would slowly mature as he labored to revise a number of his supernatural stories, often with resistance from Derleth, for the eventual Arkham House publication of Dark Carnival *(1947). Derleth also arranged for an abridged British edition (London: Hamish Hamilton, 1948), and the arrival of author's copies from England prompted Bradbury to reflect on the long editorial process behind his first story collection.*

Ray Bradbury
33 So. Venice Blvd.
Venice, Calif.

January 13, 1949

Dear Augie:

[. . .] The British editions of *DC* arrived safely and I'm quite pleased with them. A peculiar thing has happened—for the first time in two years I am able to reread *DC*. Now that it is in a fresh new type on new paper I am able to go through the book once more, a thing which I found unbearable up until this week. I suppose my inability to do so before this time is the result of my long siege of rewriting and proofing the stories two years ago. I felt rather lost, not being able to read my own stuff, but now, by God, I'm reading away at it, and finding that at least some of it reads very well. This may sound very egoistic. I don't mean it to sound that way. I mean to express my surprise and amazement more than anything, because, regardless of reviews, my growing opinion in the last 24 months was that my book was quite shoddy. Perhaps this new type-face has hypnotized me, perhaps I'm only fooling myself. Anyway, it's rather like reading someone else's book, with a fresher objectivity, and the errors, when they pop up, are *really* obvious now. You can probably cite a similar series of circumstances arising from publication and re-publication of your own work. I can only say I find it startling and fun. [. . .]

More from me later.

Yours,
Ray

Although Bradbury had grown beyond August Derleth's editorial influence by 1950, he would occasionally reflect on the reading memories preserved in Derleth's genre anthologies. Just as The Martian Chronicles *reached print, Bradbury recalled the 1930s stories reprinted in Derleth's* Beyond Time and Space *(1950) that had most impressed him as a teenage reader, discussing these tales and their authors in ways he would rarely attempt in more public writings.*

May 18, 1950

Dear Augie: I've just received and glanced over *Beyond Time and Space* and must write to congratulate you upon this fine idea and your handling of it. I don't understand why someone else didn't do this years ago, but now you have done it beautifully, and it is, as you say, a cornerstone for any s-f library.

It struck me as appropriate and oddly coincidental that three stories which rise above the years in my mind are included in your volume.

It is always a moving experience to recall a story down the calendars, and then find, one day, that a friend has written it. I had long ago forgotten that Edmond Hamilton had written "Fessenden's Worlds"; I had forgotten both author and title, in fact. And now you've revealed them to me again. You have also revealed to me the fact that "Colossus" was written by Donald Wandrei;[8] I have told this story from memory to many friends in the past 15 years, but, as usual, forgot who had written it, or the title. Now everything fits together. I am also indebted for your reprinting "The Revolt of the Pedestrians."[9] These three stories, it seems to me, are the essence of the 1928 to 1938 era of s-f in America. There was a complete, and miraculous, preoccupation with wonder and oddness and distances, with hardly a backward glance, save in the Keller story perhaps, to characterization. But as I finished the Hamilton story last night, I found myself saying, "For this once, by God, to hell with characterization; he has done something here to be proud of, he has shaken down the clinkers in my mind and refocused my views of the universe." And then it came to me that it was a shame that so much of the wonder and startlement of the early *Amazing* and *Wonder Stories* should have been lost in vast morasses of bad or dull writing. The field, today, it almost seems, could use a little more of that early wonder, combined with the knowledge we have gained in plot construction, motivation, and characterization. Sometimes it seems that we have been around s-f so many years that we have actually forgotten that one day man *will* fly into space. If I could remember this more often, and really achieve the sensation, the taste in the mouth, of wanting to get off Earth into space, I think I could be very happy on occasion doing a real bang-up, old-type, adventure tale. You have set me thinking here; nostalgia is a Prime Mover for me, and I hope to prowl back through my magazines over at my office and see if I can't do a few tales that combine the two approaches. I have been so busy humanizing the s-f story the last few years that I have forgotten the stars, and that's a hell of a thing to forget. Of course I had a reason for doing this, I had once thought, and still do think that man was too preoccupied with the so-called romantic glories of space travel and not enough involved with the realities of adjusting to alien environments. Well, I've had my say about a lot of this now, and it would be a challenge to me to step back a step

now and take a long squint at the stars and try to feel the way I felt in
1928 when I picked up and read the "World of Giant Ants" by A. Hyatt
Verrill.[10] In fact I am planning a book now for Doubleday titled *The
Space War*, which I hope will be a totally different approach to an old old
theme.[11] Half the fun of writing, it appears, is seizing upon old problems
and resolving them in one's own special way.

But I've run on a long way here. Needless to say I won't throw
overboard my people, my humans, and their problems. But I would
like to, on occasion, do something as amazing and wonderful as Mr.
Wandrei's "Colossus," the sort of story that lasts a lifetime in the
memory because of its sheer imaginative power. [. . .]

Yours,

Ray

33 So. Venice Blvd.

Venice, California

---

*Along with the 1930s stories that had so enchanted Bradbury as a boy, Derleth
had also included Bradbury's story "The Exiles" in* Beyond Time and Space. *
Derleth's cover letter for the payment check arrived with a copy of his favorable*
Chicago Tribune *review of* The Martian Chronicles, *and a gentle rebuke of
the romanticized "space urge" expressed in Bradbury's previous letter.*

May 28, 1950

Dear Augie,

Thanks for the check on "The Exiles"[12] and your wonderful review
you gave the *Martian Chronicles*.[13] Your belief in my work is warming
to my heart, and I feel that I haven't spent six years in vain working
on the stories that made up the book. I only hope that I can continue
to go ahead and develop as the years pass, and not do what the typical
American writer does, rise and fall like a rocket. The case of John
Steinbeck has been a particularly discouraging one to me, and you
can go on down the line with men like Dos Passos and Farrell[14] and

Hemingway. I don't know if it is a particular psychological aspect of the writers themselves, or the commercial gravity drawing them off center, or both. Anyway, I'm in no particular hurry to get my novels finished, they'll tie themselves up in their own good time, I believe, I'm working on them right along. In the meantime, people like yourself, Fletcher Pratt, and Tony Boucher[15] have really made me terrifically happy by your reviews.

It is so good to hear you'll be doing an Arkham Sampler anthology. There's a lot of good material there that should be in hard covers.

I suppose you are right, and that my opinions on the space urge are sheer nostalgia. I suppose that, like every other writer in the field, I fear that I will forget the true wonder of space travel, and feel the need to replenish my amazement occasionally. I know, of course, that there is far greater value and variety in the more human approach. I'll look forward to your series of s-f concepts, Augie.

I was in San Francisco over last week-end and Tony Boucher[16] told me you had sold them a really fine story; he was most enthused about it, and I look forward to seeing it.

Again thank you for sending on the carbon of your review. I'll write again soon. My best to you, Augie.

Yours,

Ray

Ray Bradbury

33 S. Venice Blvd.

Venice, Calif.

As the years passed, Bradbury's less frequent letter exchanges with Derleth still held occasional surprises. Derleth's honest and even-handed review of Something Wicked This Way Comes *prompted Bradbury to drop his more public voice and speak frankly to Derleth about the underlying truths of process that shaped his fiction.*

January 15th, 1963

Dear Augie:

Thanks for your letter with the latest news, plus the clips of your
journal, your review of *Something Wicked*, and your listing of it among
the Year's favorites.

First off, I must say that your appraisal of the book is the sort of
thing I really, and honestly, welcome. Criticism from someone like
yourself can only be filed carefully and acted upon as best one is able to
in the years ahead. I appreciate it and know, intuitively, you have stated
the case well. . . . I have taken my style to the edge, the very rim, of the
precipice in this book. It was a risk, a gamble, I set for myself, knowing I
could well fall off the edge into rhetorical nonsense. From here on, I will
probably skirt back a few feet further from the edge. It is easier, always,
for me anyway, to write short stories and not risk being ridiculous . . .
for I write all of my stories in one day, first draft . . . and cut them over
a period of weeks, months, or years. Anything done in the full flood of
emotion tends to be true and the style is only a representation of that
truth. Anything done over a period of years, as *Something Wicked had*
to be, wanders from the truth, that is, wanders from what the writer
really wants on many days, often when he doesn't want to work at all
but knows he must somehow get the work done so he can forget it.
Those parts of *Something Wicked* which are close to self-parody must
inevitably be those written in colder blood. The best part of the book, to
my taste, is the long section in the library late at night, starting with the
father's browsing through the books, and going on through the arrival
of the Witch to kill him, as the boys are taken off to the carnival. This
long section was done in a few days, and has been little changed from
that draft, so reflects, like my stories, the immediacy of my feelings. The
section with the Witch in the balloon is a similar piece, which I like; and
a good part of the ending. The rest of the book, one day in the future, I
will probably see as going in and out of focus, wavering in and out of the
truth, hitting it square on often enough to make one forgive the near-
rhetoric that followed.

This is a long-winded way of thanking you for calling to my

attention, through your article, a danger I myself have sensed for some time. It is a danger I will watch for when my next novel, s-f, titled *Leviathan '99* is ready for publication, God willing, in 1965.[17]

What is your deadline for your Arkham House collection of new stories by A. H. writers? My agent to one side, if I felt I had something short in the files that might fit . . . . in fact I *do* have a story that will be out in a little review soon (*The Second Coming Magazine*) titled "El Dia De Muerte," I might let you look at.[18] It would be fun to appear with you again. Would you want to see the story? It is a study of the many aspects of death in Mexico, as seen through the eyes of a small boy.

Yes, I would *very* much like to have a copy of *Walden West*. I am happy about the wonderful reviews you are getting!

That's it for now.

Best, as ever,

Yours,

Ray

Bradbury

10265 Cheviot Drive

Los Angeles 64, Calif.

WALTER BRADBURY

Ray Bradbury's long professional and personal relationship with Doubleday editor Walter I. Bradbury (1914–1996) spanned most of the breakout books that came to define Ray Bradbury's early impact, including The Martian Chronicles (1950), The Illustrated Man (1951), The Golden Apples of the Sun (1953), *and* Dandelion Wine (1957). *Their working relationship began in June 1949, near the end of Ray Bradbury's fruitless odyssey through New York's trade publishing houses offering several story collections for consideration. His agent Don Congdon finally brought him to the Doubleday offices, where Walt Bradbury (no relation) suggested that the young author bridge some of his Martian tales into a unified cycle of stories. The first outline of* The Martian Chronicles *took shape overnight, and in the early fall of 1949 Ray Bradbury submitted a full typescript. The final contents did not firm up until the end of the year, however, and two letters between author and editor document how the final contents were locked in place.*

[ca. December 10, 1949]

Ray Bradbury
33 So. Venice Blvd.
Venice, Calif.

Dear Brad:

It was a hell of an interesting experience talking to you via long-distance a few hours ago. If I seemed somewhat bemused and forgetful, it was because it was my first long distance call, and I was somewhat apprehensive about it. I meant to say so many things, and yet when the time came my mind blanked out and I totally forgot to ask how you were, and how New York was, and I forgot to wish you a very very happy Christmas season.

All in all, however, the phone conversation seemed to have settled most of the things you wanted to know pretty well. I sort of figured that the book would be pruned when I wrote it, so I purposely added a good number of extra words so that the pruning would be painless when it came.

Bradbury at Emperor Maximilian's palace (Chapultepec Castle) outside Mexico City, October 1945. His occasional postcards to his parents offer brief glimpses of this two-month road trip through the cities and towns of central and northern Mexico. The souvenir card from his subsequent day trip to the Pyramid of the Sun at Teotihuacan (*below*) also notes his unexpected meeting with writer John Steinbeck, who was staying at the same accommodation in Mexico City. *Courtesy Ray Bradbury Literary Works, LLC.*

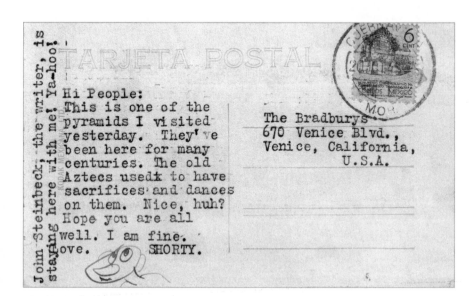

John Steinbeck, the writer, is staying here with me. Ya-hoo!

Hi People:
This is one of the pyramids I visited yesterday. They've been here for many centuries. The old Aztecs used to have sacrifices and dances on them. Nice, huh? Hope you are all well. I am fine.
Love.   SHORTY.

The Bradburys
670 Venice Blvd.,
Venice, California,
U.S.A.

Ray Bradbury and his New York agent Julius Schwartz, August 1941, in front of the Los Angeles motel court on South Norton Street, where Schwartz and Edmond Hamilton stayed while visiting with science fiction authors and friends. Four years later, as Bradbury began to move into the major-market magazines, Schwartz looked back at this moment in his September 8, 1945, letter: "Remember 'The Piper' manuscript you brought over to South Norton that day and how we went over it almost line by line to fix it up? The time seemed impossibly far off before you thought you'd be cracking the slicks, eh—but it's here!" *Courtesy Ray Bradbury Literary Works, LLC.*

Bradbury with close friends and mentors Edmond Hamilton and Leigh Brackett at an Ocean Park attraction in Santa Monica, 1948. He had stood as best man when his two friends married, and he never forgot how much he learned from them. "Of course I'm still learning," he wrote to them in June 1951, "but the older you get the slower the process becomes and you aren't learning obvious things and making tremendous strides all at once. Now the concentration is on detail and characterization and subtler things." *Courtesy Ray Bradbury Literary Works, LLC.*

Catherine L. Moore, known throughout her writing career as C. L. Moore, and her husband, Henry Kuttner, circa 1950. They wrote independently at times but often collaborated on stories and novels, using various pseudonyms that further disguised the seamless merging of talent. Kuttner was a versatile stylist across many genres and a master plotter of tales who had a great influence on Bradbury. "He was my best and most consistent teacher," Bradbury told his agent Don Congdon in a February 1958 letter, just after attending Kuttner's funeral. "He was one of the most thoughtful people I have ever known, and by this I mean a thinking man. So of course you can understand how I felt when I saw that none of the newspapers noticed that he had gone." *Photo by Gus and Helen Correl (courtesy of Don Congdon Associates, Inc.).*

Photograph of Gerald Heard, circa 1955. Heard was a central figure among the British expatriate writers in midcentury Los Angeles. Bradbury met him through Christopher Isherwood, and he enjoyed occasional tea at Heard's cottage with other expats, including Aldous Huxley. Heard was drawn to the poetic, metaphor-rich style of his young friend. "One day, you know, I hope you'll publish poems," he told Bradbury in a January 1951 letter. "It is not merely a truly original invention that carries your own writing into its own stratosphere—it is the rhetor's power of fusing an image with a phrase & in the natural flow of narrative." *Photograph by Jay Michael Barrie (courtesy of the Barrie Family Trust).*

Nobel laureate Bertrand Russell with his copy of *Fahrenheit 451* on the armrest of his reading chair, 1954. Bradbury's London publisher had sent Lord Russell copies of *The Silver Locusts* (the British title of *The Martian Chronicles*) and *Fahrenheit 451*, a novel that Russell found to be a most powerful reading experience. "The sort of future society that he portrays is only too possible," he wrote in his March 1954 response; he went on to invite Bradbury to his home, where Bradbury met Lord Russell on April 7, 1954. *Bradbury's presentation copy courtesy Ray Bradbury Literary Works, LLC.*

The prominent Italian Renaissance historian and attributionist Bernard Berenson in the gardens of his villa, I Tatti, just outside Florence, Italy, late 1940s. Bradbury's 1954 and 1957 visits triggered his discovery of Renaissance art, and he would often relate his most creative moments through letters to Berenson. In August 1955, he told Berenson about the creative fever that gripped him as he wrote about a dark carnival that became the basis of *Something Wicked This Way Comes*: "After a number of days of absolutely glowing in the dark, and feeling somewhat drunk, the carnival let down its black velvet tents and stole away, leaving me exhausted but happy, at my typewriter." *Alamy.*

Ray Bradbury's parents, Leonard Spaulding Bradbury Sr. and Esther Moberg Bradbury, early 1950s. Even as a man in his thirties, Ray's letters home maintained the tone and simplicity of earlier times. His August 1957 letter to them, written from London, discussed that earlier life as presented in his new novel, *Dandelion Wine*: "It is a work of real love, evoking many of the memories of those summers which seemed perfect to me, regardless of how they may have seemed to the adults around me, such a long time ago now. I wish Grandmother could have lived to have read this and seen herself in book form." *Courtesy Ray Bradbury Literary Works, LLC.*

Aunt Neva Bradbury was only eleven years older than her nephew Ray, and for most of his Waukegan childhood she lived next door with his grandparents. She was a designer who loved theater, and Bradbury wrote to her in the summer of 1957 with an account of seeing Laurence Olivier play the lead in *Titus Andronicus* on the London stage: "We . . . were introduced backstage to Sir Laurence and Lady Olivier. What a shock to meet a quiet, beautifully mannered man in a pair of soft-grey horn-rims and a correct suit, half an hour after seeing him play Titus, whose sons are slain right and left." *Courtesy Ray Bradbury Literary Works, LLC.*

Maggie and Ray Bradbury in their Clarkson Road backyard, 1952, with daughters Susan (*right*) and Ramona. Bradbury had to leave home for New York on publishing business just after Ramona was born, but this unavoidable trip allowed him to put his love into a May 1951 letter home to Maggie: "It is good to be away so that I can bring myself to put these things on paper to you, for it is important that people who are as close as we can sometimes stand off and repeat aloud what we know in our hearts." *Courtesy Ray Bradbury Literary Works, LLC.*

Bradbury carrying a 16mm print of *Icarus Montgolfier Wright*, with Forrest J Ackerman, who holds a first edition of *R Is for Rocket*, with *Something Wicked This Way Comes* under his arm. In the years before World War II, Forry had helped Bradbury navigate the world of science fiction fandom and amateur fanzine publishing, and he had witnessed the postwar rise of Bradbury into the literary mainstream. "You'll be glad to hear that I have broken into the slick market, at last, with a science fiction story!" he told Ackerman in a January 1948 letter. He had earned 20 cents a word, "an exceedingly high raise over the usual 1 or 2 cents a word for the average sf yarn." *Courtesy Ray Bradbury Literary Works, LLC.*

In an early 1951 letter, the emerging science fiction writer Richard Matheson expressed high regard for Bradbury's new novella, *The Fireman*. Bradbury's response hinted at the ways that he would soon expand the novella into *Fahrenheit 451*: "I want to re-emphasize the fact that we haven't time to think anymore. The great centrifuge of radio, television, pre-thought-out movies, etc. give us no time to 'stop and stare.' Our lives are getting more scheduled all the time, there's no room for caprice, and caprice is the core of man, or should be the tiny happy nucleus around which his mundane tasks can be assembled." *Photograph by Bill Idelson (courtesy of Don Congdon Associates, Inc.).*

Director François Truffaut (*center*), flanked by costars Julie Christie and Oskar Werner, during the filming of *Fahrenheit 451*, in February 1966 at Pinewood Studios, Buckinghamshire, UK. Bradbury wanted Truffaut's production to remain free of authorial interference. In his September 18, 1966, letter to Truffaut, written after the film premiered, he explained his rationale: "By working against my material often, you created my material. . . . You, by quietly cutting back on the mechanical foliage, have given me a lesson in taste and quietude." *Alamy.*

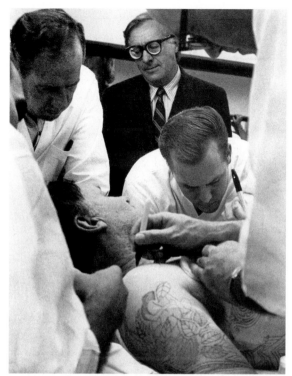

Bradbury and Rod Steiger at Warner Brothers, 1968, during the laborious makeup sessions required of Steiger for *The Illustrated Man*. Bradbury had known Steiger since the mid-1950s, and he was thrilled with what Steiger and his wife, Claire Bloom, brought to the film. Bradbury was concerned, however, with the rapid pace of the rough cut. "It is one of the few films I have seen in recent years that I wish were longer," Bradbury wrote to his two friends after shooting ended. "A hard thing to describe in a letter, but it has to do with an audience perceiving and understanding what it watches." *Photo by Floyd McCarty / Alamy.*

Arthur C. Clarke and Ray Bradbury at Cal Tech on the eve of the *Mariner* 9 landing on Mars, November 1971. The two friends engaged in a friendly debate with astronomer Carl Sagan and future Jet Propulsion Laboratory director Bruce Murray on the possibilities of life on the red planet. Clarke, Bradbury, and their friend Isaac Asimov were sometimes known as the ABCs of science fiction, even after Asimov's passing in April 1992. "Still feel sad about Isaac," Clarke wrote to Bradbury on August 11 of that year. "It's getting lonely up here on Dinosaur Plateau; isn't it?" *Photo by Floyd Clark (courtesy of the California Institute of Technology archives).*

Ray Bradbury as host and narrator of the ABC television documentary *Infinite Horizons: Space Beyond Apollo*, in 1979. His script (coauthored with director Malcolm Clarke) won an Emmy. In his April 1962 letter to historian Arthur Schlesinger Jr. at the Kennedy White House, Bradbury had predicted his evolving media role as a space-age visionary: "There are many people who know the facts about the various projects headed toward space. There are only a few who interpret, aesthetically or otherwise, our entire purpose in Space." *Alamy / CSU Archives, Everett Collection.*

Don Congdon represented Ray Bradbury as his literary agent for more than sixty years, quickly becoming a reliable sounding board; more than any other influence, Congdon helped Bradbury discover his strengths as a storyteller who transcended genre boundaries with his distinct style and emotional truths. "You should have more faith in yourself and in your achievements from day to day," Congdon wrote in August 1953, just before the publication of *Fahrenheit 451*. "You will always be struggling with this, and in many instances, it is not for you to say what is your best, or worst work. The public and the writer seldom agree."
Courtesy Don Congdon Associates, Inc.

Artist and illustrator Joseph Mugnaini with Ray Bradbury at a post-performance party during the February to August 1965 Los Angeles run of Bradbury's stage adaptation of *The Wonderful Ice Cream Suit* at the Coronet Theater. For nearly four decades, Mugnaini's interior art and cover illustrations became synonymous with Bradbury's best fiction, including their Academy Award–nominated 1962 collaboration with George Clayton Johnson on *Icarus Montgolfier Wright*. "Ours has been a phenomenal friendship," he told Mugnaini in an October 22, 1983, letter, "and I am deeply in debt to you for the ways you have enriched my life." *Courtesy Ray Bradbury Literary Works, LLC.*

July 28, 1980

Dear Joe: Here are some notions that I hope you can use!
1.

The Dust Witch in SOMETHING WICKED THIS WAY COMES
suspended in her great evil balloon, gliding over the
housetops of the small town. Below her, on his roof,
Will Halloway looks up, bow in hand, having just
released the arrow that will 'kill' the Balloon. Perhaps
the Balloon is already struck...we can see the arrow
in the "skin" of the balloon, and the air gusting out
around the arrow...the 'skin' of the balloon is beginning
to shrivel, grow ancient, but we can see the designs of
spiders and monsters and strange beasts enscribed on
the balloon's surface. Below, in her basket suspended
under the balloon is the Dust Witch, her eyes sewn shut,
her hands outreached to fend off the arrow - too late!
Her face, if we can see it, is terrified. The boy is killing
her balloon!
Joe, re-read this section of SOMETHING WICKED...it comes
somewhere in the first third of the book. Wish I could tell
you which page...but I don't have the book with me on the
train! If you don't have the book, get a paperback...places
like the PICKWICK in Hollywood carry all my paperbacks!

MAYBE
SHOW 3
ARROWS-
TWO
"PHANTOM" LIGHT
ONES IN FLIGHT
PLUS ONE REAL
ONE IN BALLOON!

ARROW

WILL

HORIZON→
LINE
DARK HOUSES
IN SILHOUETTE
MOONLIT ROOFTOPS

LOVE!
FROM
Ray

Joseph Mugnaini had a special gift for accurately interpreting pivotal scenes from Bradbury's stories and novels. In this page from a July 28, 1980, letter to Mugnaini, Bradbury used both words and a rough sketch to imagine a scene from his 1962 novel, *Something Wicked This Way Comes*. Mugnaini's interpretation was quite different; he generally shaped his own interpretation of a scene, and Bradbury was never disappointed with the artist's vision. *Courtesy Ray Bradbury Literary Works, LLC, and the Joseph Mugnaini estate archives.*

William F. Nolan's midcentury efforts to document Bradbury's prolific and wide-ranging publication history led to an enduring friendship; within a few years, Bradbury's encouragement and advice led Nolan into a long writing career of his own. Nolan would often get Bradbury to describe his working environment as well as his writing, as he did in his October 30, 1953, letter to Nolan from Ireland, where he was working on scripting *Moby Dick* for director John Huston: "We went fox-hunting last Tuesday; and it was a beautiful autumn day—my first autumn in more than 19 years. All the leaves on the trees ablaze with autumn." *Photograph by Roger Anker (courtesy of the photographer).*

Ray Bradbury and Italian film director Federico Fellini in conversation at the Hotel Hassler above the Spanish Steps, Rome, July 1991. Even in their letters, they spoke candidly about life and creativity. "In this life which is so dramatical and desperate," Fellini observed in his December 28, 1980, letter, "making a movie seems a very frivolous thing to do. On the other hand, it's all I know how to do." *Courtesy Ray Bradbury Literary Works, LLC.*

Bradbury and Thomas Steinbeck at a Santa Monica NEA Big Read lecture, October 2009. Their common bond centered on the Bradbury stories that Nobel laureate John Steinbeck read to his sons when Thom and his brother were boys. "I distinctly remember the first Bradbury story my father ever gave me to read," Steinbeck recalled in his June 27, 2003, letter to Bradbury. "It's called 'The Flying Machine,' and I loved it from the first sentence." Steinbeck introduced Bradbury at Santa Monica's Lobero Theatre for the 2009 event. *Photograph by John King Tarpinian (courtesy of the photographer).*

Bradbury with President George W. Bush and First Lady Laura Bush in the White House Oval Office to receive the National Medal of Arts, November 2004. The president's congratulatory note thanked Bradbury for bringing a gift copy of his latest story collection, *The Cat's Pajamas*, with a cover illustration penned by Bradbury himself. *Photo by Susan Sterner / Alamy.*

First Lady Laura Bush in Cairo, 2008, participating in a Big Read event at the American University that featured Ray Bradbury's *Fahrenheit 451*. Shortly after participating in Bradbury's National Medal of Arts presentation in 2004, she noted in a letter to Bradbury that, as a former teacher, she valued *Dandelion Wine* as her Bradbury favorite. *Photo by Sarah Malkawi / Getty.*

"Back in 1960, in the basement with my daughters, I painted a picture of a tree loaded with lit pumpkins. I called it *The Halloween Tree*." The painting that Bradbury described in his March 2007 letter to his Knopf editor Kathy Hourigan inspired a screenplay and a novel. "From this a wonderful thing has happened during the last twenty years or so," he continued. "If you cross the yards of America on Halloween night, you'll find Halloween Trees beginning to be lit in yards here and there." Bradbury occasionally used his painting as a letterhead image during the fall season. *Courtesy Ray Bradbury Literary Works, LLC.*

Joe mugnaini - illustration for THE MARTIAN CHRONICLES.

bradbury - 10265 cheviot drive - los angeles 90064, calif.

Bradbury adapted many of Mugnaini's illustrations into letterhead designs for his correspondence. Mugnaini's Martian, carrying a peace offering, was created for special editions of *The Martian Chronicles* story-chapter called "The Off Season." For nearly forty years, each Mugnaini illustration masterfully communicated the mood and theme of the story behind it. "You and I are on the same search for the same truths," Bradbury told him in his October 22, 1983, letter, "whatever in hell they may be." *Courtesy of the Joseph Mugnaini estate.*

So we yank out "They All Had Grandfathers," "The Disease," "The Fathers," and "The Wheel."[19]

Let me know what you finally decide about "The Off Season," will you? Whether, that is, you want it out or in the book. Or if you'd like it cut down about a thousand words, it would be very simple if we simply eliminated the chase sequence where Parkhill flees in his sandship pursued by the Martians. I'd be glad to fix this up for you if you wish. Or if you decide to yank the whole story, then I could add some more to "The Luggage Shop" or "The Watchers," combining the two interim pieces to make one, perhaps, to explain what goes on, and show the explosion.[20] [. . .]

I am enclosing the copyright data you asked for. Incidentally, I want to be certain that the copyright page for *The Martian Chronicles* contains none of this copyright data at all. I understand that the entire mass of material in the book can be re-copyrighted in my name for the year 1950, is that correct? I want the book to have a fair shake with the critics, so mention of the magazines where the material appeared should be absolutely verboten. I know you agree with me on this, for I believe we mentioned this when I saw you in June. I have met up with several critics already who, because a piece has appeared in a pulp magazine, automatically condemn it. This sort of snobbism brings me to a boil, and I want to protect my book from it. I write all of my stories with the same typewriter and the same interest and time interval given to each in its turn. I don't know the mechanics of copyright on a deal like this, but perhaps you or Don could fill me in on this.[21] I notice that the copyright page on John O'Hara's book *Here's O'Hara*, for instance, does not give copyright data on any of the magazines where his stories appeared, but simply says Copyright, 1935, 1938, 1940 by John O'Hara. I'd surely like to follow this example with *Chronicles*. Eudora Welty's book of stories *The Wide Net* follows the same pattern.

Will there be an advertising budget on *Chronicles*? And have you any idea of what the initial printing will be?

These questions are probably superfluous at the present time, so I'll shut my mouth.

About the new book idea *The Space War*. I'd like to sort of register in this title with you people so that, ethically at least, no one else can snatch it. I've sort of outlined in my mind and done a few pages of work on this novel which would be about fifty thousand words, detailing the complete human adventure of a man taken from his home in Illinois, trained to become a soldier aboard a Rocket in space, and then I hope to tell as much as I can imagine of what a war in space would *really* be like.[22] I don't mean logistically, or mechanically, or scientifically, but humanly and with understanding of the human problems to be faced in such a great and foolish undertaking. What it would be, or what it would seem to *me* to be, of course, would be the multiplication of man's errors, and the magnification of man's idiocy. If wars on Earth have been total wastes, in spite of their ideological rightness, it would be interesting to compute the total waste and senselessness of a space war with its impossible burdens of loneliness and distances, its special neuroses and insanities and humors. [. . .] If you like, later, perhaps I can give you an outline on this, through Don, and a chapter or so, and perhaps we can make a contract on it. In the meantime, I hope to be beginning work on *Frost and Fire* in a few weeks.[23] The exigencies of just producing short stories to keep us alive, has taken all of my energy since completing *The Martian Chronicles* eight weeks ago. [. . .]

This is a very disjointed letter. And *that* was an understatement. About "The Earth Men." You said that it seemed not quite to fit into my concept of the Martians in the other stories. If you people would like to point out the inconsistencies to me, I'd be more than happy to do a bit of rewriting here and there in that story to make it fit better, if you think rewriting can do it. Of course, if it's the concept of the story that is off, that's another matter. I'm so close to the book that I fail to see certain things that should be absolutely obvious to me. I'd like to see "The Earth Men" stay in, naturally, since it has been popular with everyone since its publication. Let me know what you decide.

About "Usher II." I certainly appreciate your attitude of sweet reasonableness. There is no reason why I shouldn't say that I think you're the nicest damn editor I ever met, willing to put up with crackpot authors at the drop of an intransitive verb. I'm pleased that "Usher II" will stay in, even though you are a mite doubtful on it.

I look forward to my visit to New York in May, which, come to think of it, isn't very far off now. Thank you for arranging to have the book released on May 4th, a few days after my arrival.

I have never believed that an author should fight to the last ditch for the wordage in his books. The reason why is simply that most authors cannot be objective and God knows most books would be better if the editors had been a bit more cruel with the blue pencil. I am glad that we have dropped a little suet from the *Chronicles*, and I only wish Derleth had been a bit harder with me on *Dark Carnival*; there are about four stories in it that never should have been published.[24]

Enough of this. I enjoyed the telephone conversation a lot, even though it made a nervous wreck of me. I now wish I could afford such an expensive pastime more often. Thank you for everything, Brad. Let me know about these various items when you have time. I look forward to a long and pleasant relationship with a swell editor and a fine house. My best to you.

Yours,
Ray

————————————————————————————

December 14, 1949

Dear Ray:

Thanks for your full and gratifying letter following our phone call. Again I apologize for slightly unnerving you with the phone call: it just seemed to me a simpler way to handle the matter.

As you say, it settled most of our immediate problems. Thanks for the copyright information on the stories. Don and I will split up the matter of getting these copyrights assigned to you. The copyright page of *The Martian Chronicles* will contain no names of magazines. The original dates will appear and that's all—so you need have no fears about that. We shall keep in "Usher II" and "The Earth Men." We shall delete "They All Had Grandfathers," "The Disease," "The Fathers" and "The Wheel." For the time being I think we had better leave "The Off-Season" in, and see how long the book will run when we get it set in type. If it seems impossible, later on we can cut it in the galleys and make the necessary transitions there. You see, we are not only compelled to watch the actual wordage here, but in this book there will be a great many chapter breaks which involve losing one-half to a full page of type so that the transition pieces and new chapters can start on a right-hand page. This difficulty makes *The Martian Chronicles* run longer than a standard novel would, even though the wordage might be the same length. However, we will see when the designers get to work on it.

Your idea on "The Space War" sounds intriguing. We shall consider the title "registered" with you, and I will look forward to hearing more about it.

There will be an advertising budget on *Chronicles*, but at this time I cannot tell you what it will be. It, and the first printing, will depend upon the way that advance sales come in. For the record, May 4th is our definite publication date; it's an excellent idea to bring the book out while you are here in New York.

Thanks for all your kind words, and a very merry Christmas to you, too.

Yours,
Brad
Walter I. Bradbury

Through a chance encounter, the influential British writer and critic Christopher Isherwood became an early supporter of the themes and style of The Martian Chronicles. *He would write influential reviews of the book in America and Great Britain, and he introduced Bradbury to Aldous Huxley and other expatriate British writers in Los Angeles. Isherwood became an ally in his uphill battle against mainstream critical bias; in his next letter to Walt Bradbury at Doubleday, Ray Bradbury used the Isherwood discovery to advance his hope that Doubleday would seek out other mainstream critics to review the* Chronicles. *Walt Bradbury would urge restraint in his response, however, noting that at this late post-publication date, "it is not only impossible to force such a procedure, but also dangerous to try. Such things sometimes backfire."*

Ray Bradbury
33 South Venice Blvd
Venice, Calif.

July 22, 1950

Dear Brad:

[. . .] You will be glad to know that Christopher Isherwood telephoned me the other night in a state of high excitement. To quote him: "I've just finished *The Martian Chronicles* and I'm insane about it. It's a really amazing book and I congratulate you on it."

Isherwood will do a review on the book for *Tomorrow*.[25] This is the first decent break in the open field that the book has had. Now if we could only get one from Edmund Wilson or Fadiman. If there was only some way you could get to these people and say, "Look, this book is being neglected, for various reasons; not because it is a book that people have read and not liked, but because it is a book most of the big critics have never even laid eyes upon." I think the Isherwood plug might be the first in a series of discoveries by fine critics. And all because I happened to run into Isherwood two weeks ago and gave him a copy of the *Chronicles*. Pure coincidence. Isherwood said that people had come to visit him three nights in a row and had sat reading the *Chronicles* instead of talking. I am delighted.

Do you think there is anything we can do, something special, a few phone calls, or a special delivery copy of the book, to Fadiman or Hamilton Basso or someone, at this late date?[26] I suppose not, but I can't help thinking that something might be done; this Isherwood incident has encouraged me no end.

But enough of this chatter, Brad. In closing, again let me thank you for all you have done for me in the past year, and for these new allowances and licenses to keep your author happy. The next year looks fine indeed. My best to you, Brad.

Yours,
Ray

After the early success of Doubleday's The Martian Chronicles *and* The
Illustrated Man, *Ray Bradbury met with Walt Bradbury in the summer
of 1951 and signed a contract for a mainstream novel based on the stories
that had emerged from memories of his childhood years in Waukegan, Illinois. He had been fusing an increasing number of these stories into a book
concept since 1945, and he convinced Walt Bradbury that his momentum
would carry him through to the completion of what he now called* Summer
Morning, Summer Night. *Along with Don Congdon, both Bradburys saw
this book as a natural evolution into the broader reading market. Ray Bradbury was not yet confident sustaining novel-length fiction, however, and in
March 1952 Walt Bradbury made his concerns clear. That letter, and Ray
Bradbury's response, provide intriguing context for one of the few serious
writing blocks he would encounter in his long career. It would take five more
years before part of this novel was published as the novelized story-cycle*
Dandelion Wine.

March 10, 1952

Dear Ray:

Your letter of March fifth is really disappointing, although I'm afraid I
expected it.

I had wanted very much to publish *Summer Morning, Summer Night*
this fall, and I think it's necessary for your book market and for your
general standing not to delay too long with another title.

I appreciate the difficulty in assembling the material. But to put it
bluntly, you will remember that this book was virtually completed a year
ago, and it is, after all, not a new theme and plot which has to be worked
out, but an already accepted framework which needs only the fitting
of parts. It is difficult to understand the delay, and it's a temptation to
assume that one of two things is happening: you are either putting it
aside too frequently and too casually, or you are up against a block in
the completion of it.

The precise date of publication is something that can always be adjusted, of course. The thing that is more dangerous is that you will never finish it at all.

In spite of your protestations to the contrary, there is a great danger that it will never be finished if it's a case of a block in writing. Your explanations and predictions in the last few letters have an ominously familiar ring. I have seen this situation before with other people.

If the difficulty is that you are stymied and just can't seem to go ahead with it, I have a suggestion to make. When you get this letter, would you put everything else aside and sit down and write me a long, long letter explaining just how you feel about this book. This will be confidential between us, and in it I want you to tell me all the things that are good about the book idea, and anything which might be bad about it. You might also include a detailed outline of how the story is shaping up. In other words, talk it all out until you can't think of anything else in the world to say about it. Now this obviously is a long distance, air mail, analyst's couch, and while I don't purport to be a psychologist (or even a dianeticist) it may break the dam for you.

Of course if it's something besides this kind of a block this isn't going to help any, but in any case I hope you will be honest with me and let me know exactly what you are up against. Believe me, I'm not interested in putting pressure on you, or being vindictive: I want to help.

Best regards,
Brad
Walter I. Bradbury

Walt Bradbury's concern over lack of progress on the Illinois novel, then titled Summer Morning, Summer Night, *prompted Ray Bradbury to immediately articulate a vision for the work in a letter that extended into one of his deepest explorations of his writing process and the truths he hoped to unfold. Most of the stories he describes here would eventually be extracted, with others, to become* Dandelion Wine (1957). *The surviving full draft is dated March 13; an unlocated final version went out to Doubleday on the fifteenth, prompting a more positive response from his editor.*

March 13, 1952

Ray Bradbury
10750 Clarkson Rd.
Los Angeles 64, Calif.

Dear Brad:

I can't say how much I appreciate your good and friendly letter of March
10th. Your offer of help is a fine, sincere gesture, and I will keep it in
mind should I really feel the need to turn to someone.

However, I am not as disappointed in the book and my failure to
complete it, as you are. I feel very well about it. If I felt very badly I
would be the first to throw myself into your friendly arms, have a good
cry, and proceed from there. But I do not feel badly. There are days
when the book bores me stiff; on those days I am wise enough to let it lie
and work in the file. I am a great believer in trusting my subconscious.
It hasn't failed me yet. It's like feeding information into one of these
new-fangled calculators, then going to bed; in the morning, there, on
a crisp new white sheet of paper, is the answer. Carry this simile over,
yet stronger, to my book or—for that matter—to all my work, and you
have my attitude toward "creativity." I never push. I'm afraid of locking
gears or breaking a tooth off. I know that a bad three days now means a
good two days at the end of the week. When I hit a bad spell I don't just
sit there, I go paint a window sash, read a book of poetry, or take a long
walk. I'm damned prolific anyway. After three bad days I will have a run,
like I had recently, when I wrote five short stories in five days. I wasn't
pushing, I wasn't trying to break any Derlethian records,[27] I was simply
happy getting all the totals out of my mind that had been gearing around
quietly in there during the bad days, even though I didn't know it. Three
of the new stories will go into the Illinois book. These stories were only
first drafts, of course, and will have to have 2nd, 3rd, and 4th goings-over.
But I know by now that the good stuff comes quick, and the bad stuff
slow, for me anyway. If I fuss and fidget and tinker and monkey, it's bad.
If I let it flow and get excited it's good.

So there you have it. The book is going slowly because I won't fuss and fidget and push and monkey with it. I wait for the excitement. Not a passive waiting by any means; not neglect, at all. I read a hell of a lot of Robert Frost, I find he excites me and drives me back to my typewriter. I get the old motor warmed up with Frost anti-freeze and then conk along merrily on all eight. I've even, belatedly, found inspiration in some of Shakespeare's sonnets (which had been ruined for me in high school). The book is never out of my mind but, more important, it is never out of my subconscious. I wait for those good fast, wonderful first drafts of material to come, Brad, and then I know I'm on the track and heading for the truth. Every good story I ever wrote is the product of a fast first draft; the later rewrites, up to a total of seven, simply reshaped the material a bit, and cut it down. Cutting seems to be half the problem. The mind, in emotionalizing, babbles a thing twice; it's the duty of the literary censor, next day, to step in with shears and cut away the waste material. It is my contention that people like Jean Stafford, who started out brilliantly, are working themselves away from the truth in themselves by either doing a slow, and embroidery-like first draft, or else editing the soul out of their material later. A fine balance has to be maintained. A writer's own truth is in the violent spurt of first work; if he lets the quasi-truth, the literary and style-conscious truth peer over his shoulder too often, he's a duck under glass, beautiful but, like a cooked fowl, heartless, gizzardless, gutless.

Don may have mentioned to you an incident that occurred to me about ten days ago. I was on a bus coming home from Hollywood when a boy, fourteen, leapt on, ran down the aisle, swung himself with a resilient ape-motion into a seat and, minutes later, at his own stop, leapt up, bounced off the bus and ran, the happiest gazelle in the city, off home. I was absolutely entranced with his energy; I'd seen him do the same thing other days. He never walked, he ran. The world never stopped for him; he saw it only as flashes going by. And why? Well, I discovered one reason that afternoon. He had on a pair of new tennis shoes. Do you remember what a new pair of tennis shoes meant to you when you were a kid, Brad? I remember very well. There were two big events every summer; one taking off your winter shoes and going barefoot in the fresh new grass. God what a feeling! And number two? Well, in order to get you back into *any* kind of shoes at all, during the summer, your parents had to be shrewd. There's only one better thing than being barefooted. And that is having a new pair of tennis shoes! They are a gift from the old Grecian gods. With them, you are quite obviously transformed to Mercury. Somebody has taken the resilience of the antelope, and mixed it with equal parts of lightning and India rubber and shaped them to your soles. Why, on a summer afternoon, a boy with a new pair of sneakers (much like the Red Shoes legend) can't stop running or trying new feats of dare-devilry and skill. One can leap mountains, rivers, ten story buildings and even—four foot bushes! Do you remember the feeling in your feet, of suppleness and magic! I had forgotten. Until that day when I saw the boy run *everywhere*! And I remembered it all. The first days with new sneakers are rare fine days. The magic must be taken advantage of, however, for in a few days, the gravity of a terribly realistic earth, drags one back down out of the sky, one is earth-bound again. Until the next summer, the next new pair of shoes, and the re-enchantment.

I mention the above small incident because it will be part of the book. It is a true thing. Everybody knows that truth. It will appear in the book as no more than four or five hundred words, more or less, a small thing indeed, but the small things go to build the big things.[28] From the small truths, big truths. If the reader nods to himself, you are well on the way toward capturing him *en toto*. If he shakes his head, you have missed the truth and thrown him off. I have made haste slowly to finish the book up with such truths as the above one blended into the whole. The book will be remembered if at all, for the little truths I have found here or there by lifting up boards or rocks or by surprising them sunning themselves on a river bank. I want this to be my finest book, as each new book must be finer than the last. I believe in it and am happy with it and will send it to you when I am happiest of all.

The truth is, I only *thought*, and convinced you of it, too, that the book was near completion, when I brought it to New York a year ago. Yes, most of the stories were complete, but the framework which seemed adequate, needed an amazing amount of fleshing out and slow feeding. I hold myself responsible for giving you a finish date which I later found impossible. I hope I never predict a date on a book again. The real essence of a book doesn't rise by the clock or the calendar, unfortunately.

I have a new story in the book about an inventor in my home town who tries to build "The Happiness Machine," something to make everyone happy for-ever. I have completed a new short about "Dandelion Wine" and I have added one in which a small boy, 12 years old, for the first time in his life, finds out that he is alive![29] There are two great shocks in every person's life. One comes on the day when one discovers that one is a living, breathing, seeing, feeling creature. I seem to recall I first discovered this when I was about ten. The other shock came, belatedly, when I was fourteen. I was in a motion picture one night and for no reason I could recall, I suddenly realized that some day I must die. I was absolutely panicked. The panic passed after a moment, but that cold fist gripped my heart and froze my blood. I came from the theatre, forgetting the incident, sublimely certain I would live forever, as most children believe. Nevertheless, I was shaken. I suppose that these two basic shocks mark the beginnings of philosophy—or, rather, conscious philosophy—for everyone. It's what we do with these two new knowledges that decides the pattern of our lives.

Jesus God! In writing that last paragraph to you, I have solved another minor problem in my book. Now I'll have to retype that paragraph into my notes for use this afternoon.

This is a long letter but, dammit, I enjoy talking to you. You asked for it. Bend an ear. I have a new story called "The Beautiful Child" and the problem that has faced us all when, in passing along a crowded street we have seen, bourne through the world, a child so radiant with beauty and curiosity that it can unlock the steel heart of the future. Surely this child is marked for superior things, for fame, fortune, for love, security, for poetry and the arts. And then, in looking down, we see the face of the father and mother carrying the child. Depression, rancor, ill-will, stupidity, slovenliness, bad grace, prejudice, and ignorance, the rejection of love and beauty, here. And this child, born of such as these!? Impossible. And this child left to their ignorant mercies? Murder! Murder most foul. Seize the child, then, and run! Make the child your own, give it what you *know* they cannot give it. For Christ's sake, stop the Murder![30]

This is merely the jumping off place, the theme for one of the new stories. This story, as do all the others, illustrates my basic theme

and conflict: Love. This book is nothing else if it is not a book about
love. Every story touches upon and illuminates the problem of love
as the nucleus of life. Even the Lonely One, poor unhappy bastard, is
a symbol of love gone wrong. My boy asks, why grow up, why become
an adult, to face only war, disease, depression, and death? Is it worth
it? My answer is not a manufactured one, it does not falsify the facts.
Yes, life is worth the effort, maturity is worth taking a crack at—if you
have love. Without it, you might as well go off and dig your own pit.
Love is the great lubrication that keeps the machinery of friendship
and business and marriage going. Without it you get Hitlers, Stalins,
McCarthys, gangsters, insane asylums, and so on down the list. I haven't
any panacea to sell, I'm afraid I'm more realistic about this theme than
say, Saroyan; I certainly hope I'm sincere. Anyway, you're going to get
a better book than the one I showed you in outline ten months ago.
Better in ten thousand ways, because I've been trying to isolate the non-
filterable virus Love and I think I have enough of it to make my book
glow, if only faintly, in the dark. [. . .]

Time to wind this up. The book will continue slowly, but, I feel, will
gain momentum from here on. No predictions; I've sworn off. [. . .]
Nothing I can do now can make people remember me if they don't
want to. I hope that with *Summer Morning, Summer Night* I can at least
snap my fingers to get their attention for just one evening in their life.
Everything after that is gravy. Thanks for your good, friendly help!

My very *very* best wishes!

Ray

ANTHONY BOUCHER

*The accomplished genre critic, editor, and writer Anthony Boucher (William
Anthony Parker White, 1911–1968) considered Bradbury a major storytelling
talent throughout the 1940s, and in 1949 he moved quickly to buy Bradbury
stories for his new digest-format* Magazine of Fantasy & Science Fiction. *A
rich correspondence ensued, at times discussing Bradbury's creative vision and
themes; this particular in-depth response was prompted in part by "Ray Brad-*

bury: Beginner," an essay that Boucher had recently placed in William F. No-lan's Ray Bradbury Review.

Jan. 10, 1952

Dear Tony:

Thanks so much for your letter and for your article in the Bill Nolan magazine. I was on the point of writing you when your letter came. There is no doubt in my mind that yours is the best balanced and fairest article in the book. Mag and I especially liked: "Immediately after puberty seemed to set in the Fall of man's year—"

Incidentally, it wasn't good commercial advice that took me from the *Weird* field over into s-f. The fact is, I was writing s-f as far back as 1935 when I was 15, with only an occasional venture into the supernatural. In fact, *Dark Carnival*, to me, is an irony. I never intended writing in the weird field. I didn't much care for it, it had been run into the ground. All of my first submissions, from 1936 to 1941, were s-f, and very bad. I got so many rejections that I decided to try a few weird stories. Thus, my entry into the weird field, was a commercial accident. And once I got going and seeing my way clear in the field, I began having fun, writing what I thought were variations or reversals on old themes. Later, in 1946, I knew that I had come to the end of the trail. I knew that I could go on writing weird stories and selling them to WT, but I also knew that from that year on they would not be good weird stories, for my vein was run dry and I would have to *force* to keep going. Only then did I turn my full force around and point it at s-f, where I had originally intended to go.

Your point about my doing certain themes over again is very interesting. I got to thinking about it this morning, tracing back the formation of certain stories like "The Exiles," "Pillar of Fire" and "Usher II," which are all cousins. These were all done because I felt there was still something to be said about that particular problem.[31] I tried to keep them different, and yet, invariably, resemblances crept in. Looking back now, I find I don't care much for "The Exiles," but prefer the ending on "Pillar of Fire," and "Usher II," *en toto.* I know you'll find this hard to believe, but I wrote none of these with the thought, "if that sold, this ought to too." I just had fun. I've always had a helluva lot of fun working out ideas until I, and God help them, everyone else, is tired of them. I think I've been terribly lucky here, because until I was 27 and got married, I never needed money so badly that I had to slant, and I said to hell with everything and wrote what I wanted to write, and if it sold, fine! but if it didn't, I went on and wrote something else. I trained myself, when young, or rather the Depression trained us, as a family, not to think about money if we didn't have it. Our family was on relief in 1938, the year I graduated from high school, and my allowance was 25 cents a week. In 1939, while living at home, I got my job selling newspapers on a street-corner, which paid me from 5 to 10 dollars a week until 1943 when, with a few story sales under my belt, I gave up the corner. But I was so conditioned to being poor by then, that when, in 1943, I made about a thousand dollars writing, I thought I was rich, and used it sparingly and with gratitude. When my income went up to $2000 in 1944 and then 3000 dollars in 1945 I thought I was the luckiest guy in the world, it was all gravy, I was still living at home, and I could afford to say to hell with everything, let's just have fun writing what we want to write. The few times in my life I slanted, i.e., "The Candle" (*WT*) "The Monster Makers," "Morgue Ship," "Lazarus Come Forth" (from *Planet*) the results were so frighteningly bad I soon learned to go back and relax and try to find my own way through the morass.

All of which is to say that the Martian stories, the censorship stories, the weird stories, each in their own time, and vein, came about in a leisurely and sloppy way which is my way of living. I didn't plan or hope to commercialize forever on each vein, I just wanted to work my way through it to the end of the tunnel, and along the way, I'm sure, I bored a lot of customers stiff. But, in the end, I was able to discard all the repetitions and put the *Chronicles* together and *Dark Carnival*, and now, with my latest bent, my Illinois book. After that? Only God knows. [. . .]

My very very friendliest wishes to you, Mick, Phyllis, the handsome well-behaved boys, and all and everyone in the Little Men's group.[32] And my gratitude and appreciation to you, again, for the *fine* article. As ever,

Ray

"A Sound of Thunder," with its famous butterfly effect, has always been one of Bradbury's best-known and most often-reprinted science fiction tales. Its first appearance in the June 28, 1952, issue of Collier's *was marred by an editorial suppression of the dramatic ending.* Magazine of Fantasy & Science Fiction *cofounders Anthony Boucher and Mick McComas often purchased second serial rights for Bradbury stories, but they balked at this one: "Ha! We don't believe a word of it." The following letter did not change his friends' minds ("sorry we're such obtuse bastards"), but it did set out Bradbury's essential rationale for one of the most popular stories in Doubleday's* The Golden Apples of the Sun *(1953).*

August 7, 1952

Dear Tony & Mick:

Enclosed, find carbon of "A Sound of Thunder." I have done a rewrite on this, which will go into my new Doubleday book. I have restored my original ending, which *Collier's* cut without telling me; and I have added another two hundred words to the ending which may be somewhat more to your liking.

Mick, I got a helluva bang out of your note on this. Where you say, "A minute change in time would have infinitely wide ramifications . . . but *not* such minor changes—a world apparently just the same save for spelling & who won the election!"

Mick, old bean, why didn't you *tell* me you owned a Time Machine!? I could have come to you for technical advice.

The point is, we *don't* know whether a small change in the Past would result in a big change in the future, a small change, or *none at all*. Or, for that matter, whether a big change in the Past would make a catastrophe in the future or none whatever. I thought I had made this clear in the beginning of my story where I have the Time Safari people say "We don't know." "But until we *do* know we're playing it safe" or words to that effect. The irony of my story lies in the fact that a *small* change in the Past produced a *small* change in the future. I planted this fact when I mentioned the balance between insects and crop harvests, early in the story. And a lack of certain insects could result in a change in harvest, and thus change a political aspect a slight bit, in the Future, thus putting into power a Fascist, instead of a sensibly progressive, government. I was certain that the reader would draw conclusions such as this from the plantings I carefully put in the story. Also, I thought the reader would be delighted with the irony of the *small* change, instead of the great chaos often portrayed in other stories. And my final irony is that while it *seems* a small change, it is a major change, a disaster, for Travis and Eckels who must now live under a tyranny instead of a democracy. It is all relative; and therefore I thought I had accomplished a neat, and relative, irony.

But anyway, without changing my basic irony in any way, I think I have clarified the ending, with something of a McComas fast-ball breaking over the plate. Hope you find it a more logical yarn, this time through. My best to both of you!

Yours,

Ray

The publication of Charles Beaumont's "Free Dirt" in the May 1955 issue of Fantasy & Science Fiction *led Bradbury to relate how his and Beaumont's creativity crossed paths in a letter to F&SF editor Tony Boucher. Using the same title, Bradbury would finally find a way of writing his story without encroaching on Beaumont's original in 1996. The letter documents how Bradbury's early concept for the story varied from Beaumont's.*

[late March, 1955]

Bradbury
10750 Clarkson Rd.
L.A. 64, Calif.

Dear Tony:

[. . .] I was delighted to see the Chas. Beaumont story in your current issue. Did Chuck tell you? when I was younger (about eighteen) I used to live by the same graveyard, near Washington St. and Normandie, where the sign FREE DIRT hung. I used to walk past that sign every night, and when first I saw it, put down notes for a story.[33] I still have notes in my files on it. What a shame, my story was never finished, so that I could have sent it on to you as a follow-up of Chuck's handling. It's always fascinating to see how two people approach the same stimulus. As I recall, my notes on the story are in some ways startlingly similar to Chuck's; the main use of the FREE DIRT being to cover a garden in a backyard. However, my story would have concerned an old couple who use the dirt and are then horrified at the strange grasses and flowers and bushes and trees that spring whitely up from the dark soil. How I would have ended it, I still don't know. Anyway, Chuck got there fustest with the mostest;[34] I'm happy for him. [. . .]

Yrs.

Ray

As Bradbury worked through his first full draft of Something Wicked This Way Comes, *he related his first impression of the post-*Sputnik *reissue of* The Martian Chronicles, *and the new introduction by Clifton Fadiman, which portrayed Bradbury as an anti-technology writer who believes "that human beings are still mental and moral children who cannot be trusted with the terrifying toys they have by some tragic accident invented." In closing, Bradbury alludes to Boucher's retirement from his founding editorship of* The Magazine of Fantasy & Science Fiction.

August 7, 1958

Dear Tony:

Thanks for yours of July 7th . . . this month went fast, with working on a new novel . . .

By the time Doubleday pointed out that they would have to re-set *Golden Apples of the Sun* and *The Illustrated Man* in order to give me my British version of *The Martian Chronicles*, all of which they said might be confusing to various readers who may have bought one or the other of the books, I caved in and said okay okay, let's do the *Chronicles* as is and save revisions for the day when, many years from now, some sort of other special edition is due.[35]

No, I assure you, I'm not as anti-scientific as Fadiman makes me out. I'm saddened by the things we humans do with the devices given us. And I'm excited to think these same devices, with changes, might someday give man the channels whereby his most murderous qualities could find release, could be short-circuited before they ricocheted among men themselves. I have always, as you know, been fascinated by robots and wonder if the day mightn't come when it would be feasible to do bloody murder on mechanical forms, thus releasing our furious destructive energy. All kinds of problems arise immediately, of course, in law, psychology, philosophy, ethics, you name it. But I would like to go into these more, in the future. I've been rewriting my old robot story recently, "Punishment Without Crime," and have done one about a humanist-disposed Grandma who raises children to be better humans than their own mother could.[36] I won't go into this in this letter but will hope for many good hours of talk with you and Phyllis when you hit L.A. [. . .]

If you haven't seen Disneyland before, you'll go crazy over it. The Peter Pan ride is absolutely wonderful, as is the Jungle Boat Ride. My first trip out, I went with Charles Laughton. You can imagine what a ball we had. [. . .]

The thing I'm most curious about is your reaction to *Dandelion Wine*. It may well be the book didn't come off for you. It got bad reviews all over England, while being very well reviewed here, save for *Harper's*.

My new book, *A Medicine for Melancholy*, is at the typesetter's now, for Doubleday. 23 stories. Out next February. S-F, fantasy, stories of yesterday morning, this noon, and tomorrow midnight, a little of everything in it. Brad seems happy.

I hope this long vacation away from *F&SF* has meant all kinds of goodies for us in the next year. One always hopes for another Boucher mystery, but a Boucher s-f novel will serve mighty well!

Enough! Hurry down here! Bring everybody!

Best, as ever,

Ray

ROBERT A. GOTTLIEB

Beginning as an editor with Simon & Schuster in the 1950s, Robert Gottlieb (1931–2023) became editor-in-chief of this major trade publishing house before moving on to Alfred A. Knopf as editor-in-chief and eventually as president. In these roles he was able to bring Ray Bradbury to Simon & Schuster in the early 1960s and was instrumental in Bradbury's late 1960s shift to Knopf as his primary trade publisher, where the author stayed for nearly a quarter century. Bradbury and his agent, Don Congdon, felt that Gottlieb could provide the best possible marketing support and editorial guidance for Something Wicked This Way Comes (1962), *the author's first full-length novel. With Congdon, Gottlieb was able to guide Bradbury through the last of four drafts of the long novel in spite of the household challenges that the author narrates here.*

January 7th, 1962

Dear Bob:

This is a report on the mumps, the measles, and the virus. If you think this was a week of steady progress on the novel, you are way off in left-field somewhere and no one is popping flies to you. If anyone asks you what S&S writers do in their spare time, outside of fighting with the gardener, buttering the sitter, and putting out the trash, you can say that Bradbury, this week anyway, went around rinsing the gummy substances off the doorknobs. Whenever doorknobs get gummy, you have a sick house. The children run about with gelatinous noses and glutinous fingers—thus the doorknobs. There are days when one does not know whether to hose out or burn down such a menage. Four daughters, four varieties of illness, a sick wife, a fixed cat, and—despair.

This is to say, therefore, that the novel stands at 320 pages now. I had hoped to go higher—but I was strafed out of action on innumerable occasions . . . in fact found myself hoping I, too, would come down with something, so I could take myself to bed and hide from the walking wounded in the halls. But, no luck. The moving finger writes,[37] but only slowly . . . which leaves us, still, with about 100 more pages to go.

More from me, in one week, on *Wicked*. [. . .]

God willing, the doorknobs will get unstuck . . . as will the typewriter!

Cordial wishes from,
Ray
Bradbury

Even before the release of Something Wicked This Way Comes, *Bradbury and Gottlieb had established an extended dialogue concerning the contents of a new story collection, eventually titled* The Machineries of Joy (1964). *These discussions often included the fate of Bradbury's Irish stories, and extended to include* Leviathan '99, *a new stand-alone book-length project that transformed his very successful* Moby Dick *screenplay into a parallel Space Age adventure set two centuries in the future. Bob Gottlieb's guiding comments below prompted an animated response from Bradbury.*

5/14/62

Dear Ray,

Tried to get you by phone today, but apparently you're off to the Fair.[38] Hope it was fun.

I can't call again because *I'm* off to Dallas and New Orleans, for a strange kind of vacation, and won't be back till June 6. But before I go, I wanted to tell you the following:

Your galleys arrived; all is well, and we'll be sure you see pages.

The production department is coping with the title page crisis, and (I hope) will have solved it to your liking.[39]

What are we missing for the story collection? And do you definitely want to include everything we've got? You were undecided about the Irish stories when we discussed it. It's completely up to you, but if you want my opinion, it's that they strike an odd note. Still, you're an odd-note striker.

Moby. I was caught by your "presentation," and am very enthusiastic about the whole project. I want to read it. My only worry is this—that in the sample pages I read at the beginning, it seemed to me that although it was alright to quote Melville directly, it was less wise to paraphrase and echo his sentences. In other words, I think we should talk soberly about the *language* of the book, the part you're writing. Perhaps I don't understand your purpose yet, but I think that a book written in modern language, following the structure and drama of *M.D.*, might be more acceptable than a comparable book written in Melvillean prose— which itself, as you know, is an echo of Jacobean prose, and not always successful at that.

Maybe this is what you already intend. Maybe it isn't, and what you're thinking of is better. Let's talk about it before you've really plunged in.

Whale Ho! [. . .]

Bob

June 3rd, 1962

Mr. Robert Gottlieb
Simon and Schuster, Inc.
630 Fifth Avenue
New York 20, New York

Dear Bob:

Thanks for yours of May 14th, just prior to your jaunt to Dallas and New Orleans. I hope your trip was a stimulating and eventful one for you all.

About the story collection *The Machineries of Joy*. If you send the manuscript back to me now, I'll work on it during the summer. There isn't much to be done to most of the stories, but I will go over each one for minor cuts and deletions, especially on some of the older science-fiction tales, parts of which are now a trifle naïve in the light of our fast-advancing Space people.

As for the Irish stories, I feel they should remain in the book to make it a richer mixture. One of the troubles I've had over the years with snob critics and snob readers is them running up on stage while I'm playing the harp and crying out, "Sure, but can ya play the tuba!?" I then play the tuba. "Sure," cry they, "but can ya play the oboe!?" I play the oboe. "Piano!" cry they. Piano. "Now," they say, "would you mind letting down the sandbags and putting up the curtains, and take a few tickets while you're at it. . . . ?" I do all this. And, having done it, am still, in some quarters, patted on the head, no better than Dr. Johnson's dog.

So, as in the case of *A Medicine for Melancholy*, I think it is best to have both frontal, backel, sidal, and topal attacks[40] on the reader. Let us be rocket men, let us be sea creatures, let us be Irish, and let us be dogmatic priests bewildered by the whole damn affair. Let the book be a revolving door, and you never guessing if you'll come out in patio or lobby, raw air or false illumination. Let us throw the compass overboard, Bob, and steer for the rocks.

I'm glad for your excitement *re Leviathan '99*. I don't think we'll have to worry too much about the style in which I write it. Once into the task, it will come of itself, and much of the self-conscious stuff you see in the early work, will dissolve away. Later, when we stand back and look at the finished book, we can spot the errors and trim them to size. The essence of Melville is what I'm after, the spirit, not the style itself. And gradually even the essence, of course, will suffer a sea-change from brine to meteor-dust, from island coral to mineral fire sifting in space. Melville will give me my transfusions, but I must, finally, live for myself. His symbols will be transmuted. His hermit life among people can never quite be mine. His sexual naiveté, or his suppression of his sexual knowledge, if you wish, cannot be mine, for, after all, he lives off there in the 19th Century, and I stand here on a pedestrian island on a shrieking continental Turnpike in the mid-20th. All the more reason to be fascinated and excited with the job of tenterhooking the gizzard of the *Whale* and make him star-Leviathan.

How soon do I see a proof of the jacket of *Something Wicked*? I am fantastically greedy to have one to carry about and show people. How *fine* it is.

I hear from France that Truffaut definitely moves ahead to make

Fahrenheit 451 there. In a letter over this weekend, Truffaut also
mentioned meeting Barrault and hearing from him that Barrault will
use not only live actors but gigantic marionettes in order to stage *The
Martian Chronicles* this winter.[41] Sounds great.

That's all for now. Best to you and yours,

Ray

The fall 1962 release of Something Wicked This Way Comes *led to a discussion between Bradbury and Gottlieb over various reviews of and influences on the novel. These letters played out across the final days of the Cuban Missile Crisis, prompting the allusions to it that both Gottlieb and Bradbury make in context. The core of the discussion, however, centered on Charles Finney's 1930 novel,* The Circus of Dr. Lao. *Finney's frustrations dated back to the 1956 publication of the Ray Bradbury–edited story anthology,* The Circus of Dr. Lao and Other Improbable Stories; *against Bradbury's advice, the anthology went to press with Bradbury's name positioned in a way that appears to suggest authorship of the short Finney title novel. Bradbury's comments below on his successful four-year court struggle over* Fahrenheit 451 *emerged in large part from the United States Seventh Circuit Court of Appeals 2–1 reversal of a federal district court decision in favor of CBS, which paved the way to a final settlement in Bradbury's favor.*

October 30, 1962

Dear Ray:

This seems to be the week for bad reviews. I've just got an advance
copy of this one, from next Sunday's *N.Y. Times*. I don't know who
Lillian de la Torre is, but she doesn't seem to like us.[42] What I want to
know is: what is this style of yours that these reviewers are objecting
to? I recognize the symptoms they note, but they seem to me exactly
appropriate to the content and tone of the novel. It's very upsetting—
not only because it's an attack, but because I'm beginning to think I
don't know how to read.

But I do know how to read.

Also enclosed is an extraordinary letter from Charles Finney, which seems to me almost impossible to answer. Lawyers would probably have us not answer at all, or at least let lawyers answer it. But I want you to see it first. Perhaps you'll send it back to me, with comment, and we'll cope from there. Or maybe you'll want to answer it yourself. But if you do, you probably *should* show your answer to your own lawyer, or to ours. Law suits, expensive even when won, have been started from far less than this.

Enough bad news. The good news is: a) we seem to have achieved a nervous peace, after the terrible fright of last week. And this is the best news I've ever known. b) sales continue. Last week, over 200, bringing the total to 8,237, if you can believe our "stock status reports"—which you can't. The best thing about them is, that we can have sold either fewer copies or more copies than they indicate. Don't worry, though, all will come clear on royalty statements.

I'm sending you half-a-dozen copies of *Something Wicked*, in case you've run out. Thanks again for helping out the stores.

Best,

Bob

Hallowe'en.

October 31, 1962

Dear Bob:

I appreciated your two protective and warm letters this week, first about the *New Yorker* review, which I haven't seen as yet myself,[43] and now about the de la Torre *NYTimes* review and Finney.

To take first things first, de la Torre's review sounds like a frustrated, and therefore slightly vindictive, would-be fantasy writer's attempt to take off my skin. The harder she tries, the more she fails. This review didn't begin to get to me the way Prescott's did,[44] for he injected an unfair reference into his piece, intimating that I had based my novel on a television script, which of course riled me. Sour grapes is the best answer to de la Torre.

Finney's letter is one that shouldn't be answered by you or me or anyone. He obviously hasn't read either my novel or his own novel, lately. When I was working on *Something Wicked*, over the years, I had heard of *Dr. Lao* from friends, and purposely delayed reading it until I had laid out the choreography of *Wicked* and done a first draft. I have always been fearful of and careful of influences. That's why I rarely read in the s-f or fantasy field anymore.[45] I don't want, even unwittingly, to carry something into my work from someone else. If I should carry some of Robert Frost into my stories, well and good. He is a poet, and I love to read poets and, if lucky, unearth single lines that I allow to germinate and become short stories. I have written Robert Hillyer and told him that a single few lines of a poem about a mermaid found near Plymouth Rock inspired me to write "The Shoreline at Sunset" story in my *A Medicine for Melancholy*. But inspiration is one thing, indirect or unwitting or direct plagiarism is another.

Anyway, I didn't read *Dr. Lao* until it was time for me to write my introduction to the Bantam book, and then, embarrassingly, after I had agreed to do it, found the book to be very sparse, only fitfully imaginative, somewhat vulgar, and not at all the set of fireworks my friends had led me to expect. If you read my introduction you'll find I hedged my opinion all along the way.

So, in sum, the only resemblance between Finney's novel and mine is he wrote one about a Circus, I wrote one about a carnival. Beyond that gapes the Abyss. The best test would be to ask any competent fantasy or s-f editor who knows both books, rather than take Finney, or myself, at our word.

But I'm an expert now, at plagiarism law, having fought my suit against CBS and *Playhouse 90* all the way to the United States Supreme Court on their stealing *Fahrenheit 451*, and winning. We settled, as you know, about a year ago.[46] And in the process I helped write part of the new law, the papers and analyses of what plagiarism really is. I'm proud of the clarification I hope my case has provided for other writers. The whole thing boils down to: Ideas cannot be copyrighted or protected, but "sequences of texture, sequences of events, based on an Idea, *can*." For instance, I can write a story tomorrow called "To Build a Fire," using Jack London's title and idea, as long as I challenge my hero differently, and adventure him in such a way that all the textures and details are different and in no way resemble "in sequence" or "any inferred sequence" London's story. Just because London wrote a story about a man freezing to death in the wilds doesn't mean all writers after him must give up trying to write about death by freezing . . . It means they must find fresh ways to use that idea, so as not to infringe on his sequential originality.

Enough. If Mr. Finney ever takes the two books to a lawyer, he will come a cropper, immediately, for no honest lawyer would take on a case where there is none. His letter makes me sad, for it is unfortunate if he is making himself unhappy because of a book that does not resemble his own. This is needless grievance-collecting. I hope he gets to work on something new and puts his mind where it belongs, on vitality and creation, rather than on fruitless comparisons.

I am enclosing Finney's letter, for your files. Again, I don't think it should be answered. Thanks.

The sales report on *Wicked* is heartening. I am, sir, working, right now, on the stories to go into *The Machineries of Joy*.

I, too, am relieved at the turn of events in the last week. The first day, I was rather stunned, and then I began to think again of the fact that parties and policies no longer run the world but, to quote the old familiar "things are in the saddle and ride men." So the atom bomb controls, in the final analysis, both Kennedy and Khrushchev, whether they like it or not. To look into the face of Annihilation can be satisfying only to a mad man. Luckily, neither is mad.

I have sent on to Don some color transparencies plus some story-board sketches from our just finished film *Icarus Montgolfier Wright*, the 15 minute semi-animated project which we have been working on for the past two years here. [. . .]

Icarus is being screened at the White House this week. This, I hear, from Arthur Schlesinger's secretary. Whether or not the president will sit in, I doubt, with the huge problems confronting him. But Schlesinger will screen it anyway, along with George Stevens, Jr.[47]

That's all for now. Thanks again for your helpful words, given me at just the right time.

Best to you all,
Ray
Bradbury

AVRAM DAVIDSON

The Hugo Award–winning and often genre-defying fantasy, science fiction, and mystery writer Avram Davidson (1923–1993) edited The Magazine of Fantasy & Science Fiction (F&SF) *from 1962 to 1964. During his tenure as editor, Davidson began the tradition of occasional author-specific issues of the magazine by publishing issues celebrating Theodore Sturgeon (September 1962) and Ray Bradbury (May 1963). Davidson and Bradbury were friends, due in part to their mutual transcendence of genre rules; in his 1970s introduction to Davidson's collected stories, Bradbury proclaimed, "This is what storytelling once was, and can be again, if we leave it in such capable hands." The following letters show how the special Ray Bradbury issue of* F&SF *grew out of this personal and professional relationship.*

August 13/62

1050 Fell St.
SanFranCal

Dear Ray,

Sorry that our messages got all interbollixed so that we never got together again. I was going to write to you soon about something but a letter in today's mail made me decide to do it Now. Joseph Ferman, the publisher of *F&SF*, and I had discussed the possibility of a Special Ray Bradbury Issue of *F&SF* even before the Special Sturgeon Issue came out. He liked the idea and felt we ought to do it when we got a story from you, provided the story was long enough. Following publication of the Sturgeon number several fans wrote in suggesting special Bradbury and Heinlein numbers (Mr. F. and I had also discussed the idea of one for Heinlein. We have not considered any other "specials," nor do I think we will, than these three). Then today I got a letter from Bill Nolan making the same suggestion, plus. Plus a rewrite of his profile of you in *Rogue*, plus an index to be prepared by him, plus "Time Intervening" if you agree. He wants to start right away as he is in between assignments on his auto books. I feel that we might well give him the assignment if you feel that you can give us a semi-firm commitment as to when, approximately, we might expect to have a story from you. I do not expect a *date*; right now I think just letting us know what quarter of the year—and what year!—might be sufficient.

Right now I can only offer (besides three cents a word) my own personal enthusiasm, plus that of my publisher, for this project, as inducement. I don't have to say that this enthusiasm is based on more than magazine sales, and I won't insult you with praise.

I just hope, hope, hope you say Yes.

Grania is, th. G.,[48] fine, and I have already felt the baby kick, myself, so I guess he/she is fine, too.

Our warm regards to Maggy and the two littlest angels.

Prosper and flourish,

Avram Davidson

August 16th, 1962

Dear Avram:

The Sunday before you left town we, the family and I, came in search of Vista Place, just to drop by a signed copy of the English edition of *The October Country*. Needless to say we did not ever find Vista Place, save on the crinkled map, on the way home. Under separate cover, to assuage everyone's discouragement, said book goes off to you.

Your letter of the 13th is wonderful wonderful indeed. It is the kind of letter you never dream you will ever get in your life. I remember when I was 18 years old and corresponding with Edgar Rice Burroughs, trying to get him to come down to the science-fiction club to give a talk (he never did; he was very shy about such things), if anyone had told me that some time later in my life an offer such as yours would come along my ego would have rejected the idea totally as really much too good.

Yes, I want the special R.B. issue as much as you do. I have several short stories in my files, which I have been working on for some years. I hereby promise to deliver to you, some time in the next eight (8) weeks, the new short story you ask for. This is a definite commitment.

So you can go ahead then with dear friend Bill Nolan, bless him, and have him start work on his Index.

This news, plus the fact that *Life* telephoned ten days ago and put me to work on their lead article for an issue on Project Apollo and beyond, which will appear in four weeks, has made this two week period incredible for me.[49]

Is "Time Intervening" good enough? I take it you want to use it, *plus* a new story by me? I'll re-read "Time Intervening" in the next few days, to see what I think of it. We may all decide it is a weak sister.[50]

Enough for now. You've made me very happy. Give Grania a bear-hug for me, and one for yourself! Take care of that family!

Thank you, thank you,
Ray

Bradbury's further refinement of the special May 1963 issue of F&SF *evolved through three letters to his agent Don Congdon and F&SF's Avram Davidson.*

August 19th, 1962

Dear Don:

[. . .] Avram Davidson has approached me to do an entire issue of *Fantasy and Science Fiction* dedicated to me. Boy, I think this is great! Joe Mugnaini will probably do a cover portrait of me. Bill Nolan will make up a complete Index of my published stories, which would be handy for us all. Davidson wants to publish an old story of mine from Nolan's *R.B. Review*, plus a new story I will write in the next 8 or 10 weeks, gladly. I'll probably let them reprint an article of mine from *The Writer*, also. And they will use an article by Nolan he did for a west coast magazine on me. All in all, a very flattering and happy thing. [. . .]

Best,

Ray

November 9th, 1962

Dear Avram:

I am still working on "One Way to Chicago Abyss."

It will run, as you suggested, about 5,000 words.

So, you need a second story, as you suggested in your last note.

So here is that second story, "Burning Bright,"[51] for you to read while you are waiting for me to send on "Abyss."

This enclosed is a curiosity. I wrote it back in 1947–48 and it remained in my files over the years, going out only a few times to quality markets like *Harper's Bazaar* or *The Atlantic*, where it was dismissed. It lay in my files and collected about it many ideas. These ideas grew large and became . . . *Fahrenheit 451*.

So here is a new, unpublished story, which I have freshened with a revision during the last two weeks. Some of your readers, I hope, will be interested in this because it was the starting point for one of my longer, and popular, works. I also hope they enjoy it as a single pure experience, to itself.

I'm going back to work on "Abyss" now and hope to get it in the mail on the 15th, as promised.

Joe[52] is working feverishly on the cover illustration, and it goes very well indeed.

More, next week. Best, as ever,

Ray

November 20th, 1962

Dear Don:

Under separate cover during the past week I have sent off two short stories to *Fantasy and Science Fiction* which will appear in their Bradbury issue come Spring.

One story, "Burning Bright," is the genesis of *F.451*, a tale I wrote many years back, which changed and became the Fireman novel. So, as a four thousand word bit of curiosa it is fascinating, but would have been unsalable to any large magazine in the USA.

So you can rest easily, considering "Burning Bright," for I know you worry, and correctly so, about my giving away good ideas to small markets.

The second story "One Fare to Chicago Abyss" deals with an old man in the future whose career is "remembering."[53] He remembers what cigarette packages looked like, what the dashboard of a Cadillac looked like, what coffee was, and how certain toys worked. He lives in a devastated area, after a nuclear war, and his strength is merely, and simply, being a mediocrity capable of total recall of mediocre things. This story might have sold to a larger market, but, on occasion, we must sacrifice, especially since *F&SF* is doing this R.B. issue.

Will you contact Mr. Ferman at *F&SF* now and find out about price, please? I sent the stories directly on to them, for they have a time-and-printing problem and I wanted to save them delays. If you wish, I'll send you carbons as soon as I have extra copies made, okay?

The issue will contain my 2 stories, an article about me by William Nolan, and a complete Index of my work.

More from me, in a few days, with another story, "The Vacation," just for *you*!!!!![54]

Best,
Ray

DAVID MANESS

Bradbury's role as a Space Age visionary began even before his 1950 publication of The Martian Chronicles, *but his deepening relationship with NASA was greatly advanced as* Life *magazine editors convinced him to write three major features on our destiny in outer space. These 1960s essays celebrated our search for life on other worlds and the massive Saturn V rockets that would take the Apollo astronauts to the moon. But Bradbury reached a crucial decision point in early 1969, as his desire to celebrate family milestones with an extended overseas vacation came into conflict with NASA's scheduling window for the Apollo 11 lunar landing in the summer of 1969. That dilemma, as well as his account of a rare Bradbury story-essay that apparently got away unwritten, informed his March letter to longtime friend and* Life *magazine editor David Maness.*

[ca. early March 1969]

Mr. David Maness
Life Magazine
New York

Dear Dave: On the way to the office today it suddenly struck me to think of astrology and the way it has had a sudden resurgence the last few years, all over the place, in women's magazines high and low, and among young and old, a thing we all saw happening forty years ago repeated again now. Crazy, wild, strange, silly, etc., etc.

I also suddenly thought of Hitler and the fact that behind Hitler was an astrologer. And the further thought that many of the crimes, really, should be laid at the astrologer's doorstep, for he advised, did he not? Yet was he ever brought to trial? For what? How? Where? Is he still alive? If dead, how did he die? Or is he around in So. America advising dictators, or hiding out at the LBJ ranch?

Few articles have ever been done on Hitler's astrologer. Did you ever do one? Would you be interested in a short familiar essay on him, tying him into this new upsurge in mysticism, for up front in *Life*, where Loudon Wainwright often tries out his familiar essays? Or for a bit longer article toward the back? I'm working in the dark here, for I have heard nothing about the man for many years. If *Life*'s researchers could pitch in and help me, I think I could do an ironic, wryly amusing one on the crazy-tragic aspects of all this.

Also, I have purchased tickets for the whole family to sail on the S.S. *United States* from New York on June 24th. We will spend the summer in London, returning Sept. 9th to NYC. How this will affect my helping out on the Moon Shot Landing, I don't know. I take it the dates are all tentative, and depend on the success of the next Apollo missions. I thought I should let you know the above . . . it may be the last time we will have the family together in one place for one summer . . . so I have moved ahead, since Apollo plans seem fairly nebulous . . . and, let's face it . . . I don't necessarily have to be in Florida to write a story. In fact, as we have seen in the past, distance really does wonders for me and my ideas. Let me know what you think of all this: Hitler's Star-Gazer, and Bradbury as Star-Gazer for Apollo.

Best, as ever, yours,
Ray

NANCY NICHOLAS

During the 1970s and early 1980s, Alfred A. Knopf editor-in-chief and president Robert A. Gottlieb gave Nancy Nicholas a new role as Ray Bradbury's principal editor. This transition began as Gottlieb, who had edited Bradbury's books since the early 1960s for Simon & Schuster and then Knopf, finished editing Bradbury's short novel The Halloween Tree (1972). *Nancy Nicholas's background in poetry led to the publication of three volumes of Bradbury's verse during these years, carefully edited through long letters to Bradbury as he sent her poems for each successive collection. Nicholas would also edit Bradbury's fiction volumes, includ-ing* Long After Midnight (1976), The Stories of Ray Bradbury (1980), *and* Death Is a Lonely Business (1985), *before leaving in 1985 for Simon & Schuster.*

She established her close working relationship with Bradbury through the editing of his first poetry collection, When Elephants Last in the Dooryard Bloomed (1973); *the letters that follow provide a sense of how writer and editor refined these expressions in verse, a form that Bradbury loved exploring even as his creativity remained ever focused on fiction and the adaptation of his stories and books to stage and film.*

August 25, 1971

Dear Mr. Bradbury,

Bob Gottlieb has asked me to write you about your poetry in a dual capacity as a poetry handler here, and a Bradbury fan of old. I have gone through the collection and made some suggestions which I hope will be helpful, but please discard them if they seem wrong to you. You know best what you are doing. [. . .]

A few general comments:

As you can see, I have Xeroxed and marked some poems with ideas of how I think you could perhaps improve what you have done. Basically you have such a good economical poet's mind—it works in images and tight, whole parts. But sometimes I think you strain for a meter for a filler. But you will see.

Also, if there is one general suggestion about making a collection, a book, rather than a group of your poems, it is that there should perhaps be more humor—not parody, but the rather malicious fun of some of your stories. Also, because you are already well-known and have a following for your prose, maybe you should do more with the themes fans expect from you and which are so good. For instance, could you try a cycle of Martian poems; that world is so vivid to anyone who has read the *Chronicles* that it could be either the literature of the Martians or poems about the coming of Earthmen or just poetic descriptions of the planet as we know it from your stories.

And what about some more autobiographical work? Would you consider some Hollywood or California poems? Or geographical ones— more about Mexico or some to go with the Irish stories?

I hope this has been some help, but if you disagree with any, just toss it out, and if you have any questions or if there is anything more specific I can do to clarify for you, please let me know.

Sincerely,
Nancy Nicholas

Bradbury allowed some of the internal touches and refinements that Nancy Nicholas suggested, but in spite of her recommendations to discard some or choose between two closely related poems, he retained almost every poem that he sent to Knopf. Bradbury's response to her August 1971 critiques set out his basic approach to writing light verse as an exercise in joyful spontaneity rather than serious poetic ambition. She was able to accommodate his point of view without lessening her steady and careful critiques of the poems that continued to come in over the next year.

September 15th, 1971

Dear Nancy Nicholas:

Thank you for your long and most helpful letter. This short response just to let you know your large envelope arrived safely and I will be brooding over your suggestions and ideas for the next week and write you again.

Your idea for more humor might result in my revising a long poem
I have been working on for a year about . . . W. C. Fields! I met him only
once, when I was fourteen. I ran up, got his autograph, and he handed
me back the pencil and paper and said:

"Here you are, you little son-of-a-bitch!"

I have never forgotten.[55]

I also have a few other s-f poems I will glance at.

You didn't mention my new poem "If I Were Epitaph" which I sent
a Xerox of, to Bob, about a month ago. Did it arrive safely and was it put
into the manuscript box with the other poems? I have also sent another
new poem to Bob this week, which you might ask him about. I would
welcome your opinion of both these new ones.

I think you should know now that of course I do not know, on a
conscious level, what I am doing. I have loved poetry since I was a child
and it has taken me roughly 35 years to begin to let the wonderful stuff
come out my fingertips unhampered. But everything I do is intuitive.
I don't know the names, labels, or theories that go with various rhyme
schemes, rhythms, etc., etc. I have never been able to learn technical
things in a technical way. I learned to write poems, as I did stories, by
writing them and failing, writing and failing, until I began to stagger,
walk, then run.

I didn't put the poems in the manuscript in any special order.
Later, we will have to decide which strong ones to open and close the
book with.

Again thanks! More from me, in about a week!

Best,
Ray B.

PS. Has there been any preliminary discussion on just how long the
book must be? How many poems we really need? How many pages in
the book? I realize much will depend, also, on type-size. The larger the
type, the fewer the lines, the fewer poems needed. But?

R.B.

November 10, 1971

Dear Ray,

Yesterday your new poem, "Remembrance" arrived and I like it so
much. In many ways the best of any in the collection—partly because
of the idea and the real sense of memory you put into it, but also partly
because I choose to think it is the same ravine you described in a
story (called maybe "The Ravine") about a woman coming home from
the library across a ravine—a story which has always been one of my
favorites of yours.[56]

I have a few minor quibbles, as usual, but as usual, they are tiny and
only intended to be help. About a third of the way down the first page,
the line "The days being short . . ." This seems to be an unnecessary
poeticism and especially since it scans less well than the straighter
version, "The days are shorter now, I simply had to come." [. . .] Page
3, the last line of the first stanza, for the metre can you insert another
"the"? "The squirrel's hole and the long-lost . . ."[57]

Again, my compliments to the poet.

Best,
Nancy

December 3rd, 1971

Dear Nancy:

Thanks, at long last, for your new letter.

The other three which you enclosed, by Xerox, of course, had never
been seen by me before. Somewhere along the line they were lost. It's
hard for me to believe all three were dumped between NYC and L.A., or
mislaid *in* L.A. Recalling your Mail Dept. back in August, which delayed
sending out your first letter by some two or three weeks, I would
suggest you dredge around your basement / attic / laundry chute. You

will probably find the missing letters under a retired elephant in the Knopf underground zoo.

Anyway, glad to have them. Will read them over. Will double-check all suggestions. We really are well on our way to a finished book. Would like to run all the semi-dubious lines in certain poems through my typewriter again before Christmas. Would be great to have the whole book finished and off to you by then, so I can go back and finish up *The Halloween Tree* for Gottlieb, who will change his name to Satan's despise if I don't watch out!

Anyway, here is *another* new one, enclosed. Much fun.

Did I tell you? *Ladies Home Journal* bought "Remembrance" a few weeks back, and will run it on a double-spread some time next year. Not often one gets real money for poetry. Huzzah!

Thanks for your help. More in the next two weeks! Glad we are back in touch!

Yours,
Ray

Dear Nancy:

This is one of those peculiar situations where Alfred A. Knopf is in competition with Alfred A. Knopf.

Which is to say I am taking from Nancy Nicholas in order to feed Bob Gottlieb. . . .

I have a deadline on my *other* Knopf book of the 2nd or 3rd or 4th of Feb. to finish *The Halloween Tree* in order to publish in October. Since Bob has pleasantly pressured me to by all means finish up, I knew that you would understand if we delayed the Poems a few weeks, since we are not under the gun for an autumn date to the same extent, yes, no?

So right now I am sweating out revisions on *Halloween Tree* and hope to get back to the poems and you, dear lady, some time in Feb.

Plus completely rewriting my musical *Dandelion Wine* which opens here March 10th, plus revising my Space Age Shakespearean-type three-act drama *Leviathan 99* which opens here March 22nd![58]

A full year, already!

Thank you for the gentle nudge, much appreciated by, good old *half-*dependable

Ray
Bradbury
January 19th, 1972

Bradbury's fifty-poem final order of contents for When Elephants Last in the Dooryard Bloomed *was accompanied by this cover note reaffirming his desire to maintain a sense of humor in the celebration of everyday things and extraordinary people that would distinguish his verse (but not necessarily his themes) from that of more serious poetry.*

[ca. June 18th, 1973]

Dear Nancy:

Here's what would seem to be the final order of the poems in my book, okay? I have tried to space things out properly, with, on occasion, a small clump of poems of a certain type . . . but mainly keeping space poems away from space poems, and remembrance poems away from remembrance poems . . . so that people diving casually into the book will be, I hope, refreshed and surprised on every page as I try, and sometimes succeed, to balance on-point while hitting a cantaloupe with a mallet. . . .

Hope all this is totally confusing and amiably mad . . . It is 103 here today. So you are probably better off in New York!

Best, as ever,
Ray

As Nancy Nicholas edited Bradbury's successive poetry volumes and his new fiction volumes, she also oversaw a new hardbound trade edition of Dandelion Wine *(1957, 1975), which had gone out of print with its original trade house. In early 1975, Bradbury responded to the new* Dandelion Wine *edition with reflections on the childhood memories that he had transferred into Douglas Spaulding, his largely autobiographical central character.*

Dear Nancy:

The first copy of the new edition of *Dandelion Wine* has just arrived and I am touched and pleased, delighted and saddened, grateful and humbled (not an easy thing to do to me) by its presence. The first edition of this book came out the month in 1957 when my Dad became ill and died. My first thought then today was of him, and how he and my other relatives and friends live in the book. I am immensely grateful that my parents raised me well, and cared for their crazy son so he could survive and do books like this. Anyway, it is a strange day of bright sun. You have brightened it more. Thanks for keeping my family alive in this way. Blessings to you and Bob from Douglas Spaulding who goes around calling himself . . . Ray

Ray
Sat. Feb 15, 1975

In 1980, Bradbury's massive 100-story retrospective collection The Stories of Ray Bradbury *was published by Knopf. The selection and ordering of contents came after three-way discussions between Bradbury, Nancy Nicholas, and editor-in-chief Bob Gottlieb, who was now also president of the house. Bradbury made his selections from the contents of his various story collections, but in June 1979 Nicholas noted that the contents were "a little heavily weighted toward the later stories. It is the early ones which are lodged behind everyone's pineal lobes and which they will expect." Bradbury accepted the changes in story order suggested by Nicholas in February 1980.*

February 26, 1980

Dear Ray,

Here is our final list of contents in order.

As you will see what I have done is essentially keep to the chronological order of the book publication with a few cheats. For instance I took some stories from *October Country* and put them back with *Dark C[arnival]* because they are strong stories and very "you" and we wanted them toward the front of the book more.[59]

Also I pulled "The End of the Beginning" out of order because I think it makes such a good finale, sort of summing the book up.

Please let me know if you have any suggested changes or replacements, etc. Meanwhile, I look forward to the intro.

Love,
Nancy

KATHY HOURIGAN

Kathy Hourigan had been Bradbury's editor at Alfred A. Knopf since the mid-1980s, developing the same kind of warm personal and professional relationship that Bradbury had enjoyed with most of his major trade editors. Her gift of director Peter Bogdanovich's Who the Devil Made It: Conversations with Legendary Film Directors *triggered a cavalcade of Hollywood memories in this 1997 letter, which also offers Bradbury's first account of his state-sponsored visit to Argentina. The distinguished writer Jorge Luis Borges had sparked Bradbury's popularity in the country by publishing the introduction to an early Argentine edition of* The Martian Chronicles.

May 15, 97

Kathy Hourigan
Editor
Random House

Dear Kathy:

Thanks, much thanks for the Bogdanovich book of director interviews. It is truly a special gift for me. I knew at least half of the directors at one time or another, some of them intimately as you recall from *A Graveyard for Lunatics*. Fritz Lang, for one, used to call and yell "son of a bitch!" at me. I met Hawks on the set with Bacall, Bogart, and William Faulkner in the spring of 1946 when my friend and teacher Leigh Brackett introduced us.[60] I will really curl up with this collection!

I'm just back from Argentina where the whole city celebrated. Can you believe that? My face was on the front page of every newspaper, they put on a Martian show at the planetarium and at the finale, my image came floating down out of the Cosmos! I received an honorary degree from the University of Buenos Aires and spent an hour with the President. No, I didn't sing "Evita!" When Maggie and I were having lunch near the Rio de la Plata a couple passing, stopped and paid our bill! Everywhere I went on the street, crowds gathered. The sum, of course, is that I have been taught in all the schools and colleges for 35 years. Borges is responsible. He wrote the introduction for the *Cronicas Martianas* in Buenos Aires way back in 1953! When we got on the jet to fly home, there I was on the jet-TV. Everyone up front on the jet looked, turned, stood up, yelled and pointed at me. Dear God, Kathie, I wish you had been there to share with me. I hated to come home to plain, simple, and uneventful L.A.

Again, thanks for the Bogdanovich. Love,

Ray

Of all the titles that Bradbury published during his years with Alfred A. Knopf, The Halloween Tree (1972) held a special place in his heart. He didn't always agree with Knopf's decisions to publish the book as a juvenile novel under various house imprints, but he worked with Kathy Hourigan to ensure that the book would remain in print with the original illustrations by Joe Mugnaini and the newer cover art of Diane and Leo Dillon. His retrospective letter to Hourigan helped reinforce this continuity just as the projected 2007 Disneyland celebration of the book blossomed into an annual Halloween Tree event.

March 28, 2007

Dear Kathy:

I hope all goes well with you.

I'd like to tell you, briefly as possible, a story:

Back in 1960, in the basement with my daughters, I painted a picture of a tree loaded with lit pumpkins. I called it The Halloween Tree. I showed it to my animator friend, Chuck Jones, one day at lunch and he said, "My God, that's the genealogy of Halloween. Would you like to write a screenplay about that for me and I will animate it?" So I wrote a screenplay for Chuck Jones, whereupon MGM animation studios went out of business and I was left with the screenplay, which I then adapted into a novel, which I sold to you good people at Knopf. I then wrote another screenplay which was produced as an animated film over ten years ago and I won an Emmy Award for it.

From this a wonderful thing has happened during the last twenty years or so: If you cross the yards of America on Halloween night, you'll find Halloween Trees beginning to be lit in yards here and there. When I came through L.A. two years ago on Halloween night I found four or five yards with Halloween Trees in the front with pumpkins with lit candles in them. I never guessed that I was going to change the history of Halloween, but that's what seems to be happening. Imagine what it will be fifty years from now or a hundred years from now when there will be lit pumpkin trees all over America. Before my book was published or my film was made there were no Halloween Trees anywhere in the world. Now they are being born.

This Halloween out at Disneyland I hope to convince these good people to have me there and have all the animators bring pumpkins with candles lit in them and put up the first Halloween Tree in Disneyland. I believe we'll get all kinds of advertising about it in newspapers across the country, because I'm changing history.

This Halloween I think it would be great if you did a new hard cover edition of *The Halloween Tree*, or lacking that, at least a bigger edition of the paperback, so that you could be part of the celebration of me becoming part of history because I never dreamed that would happen, but it's happening.

Get back to me on this when you can and we'll see what we can do.

I send you big hugs and much love,
Ray

LOU ARONICA

During the mid-1990s, Bradbury moved to Avon Books on publisher Lou Aronica's (1958–) promise that his enduring titles would remain in print as hardbound editions. As the new small-format Avon hardbacks came out, Bradbury took the opportunity to advance the date prefixes for the Martian Chronicles *story-chapters and interior bridges. As the years passed, these new dates aligned more or less with NASA's revised mission planning. Bradbury took care to include "The Fire Balloons," dropped from the original Doubleday and Bantam editions in the early 1950s but included in a few subsequent editions in Britain and America.*

Jul 7, 1996

Dear Lou:

Just a brief note from Paris. As I have mentioned before, the dates on *The Martian Chronicles* will have to be changed for your new edition. Seeing as how they start in 1999, which I never anticipated 45 years ago, it might be best to move the dates ahead by about 30 years, yes? Hoping that the Mars Expedition, meanwhile will catch up? Please have someone there do a tentative re-dating and check it with me, okay? The first date instead of 1999 might well be 2029 and then go through and advance the numbers appropriately, yes? That will give NASA a bit more than 30 years to fulfill my prophecy. On the other hand, what I was writing was Greek and Roman and Egyptian mythology, not scientific fact. *The Martian Chronicles* will be read on Mars, friends tell me, one hundred years from now, for what it is, myth-making and imaginative conjuring which, at times, we prefer to terrible truths and hard fact.

Also, please be certain that who ever is in charge of typesetting the new edition of *Chronicles*, uses the Doubleday 40th Anniversary edition, which contains "The Fire Balloons" which, somehow, got left out of our Bantam paperback edition, a few years back. My oversight, dammit. [. . .]

Best,
Ray

JENNIFER BREHL

During the mid-1990s, Avon Books senior editor Jennifer Brehl became Brad-
bury's editor as well; she would eventually bring Avon and its authors into the
William Morrow publishing house as HarperCollins imprints. Brehl would
become executive editor and senior vice president at HarperCollins, where she
continued to publish Bradbury's books for the rest of his life. A 1997 Avon
advertisement in The New Yorker *for* Driving Blind, *his most recent story*
collection, triggered this reflection on the circumstances surrounding the pub-
lication of "I See You Never," his first appearance in that magazine a half
century earlier.

Jennifer Brehl / Avon

Dear Jennifer:

Much thanks for the tearsheet of the Avon *New Yorker* advt. Once
every fifty years, by God, once every fifty years! Fifty years ago, just as
Maggie and I got married, I sold my first story to *The New Yorker*. Just
in time, we had nine dollars in the bank the day that we were married
and Maggie had to go to work to support us as I wrote *The Martian*
Chronicles for a penny a word for the pulp magazines. I think I got five
hundred dollars, which paid our rent in Venice, California for more than
a year (30 dollars a month!)

   Now, fifty years later, this splendid Avon advt. I haven't sold another
story to *The New Yorker* since, although they have seen at least 300!
That's one helluva lot of rejection slips.[61] Thanks for getting me into the
magazine, again!

Love,
Ray
September 21, 1997

Somewhere a Band Is Playing, *the idea of a small town that existed both in and*
out of time, was a long-deferred novel concept that caught Brehl's interest in the

1990s. This letter offers Bradbury's interim synopsis for the plot of Somewhere a Band Is Playing, *which finally evolved into a novella published, along with his novella* Leviathan '99, *under the single-volume title* Now and Forever (2007).

April 28, 1998

Dear Jennifer:

You ask about *Somewhere a Band Is Playing*. So, briefly, its history goes back some 30 years when I commenced work on it, then put it away.[62] About six weeks ago I came upon the original manuscript, some eight thousand words, and it sat up in its tomb and gasped for breath. What could I do but cry, "Lazarus!" Now, whether or not the darned book will be finished soon, I can't say. I am up to about 25,000 words as of this week, and it seems to be going well, and I hope to finish a first draft before Maggie and I leave for Paris, June 22nd. It is a semi-fantasy about a small town in the midst of the Arizona desert where some genetic "sports" gather, men and women from all over the world whose lives span one hundred to two hundred years, yet they look only middle-aged or younger. While all their friends grow old and die, they remain young, which is, of course, embarrassing. So, to protect themselves, they accumulate in this mostly unknown small town. A young reporter arrives with some bad news which he has not as yet told them . . . that in the near future a super highway will thrust across the desert and impale or threaten their town. Pandemonium. Because that means the town, as yet unvisited by the outside world, will be afflicted by cars, people, newspapers, etc. The young reporter, meanwhile, has fallen in love with the town beauty, a lovely young woman who, in reality, is close on to being one hundred years old or older. She offers him semi-immortality and he has to decide to go home and say goodbye to all his friends who will age and die while he remains young, not an easy decision, a guilty one. That's the main thrust of the book, with all its ramifications and problems.

The young reporter when he arrives, does not know what the town is all about, he must solve the puzzle when he notices there are no children in the town, and the graveyards are, in fact, unoccupied. He, in turn, has not told the town people his secret, the fact of the highway arriving in the near future, to explode their peaceful existence.

I don't know, yet, if I am succeeding or will succeed with this novella. I never know until I am finished with the last word on the last page. It is a delicate subject in which I must put my foot right with every page and judge every word, finally, to see if I have been too fanciful. There is always the danger of being saccharin, which would be fatal to the entire book.

Meanwhile, I am doing further revisions on *The Martian Chronicles*, hoping to please the overlords at Universal Studios.

Glad to hear that your art director liked my metaphor for the cover image of *Death Is a Lonely Business*. Wonderful!

Carpe diem, dear young lady, *carpe diem*!

Ray

September 7, 1999

Dear Jennifer:

Just a brief note, belated, to thank you for the advance copy of the new edition of *The October Country*. Another beauty! What a line-up all these hardcovers make. And people in bookshops, at signings, seem to react to them wonderfully.

All else goes well. I am busy revising *Let's All Kill Constance* and putting together 35 stories for a new collection, tentatively titled *One More for the Road*.[63] No news from Mel Gibson on *F.451* and further delays on *Martian Chronicles* at Universal.[64] So what else is new! I have written an article for *Playboy* to be out in December,[65] once more declaring to millions of people, who will ignore it, that the Millennium doesn't start until January 1st, 2001. But what the hey, a billion bucks will be exploded right after this Christmas to celebrate the non-holiday. I will go hide somewhere.

Again thanks, much thanks.

Love,
Ray

Although Bradbury's novelized story-cycle of the supernatural Elliott family
had been evolving in his mind for a half century, his bridging chapters and a
few newer stories did not form a final seamless sequence until after submission.
Bradbury accepted a final adjustment to the story sequence and minor character
names as suggested by Brehl just a few months before publication of From the
Dust Returned.

October 1, 2000

Ray–

I've just finished putting the manuscript together, inputting your
corrections, restoring the new version of "West of October." The final
Table of Contents follows.

You'll notice that I placed "West of October"[66] as Chapter 10, rather than
Chapter 21. This is because in "Return to the Dust" (formerly Chapter
20), we witness the demise of the House, and so Grandpère's train ride
with the four obstreperous cousins and Cecy seems out of place, coming
so late in the book. I think it works as Chapter 10, coming after the
Homecoming, and after we've learned of Cecy's peculiar talents.

Of course, you may think it should be placed later in the book; please
let me know. Nonetheless, I really think this story, which is about the
Family in its prime, should come well before "Return to the Dust."

Another possibility: It might work well between "The Whisperers" and
"The Theban Voice," two rather short "interlude" chapters.

Another thing is that I think two of the cousins' names should be
changed. The four cousins in "West of October" are Tom, William,
Philip, and John. However, Tom is the name of Cecy's love in "The
Wandering Witch," and he reappears in "The One Who Remembers."
And John is the name of the evil uncle in "The Traveler."[67]

Therefore, I suggest changing Cousin John to Cousin Jack (pretty close). I don't know what to change Cousin Tom's name to. Peter? Arthur? Robert? What do you think?

That's it for now. I am at home, if you'd like to call later and let me know what you think. [...]

Love to you and Maggie,
Jennifer

A Sound of Thunder (*Warner Brothers, 2005*), *directed by Peter Hyams, was adapted from Bradbury's enduring 1952 time-travel story. The original re-mained in print through* The Golden Apples of the Sun and Other Stories, *but the film led Brehl and HarperCollins to release a parallel edition titled* A Sound of Thunder and Other Stories *with the movie poster as cover art.*

September 1, 2005

Ray–

I saw the movie A *Sound of Thunder* last night. What fun it was! There were, perhaps, one too many near-death escapes (I didn't see how they'd ever get out of the submerged subway car with the tunnel caving in and that mutant sea monster attacking!), but I loved the time travel sequences, and the simplicity and awe of the realization about the ramifications of the crushed butterfly. And, I have to say, I loved watching Ben Kingsley ham it up at his greedy, nefarious best!

I hope it makes buckets of money.

XX
Jenny

7

AGENTS

Doubleday, as I imagined, did not panic for the exits
when they heard the news that the flea was packing his
tiny trunks and leaving. All the elephants watched as the
microscopic author marched past their stables, leaving his
infinitesimal footprints on the shifting editorial sands . . .
—*Bradbury to Don Congdon, July 24, 1960*

FREDERIK POHL JR.

At various times in his career, Nebula and Hugo Award winner Frederik Pohl Jr. (1919–2013) interacted with Ray Bradbury as a fellow writer, an editor, and, very briefly, as an agent. Their friendship dated from the inaugural 1939 New York World Science Fiction Convention; Pohl was less than a year older than Bradbury, but his early connection with the "Futurian" nexus of fan-writers in New York fast-tracked Pohl into the profession. For roughly a year and a half after the 1939 Con he agented for Bradbury, who was still an amateur writer at the time; their contact was intermittent, and none of Bradbury's submissions made the grade before the more experienced Julius Schwartz agented his first professional sales. The three letters that follow capture Bradbury's first tentative steps toward the professional genre pulps during the prewar years.

[August 1939]

Dear Fred:

While in New York I meant all along to have a serious discussion with you about your agenting my stories. But, since no such occasion came about, may I petition you to be so kind as to become my agent in the near future? I realize of course that there are certain rules and regulations to having an agent, and if you would please write me as soon as possible telling me your terms and any other data, I would be pleased immeasurably.

I have decided that it is time for Bradbury to sell a story, and since you have already done alright by Rothman and Asimov[1] there is no reason why, after due deliberation of plots and stories and facts, that we can't work out a selling combination.

What do you think? Please do not judge my stories by the stuff you may have seen of mine in fan mags, I really think I am improving my style and someday might come out okay as a professional. But you, being in contact with the editors, constantly know when they want something, what they want, and how they want it, would be my most likely bet for selling.

Let me, at this point, say that I enjoyed the Futurians publication
In Your Teeth, Gentlemen, immensely. I think you are right. Taurasi,
Moskowitz and Sykora are the bad little boys of science-fiction.[2] [. . .]
I wouldn't want to incur their enmity at any time, because, after all, no
matter who you sympathize with you must remember we are all fans.

I would like to get some comment from the Futurian Group on
my mag *Futuria Fantasia* if they have seen it . . . if they haven't . . .
please inform me and I'll send back a couple copies. Get comments of
Wollheim, Lowndes and Michel especially . . . and yourself.[3]

I arrived back in L.A. last Sunday. The San Francisco Fair stinks![4]
I shall never forget my trip to New York . . . it was, without precedent,
the happiest five weeks of my life. Hope I can see you all in Chicago
next year . . . or perhaps in New York again. I love New York (next to
L.A.).

I am rushed for time, so will end this missile with a plea . . . . . .
please write immediately stating agent terms, etc. . . . facts about
manuscripts . . . will you handle stuff from me to *Argosy*? *Blue Book*? Or
am I shooting too high? Rush reply

Scientifictionally yours,
Ray Bradbury
1841 S. Manhattan Pl.
Los Angeles, Calif

---

19 August 1939

Dear Ray:

I will handle your stuff to any magazine in New York City, to any science
fiction magazine in the world, or to any of half a dozen other magazines,
neither science fiction nor in New York, where I keep in close contact.
My commission is 20% up to $500, 10% thereafter on all American sales;
on foreign sales, since extra expenses are involved, the commission 25%
to $500, 20% thereafter. In return for that I do all sorts of nice things, all

of which reduce down to getting money for you when it is at all possible.
All you need do is send me your stories. As soon as I've sold one story,
I'll send you an affidavit form to fill out which is a sworn statement
from you that you are not a nasty plagiarist. This I have to have before
I cash any checks on your work, as there are eighteen counts at law on
which plagiarism can be punished, and editors hold agents responsible
for everything they handle.

A few suggestions might not be amiss. Lay off mystery stories in
stf. Slant your stories as much as you can for a particular magazine,
preferably *Astounding, Amazing,* or *Thrilling Wonder,* as they pay the
highest rates. (1¢ per; sometimes higher.) Double space mss., of course.
Don't make too many mistakes in typing and keep penciled corrections
to a minimum. Don't depend on smash endings, or O. Henry endings.
Don't use puns or other low forms of humor. Keep your stories between
3,000 and 8,000 words at first. If there is an epidemic of robot stories
in the magazines, don't write robot stories. Don't depend on super-
scientific ideas: either fast action or smooth style is necessary to sell.
Have your characters speak naturally. Etc., et al.

Do svidania,

Ø

[ca. January 1941]

Dear Fred:

It's been a long time since I submitted anything to you, but I've been
busy getting about ten stories ready, so you can expect a bombardment
of stories, beginning with this one, during the next six months.

In the near future Henry Hasse and I may do some stories together.
We just did one called "Pendulum" which Julie Schwartz is agenting.[5]

Latest Bok illustrations in your mags are very very good. The mag
continues to improve, showing how much you have learned about
editing in the time that has passed.[6]

Hope you like this yarn.[7] Any suggestions or criticisms you have about it will be thankfully received.

See you again,
Ray

JULIUS SCHWARTZ

Between 1941 and 1947, Julius Schwartz (1915–2004) agented the young Ray Bradbury through more than seventy-five sales to the genre pulps. Schwartz used his proximity to the New York publishers to develop what was, essentially, the first agency for science fiction writers. His sales extended across genre field boundaries as Bradbury became a popular author in the weird tale, fantasy, detective, and science fiction pulps. Schwartz gradually left the agency field as he moved into a prominent role as a comic book editor, and this transition coincided with Bradbury's gradual move into the major market magazines. In many ways Julius Schwartz was central to the network of science fiction authors who mentored Bradbury and became lifelong friends. But Schwartz knew he didn't have the time or expertise to represent Bradbury in the broader literary marketplace, and the first letter offers his blessing and a few words of advice.

255 East 188 Street,
New York 58, New York,

September 8, 1945.

Dear Ray,

The news of your sales to *Collier's* and *Mademoiselle* is *wonderful!*[8] Congratulations—and I'm very proud of you. You've certainly come a long way from 1941 when I first saw your attempts at writing. Remember "The Piper" manuscript you brought over to South Norton that day and how we went over it almost line by line to fix it up?[9] The time seemed impossibly far off before you thought you'd be cracking the slicks, eh— but it's here! Now please take it easy and don't imagine that everything you write from now on is going to turn to gold. Keep a level head, sweat your stuff out and you'll be a real author by and by . . .

Incidentally, did you just send your stuff around blind, or did you have an agent take care of that angle for you? If the former, my guess is that in the near future you'll be getting correspondence from various agents asking them to represent you. If you do pick one—and I advise this—be sure he's a good one. In any event, let me know how this progresses and if I can advise you in any way I'll be happy to do so.

And did you definitely sign that contract with Derleth yet? If not, I think you'd better turn him down.[10] I feel that book companies and maybe even movie companies are going to start parking on your door and there's no reason why Augie should grab himself a 50% chunk on some of your early stuff.

Ed Hamilton blew into town yesterday. Mort wants him to write a few *Batman* stories for him. Ed's never done comics before, but he says he's going to have a whirl at it. If guys like Binder, Wellman, Kuttner, Bester and others have made a success at it, no reason why Ed can't.[11] He says he may head out for California again this winter . . . Haven't seen Otto in some time. Every time I saw the fellow I asked him to come around to the office for lunch or dinner, but he never got around to it. [. . .] Didn't know Jack Williamson had a yarn in *Blue Book*. Was it a fantasy?[12]

I was very pleased you liked Kid Ory and his Creole Jazz Band. I was a little afraid you'd come out of there saying something like, "Slick Jones has got Ory beat a mile!" Some L.A. fan, Francis Laney,[13] had an article in a fan magazine discussing jazz. I wrote him a letter and he's just answered, so maybe we'll be getting up a hot jazz correspondence. Do you know the guy?

Guess that's all. Drop me a line before you leave for Mexico—and have a good time . . .

Best,
Julie.

In spite of his growing editorial responsibilities with the emerging DC Com-
ics syndicate, Julius Schwartz conscientiously continued to shotgun Bradbury's
pulp offerings around the pulp universe after World War II. This spring 1946
letter, written as more of Bradbury's stories were appearing in the mainstream
magazines, shows the typical range of Schwartz's ongoing negotiations with the
remaining pulp stories.

255 East 188 Street,
New York 58, New York,

March 25, 1946.

Dear Ray,

I don't think there's going to be much of a difference between the $35
paid for "The Watchers" outright, than if you sat back on your can and
waited for the royalties to roll in. The book got bad reviews anyway.[14]
So keep the check. Don't bother to send me the commission on it
because . . .

Planet is taking your "Rocket Summer" which Campbell turned
down. Campbell said it "has rather a good idea, but I feel that the
treatment is too heavy-handed and that he pushes too hard." Reiss
said, while the story "isn't really our style, it's too good to turn down.
It certainly makes one think."[15] Check for $63 will come thru in a
couple of weeks and I'll take "The Watchers" commission out of that.

Campbell also bounced "The Irritated People."[16] He found it
"amusing, but not strong enough. He has been a bit too blatant about
it to make it a dramatic story and his humor is too slap-stick to go over
well. The essential idea is the same as that of Manly Wade Wellman's
'Nuisance Value' some years back."

Incidentally, I sold "Rocket Summer" under the Bradbury name.
Frig Campbell if he discovers the trickery . . .

Glad to hear of the sales of "Riabouchinska" and "The Baby."[17] In
what sort of an *E. Queen* anthology is this slated to appear?

Don't know anything about *New Worlds*.[18] Maybe this is the
magazine Ted Carnell is supposed to be getting out.

How can I keep telling you that I thought that "The Children's Hour" was terrific, only a few weeks from now I'll probably have to tell you that Campbell bounced that too.[19] Well, I'm still waiting to be proved wrong.

I told Bloch the latest story he had done for *WT* was just about the best story he ever wrote. He replied that he thought it was as good as a *poor* Bradbury ("there's a guy that can really write for my money"!) Make you feel good?

Damn it—where are the stories for Tilden???[20]

Best,
Julie

DON CONGDON

In Don Congdon (1918–2009), Bradbury found the agent who would guide him through the world of publishing for the rest of the twentieth century, and beyond. Through his experience as an editor with Collier's *magazine and the Simon & Schuster trade house, Congdon knew the business of magazine and book publishing from an inside perspective. As a very young man he had also worked with Lurton Blassingame's literary agency, and in 1947 he left editing to join the Harold Matson agency, where he would remain until launching his own agency in March 1983. In September 1947, Don Congdon became Bradbury's representative in all markets. Of Bradbury's many books, only* Dark Carnival, *published in the spring of 1947, would not be published under the guidance of Don Congdon or his son Michael.*

In late August 1945, Congdon's former colleagues at Collier's *told him of a promising but unknown writer using the name William Elliott.* Collier's *editors soon bought "One Timeless Spring" and discovered that the writer's real name was Ray Bradbury. By now Congdon was with Simon & Schuster, and he reached out to "William Elliott" hoping that this mainstream potential would extend into book-length fiction.*

8/27/45

Dear Mr. Elliott:

The people in *Collier's* fiction department, of which I was a member until a month ago, tell me you write very well and might be interested in doing a novel. If you are considering anything of length, I'd very much like to hear from you.

Cordially,
Don Congdon

Bradbury's correspondence with Congdon quicky evolved, in spite of Bradbury's extended automobile trip through Mexico in the fall of 1945; one of Congdon's letters followed Bradbury all the way to Guadalajara. Two years later, Cong-

don became his agent and began to focus on introducing Bradbury's work to the major publishing houses. Unexpectedly, Harper's asked Congdon if Bradbury might be interested in editing a volume of fantasies by other authors instead. Such a collection never materialized, but it sparked Bradbury to suggest his own dream of persuading mainstream authors to write stories and poems about the next human frontier: Mars.

December 30th, 1948

Dear Don:

Your letter concerning Harper's publishers has set all sorts of things stirring in my mind. I would be fascinated, naturally, with the task of putting together a book of fantasies for them. The only possible drawback would be the money, of course. Suppose you feel them out on the maximum amount they might guarantee me for a book? I don't feel it would be worth my while to do it for less than $700 and I would like $1000 if possible. Quote them the $1000 price and see what happens to their eyebrows. Then decline slowly to the $700 and see if the color returns to their faces.

I have been considering for a year two ideas for two books that might be tied into the above book somehow. I suggest that we try these ideas with Harper's and see if they might be interested. Here they are:

The Martian Chronicles. Edited by Ray Bradbury. We contact Evelyn Waugh, V. S. Pritchett, Eudora Welty, Elizabeth Bowen, John Steinbeck, Truman Capote, Walter Van Tilburg Clark, Elizabeth Parsons, Margaret Shedd, J. F. Powers, Robert Lowry, John Collier, John Hersey, Wallace Stegner, E. B. White. Within a specified time, long enough for thought and creative effort, we ask each of the above to write a story concerning the first trip to Mars, the colonization of Mars by Earth people, or any aspect of later life on Mars, once colonized. What would Waugh people do on Mars? How would Welty people react? Suppose Capote landed there? How different the reactions of Robert Lowry and John Collier, Margaret Shedd and John Hersey, Steinbeck and E.B. White. They can write on any aspect they please. They can let their minds fly.

No rules, no regulations, all the artistic freedom necessary. It is, to me, an exhilarating idea! The time of the Future (with capital letters) is fast approaching. The time of the rocket is upon us. If Harper's would back me on this idea, we might guarantee the authors something like a hundred dollars per story *plus* the inevitable sale of the series, *en toto* or in part to *Harper's Magazine* or *The Atlantic* or *Harper's Bazaar*, or *Mademoiselle* or any one of the big magazines which would be only too glad to run such a series. Perhaps the stories could be sold in clusters of five; five to *Harper's*, five to *Town and Country*, five to *Collier's*, and so on. I think the authors themselves might be as touched and excited by this new vista for writing as I am! It would be science-fiction fantasy with a vengeance.[21] And the sales! My God, the sales!

Book number two:

The Martian Poems. Edited by Ray Bradbury. Similar in plan to the above book, this would be a volume of 30 poems by 30 poets. Marianne Moore, Auden, Eliot, Kenneth Fearing, Spender, Cummings, De La Mare, et cetera. We would contact them and ask them to write poems as if they themselves were inhabitants of a Martian culture. An old culture, and a wise and beautiful one. There would be more than enough poetic freedom in the idea. Poems about Mars, the nights and days and temperatures and colors. Poems about love and hate and death, not far different from that on Earth. I think that these poets might leap at the opportunity to put their fertile imaginations to work on such an amazing idea. The poems could be published as a series in *Harper's* or elsewhere, prior to book publication.

Perhaps these two books might be published simultaneously, or, at least, in the same year. The authors and poets would be given a good long period to mull ideas over—say about six to eight months.

I, of course, cannot be objective about the above ideas. I'm really hepped on them. I look forward to hearing from you on them. [. . .]

Thanks for the letter which has set me off like a firewheel!

Yours,

Ray

Harper's declined Bradbury's idea for the multi-author Martian anthologies, yet his Martian Chronicles title soon found its way to a 1950 novelization of his own Martian tales solicited by Doubleday in June 1949. Bradbury was unsure if he could bridge and sustain such a long work of fiction, however, and he missed his first two deadlines at press. Earlier plans to novelize his supernatural Elliott family stories and his more realistic "Green Town" Illinois tales had so far failed to interest publishers. At this point, Don Congdon provided the perspective that Bradbury would need to develop unified book-length works of fiction in the years to come.

October 7, 1949

Dear Ray:

First question of the day, where's *The Chronicles*? Don't labor too long over this, to reach the acme of perfection. I know you can worry over this kind of thing to the point of thinking a story or book isn't good, and you shouldn't. You are prone to strive for the perfection you feel you must have, often I think to the point of seriously reducing your production. And I hope *The Chronicles* hasn't been bothering you in this way. I think the other book tries licked you in this way, and you're too good a writer on the drafts of stories I've seen to have any need to doubt the skill and quality of your writing.

From talking to you while you were in New York,[22] I could see that the endless number of stories you have in your head and which excite you and drive you are jammed up against a very high ideal of yours for literary perfection. Not for a second do I think you should sacrifice your own sense of artistic perfection, but as I hope you saw clearly last June the magazines and most book publishers put very little appreciation on this count *when it comes to the difference between acceptance and rejection.* Consequently on the majority of stories and projects you do, I think you should strive to free yourself of the perfectionistic reins you hold on yourself, let the stories get away from you more easily. Save the intense honing you give your work for the parts you know are closest to your heart and which satisfy your own artistic ideals, and which is done for these reasons more than for money. On those things for money, you should deal more objectively and efficiently with them.

Sorry I leapt out immediately with this, but you have promised the book twice and the deadlines have gone by. And I'm jumping the gun on you because I think this point is bigger than just the *Chronicles*. [. . .]

Let's have some news. And I hope a couple of new stories.

Yours,
Don

The bridged stories of The Martian Chronicles *did little to ease Bradbury's anxiety over sustaining a novel-length work of fiction. Congdon continued to break down the paralyzing reverence Bradbury felt for the novel form, reminding him that the unpublished "Interval in Sunlight," a prequel to the masterful psychological realism of "The Next in Line," formed the foundation for the Mexican novel that Bradbury hoped to write. These two stories would instead appear in his story collections and eventually merge into a stage play. Bradbury felt his way toward long fiction by extending "The Fireman" into* Fahrenheit 451, *and the story of a dark carnival into* Something Wicked This Way Comes.

January 12, 1951

Dear Ray:

[. . .] I hope you'll have a flurry of short stories in here in the next three months. You made a mistake to tell me of all the yarns in the file, and I expect you to get a few of these rounded into shape when the financial pressure is on you. There's certainly the revision of "Interval in Sunlight"—which even if not revised I'd be glad to try around some more. But if you could make the changes for *McCall's*, I'd think we'd have a pretty sure sale.[23] [. . .]

On length—I'd like to see you give a very hard try at something this spring to bring out with you in May. If we had something to talk about specifically—say half a novel or a play, I think we might be able to straighten out any kinks so that by the summer you'd have a long work in hand.

I've had people in the science-fiction field tell me they didn't think you'd ever write a novel, that you were too much of a short story man in conception of plot. This is about as glib a comment as anyone can make about any writer, and I hold no part of it is true. I do think you have some kind of anxiety about not being able to handle a form you hold in too great a regard. One great form of the novel is nothing more than an elongated short story; in which the incidents that happen are the story, and they happen to the major character, without actually changing him. *Vanity Fair* is a good example and the suspense novel is another. With the several wonderful ideas you've already mentioned for novels I can't see any reason why any novel you start shouldn't flow pretty smoothly and once done be a good one. Until you have actually finished something at forty to sixty thousand words, you can't know nor can anyone else that it isn't going to be good. I have every confidence that it will be a humdinger.

More next week.

Sincerely,
Don

"The Whole Town's Sleeping," perhaps Bradbury's best-known and hardest-hitting suspense story, presents the last hours of a young woman who slowly realizes that she may be the target of a murderer—a silent serial killer who sometimes strangles his young victims in the town's dark ravine. As both a radio drama and a McCall's *magazine short story, it attracted the attention of Ellery Queen Mystery Magazine founder Frederic Dannay (1905–1982), who had corresponded with Bradbury since the mid-1940s. In the summer of 1952, Dannay approached Don Congdon with an unusual offer, prompting Bradbury's direct response to Dannay himself.*

August 6, 1952

Dear Ray:

Fred Dannay of *Ellery Queen* called last week to suggest an interesting proposition. He has read "The Whole Town's Sleeping" and likes it very much and would like to reprint it. However, he thought the story might very well have a sequel, if you took up right at the end of the first story and wrote another four or five thousand words as to what happened to the woman and established whether the killer was the lonely hearts killer, etc. He said that he thought he would like to enter the sequel in the *Ellery Queen* contest. He says, as a matter of fact, that if the sequel were a good story he thought of the idea of putting "The Whole Town's Sleeping" as the first story in an issue of *Ellery Queen*, and the sequel as the last story, a kind of binding the whole issue idea.

I don't know whether this appeals to you, and for that matter we probably would have to clear the idea with *McCall's* since they published the first story, and also because they control the second serial rights. However, my hunch is that they would not want to run the story, even though they might want to see it. Before we take up that matter, however, I think you should decide whether you think you could write a sequel. Insofar as a price for this story, Fred says that he thinks if the sequel were any good at all that it would take one of the top prizes; although, we have no definite assurance of this, you understand. The contest closes in October.

Regards,

Don

Just got the book script—Good!²⁴

Just got the book script—Good![24]

Ray Bradbury
10750 Clarkson Road
Los Angeles 64, Calif.

August 10, 1952

Dear Fred:

Don Congdon has passed on your interesting idea about a sequel to my story "The Whole Town's Sleeping." I certainly appreciate your good thought.

At first, in reading Don's note, in which he synopsized the general idea you were after, I thought the entire project an insurmountable one. But I have learned once more, even as I have learned in the past, that the subconscious is a mighty friend, and that the enemy of the subconscious mind is the gahdamned insolence of the conscious mind that says, "No; it can't be done!" I put Don's letter aside last night and during the evening did a bit of reading from various books, including some poetry. Late in the evening I came across the first line of a poem by Edgar Allan Poe, which gave me the title for my sequel: "At Midnight, in the Month of June."[25] This morning, God bless us all, my subconscious delivered, and I have some fifteen hundred words done on the story. I know where I'm going, I have my beginning, my middle, and my end; what remains is to flesh the skeleton. I hope to have the story sent off to Don sometime during the next month. I feel much indebted to you for having given me that fabulous thing that Henry James spoke of: The Minimum of Suggestion.[26] God bless you!

Strangely enough, I had been thinking about writing you recently, not only to say how pleased I was that you purchased my story "Touch and Go"[27] for reprint, but to suggest one other of my stories for possible future use. I think you know the story (I think Boucher has mentioned it to you) but I am enclosing it herewith, anyhow, and perhaps you will consider it anew for *EQMM*. The miracle of the story, "Pillar of Fire," is that I was writing a detective story, deduction and all, without being in the least aware of what I was doing. Ah there, Subconscious, you *dog*, you! I think this yarn might well prove to be a fascinating experiment for you and *EQMM*; anyway, I'd be glad to hear from you on it. In the meantime, again thanks for the "Touch and Go" sale, the sequel nucleus, and your continuing interest. My best to you, your charming wife, and that s-f reading son of yours!

Yours, as ever,
Ray

Bradbury's race against time to complete his expansion of "The Fireman" into Fahrenheit 451 *played out during the spring and summer of 1953. His well-*

known return to the typing room of UCLA's Powell Library to complete this
transformation in May and June continued with heavy revisions through July,
as Bradbury struggled to send installments on to Don Congdon in New York.
The following three-letter exchange between Congdon and Bradbury sheds new
light on Bradbury's largely internalized struggle to fulfill his vision for Fahrenheit 451 *while facing a deadline with publisher Ian Ballantine that was already*
stretched to its limit.

July 24, 1953

Dear Ray:

[. . .] The last 20 pages reached me Wednesday and I gave them to
Ballantine right after lunch. I think the story is continuing to build and
definitely has a very strong impact. I do wish I didn't have to read it in
these short gulps because it is hard to assess one's feelings accurately. I
do agree that more work on the young girl would be useful.

Do your very best to finish up the book this week; as I've said all
along, there will still be time to work on it once the whole thing is
finished, in the mail, and you can have a breather of a couple of days.
Particularly because Ballantine is in a hell of a spot with his printer.

Yours,
Don

P.S. It's occurred to me that it might be wise in the future to use me as
an earlier sounding board when you are working with a delivery date up
ahead. For instance, if you had let me read "The Fireman" a couple of
months ago, it is just possible I might have been able to give you some
suggestions and advice which would have both provided stimulus and
more certainty on your part that you were headed in the right direction.
In the present circumstances, as in the past with Doubleday, you've
held on to the manuscript until the very last minute so that neither
editor nor agent can act as a proper sounding board for you. I do think a
sounding board is valuable, and I think a lot of the tension, pressure and
anxiety could have been reduced, if not avoided, had you followed such

a course. In other words, I don't think you should be afraid to show me work which you consider unfinished, to get another opinion. I wish you would give this some thought.

D.

Bradbury

July 30, 1953

Dear Don:

Thanks for yours of the 24th.

[. . .] Thanks for your continuing offers to be a "sounding board" for me. You always have been, of course. And I have always been very much indebted to you for your help. The trouble is, in the case of "The Fireman," you couldn't possibly have helped me several months ago, or saved me any uncertainty or any time, really, for several months ago I had nothing to show you. Only now, at this time, do I have anything to show you, and you are seeing it as it is finished. But four months back, there was only the original version of "The Fireman." I had done work on it, of course, and thrown the work out. And started over fresh. When I know that something drastic is wrong with my work, I just pitch in and do it. Then, when I think I have something decent on hand, but suspect some hidden errors, I need Congdon so much it isn't funny. I need you now, and I hope you will be as frank as possible with the finished new version of "The Fireman." It's never too late to do forty new pages of material. I am always willing to do this and Ian will have to wait if necessary, for me to get this thing right. It's coming better every day. Over this weekend I'll have the last pages of the third and final section in the mail to you. Next week, early, I hope to have the early section, on the meeting between Montag and Clarisse, cut and touched up to make her come more alive. Plus some work on the transitional nervousness of Faber, who moves from cowardice to a semblance of strength and back to cowardice again, in his face-to-face meeting with Montag. It is a little rough, I feel.

The trouble with all my relationships with publishers so far has been my agreeing to deadlines. I work right up to the very last, writing and rewriting and fixing, and then we lose out in the magazine markets. I don't know how to remedy this, for I don't want to show you anything that I *know* is wrong. I don't want help in the things I feel aren't ready, and then by the time I get them ready, there is usually little time for you to help me with the subtle things that may have escaped me. Yet one *does* have to have some sort of deadline to work toward. In the future, I hope to finish a book here or there, without making a contract on it, really get it all done, and let you look at it before we even show it to a publisher. But I've had such a damn funny career, in a way; I've always sold books to publishers without showing them a completed script, sometimes only an outline. Other authors usually submit finished work, and there is time for agent and editor to jump on it. I've always signed contracts for work-in-progress, and because I've always had a relaxed, let's-have-fun philosophy of working on these stories, it might be ten years from Christmas before I actually finished up a book if I didn't have pressure. It's a damned paradox; I need the pressure to finish the long drudge of a book, but the fact that a publisher sets a deadline to publish, prevents my getting the "sounding-board" help from you that, when it is time, I need so much.

I've been able to get much done in the last three weeks by thinking only one thing and relaxing as a result of the thought: Ballantine isn't important, the deadline isn't important, getting the book out this year isn't important. Only one thing's important now—doing a really wonderful book, doing a fine book, because if the book comes out and is bad, I'll be dead, but Ballantine will go on living. And even if the book doesn't come out, Ballantine will live. So let's have fun, let's do wonderful work, lets knock down all the damn lousy writing that is in the original version of "The Fireman," and put every single stone back together again to make a more solid structure, a better thought-out, and more firmly fleshed book.

The frightening thing to me is the fact that I might have at one time agreed to let "The Fireman" go into galleys in its original version, to be corrected that way. It would have killed me from shock to have had that happen and to discover, belatedly, how bad the original was. So much of this belated nervousness is the result of my own stupidity in not re-reading "The Fireman" entirely, long long ago, when we first signed the contract. But I was living on my remembrances of the original story. After all, I told myself, originally I did some seventy-five thousand to one hundred thousand words of writing and rewriting to get the *Galaxy* version of "The Fireman"; it must be pretty decent, it must be perfect, save for the beginning, where the new work will go. But I've learned a lot about character and transition and growth in those three years, and now the original structure seems skeletal and inadequate in the extreme.

And then, of course, my political and sociological knowledge has built up a bit more of a reservoir in the last 36 months. I'm beginning to think for the first time in my life. Only now, am I on the outer periphery of really thinking about things with some degree of logic. It's great fun to feel the old boundaries moving out an inch here or there. And I can pick up Ortega Y Gasset or Toynbee[28] or the others and actually know what I'm reading. God, it's taken a long long time. And the exciting thing to discover, a thing which I discovered only last week, is that some of my new thinking, which went into *Fahrenheit 451* here or there, is echoed in Ortega Y Gasset and in Mumford's *Art and Technics*, which I got around to only a few days ago. I came by many of my ideas slowly, over a long period of time, looking and feeling, and recently, seeing Cinerama, I came out realizing that it was the quintessence of nothingness. Incredible, amazing, stupefying; but with a vacuum at its center. And if the government of a country wanted to really control its people, how wonderful a device would be this Cinerama item, so big, so encompassing, like an Environment itself, which could be carefully trimmed of any roots that led directly to reality. Keep the marionettes off the floor of the stage! By all means. Don't connect up the blood stream of the nation with the heart of reality, for God's sake. I came to this conclusion and put it in *Fahrenheit* and then turned to Mumford and Y Gasset and found it echoed there. Very exciting indeed. I don't ask to be original now. I ask only that I find myself thinking things out and then discovering that someone else, who thinks much better, has tickled the same problem in the ribs. It is good to see myself moving. And it is particularly heartening to know that I can on occasion say something that brings, as it did several weeks ago, a letter from Bernard Berenson, in Italy, his first fan-letter, he said, in some 80 years, re my article in *The Nation*.[29]

Do I sound like a kid with a toy? I am. I certainly am. Montag and I have much in common. I was raised by a father who was Republican, anti-Jewish, anti-Catholic, anti-Negro, anti-everything. It's taken a good many years to move out of those jungles of thought into the clean air of noon and stand in a clearing of my own. My machete is damn small and it hasn't much of a cutting edge, but by the time I'm fifty I hope I can make a nice path right straight down through the center of life. I'm still awfully young and naïve, which seems to be pretty typical of most of the guys I've known in my traveling around in this country, but I'm having one helluva good time. As long as I'm having a good time, piecing ideas together, and figuring out ways to emotionalize rational concepts, I'll keep right on jogging along, falling off cliffs, tripping over creepers, with my ignorance held in my right hand where people can see it and hit at it for me and put a sharp edge on it until some day it won't be ignorance at all, it'll be that machete I talked about a little space back.

All of which is to say that if *Fahrenheit 451* turns out only fairly, I'll be happy, for it says more now than it ever said before. Five years from now it could say more, I know, but since it *isn't* five years from now, it's only July 30th, 1953, I guess I better shut my yap and go back to figuring out Montag and his troubles.

Believe me, you are the most valuable sounding-board in the world, and you must always tell me when the slightest doubts come into your mind on certain stories of mine. I'm always delighted to hear from you and it only seems right to me that this book be dedicated to you for your friendship right on down the years.

More from me very soon. No reason why the last pages of the book won't go into the mail on Saturday the 1st of August.

Love and regards to you, Sally, Mike, Hal, Marie!

Ray

August 18, 1953

Dear Ray:

[. . .] Now that *Fahrenheit 451* is done, I'll comment on your letter of
July 30th which I found fascinating, and helped my own understanding
of what you are trying to do in your work. I was particularly impressed
with what you said about your own intellectual development, a frontier
where you can learn much that will deepen and broaden your work. At
the same time, you are not a writer primarily of the intellect; to date
you have been a writer primarily concerned with dramatizing a story in
which there is generally a single idea, and the intensity and vitality with
which you infuse the dramatization is why you are on your way to being
one of the most widely read writers in America.

Your emotional response to this "idea" in your story has always
been true and never false, but sometimes in the past, you've not had
the depth and breadth of knowledge or experience with the idea, and
this has left you exposed occasionally to the attack of being naïve or
excessively emotional.

There is much cold, intellectual writing on the part of our writers
in this country now, that your very fault sometimes seems an attractive
virtue, but the growth you have been demonstrating in the last 4 or 5
years, and the conscious deliberation set forth in your letter of July
30th, makes me very confident that you will gradually eliminate the
aforementioned problem.

But your ability to tell a story, to dramatize your idea, that
should never be tampered with. A writer must be born with this
passion. At this, you are a master and it is why you have such a
tremendous power of communication to all sorts of minds and to
peoples of all countries. It is imaginative genius. It is also something
that is held in contempt by the intellectual elite—for instance, the
New Yorker crowd seems to feel it is one of the lesser virtues, even
though they occasionally do stories by Dahl, Robert Coates, and a
few others who work with highly imaginative situations. One of the
things that seems to unsettle these people is the freshness, almost
the surprise, with which you set upon the dramatization of such

an idea; to them, such ideas would presume to be more commonly known, and they demand consequently, a more restrained, almost ironic approach to the idea, so that no one could ever accuse them of having joy at such discovery. It's just this appreciation of discovery, and the intense feeling you inject into the dramatization which makes them shy away, in my opinion.

But still, since your stories have given great pleasure and satisfaction to people who can be considered members of the intellectual elite, I do not see why you should ever be concerned with the malcontents. The great thing, which is pure, distilled Bradbury, is the skill with which you dramatize an idea and entertain the reader while he is absorbing it. The more you deepen your own understanding and experience with ideas, the more effective you will become.

Having said this, I would then hazard a guess that your anxiety over "good and bad writing" derives from certain compensations you have set up in yourself. Your overconcern with phrasing is, in my opinion, just overconcern and nothing more. As you seem to say yourself in your letter, your struggle with "The Fireman" was with your perception of Montag's character and being sure of his motivation within the idea with which you engaged him. I feel that the more you settle in your own mind your own growth and experience with ideas, the more you will relieve yourself of the anxiety that the writing is either bad or good. Your writing is professional and completely satisfying on any literary level. I think you will eventually discover that you are wasting time and energy rewriting and rewriting, because I doubt that you are improving the text, but you *are* trying to sink down deeper in your characters and in their motivations.

I think this is all very understandable when one is aware of your development as a writer. You have said yourself many times, that you write out of an inner emotional experience and often it requires a passage of time for you to understand the implications of that emotional experience with your mind. This intensifies your struggle because you are instinctively aware of your responsibility as an artist to communicate on the level of ideas, as well as a true emotional experience. I do think that you should try to quell as much as you can,

your fear and anxiety that some reviewer or critic or friend may find
a phrase or a paragraph which is unworthy of you. There never has
been a writer who has been completely impeccable, and as soon as
such a thing emerges in them as the cardinal virtue, the blood seeps
out of their work. I am sure you are working this out yourself—your
letter very clearly demonstrates this, as I said earlier—and I have
the greatest faith that you will achieve everything you wish to. I feel
strongly however, that you should not mis-label your own struggle,
nor fritter away your energies in directions away from the real
problem.

Of course, you can't shut off your production until you reach
a certain pinnacle which will satisfy you, because no one can ever
reach that pinnacle. You should have more faith in yourself and in
your achievements from day to day and not be afraid to publish and
communicate while you are struggling; as I say, you will always be
struggling with this, and in many instances, it is not for you to say
what is your best, or worst work. The public and the writer seldom
agree.

The business of being a "sounding board" is merely a crutch for you
along the way, and indeed more or less a crutch right *now* while you are
going through what I think is a basic realization in yourself. Someone
like Stanley[30] or myself can be of use to you while a piece of work is
in the half formed stages, because you can use us to find out whether
an idea has jelled sufficiently, whether you've sunk the piling down far
enough to get the meaning strong and clear.

Well, enough of this; I didn't mean to get you off on such a long
explanation, but your letter was so stimulating that it provoked a bigger
response in me than I at first thought it would.

Yours,

Don

Bradbury's 1953–54 screenplay adaptation of Moby-Dick *for John Huston soon
brought Bradbury offers for a number of films. He was considered for the 1956
British production of George Orwell's* 1984 *and was asked to adapt Jessamyn*

West's The Friendly Persuasion (1956) *for producer William Wyler, whom he*
had met through Huston. But he was at a creative impasse with his long-overdue
Illinois novel, and passed on both projects while he crafted portions of the novel
into the bridged story-chapters of Dandelion Wine (1957).

Bradbury
10750 Clarkson Rd.
Los Angeles 64, Calif.

                                                          March 31, 1955

Dear Don:

Thanks for yours of the 29th. I think Ian and Stan[31] are wise in
scheduling the hard-cover *October Country* first, with the soft-cover
three months later. It will be interesting to see how sales go, with this
arrangement. I'm certainly all in favor of it, anyway.
      [. . .]
      Fascinating news to hear that the Peters people have put my name
in as a possibility for the Orwell 1984 job.[32] That would be a corker. So
much depends, of course, on how the summer goes. I travel in so many
directions every day, every week, every month. Anyway, it would be
good to hear an offer made and decide, on the basis of time, summer,
and the Illinois book, whether I could do it.
      Here on the Coast, I hear that Wyler and his company have still not
picked a writer to do *The Friendly Persuasion.* Ben talked to me about
it again two days ago.[33] I told him approximately the same thing—if
they would be willing to wait until autumn for me, I can hardly imagine
a screenplay that would be more heartwarming for me to do. I have
always felt that this book would be around on the American scene
long after many Hemingway books were lost in the past. A drastic
observation, perhaps, but it's a natural feeling I have for West's ability,
especially in that one volume. [. . .]
      Guess that does it for this time. Save to say that I've had some
wonderful mail on the Verne article, so far, and most people who've read
it around town here seemed sincerely pleased about it.[34] Thank God

for that, too. I held my breath up until a few days ago, waiting for an
avalanche to fall on me, hard. . . .

Love to everyone!
Again thanks for everything!
Yrs,
Ray

---

*Over a period of thirty years, Bradbury would eventually write nearly twenty stories
inspired by the people, towns, and countryside he encountered in Ireland during the
fall and winter of 1953–54. As he worked to refashion these tales into stage plays and
finally into the novelized story cycle* Green Shadows, White Whale *(1991), his
submissions to Don Congdon would often include the memories that shaped them
and his hopes that they would find success as Congdon circulated them.*

April 8, 1955

Dear Don:

Here's the first of my Irish stories to come to you—"Ireland Green in the
Morning."[35] It was a long hard cold time in Dublin a year and three months
ago when the family went down to Sicily and I stayed on writing the *Moby
Dick* script over and over. Some days I simply sat at my typewriter and wept
silently, for it seemed I'd never be done with that damned Whale, and I'd
never be done with Dublin and the dreadful winter. On days like that, out in
the street, I often came upon this little lady playing her harp in the gutter.
Out of my encounter with her—this story.

Very hard to predict who might like it; but our last sale to *The Post*,
on "The Sound of Summer Running,"[36] was a bit of a surprise, so, who
knows, perhaps this Irish bit will please them. Look forward to your
opinion on it, anyway. [. . .]

Best to everyone!
Yrs,
Ray

_____

Many network television producers approached Don Congdon during the 1950s to discuss potential adaptations of Bradbury tales. The first serious offer to televise Fahrenheit 451, *discussed here between Bradbury and Don Congdon, would come to naught, but it showed the strong interest that this work already commanded in the Hollywood marketplace. Nothing would come of network interest in "The Next in Line" either, but the discussion allowed Bradbury to explain in depth the masterful subtleties that made it one of his most highly regarded stories of the 1940s. It remains a high-water mark of realism in his fiction, and forms, along with "Interval in Sunlight" (1954), the basis for his unfinished Mexican novel.*

April 12, 1955

Mr. Ray Bradbury
10750 Clarkson Road
Los Angeles 64, California

Dear Ray:

Got the television contracts for "Zero Hour" this morning and have sent it over to J. Walter Thompson.[37] I talked with one of the people there today and they said they're also interested in "Next in Line" for a live half-hour show. I know you've had this one on the list of prohibited for television, but I think a short-term lease for live wouldn't hurt a bit. Is it all right with you to negotiate this if they finally decide to use it? Their problem is what kind of plot motivation can be inserted to let the audience know why the husband kills the wife, and also how he does it. You don't have any bright ideas to immediately slap down on paper by chance? [. . .]

Television Playhouse has asked whether you'd consider a live hour show of *Fahrenheit 451*. They're not ready to make a definite offer yet, but I thought I'd ask you at this time whether you want to consider it. It seems to me that only two or three months ago I wrote you about it in some connection or other, and suggested waiting until you decided about the play. However, the fact that *Television Playhouse* is interested, and in my opinion they are consistently the best hour live show there is, and because Bob Aurthur is a great fan of yours, I've warmed up a bit more to the idea.[38] As a matter of fact, it just might possibly stimulate a higher level of interest both from theatrical producers and motion picture people if *TV Playhouse* came up with a stunning production. You'll remember that when *Studio One* did *1984* by Orwell that there was considerable talk for two or three weeks around the country. Let me have your reaction on this one, too. [. . .]

Sincerely,

Don

Bradbury
10750 Clarkson Rd.
Los Angeles 64, Calif.

April 18, 1955

Dear Don:

Thanks for yours of the 12th. Glad to hear there is interest from J. Walter Thompson on "The Next in Line." No reason, really, now, why we couldn't let a live version be done on TV. If they decide to use it, you can go ahead with negotiations, Don; thanks. The problem about plot motivation, concerning the reason why the husband kills the wife is in the story, but perhaps not emphasized enough. The real reason why the husband kills the wife is, gruesomely enough, he is simply bored with her and the life they have had. The real terror of the situation is in the casual way the husband allows her death to occur. He keeps himself remote from her death and therefore can never really acknowledge his own guilt after her death. He hides the murder in his own heart from himself under a swarm of inconsequential detail, the details of the trip, the rooms, the gas and oil problems of the car, the breakdown

of the car. All of these, interfering, prevent their escape from the
environment which, by frightening her, will destroy the wife. If he
had really wanted to save her life, he would have not let these details
interfere, he would have provided an escape from the nightmare
of Mexico for his wife. The true horror of the story then lies in the
reader's recognition of the fact that the husband is letting Mexico
kill his wife for him. Whether or not the husband will ever really
face up to his own deed, there is no way of telling; in all probability
he will rationalize the experience the rest of his life. Under the
circumstances, the motivation for his killing his wife via the "feeling
of mortality" in Mexico, is merely, as stated above, his boredom with
the marriage. At first glance this may not seem sufficient motivation,
but to a truly selfish and childish person, it is more than enough, and
it adds, yet again, even more nightmare to the situation. I think that
whoever adapts the story for live TV could point up the ordinariness
of the motivation, in the husband, and thus more clearly delineate
the nightmare lying just beneath the surface of the husband-wife
relationship.

As for how the husband kills his wife, I have already indicated, above,
that he uses Mexico for his weapon, knowing his wife's mortal fear of the
country, and its effect on her bad heart. The adaptor might well have the
wife say something to point this out to the viewer. She might possibly
observe that her husband is a murderer and that he is using Mexico as
a cold machete with which to chop at and destroy her, bit by bit. A little
death here, she says, a little death there, and finally, the large death for
herself. The weapon lies all about her, killing her with its symbols—
the El Dia De Muerte skulls and little plank-board funerals and floral
wreaths. Only he can save her life, she says, by taking her away from the
weapon that surrounds her like a mouth with a thousand teeth. . . .

He refuses, of course, laughing mildly at her "childish" demands.
[. . .]

A *live* TV use of *F451* would certainly be worth thinking of, and
if TV *Playhouse* continues to be interested, perhaps it might well be
the turning point for acceptance of the book here in Hollywood. I've
talked to so many people who've wanted to film it, but lack the final
ounce of guts to make the move. Perhaps a live TV show, if successful,

would push them off the cliff. It's something for us to approach, anyway, and if you can make the sort of deal that would be happy all around, then perhaps we should go ahead. If possible, I would like to have some sort of opportunity to look over the script, when finished, and make suggestions for it, if this can be arranged. I would be willing to make necessary changes for the *TV Playhouse* people, if I felt I could improve the script, in any way. Let me know how you feel on this, in any event. [. . .]

Had a wonderful time last week one night, out at Cal-Tech, lecturing to about a hundred young and enthusiastic scientists and scientific engineers on science-fiction, philosophy (ha!) and their own work. They kept me stepping to a fast pace, but I got through with my skin pretty much in one piece.

Guess that does it for this time. Thanks for all the news.

Best to you, Mike, Wendy, Sally,

yrs,

Ray

The depth of Bradbury's abiding friendship with Don Congdon was often seen in little asides such as this letter, where Bradbury conveys private emotions that only a close friend could understand and appreciate.

May 5, 1955

Dear Don:

[. . .] The result of our changing our phone number has been a rash of indignant letters from "acquaintances" who took our self-rescuing move toward sanity as a direct assault on their "friendship." I have been moved to philosophize about this untoward reaction and I would sum it up something like this: *only a real friend can understand why in hell you would have your number changed. All the rest are insensitive dwarfs, midgets, and adults whose entire babyhood was spent keeping everyone awake by crying all night.*

The other night I looked up from my book, tilted my head and whispered to Mag, "Listen!" She cocked an ear. "What?" she cried. I closed my eyes and listened for a moment myself. "Silence," I said. "That strange sound emanating from the telephone. My God, isn't it wonderful!" In tears, my wife could only nod dumbly. After a brief cry myself, I settled down with my book, and the evening passed with only the sound of our clogged sinuses in the room.

Nearest thing to a long ocean voyage I can recommend.

Refreshedly yrs,
Ray

The launch of Russia's Sputnik, *the first artificial Earth satellite, spurred on Bradbury's efforts to get a new hardbound edition of* The Martian Chronicles *back in print. But the night before the launch, the popular CBS* Playhouse 90 *dramatic television series broadcast "A Sound of Different Drummers," which had striking similarities to Bradbury's* Fahrenheit 451. *Bradbury's decision to file for plagiarism against CBS would take nearly four years to resolve.*

Oct. 4, 1957

Dear Don:

Here is a copy of *Report from Space*[39] which I thought you might want, to show to Stuart Scheftel or any others that show interest. With the Russian satellite in the sky today, you'd think one of the networks would get *busy* . . . ! But . . .

I've had more phone-calls. Last night and this morning, it's amazing how many people have been incensed about the *Playhouse* 90 business. People I haven't heard from in a year or so, have been calling.

Jack Sher, a motion-picture writer who has won three plagiarism suits, called, and suggested something you and I hadn't as yet discussed, the fact that this 90 production has endangered, in many ways, my plans for some future time finally rewriting and putting *F.451* on the stage. Something to remember when we tote up our list of possible damages. More from me, next week. Ben called CBS and talked to the business-head. Their lawyers are reading *F.451* now. Ben will call them on Monday or Tuesday, I gather. Best to everyone,

Yrs,

Ray

CBS allowed Bradbury to view the kinescope recording of the live Playhouse 90 performance of "A Sound of Different Drummers." He now worked with Don Congdon to develop a timeline for earlier negotiations with several studios for rights to Fahrenheit 451. *One of these negotiations had involved writer Robert Alan Aurthur, who subsequently scripted the* Playhouse 90 *broadcast.*

October 14, 1957

Dear Don:

Here is my list of observations made by me following the showing of the kinescope of A *Sound of Different Drummers* the other day at CBS. If you feel I have been unreasonable any where along the line, please tell me.

Your list-history on "The Fireman" and *F.451*, as I said in my other letter, is mighty impressive. Do you feel that this list might be sent to CBS-TV in New York and here in Hollywood at this time, to acquaint them with the facts concerning Robert Alan Aurthur and his close connection with my story in the last few years? It might conceivably save us much trouble. I would certainly like to get all this over with and forget it, for it colors one's thoughts constantly and is really a very upsetting thing to deal with, especially if it continues for too long a time. I would like your opinion on whether you think Ben should show your "history" to the people in charge over at CBS, and whether you will do the same in New York. I may be wrong, of course, and even with the history before them, they may elect to ignore us.

I will probably be calling you again, on all this, Wednesday, after you've looked over this enclosed brochure of mine.

Until then, best to everyone there.

Yours,

Ray

P.S. Will you please send a photo-reproduction of this outline back to me? My only other copy is with Ben. Thanks,

R.

Bradbury's fortunes with his Fahrenheit 451 *plagiarism lawsuit would not rest with corporate lawyers. In early November, Don Congdon pointed out why Ben Benjamin and the Famous Artists Agency would be limited in what they could provide in terms of legal counsel. Acting on Congdon's advice, Bradbury soon retained the Los Angeles law firm of Carter and Marks, who would represent him throughout the progress of the case to the highest levels of the federal justice system.*

November 6, 1957

Mr. Ray Bradbury
10750 Clarkson Road
Los Angeles 64, California

Dear Ray:

I got Ben's note about "sitting tight" waiting to hear from the CBS attorneys.

It seems to me probably the best thing for your own peace of mind is to set for yourself a deadline, which you will not go beyond, to get your own attorney, and assuming there is no satisfaction from CBS before that deadline. One has to be aware of the fact that Famous, or any agency for that matter, does a tremendous amount of business with CBS, and they are not equipped to think entirely from your point of view, as would an attorney. [. . .]

Yours,

Don

By 1958, Bradbury had added The October Country *and* Dandelion Wine *to the run of books that would remain in print for generations of readers. In April 1958, he sent the first major hardbound reissue of* The Martian Chronicles *since its 1950 publication to Don Congdon, prompting Bradbury to reflect on the making of that book and the slow but sure path to success for other midcentury Bradbury tales.*

April 16, 1958

Dear Don:

[. . .] The list I was referring to on the phone yesterday, of the stories I brought with me to New York to show you, in May 1951, was as follows: "Interval in Sunlight," "A Scent of Sarsaparilla," "The April Witch," "And the Rock Cried Out," "Lime Vanilla Ice,"[40] "The Magical Kitchen," "The Great Wide World Over There," plus three or four others. It's good to look at a list like that, and remember how discouraged I was when I left New York after 12 days without selling one of those stories. But they all *did* sell, eventually, though it took from six months to three years to do it. I find, in going over my file here today, that on the average, it has taken at least a year or more to sell most of my stories. I had never really considered it seriously, but the record is there. [. . .]

The best remedy is time, and *more stories* coming to you, by God!

Under separate cover I'm sending on a copy of the new edition of *The Martian Chronicles*.[41] Looking it over, I remember the night Brad came to your apartment in the Village and we talked until suddenly the *Chronicles* sprang to life. It's nice having the brainchild still around after all these years, and in this fine new dress.

Did I ever tell you my experience with the *Chronicles* when I trained to New York in late April, 1950? The book had been published that week and I was making my annual jaunt to see you and the editors, and all, and I was very uncertain and uneasy about the *Chronicles*. I remember giving a copy of it to a friend who was traveling with me on his way to Europe. He read it sitting beside me, all the way to Chicago, and liked it. *Liked* it. Well, I felt a bit more uneasy. Liking isn't enough for a writer. I got off the train in Chicago and it was a cold wintry day, with some snow still on the wind, and I trudged over to the Art Institute, as all good travelers do, to look around, and to meet two friends, two science-fiction readers, there.[42] But when I arrived at the Art Institute I found that not two people but twenty were waiting to meet me there. *The Martian Chronicles* had been out long enough in Chicago for some readers, and God Bless everyone, some fans to accumulate. I was taken to lunch, feted, wined, made over, and sitting there, blushing with glory, I thought, "I'm a writer!" It was the first time I really felt some of the things I always guessed writers must feel when they are finally accepted. Two hours later I got back on the train, absolutely singing, and came on to New York.

End of story.

End of letter. [. . .]

Best to everyone,
Yours,
Ray

Bradbury's intermittent odyssey as a contract writer with the independent Hecht-Hill-Lancaster Hollywood production company (H-H-L) paved the way for him to work with Sir Carol Reed in London during the summer of 1957 on a screenplay for his 1953 story, "And the Rock Cried Out." However, when Bradbury returned to work at H-H-L the following year, the highly successful consortium was overextended with unproduced properties as the partners prepared to head in different directions. Bradbury found himself adapting The Dreamers, *a postcolonial supernatural novel written by British film critic Roger Manvell, so that he could buy back his rights from H-H-L for "And the Rock Cried Out."*

The eccentricities of the daily routine became the satirical plot for this update to
Don Congdon.

Oct. 24, 1958

Dear Don,

Just a note to let you know I am imprisoned in this Chinese Fortune
Cookie factory and am stuffing this message in the next confection that
goes into the oven and thence to you!!!

Don't need help now. All goes well. [. . .] John Huston arrived
yesterday to liven things up with his own production here. Lancaster
is flexing his muscles, Jim Hill is drinking quietly on the side, Harold
Hecht is ebullient as ever, running in and out with original El Grecos
and Picassos under his arms. . . . We are mostly sitting here this week
talking and I am writing treatment pages to fill in all the material Roger
Manvell conveniently, and with malice aforethought, left out of his
book. I am enjoying this, really, and am sure I will do a fine script. No
ego here, I just feel that way about the property. [. . .]

The baker is coming now, so must stuff this in cookie and run!!! Yes
sir, Mr. Hill, no, sir, Mr. Hecht, maybe, Mr. Lancaster!

Yours, as ever,
Ray

P.S. Did the people at Columbia Pictures there in NYC get in touch
with you about your sending over a copy of the script of *And the Rock
Cried Out* for them to read? Carol Reed wrote me from London that he
was going to try to make one last pitch while traveling through, which
I think I mentioned to you in a letter a week ago . . . I had hoped that
Reed might finally get a chance to meet you there . . . but the latest news
is he is in Cuba and might not be back to NY for some time. Anyway, I
hope that Columbia has followed through to get the script. If not, you
might tell me, and I'll see what I can do to move things along.[43]

As Bradbury continued to work, intermittently, under contract to the fast-paced Hecht-Hill-Lancaster film production company, he would often use the intervals to work on his latest creative passion—the transformation of his Irish stories into one-act stage plays. Despite the relatively narrow appeal of these romantic stereotypes, they formed a bridge to his real-life experiences through the cold Dublin winter of 1953–54. As this letter shows, these encounters with everyday Irish life had helped him endure the stress of writing the Moby Dick *script for the hard-driven John Huston.*

Dec. 24, 1958

Dear Don:

Three weeks ago, as you recall, I sent you the teleplay version of *The Great Collision of Monday Last.* Now here, enclosed, is my stage adaptation of *The Great Collision.* Can you help me decide now which medium we submit it to, first?

The same situation applies to *A Clear View of an Irish Mist* which I sent you earlier this week. [. . .]

These could be fun, I think, with strict Abbey Theatre type–casting. I'd love to see people like Barry Fitzgerald and Thomas Mitchell and Arthur Shields water their mouths over roles like these.

Have you ever seen O'Casey's *Pound on Demand* staged? It's one of the most hilarious half hours in stage history if put in the hands of real actors who savor the whole thing. It's delicious. I suppose, in a way, that's why I've done these plays. I haven't at any time, consciously imitated O'Casey; I have, in fact, stayed strictly away from his plays during this time, for fear of taking on too much coloration. I wanted, mainly, to imitate his driving zest and the irrefutable illogic of his lovely characters. This, plus the fact that I *do* have 7 months of Irish time under my belt, made the task easier.

I used to walk through the rain from the Royal Hibernian Hotel up around to a little candy and magazine shop near a theatre in Dublin, so I could talk, but mainly listen, to an old lady there who had harps for vocal chords and the sweet wisdom of pure intuition in her selection of words. The woman was a poet, or seemed so to me, but I imagine, all languages, in the hands of proper people, heard by foreigners, become magical. If I have any of the lilt of the Irish in my stories about them, it comes from my nights in the candy-shop chewing Cadbury's Milk Flakes and listening to Edna St. Vincent Millay's great-grandma, or driving out to Kilcock and back 4 or 5 times a week with Mike, my driver, one way, and Nick, my village chauffeur, coming back.[44] They both breathed blarney and barley. [...]

Love to you and the family,
Ray

Bradbury's Fahrenheit 451 *plagiarism* suit against CBS did not come to trial *until May 1959, more than eighteen months after the broadcast of "A Sound of Different Drummers." Bradbury's lawyer, Gerson Marks, set out to prove that the CBS screenwriter, Robert Alan Aurthur, was familiar with the novel prior to writing the script.*

Ray Bradbury
10265 Cheviot Drive
Los Angeles 64, Calif.

May 30th, 1959

Dear Don:

This has been a most upsetting week. We went into Superior Court on Tuesday and got out of Court late Friday on the suit concerning CBS and *F.451*.

We started out with two-and-a-half strikes against us. Judge Yankwich, in his mid-seventies, is senile, irascible, and was quite obviously prejudiced when the case began. This is not just my opinion. I have run into some other lawyers, over and above my own, in the past week, and each shook his head and protested that Yankwich should have been removed from the bench years ago.

As if this weren't bad enough, the judge accepted everything Aurthur said on the stand. As a result, we were not ever able to even prove *access to my material*!!!

I hope you will forgive me if I say, in passing, that I am unhappy about Bernard Wolfe's not coming out. If he had accepted our invitation to be flown out free of charge, we could have proved access. I understand his reasons for not coming, but right now with the roof falling in on me, I'm afraid I don't like him very much, anyway. This will pass, and I will be more forgiving in a few days or weeks.

Yankwich will deliver his decision in a few days, but Gerson Marks and Sandy Carter agree with me our chances are miniscule to say the least. We did everything we could, but Aurthur is a very clever man on the stand and claimed that even though he was story-editor and associate producer on Philco Playhouse, he didn't bother to read my novel. And the judge believed him!

I have lost 10 days out of my writing schedule, preparing the case and being in court. I hope to get back to work on the Irish play in a few days. Thanks for your encouraging letter on the 1st Act. I'm happy to hear, also, that the contracts are working out fine.

Best, as ever, yours,

Ray

[Received June 19, 1959]

Dear Don:

I suppose you've already seen this [clipping]:

There isn't much to add to it. Luckily, Yankwich denied attorney's fees, so I won't have to assume Aurthur's expenses.

We're reading over the Yankwich decision now, so we can file our Appeal in the next week or so.

The Clerk of the Court, when he telephoned Gerson the day before yesterday, to break the news, said, confidentially, that he felt that if we appealed to a higher court, we had a good chance of winning. Who knows? Certainly I don't, any more. But it is interesting to have everyone on the Court staff on our side, save the Judge himself.

I won't let myself be built up again. This has been the unhappiest month in my life, mainly because it has shown me a side of myself that I don't enjoy seeing. It has made me nervous, lousy company, mean, high one moment, low another. A single pine-needle has fallen off a tree and tapped me on the brow and I have reacted as if an avalanche came down a mountain and buried me a mile deep. If a *real* crisis came up in my life, I begin to wonder what kind of pasteboard I'd be made of.

To hell with that. [. . .]

Best,

Ray

Within a month of the decision in favor of CBS, Bradbury and his attorney Gerson Marks had worked out plans for an appeal, described below. The United States Ninth Circuit Court of Appeals reversed the lower court decision in January 1961; CBS would file a further appeal with the US Supreme Court, but when Bradbury's team also filed, CBS settled out of court.

June 25, 1959

Dear Don:

Thanks for your long letter about the resolution of the trial and one's attitude toward justice and the world in which it exists, which is far away from our world. Right off, I think it is time our children were taken to court for three or four days out of each year of their life starting when they're ten or eleven. I should have been prepared for much of the impact. I feel our educational system is shirking its duties in not showing us the real thing, in detail. Perhaps more of this thing is being done—I doubt it. A quick run-through on a guided tour isn't enough. [. . .]

About our Appeal on the plagiarism suit—we are going ahead with it immediately. Hold onto your hat—it will cost me about $700 to have the record typewritten, plus another $800 to have it printed in copies to go before the Ninth Circuit Court of Appeals, plus, I hear, $250 I must put into bond to insure court costs, if necessary, later. So I will be out of pocket at least $1500 to start with, all of which shows once again, the ordinary person cannot go to court. Six years ago, I would have found such a suit impossible to sustain. Television, with its available jobs, makes ready money possible when one needs it. If my *F.451* screenplay job is delayed in any way, I'll ask you and Ben to line up some t-v assignments, which are definite. Of course, quite soon I take it, the money from Bantam should be coming through . . . ??

More from me, next week, [. . .]

Again, thanks and best,
Ray

P.S. It strikes me I may not have told you—the backer who was to pay me the weekly salary to write *F.451* for the screen dropped out of the project upon hearing we had lost our plagiarism suit. So now Ingo[45] and Roger Kay are hustling about finding new interest. I was supposed to start the 1st of July. I have now put the date off to the 6th and will further put it off until I am certain the money will be coming in each week. [. . .]

R.

Bradbury's summer 1960 letters to Don Congdon centered on his revisions to Something Wicked This Way Comes, *which would become his first Simon & Schuster title. Other projects were also in play, leading Bradbury to comment on his recent departure from Doubleday and his new contract work writing a* Martian Chronicles *screen treatment for MGM Studios.*

July 24, 1960

Dear Don:

Thanks for your letter of the 21st. I have already begun to go through the novel for the third draft this year alone. I have many delicious character and atmospheric tidbits to add, all of which intrigue me, and certainly some time this early autumn a fairly decent book should be on hand. I still blow hot and cold on the title *Something Wicked This Way Comes,* which strikes me, as well as others, as artsy-craftsy. Other titles that have recently popped into being are: *Watchman, What of the Night?* . . . *Autumn Is a Way of Life* . . . *Nightshade & Company* . . . *The Pandemonium Theatre Company* . . . *The Midnight Balloon* . . . and on, and on, and on. . . .

Doubleday, as I imagined, did not panic for the exits when they heard the news that the flea was packing his tiny trunks and leaving. All the elephants watched as the microscopic author marched past their stables, leaving his infinitesimal footprints on the shifting editorial sands . . . one second after ye little author was out the door, the elephants were back to chewing their monstrous cuds and munching on great bales of *Ice Palace, Jericho's Daughters* and *How to Make a Million Dollars Between Twelve and Tiffen.*[46] . . .

I have no signed agreement with MGM. All there is is the deal slip, which you have a copy of there. Evidently the contract will be ready around New Year's, Ben thinks.[47] MGM has elephants as well as lions, too. [. . .]

First week at MGM over, happily. Doing character work on my project now. Hope to start treatment this next week, and, with luck, get into the fun of the screenplay as quickly as possible. I would much rather make mistakes in the screenplay and have to correct them, with time and sweat, which is more fun than trying to plan, through character analysis, what they might be up to. [. . .]

Best, as ever,

Yours,

Ray

As the prospects for filming his mid-1950s dark carnival screenplay stalled, Bradbury found it difficult to transform this project into the sustained work of long fiction that the storyline demanded. Congdon provided perspective at key moments as the emerging novel, Something Wicked This Way Comes, *evolved through four drafts between 1958 and 1962. At this point in the summer of 1960, Congdon helped Bradbury develop distinctive and contrasting personalities for the two boys at the center of the novel, Will Halloway and Jim Nightshade.*

August 24, 1960

Memorandum to: Ray Bradbury
From: Don Congdon

Here are my notes, taken down while reading *Something Wicked This Way Comes*:

[...] It occurred to me that you should plant earlier the seeds of Jim's being wilder and less controllable, less stable than Will. As I think I mentioned in reading the previous version, Twain managed to get a very different quality between Huck Finn and Tom Sawyer. He got much more interested in Huck Finn the more he wrote about the two boys, of course, and I'm not suggesting that this novel go off in that direction, but if Jim were introduced as having more of a reputation in town of being a queer boy, a little more withdrawn, a boy not quite so easily ready to run off and float with the wind, but very possibly the night hours were his best, perhaps he's the one that got Will to come out at night. Will may be better playing ball or doing things during the day in the sunlight, and Jim just isn't so susceptible. But the nighttime, if it isn't pushing too much to stress this even though Jim's name is Nightshade, provides another area where you could get across the differentiation between the two boys. [...]

My main point is that there is still more work to be done to set the boys apart as real individuals, and as I said over the 'phone, that some of the emphasis upon the inability of Will and his father to reach each other is reduced. I think you hit this too hard, and I think the reader would be more impressed if there were a little less of it, but of course the point should be kept in the book. It is important.

DC

Take from this what's useful, of course.

August 27th, 1960

Dear Don:

Your long long letter concerning the work that needs to be done on
Something Wicked This Way Comes arrived a few hours ago, and once
again I find myself with a debt of gratitude that it will take me years
to work out . . . if such things could be done. Again I feel so fortunate
to be with you on these many projects where you protect me not
only from business but aesthetic mistakes. Just about everything
you say in the letter touches on some faintly sore spot in my mind
concerning the novel—things I suspected but could not fully
recognize.

I'm happy that the major construction flaw, which bothered me, has
been overcome by blending the characters of the father and janitor.[48]

All of the other things, as I move along, I will look at carefully. Later,
if I find myself in opposition to anything you've indicated, I'll drop you a
note, but right now it is just the sort of heaven-sent analysis I need. [. . .]

Again, thanks for your long and detailed criticism.

Best as ever, yours,
Ray

Bradbury was often critical of intellectual and mainstream magazine as-
sessments of the American cultural and political scene, and he felt that the
wide-ranging satire of Mad *magazine was far more effective. He invoked his*
own special kind of satire in referring to Mad *as his favorite "intellectual" mag-*
azine. Bradbury's discovery of Help! *magazine, with a staff that included many*
of Mad's *former artists and writers as well as assistants such as future Monty*
Python co-founder Terry Gilliam and journalist-activist Gloria Steinem, pro-
vided an opportunity to explain his perspective to Don Congdon as the first is-
sues of Help! *reached print.*

Bradbury
10265 Cheviot Drive
Los Angeles 64, Cal.

September 14, 1960

Dear Don:

I enclose two copies of the magazine *Help!* plus a letter from the
Editor, Harvey Kurtzman. I've glanced at the magazines, found them
in many ways like *Mad*, my favorite intellectual magazine in the USA
today, and would approve if you could arrange a reprint with Mr.
Kurtzman on one of my stories. His magazine doesn't compare with
Mad, of course, but it is a good try, and I find the old film-photos, with
captions, great fun.

Do you ever read *Mad*, incidentally? I don't know if I've mentioned
it to you in letters, in the past. But it seems to me that more often than
not it is busy doing the job of cutting our political boobs and hacks
down to size and making the sort of fun of advertising, tv, etc., that
our so-called intellectual magazines should be doing but don't do. The
highbrow magazines print articles, which are one thing, most articles
don't destroy the silliness of man's world. Good plays, like those of
Shaw, good t-v comedy, like that of Sid Caesar, and good cartooning, like
that in *Mad*, demolish the nitwit on the spot.

Nuff said. You might try to up the price on a reprint, with Mr.
Kurtzman, naturally. But, above all, I do approve of appearing in *Help!*,
and hope you agree. I've dropped Kurtzman a note telling him that I'm
sending this letter of his to you.

Best, as ever,
Yours,
Ray

---

*Don Congdon would become Bradbury's primary sounding board as the Ken-
nedy administration accelerated the timeline for NASA's spaceflight program.*

Bradbury's dreams had become the nation's Space Age dreams as well, and this process heightened his desire to remain in the vanguard of science fiction writers who identified closely with this goal. Not surprisingly, Bradbury first expressed his determination on inauguration day, 1961.

January 20th, 1961

Dear Don:

[. . .] I can hardly believe this day has come—the day of Kennedy's inauguration. The grousing Republicans have made life so uncertain, and elections so tenuous in my mind, I half expected old tricky Dick to step up and humbly accept inauguration by acclamation this morning; I am still in shock from finally accepting the great truth.

I hope, somewhere down the line, to be part of this Democratic four years. I'm sending all of my books to Kennedy, through Arthur Schlesinger, Jr., who is a s-f fan, with the word that if there is some way, in the coming years, for me to help dramatize the Space Age, I would be delighted (hell, what a weak word) to try my hand at it.

That's all for today. I look forward to your reaction to all the above.

Best, as ever,

Yours,

Ray

P.S. I have accepted an invitation to spend two weeks at Bread Loaf from August 15th to the 30th this summer, lecturing with and standing alongside of Robert Frost, Howard Nemerov, John Ciardi, and others. This is an old old dream come true, an adventure I've always wanted.[49] [. . .]

Bradbury's increasing canon of Irish stories-into-plays would soon begin to radiate out into stage adaptations of his fantasy and science fiction stories as well; by 1962, he began to form an acting company whereby he would experiment with small-venue stage adaptations for the next forty years. On the eve of this

transition, Bradbury offered Don Congdon his sense of the distinctions between
story writing and writing for the stage.

This letter also captures his last unrealized hope to salvage his Martian
Chronicles *option at MGM under writer-director Richard Brooks (an old*
friend from Bradbury's Moby Dick *days with John Huston) who was, unfortu-*
nately, unable to make time to take on the project from original producer Julian
Blaustein.

April 14th, 1961

Dear Don:

Here are three of the one-act Irish plays in their original form: *The First*
Night of Lent, *The Great Collision of Monday Last*, and *A Clear View of an*
Irish Mist.

The fourth one-act Irish play, *The Anthem Sprinters*, I have excerpted
from the long play, combining it with missing elements from the short
story, which we sold to *Playboy*.[50] [. . .]

New developments here at MGM. I bumped into Richard Brooks,
the writer-director, yesterday, and he expressed interest in *The Martian*
Chronicles. I'm talking with Blaustein about him. He may well be the
man to take over the job of working as quasi-producer-critic on the
project so we can get back to work on it sooner. He would want to
direct, which is all right with me, for I believe his powers have increased
considerably in recent years, as witness *Elmer Gantry*, which I very
much liked. Brooks not only directed, but wrote the screenplay on that
one. I'll let you know what develops.[51]

The one-acts are really piling up, eh? And over the years I hope
to do twenty or thirty more, to implement my short-story writing,
to carry it over, really, into this new field. I've begun to know the
difference between story-page, theatre-page, and screen-page, a
fascinating thing to watch the cogs in my mind ease over into new
functions, to change gears and use slightly different languages. On
the short story page, images to be read and summoned up by the
mind; on the stage, images to be heard and shaped as echoes; on the

screen, direct images to be seen, but always masking some small
element of mystery, so you give the viewer a chance to supply echoes
and shapes with his own imagination. Fascinating, fascinating. I
think a writer can really grow by learning from each to strengthen
the other.

Thanks and best!
Yrs,
Ray

In the summer of 1961, as it became apparent that his year of working on a
Martian Chronicles *screen treatment would not succeed at MGM, Bradbury*
had hardened his heart against studio collaboration where he would have no
control of the outcome. For now, he focused on finishing deep revisions to
Something Wicked This Way Comes *for Simon & Schuster. The first test*
of his resolve came late that summer from a surprising opportunity, as he re-
lated to Don Congdon. The Alfred Hitchcock Presents *television series had*
aired Bradbury story adaptations since the very first 1954–55 season, but now
Hitchcock had another idea in mind.

September 4th, 1961

Dear Don:

[. . .] All kinds of things brewing. Hitchcock is planning a film on
Daphne Du Maurier's story "The Birds." A feature film. He has called
me in to speak to me about it. I've always wanted to work with him, of
course. And while I'm already busy with the TV film project for him, it
is tempting to contemplate a further involvement.[52] After I've re-read
the story and had another talk with him, I'll make up my mind. Main
trouble is he wants me immediately, and, of course, my novel calls
piteously to me to get on to the end and get the manuscript off to S&S.

　　Here stand I in the plenteous rain with nary a spoon nor a
drinking cup.

Am also guilt-ridden by hidden self who declared, earlier in summer, no more films for rest of year.

Hard decision ahead. [. . .]

Yours,
Ray

P.S. I had a further talk with Hitchcock later today and he cannot wait the 8 weeks I asked him to wait . . . so the deal is off. Really, the novel *must* get worked on!

Academy Award–winning actor Charles Laughton was the last of Bradbury's true mentors; his 1955 stage adaptation of Fahrenheit 451 *for Laughton had failed to reach production, but Bradbury had learned much. He would learn to write light musical verse in a delightful but unstaged project for Laughton's Academy Award–nominated wife, Elsa Lanchester. Laughton revived Bradbury's interest in Bernard Shaw and Shakespeare, and often discussed his own stage acting strategies with his younger friend. As Laughton entered his final illness, Bradbury confided his grief and compassion for Laughton in two letters to Don Congdon.*

August 6th, 1962

Dear Don:

[. . .] P. S. I'm sorry to report Charles Laughton is in a very bad way. His wife called me to the house last week; I spent several hours with her and unless there is a miracle of remission, which *does* happen once every ten thousand times, his chances for survival are limited. It was a strange sad day . . . for I realized that with all their fame and money, here were the Laughtons depending on someone, really, who is a comparatively new friend . . . a situation which flabbergasts, unsettles, and touches me, by turn. I have nothing but good thoughts of Charlie . . . though he has always groused about money, and I have heard much from others . . . still I can only judge by my own experience, which was excellent.

R.

After battling cancer for more than a year, Charles Laughton passed away on December 15, 1962. Bradbury's continuing friendship with Elsa Lanchester made it easier to face Laughton's passing; he would remain close to her for the last quarter century of her life, providing counsel at times as she contemplated offers by others to write books about Laughton's life and distinguished career.

December 19th, 1962

Dear Don:

[. . .] Elsa Lanchester telephoned yesterday and we had a ten minute talk about the long strange terrible months just passed with Charles. She made it easy for me not to attend his funeral today by saying that Charles himself hated funerals and never went to them. I will go by and see her later this week. It is a good thing to be able to say when a man is dead that my own personal relationship with him makes for a flawless and happy memory. I know of other things that went on in the house and the marriage . . . which is something else again . . . but by firsthand information, on scene, I can honestly say I remember his graciousness with me, his thoughtfulness about my own creativity when I was working on the operetta with him, his wonderful treatment of my kids when they went over to swim with him in his pool, and the private performances of Shakespeare he often gave for me to prove a point he wanted me to learn. This and our first grand tour of Disneyland one day six years ago, make for a fine, fine memory of a man I vastly enjoyed being with. God rest Charlie Laughton and give him peace after this nightmare year.

More from me, soon.

Best,
Ray

In the fall of 1964, Bradbury's growing success with small-venue stage adaptations of his stories would blossom into a four-month Los Angeles run of one-acts based on three of his cautionary science fiction tales ("The Veldt," "The Pedestrian," and "To the Chicago Abyss"). As he worked with director Charles Rome Smith on this production, he wrote to Don Congdon about the ready-made Southern California audiences for these futuristic plays.

March 24th, 1964

Dear Don:

Things are popping along here with Chuck Smith and our effort to get the one-act plays in production for October. [. . .]

If we *can't* open here in the middle of the Space Industry complex, I'll eat a genuine plexiglass astronaut's helmet. With hundreds of thousands of workers and thinkers alone in the various rocket fields hereabouts, we should be able to fill the theatre. And my contacts with various fields of learning will be invaluable. My latest conquest: I have been asked to address the school of Architecture at S.C.![53] Isn't that incredible? But the rules of Creativity apply where ever you put them down. You either love what you are doing or don't love it. I teach love, jumping up and down, yelling with excitement, intuitive thought, proper hates, . . . er . . . but you've heard all this before. [. . .]

Happy Easter!
Yours,
Ray

Bradbury sensed the coming success of The World of Ray Bradbury, *his trio of one-act plays, during the final weeks before opening at the Coronet Theatre in Los Angeles, and this emotional high carried over into his comments on the recent passing of spy-novel master Ian Fleming. He had been a vocal proponent of filming Fleming's James Bond novel franchise many years before feature film productions began in 1962, and his respect for Fleming's final "no regrets" attitude is evident in this letter.*

August 20, 1964

Dear Don:

[. . .] Our opening has been delayed until October 8th, but things move
steadily and excitingly onward. I am having a ball with all this. When
you are your own producer, you never look behind and never look back,
or, for that matter, to either side. You just walk on ahead into the happy
or slightly confusing problems. But I really *love* it!!!

Did you read Ian Fleming's final words in the hour before he died,
on his way to the hospital?

"Oh, it was all such a lark."

Isn't that great? God, when I read it tears came to my eyes. It was
what I wanted him to say, what we all wanted him to say, for it was in his
books, and I've read them all. Jesus, if, when it comes our time, we can
only, fervently, with gratitude, say the same. I thought I ought to tell you,
in case you missed his farewell speech. I'm really sorry I never met him.

That's all for today.

Best until next week.

Ray

---

*Two years after his long and ultimately unsuccessful stint at MGM writing a
screen treatment for* The Martian Chronicles, *the producer-director team
of Alan Pakula and Robert Mulligan engaged Bradbury for a second attempt.
Bradbury was impressed by their success with* To Kill a Mockingbird, *and he
had high hopes when he began contract work in Pakula's Warner Brothers offices. When he opened his desk drawer, he found letterhead stationery that had
been printed years earlier for studio head Jack L. Warner, prompting Bradbury
to reflect on the magic years of MGM in a letter to his agent Don Congdon.*

November 23, 1964

Dear Don,

I found this stationery in my desk just now when I arrived to start my incarceration at the W. B. studio with Pakula-Mulligan. I thought you might be charmed. There is a certain air about a studio like this . . . memories, I imagine, of the best all around films made by any studio . . . Warner films hold up over the years . . . when you think back on the product of the thirties and early forties . . . not the musicals, no, strangely enough . . . but all of the Bogart films, all the Bette Davis films . . . all of the Huston films made here . . . Edward G. Robinson, James Cagney . . . they were story tellers and told their stories well . . . *Robin Hood*, with Flynn, is still a damned fine all around jolly adventure . . . anyway, I have respect for any studio that respects story telling . . . and my nostalgia for the place is based solidly on this story-telling background which was their symbol until a few years ago. I also respect Warner for he is one of the few remaining big Punjabs who doesn't look to New York for his orders (please forgive), but does all his own deciding here, as does Goldwyn. All the other studios have to run off to Manhattan every time they feel the need to wash their hands.

Anyway, I'm here, and will keep you posted as to my progress on the screenplay as it moves its juggernaut way through Space. [. . .]

Best, as ever,
Ray

Three years of small-venue stage ventures in Los Angeles culminated in a four-month run for The World of Ray Bradbury *at the Coronet. For this production, Bradbury stepped away from his beloved Irish plays and the romantic potential of* The Wonderful Ice Cream Suit *to stage, instead, three science-fictional glimpses of possible futures: "The Pedestrian," "The Veldt," and "To the Chicago Abyss." Stage and screen represented his first interwoven loves as a child, and the Coronet Theatre experience, with the actors of his newly formed Pandemonium Theatre Company, prompted a rare moment of reflection.*

Bradbury

February 15, 1965

Dear Don:

I had to pass on to you these few reflections on last night, when the
World of RB closed here many many months after its opening on
October 14th. Norman Corwin and Sir Carol Reed came over along with
a lot of friends for the final performance, and we had a beer-pretzel
and champagne party after, on stage, and I stood among all my friends
thinking what a fine place to have a party, at the very heart of the theatre
itself. And I thought: this is where I have belonged since I was ten. It took
a long time and a very long way around from doing magic tricks then, and
appearing in amateur theatricals, to a night like last night when you say to
yourself, I really belong. This theatre is as much my body and my flesh as
my own body and flesh are. How fortunate to be one of those who really
knows his place, finds it, and tries to tend it well and make it vital.

Claude Giroux came to the plays three nights in a row, and capped
the evening with his announcement to me and Chuck that he would like
to start rehearsals in early April in New York and open on or around the
21st.54 [. . .] He kept saying, you'll run for years in New York, and I, like
a cautious Chinaman, kept crying: Bad Rice! Bad Rice! to fend off the
envious Gods. [. . .]

With much affection.

Yours,
Ray

---

*At the end of each year, Bradbury would send Don Congdon a net assessment
of triumphs and disappointments. Sometimes a gift would mute the disappointments, as seen here in the 1965 letter, where the disappointing critical reception
for his brief October run of* The World of Ray Bradbury *for Claude Giroux on
the New York stage remained fresh in his mind. This note also shows how, in his
mid-forties, Bradbury was hoping to extend the creativity of his remaining years*

by taking more time to work alone. The lure of stage and screen, along with his growing popularity as a speaker, would challenge these wishes in the years ahead.

Monday, December 27, 1965

Dear Don:

The Michelangelo book is the most beautiful book in the art field I think I have ever seen.[55] Especially since I have stood before so many of the statues and paintings represented in the book and been stunned by them, so the book was a stunning experience. Aside, I hope one day soon you will have the one experience alone of seeing the Boy David in Florence. It seems silly to say that the encounter is like that one might have with the Grand Canyon which I saw as a boy, but the experience is absolutely the same. There simply are no words to describe the awe one has in the face of a sculptor being able to do what Michelangelo did with David alone. Anyway, because of this event in my life, your book, opened this Christmas, is very precious. Thank you.

And here it is again, the end of another year. This one went faster, as the cliché puts it, and I can see now that from here on it will be a waterfall of days and each must be grabbed onto and worked with as well as possible. I am getting more and more touchy about giving my time to people. Once I squandered it horribly, now I refuse again and again to go to lunch with anyone. I want that time to write, or walk and think about things, or go off to a book store, gallery, or what have you. I am going to ride the waterfall *my* way. So, too, I am more afraid of working with people than ever before. Claude Giroux had so little to offer me, constructively. Two years of work on the *Chronicles* seem to be coming to very little, and I begin to wonder once more if the screenplay mightn't have been closer to all our hearts desires if I had worked less closely with Alan and Bob, much as I like them.[56] Hard to figure, hard to judge, for the screenplay is such a special form.

Anyway, thank you for your part in making 1965 another fine year. The sum of it is in the main good. First, in the matter of health, we all survive and more than survive. Creatively, we have had some new and good short stories to show, and my experiment in Los Angeles theatre while not lucrative enough to help us do another set of plays, was aesthetically and critically excellent. We shall, for the time being, forget about Giroux. I seem still to be licking those wounds. I had a fine gift at Christmas from a New York fan who went on different nights, with his brother, to see the Plays. They then bought all the reviews and their comment was that the reviewers were reading things into the Plays that simply weren't there. I think I believe this also, when one sits down to sum up all the columns. I was not, as many reviewers indicated, doing a doom-laden evening, or if I was I was unaware of it.

Anyway, despite some reverses and momentary setbacks, I look at the year with overall pleasure, and set my sights on 1966 [. . .].

Much love to you all, yours,

Ray

After attending a 1975 performance by Marcel Marceau in Los Angeles at the Shubert Theatre, Bradbury went backstage and asked to meet the world-renowned mime. Marceau came out of his dressing room and introduced himself to Bradbury by saying, "You may know me, but I know you!" (Bradbury-Eller interviews, March 14, 2010). He immediately described Marceau's enthusiasm in this letter to Don Congdon.

Mar. 21, 1975

Dear Don:

Thanks for yours of March 11th.

A. I'm working on the Intro for the *Pillar of Fire* Playbook.[57]

B. Yes, it's okay to cut out Jesus and Christ if they insert in the text, in parenthesis [He swears]. I can then suggest in my Intro that what ever seems best for the age group, audience, etc., etc., can be inserted there by the director or actor, later.

C. I don't think there are any substantial changes I want made in the plays.

[. . .]

Hey, I've spent two evenings with Marcel Marceau here during the past week. He wants to do pantomimes based on many of my stories sometime in the next year or year and a half, in Paris. I gave him all my books, most of which he has already read. We got on absolutely fine from the first minute on. He opens in NYC in about a week at the City Center, I think. He will be staying at the Regency Hotel in New York, so give him a buzz and he will probably invite you to the Opening Night, okay? . . .

I would like you to meet him, maybe after that performance, or probably at a later time, some night after one of his other shows. He has dinner late most nights. He doesn't have any food until midnight, after a show. I think you will like him. He seems super fond of all my work, and of course I think it would be great if he put on a third-evening or half-evening or full-evening of my stories carried over into mime. [. . .][58]

Luck and best!

R.

Bradbury's dream of controlling his own television series was fulfilled through The Ray Bradbury Theater, *which ran on HBO and the USA Network from 1985 through 1992. Bradbury wrote all sixty-five adaptations of his stories for the series, the last of these being his script for "The Handler."*

Dear Don:

[. . .] I have, this day of April 10th, 1992, sent off copies of my final teleplay *The Handler*, to New Zealand, to Peter Sussman at Atlantis, and to Bonnie Hammer at USA-TV, NYC.[59] Thus finishing off the last of the scripts, to end the season. Unbelievable. To think, it is all done, it is all finished, at last. And without the aid, strangely sad, this late in time, for he *began* it all years ago, of Larry Wilcox. Sad, because it was he and his partner, seven years or so ago, who convinced me I should trust them and start the series!

The latest films from New Zealand are coming in, and we have, I think, the best season yet. Praise God, our actors, our directors, our various producers and, what the hell, *me!*

I waited for fifty years for this power to pass into my typewriter hands. Looks like God, He of the Remington and Underwood, understood my dream and my need.

Love,

Ray

Friday, April 10th 1992

RUTH ALBEN DAVIS

By the late 1960s, Bradbury realized that his ever-increasing schedule of speaking engagements required professional oversight. He engaged Ruth Alben Davis (1931–2020) for this role, and she would manage his schedule and negotiate his arrangements for the rest of his active life. Davis was pivotal to Bradbury's transition from rail and automobile travel to air travel in 1982, and she grew his speaking schedule into a robust national and international range of engagements. In earlier years, as Ruth Alben, she had been a television producer and for a time was part of the East Coast cabaret culture, a world that Bradbury had always found enchanting. Her recollection of popular lyrics of the 1930s triggered Bradbury's glance back to a time when, as a teenager, he avidly collected autographs from many of the actors and composers of those days.

Dear Ruth—

Thanks for the opening lyrics of "The Last Time I Saw Paris." I had forgotten that Hammerstein and Kern had created this lovely song.[60] It still works its magic, all of these years later. I met Kern on many occasions when I was 14 and 15 years old when he appeared with Sigmund Romberg and others on the old Al Jolson *Shell Chateau* radio show in 1934 and 1935 on the old RKO film lot, where I showed up with my roller-skates on my lap.[61] Kern and Romberg and, especially, Victor Young who did the lovely score for *Around the World in 80 Days*, were kindly gents to this kid. I have all of their autographs somewhere in my collections!!

Could you send me the rest of the lyrics of "The Last Time I Saw Paris," please, to refresh my memory? Much much thanks, dear song lady. Climb up on that piano, cross your legs, and belt out another for this fourteen-year-old somehow become almost 75.

Love.

Ray

7/6/95

8

WAR AND
INTOLERANCE

I would be very pleased to have you criticize the style, the
characterization (which you did), and the structure of
the story. But when you begin telling me how my theme
should be angled sociologically or politically, I am going
to pack my belongings and trot out the front door.
—*Bradbury to Leslie Edgley,* California Quarterly

BRADBURY TO THE REPUBLICAN PARTY

Ray Bradbury occasionally vented his frustrations at the intolerance of both the far left and the far right in an increasingly polarized world. He was openly critical of the totalitarian legacy of Stalinist Russia, and equally outspoken about the "climate of fear" triggered in the postwar years by Senator Joseph McCarthy and other prominent political figures in America. For Bradbury, the problem was not the election results of November 1952, but rather the hardline political rhetoric that followed. Immediately after the election, he paid to have his open letter "To the Republican Party" published (as a paid advertisement) in the November 10th issue of the Hollywood trade magazine Daily Variety; *it was subsequently reprinted for a broader national audience in* The Nation.

To the Republican Party:

You have won and the Democrats are now the opposition. And so it is time for someone to remind you of a few words that you yourselves spoke during the campaign concerning your fear of losing the two-party system.

I remind you now that the two-party system exists and will continue to exist for the next four years. Every attempt that you make to identify the Republican Party as the *American* Party, I will resist. Every attempt that you make to identify the Democratic Party as the party of Communism, as the "left-wing" or "subversive" party, I will attack with all my heart and soul.

I have seen too much fear in a country that has no right to be afraid. I have seen too many campaigns in California, as well as in other states, won on the issue of fear itself, and not on the facts. I do not want to hear any more of this claptrap and nonsense from you. I will not welcome it from McCarthy *or* McCarran, from Mr. Nixon, Donald Jackson, *or* a man named Sparkman. I do not want any more lies, any more prejudice, any more smears. I do not want intimations, hear-say, or rumor. I do not want unsigned letters or nameless telephone calls from either side, or from anyone.

I say this to you then: do your work and do it well. We will be watching you, we, the more than 25,000,000 Americans who voted without fear and who voted Democratic. We are not afraid of you and you will not intimidate us. We will not be sloughed aside, put away, turned under, or "labeled." We are a strong and free force in this country and we will continue to be the other half of that wonderful two-party system you wailed so much about losing.

Leave that system alone, then, leave our individual rights alone; protect our Constitution, find us a way to Peace, and we will be friends. But God help you if you lay a hand on any one of us again, or try to twist the Constitution and the Bill of Rights to your own purposes. We Democrats intend to remain as powerful and thoughtful four years from now as we are today, and that is powerful and thoughtful indeed, and, given provocation, we will vote you out the door in '56, with the majority, next time, behind us.

Get to your work now, remembering that you have good men in your party if you put them to work. But in the name of all that is right and good and fair, let us send McCarthy and his friends back to Salem and the 17th Century. And then let us all settle down to the job of moving ahead together, in our own time, without fear, one of the other, and with the good of everyone, each lonely individual in our country, firmly held in mind.

Ray Bradbury
November 6, 1952

WILLIAM F. NOLAN

After reading Bradbury's "Letter to the Republican Party," a Hollywood agent told him that he would probably never be able to find work in films again. A local Los Angeles columnist made light of Bradbury's words, but various off-camera studio workers and writers he knew privately thanked him for his stand. Bradbury sent his own thoughts to William F. Nolan (1928–2021) on the day of publication—a time when Nolan was trying the risky transition to a full-time writing career. Nolan's many published stories would garner recognition across the science fiction, fantasy, and horror writing communities.

Nov. 10, 1952

Bill:

Chin up, carry on!

The briefest of notes. More in a week. All is not lost. Have faith. Read the enclosed advertisement that I took in daily *Variety* today. I have been getting phone calls all day about this ad, from people who were discouraged and afraid to talk up. Now they feel better and the blood is flowing again in their veins, by God, the blood is really moving.

We will not be jumped on by McCarthys and Nixons. We will go on fighting just to be plain old Democrats and nice old Americans, as we were meant to be, Bill, and as we shall be if we keep talking, keep moving, keep out of the corners, and stay in the center of the ring, with our guard up. Does this sound like Papa Hemingway? Well, there are times when his idiom is just right. This is a time. All my best to you, Bill, and much luck in finding work! God bless you!

Yrs, as ever,
Ray

LESLIE EDGLEY

*Bradbury's course as an independent visionary and writer came into sharp
focus late in 1952, when mystery novelist and screenwriter Leslie Edgely (1912–
2002), an editor of the ultra-liberal literary journal* The California Quarterly,
*congratulated Bradbury on his anti-McCarthy letter "To the Republican Party"
while simultaneously rejecting Bradbury's story "The Garbage Collector" for
its underlying premise that Russia was just as likely to start a nuclear war as
America was. Bradbury wrote the story to point up the lunacy of assigning garbage trucks to pick up bodies in the event of a nuclear war, a procedure report-
edly under consideration in Los Angeles. The CQ rejection was based solely on
Bradbury's philosophical premise, and elicited this thundering response from
the author.*

December 30, 1952

Dear Mr. Edgley:

I must confess that I was startled, puzzled, and then a bit more than
angered with your final rejection of my story "The Garbage Collector."
I felt your criticism to be entirely invalid and politically off-bounds.
If I had wanted to write the sort of story you seem to feel this should
be, I'd have written it. I chose, however to write the story I wrote. I
wrote a protest against a world that can come so close to an atomic war
that it can accept, almost glibly, almost flippantly, with little thought,
the fact that garbage units might be used to pick up the dead in the
streets. That garbage trucks could be used for this terrible purpose
without any undue ripple in our society, seemed sufficient to me. This,
evidently, did not satisfy the majority of the people on your magazine.
You say that the story achieves its horror by the development of a lie,
and helps to perpetuate that lie: the lie being that L.A. will some day
be bombed by Russia. You would like me to approach the story, making
the character react with abhorrence to this lie. But this, Mr. Edgley, is
not my story, nor do I believe it can be my story. And you people have
stuck your noses in where they damn well are not welcome. I would be
very pleased to have you criticize the style, the characterization (which

you did), and the structure of the story. But when you begin telling me
how my theme should be angled sociologically or politically, I am going
to pack my belongings and trot out the front door. I won't take it from
the *Saturday Evening Post*, I turned down a chance to have a story in the
rotten new *American Mercury* because I knew their bias, and I won't
take it from you.[1] Either a story is a good story or bad story; it either
achieves its effect or it does not, and you should have enough courage to
occasionally publish a story that doesn't meet with your entire political
approval. Even the *Saturday Evening Post* does that, as witness my story
"The World the Children Made," which took a healthy swat at our
machine-run society which advertises widely in the *Post*. I was damned
pleased when the *Post* published this, without a word changed.[2] And I
reject and cast out your suggestions on my story as utterly impossible
and wrong-headed as all hell. I happen to believe we exist in a world
where at any moment either Russia or the U.S. could blow the top off,
I happen to believe that both are equally responsible for this mess.
I happen to believe we could get into a war very easily and that L.A.
could be bombed by Russia, even as we could bomb Moscow. I wrote
"The Garbage Collector" as a protest to both countries, in a way, not
to just one side, or the other. I'm afraid I suspect all countries, from
Plato's time right on up to our own, of chicanery, and the ability to
be pigheaded and dangerous. That means Russia as well as our own
country. But I don't see how my story can be in any way viewed by
your editorial board, as distinctly anti-Russian. What my story said
was that we should start looking around for a way to peace. That was
my inference, anyway. When we start sending out garbage trucks to
shovel up the dead, it is then time to stop and think where we are
going. How you could have misconstrued this is beyond me. It reveals
a terrible blindness on your part, and I must confess that I first began
to realize you people had this blind spot when you turned down my
story "The Flying Machine," for the same sort of political-sociological
reasons, completely invalid in that case as in this.[3] You say you are
for free speech, free this, free that, and yet you want me, as a writer,
to shift the emphasis in two of my stories, completely changing the
philosophical tone. Would you accept that sort of criticism from the
Post or *Collier's*? Like hell you would. Neither would I. A writer is

either free to think and write as he will, no matter whose toes he steps on, or he is a cipher.

   This letter is written, believe me, by a writer who has, in his time, received well over two thousand rejections, probably more, in a period of ten years or more of writing. This is not the letter of an egotist who thinks his work is above criticism, for it fails continually to please me in dozens of ways, and as the members of my own writing group can tell you (we meet every two weeks) I bring my own stories to that group for help, in construction, in cutting, and for endless reasons.[4] I am not above seeking for help and guidance. But I do not ask for nor do I welcome at any time, such suggestions as were put forth in your rejection of "The Garbage Collector" and "The Flying Machine." You were tampering with my own basic philosophy then, and when that happens, look out! There is plenty of elbow-room in the world for all of us, and I am indeed sorry that you cannot find enough room in your magazine for my elbow, dirty as it may seem, calloused as it may look. In all my years of collecting my two thousand rejections slips, I have never, and I repeat *never*, had two rejections like those you have given me.

   Therefore, I must ask for the return of the poem I submitted to you. I do not want it to appear in your magazine.[5] And I shall stop, as of this day, submitting stories to you. And I ask you now to stop my subscription to your magazine and refund to me the money remaining, immediately. I do not want to read a magazine edited with your bias, for I do not believe in tampering with other people's philosophies. If a story is good, it is good, if bad it is bad. You completely neglected to say in your letter whether my story was good or bad. *Jesus*! If you edit all your stories this way, God help your writers. I, praise the Lord, will not be one of them.

   I suppose all of this will surprise you somewhat. But I insist upon my own thoughts and beliefs and philosophy and I don't think an editor has any goddam business tinkering with me or anyone else that way. I shall continue to fight for the things I believe right, I shall oppose war, support the UN, work for peace, despise the reactionary bastard like McCarthy, Peron, Franco, etc., and I shall work as an independent thinker, voter, and actor. I shall oppose any damnfool thing we do as a country, and anything Russia does as a country. I shall go merrily on with my flag which bears a snake and which reads: *Don't tread on me*. May the *California Quarterly* collapse within the coming year.

Yours,
Ray Bradbury

LORD BERTRAND RUSSELL

Nobel Laureate Bertrand Russell (1872–1970) found great significance in Fahrenheit 451 *and asked to meet Bradbury as soon as he finished the* Moby Dick *screenplay for director John Huston in Ireland. Rupert Hart-Davis, Bradbury's London publisher, had sent Russell British editions of* The Martian Chronicles (*as* The Silver Locusts) *and* The Illustrated Man, *but it was the gift of* Fahrenheit 451 *that prompted a response. Lord Russell's letter to Hart-Davis publishing associate Ruth Simon was immediately forwarded to Bradbury, who met with Russell at his home near London on April 7, 1954.*

13 March, 1954

Dear Mrs. Simon,

Thank you for your letter of March 8 and for Ray Bradbury's book *Fahrenheit 451*. I have now read the book and found it powerful. The sort of future society that he portrays is only too possible. I should be glad to see him at any time convenient to us both, and perhaps you might ask him to ring me up when he returns from Ireland and then we can fix a time.

Yours sincerely,
Russell

FREDERIK POHL

The versatile and award-winning writer and editor Frederik Pohl Jr. had known Bradbury since the first Science Fiction World Con in 1939. He was very familiar with Bradbury's full range of Martian tales, including a few that Bradbury would have preferred to forget. In editing the Star Science Fiction *anthology series for Ballantine Books, Pohl asked for one of these, and Bradbury's response plays on McCarthy-era fears of book burning.*

Nov. 11, 1954

Dear Fred:

Thanks for yours of the 1st of November and the horrible manuscript of "Christmas on Mars" which I burnt immediately.[6] I am dismayed that you ever thought well enough of it to use it; my faith in you is shaken, believe me. I have sent a new story "The Strawberry Window," to Ian.[7] I'll pay you blackmail for the next 20 years never to mention the Christmas tale.

Otherwise, all else goes well. Am working on my Illinois book for Doubleday. Non-fantasy, non-s.f. Due for publication next summer.[8]

Hoping you are doing something else, with or without Kornbluth (I never believed that name, he *does* exist, doesn't he?) as wonderful as *The Space Merchants.*

Thanks again for letting me play McCarthy with my own story. The blaze was wonderful.

Yrs,

Ray

Ray Bradbury

10750 Clarkson Road

Los Angeles 64, Calif.

BRADBURY TO THE KENNEDY WHITE HOUSE

*Bradbury embraced the Space Age vision that emerged from the Kennedy admin-
istration's celebrations of the first two Mercury manned spaceflight launches,
but he also weighed in on what he perceived as the aggressive brinksmanship
practiced by the Soviet Union in the early months of the new presidency, including the creation of the Berlin Wall. Bradbury was strongly anti-war and
actively campaigned against nuclear proliferation; the John F. Kennedy Presidential Library preserves this Bradbury telegram, printed at the White House
communications center September 1, 1962, and forwarded by memo to the State
Department on September 8.*

THE WHITE HOUSE
WASHINGTON

1961 Sep 1 PM 7:15
Beverly Hills Calif 1233P PDT
The President
The White House

Strongly and sincerely urge Russian resumption of nuclear testing plus
Berlin situation be taken to United Nations immediately so world law
and opinion can be applied.

Ray Bradbury

FREDERIK POHL

The tensions created by the building of the Berlin Wall and the Soviet Union's unilateral resumption of aboveground nuclear testing suddenly reached new levels when President Kennedy announced a blockade of Cuba and a demand for Russia to dismantle their missile installations in the island nation. Science fiction writer and editor Fred Pohl, who had briefly been Bradbury's first agent decades earlier, offered the following proposal to his old friend.

386 W Front St
Red Bank, N J

25 Oct 62

Dear Ray:

I expect you are as concerned about the present insanities in our international affairs as I am.

Casting about for something that I personally could do about it, it occurred to me that I might try to organize some sort of effort involving science-fiction writers. I have a mailing list of something close to 4,000 slush-pile writers, mostly those submitting to *Galaxy* in the past two years or so. The question is, what form should it take?

At this point I remembered that you are one of the sponsors of SANE.[9] I wonder if you would like to send a form letter to these 4,000, enclosing one of the SANE leaflets and suggesting they join? I cannot myself send such a letter—among other reasons, I am not a member of SANE. But I would be glad to make the list available, to have my name mentioned as one endorsing the purposes of SANE, and to put up fifty dollars or so toward the cost. I expect it would cost about $200. If you think it worth doing, I think between us we could tap a few other sf writers for the balance, and also for the use of their names too.

Let me know what you think . . .

I am optimist enough to think everything will come out right in the end. I have worked out a rationale: Kennedy, like any president, is the captive of political pressures and can work toward disarmament and peace only by first establishing a reputation for toughmindedness. (I suppose I have to think that, having voted for him—for that matter, being a candidate for office on the Democratic ticket right now.) But I do wish some of the political pressures would be in the direction of peace. I'd like to see SANE with a couple of million voice-raising, congressman-writing members . . . hence the notion of this letter.

Bests,
Fred

Hallowe'en, 1962

Dear Fred:

Thanks for yours of the 25th, which I appreciated and sympathized with. But, at the present time, I am no longer alarmed, in fact am optimistic about the chances for progressive disarmament, due to the President's masterful handling of the situation. I don't think an advertisement or mailing is necessary now. Ironically, an ad placed in the *NY Times* yesterday, stating the things that should be done, was re-iterated, and thus invalidated, by the news items immediately above. In other words, those things asked for in the ad had happened on that very day. I think we should wait, keep our eyes peeled, and put pressure, later on, where needed. But I don't feel we should rock the boat. Once Russia is out of Cuba, we can hope that, eventually, we will volunteer to move some of our machinery out of Turkey, or some other spot. But not because of blackmail, only because it would be a peaceful gesture on our part.[10] This, in turn, may encourage Russia to make yet another step, and so on down the line. To sum up: I do not fear. I am optimistic. I think we should wait. Later, if things turn badly, I'll put you in touch with SANE. I'm not on the Board anymore (the L.A. Board) though I am a Sponsor. Actually, later on, if you felt you wished to, you are closer to SANE national headquarters than I am. They are right there in New York and would welcome, I should think,

your mailing list. Let me know what you think, later on. Okay? Thanks
for your letter, your concern, your idea.

Best,

Ray

DON CONGDON

*Throughout his life, Bradbury believed that the best way to recover from trauma
was to face it and revisit it through the written word. Fiction, often replayed in
variation through a number of stories, had allowed him to exorcise his fear of auto
accidents, or catacombs, or drowning. He would take the same approach in writing a long letter to Don Congdon to work through the national tragedy of the death
of a president. On that dark day he had just arrived at the office of Hollywood
producer Alan Pakula to discuss progress on the* Martian Chronicles *screenplay.*

December 1st, 1963

Dear Don:

One man decided to hold an Election. One man did. All by himself, he
dared to vote for everybody. And so . . . Election Day, November 22nd,
is over, gone, done, and one man has revoked the ballot for 180 million
Americans, put our President in the earth, and given us the most brutal
and terrifying and frustrating week in the history of our own lives,
anyway. I don't imagine your week was any different than mine. For
three days after the murder I kept taking in a bombardment of detail,
and thought, well, I have taken in everything now, it is over. But I did
not think about my subconscious and how it might want to "give out."
I have never had the two aspects of the human mind so vividly and
sadly illustrated for me as in watching my own reactions to this dread
passage of time. You think you are done with this? The Subconscious
says, no, no, for I give you this, and again *this*. And you find that on the
fourth day the hurt is worse, and the tears still start forth, and you want
like unholy anything to be back on the early morning of the 22nd so

you can run out yelling and warning the world what is going to happen. But Time Machines don't work, and you wind up being "disturbed." I have never used the word on myself in my life that I recall, but surely in the last few days that is about all I can find that is a proper label. I am disturbed and immensely sad, and the picture of the dead President on *Life*, which I saw for the first time today, by Karsh, only gave me another strike in the gut.[11] I didn't really think I cared that much, and now I find I cared a very great deal indeed, and was looking forward to meeting him in April when he was supposed to open our Pavilion at the Fair.[12] A very silly, superficial, and personal thing, of course, but now that it has been taken away, along with so much else that was of greater meaning, I find the Pavilion itself of very little importance right now. I know this will change, as it must change. My work on it is almost finished, and I will be there for any on-the-spot changes, and I will be very proud of it. But, damn it to hell, our generation has been shoved under the earth suddenly. It may not come again, this sort of time for our generation to have this power in these few short years before fifty. There was a special pleasure in having one of us in the White House. [. . .] The power that will come to our generation later, and it must come, won't be quite the same, will it, when it falls into older sadder hands? [. . .] I set out on a journey November 22nd to deliver the first 125 pages of the *Chronicles* to Pakula. I arrived at his office to find that the President had been shot. I felt the manuscript turn to ash in my hand. I carried it away with me, when, after a long wait with Alan, we heard the announcement, final and brutal, of the death of the President. I was glad I was with Alan, a fine and good person. We embraced, we held, and I went my way, to come back some other day on business that now was of no importance.

Time is passing, all this too will pass, but even tonight my subconscious is talking to me, and I do not like what it says. So, I guess this is one way, as with my stories, of getting the old poison out on paper where we can all look at it. I don't think I have ever hated one single week so much in my life, or felt worse at the death, strangely enough, even of my father, perhaps because I was ready for that.

Well, enough. I wanted to hand some part of this dark week to you as I sensed it. My Time Machine is set for "Now" from here on, and will move only Ahead, moment by moment. The incredible

Jacqueline Kennedy has shown us how to make it work. Good God, how I admire her.

That's all I wanted to say.

Yours,
Ray

Bradbury understood the need to lightly edit his published stories for his young reader collections such as R Is for Rocket *and* S Is for Space, *but he stood firmly against heavy abridgement that, in effect, bowdlerized his work. This 1966 letter to Don Congdon conveys his deep frustration with an abridgement of "The Pedestrian" (1951), one of his best-known antiauthoritarian tales leading up to publication of* Fahrenheit 451 *more than a decade earlier. Congdon's reasoned response persuaded Bradbury not to turn the incident into an editorial crusade in the major market magazines, but he would devote more than a few occasional essays to the subject of diluting classics of the past.*

Dear Don:

I have written directly to those dumbcluck people at Science Research Associates, Inc. and refused them permission to gang-rape my story "The Pedestrian" for their simple-minded book.[13] I am also having Xerox copies made of their "adaptation" to send to *The Saturday Review*, Clifton Fadiman, and some others, to illustrate once again one of the super-intellectual reasons Johnny Can't Read. Jesus Christ. I hope one of them will want to do an article on this. If not, I will myself. Subject: "How to Burn a Library Without a Match."

Jeeminently!!,

Yrs,
Ray
Sept. 20, 1966

RUSSELL KIRK

Russell Kirk (1918–1994), Bradbury's friend and fellow author of award-winning supernatural fiction, was best known as a key figure in articulating a historical basis for conservatism in postwar America; like Bradbury, he was also capable of criticizing the far right as well as the far left in American politics. An incident of book burning involving Fahrenheit 451 *soon came to the attention of Kirk, who would later include the anecdote in* Enemies of the Permanent Things, *but not before sending a similar but far more methodical book-burning adventure directly to his friend Ray Bradbury.*

July 8, 1967

Mr. Ray Bradbury
Los Angeles

Dear Ray,

Very good it is to have your news of the provisional success of *Dandelion Wine*.[14] I do pray that sponsors may be found. [. . .]

I have lectured at one or two churches—aye, even from the pulpit—on angels and devils. Your *Something Wicked This Way Comes* was one of my chief illustrations. And I have given copies of most of your works to the Newman Center at Ferris State College . . . , our newest institution of the higher learning in America.[15]

A friend of mine who edits *Practical English* (one of the *Scholastic Magazine* publications) told me recently of how a female librarian was enraged to find *Fahrenheit 451* among a shipment of books for children, and proudly announced that she had burnt that evil book.[16]

I may soon write a piece for *National Review*, and a shorter one for my syndicated column, on the subject of Librarians and *Fahrenheit 451*. Some months ago, I gave nearly a thousand books from my library to our new local public library. These were sent to the nearest agency of the State Library system for classification and the like. Nearly half of them never came back to our local library; and when we enquired, it turned out that they had been burnt, quite literally. The bureaucrat responsible had discovered that Russell Kirk, donor, was a Wicked Conservative, and therefore he destroyed virtually all the books on politics, current affairs, and economics, to be quite safe. (Actually, I gave more radical and liberal works than conservative, but he was unable to distinguish, and so destroyed the lot, except those he was sure were not conservative. I even have his confession in writing; he was proud of his holocaust. In the process, incidentally, he got rid of all the better books by radicals and liberals.)

Also he destroyed much else—on what principles, if any, I still am trying to discover. A complete set of O. Henry's works, in good print and well bound, was among the victims. Why? Written too long ago? Only Best knows. (That's the librarian's name.)

But he has caught a Tartar, since I am on friendly terms with the Librarian of the State of Michigan, and with the Speaker of the House of Representatives. Also I have a typewriter, and am published daily by several Michigan newspapers. Best complained that he didn't know we had made a list of the books donated—we ought to have warned him. [...]

More another time. Best wishes,

Cordially,
Russell Kirk

LEON URIS

After returning from his 1953–54 pre-production work in Ireland scripting John Huston's adaptation of Moby Dick, *Bradbury began to engage more actively with the Writers Guild of America (West). Those members who wrote for Hollywood were already under government scrutiny, and the August 1954 meeting agenda included a vote to deny or withdraw membership to writers associated with the Communist party, or who refused to testify if subpoenaed by congressional committees. The secret ballot defeated the measure, but an extraordinary open revote by raised hand passed, with outcries from a few opposed to the suspension of the rules of order. Bradbury made the loudest outburst, which was described in the August 27, 1954, issue of* The Hollywood Reporter. *Nearly a half century later, Bradbury reached out to one of the few surviving dissenters, prominent novelist Leon Uris (1924–2003), to see if his own recollections rang true.*

May 10, 2001

Dear Leon:

It's been almost a lifetime since I saw you last; the summer of 1954 to be exact, when we were at the Crystal Room of the Beverly Hills Hotel and saw our fellow liberals toss away their rights.

Your daughter came up to me after a lecture a couple of years ago and told me who she was. I immediately said, "Has your father told you?" and she knew what I was talking about. She said, "Yes, he told me," and we discussed the Crystal Room.

Now, very late in time, it would be wonderful if you could write me a letter and verify all the various thoughts and things I've said over the years, so I could have it with me in case people doubt what I'm saying. That night has burned itself in my memory because I recall on the first vote we writers turned down the producers who wanted us to guarantee our appearance before the Un-American Activities Committee. We rejected the offer, at which time Borden Chase, our president, leapt to his feet and cried, "We must have another vote," even though such a vote was illegal. The first vote was a private ballot and the second vote that he insisted on was an open vote with cards held up. When they took the vote our membership reversed themselves and voted to give away their rights to the producers, at which time I leapt to my feet and cried "Cowards, where is your vote now?" You were on your feet with me and perhaps another dozen other people among the hundreds of writers there that evening that gave away their rights. Borden Chase pointed at me and shouted, "Throw that man out!" I said, "Don't bother, I'll throw myself out." I went outside, sick at heart, and didn't go to another meeting for quite a while. Thank God things finally reversed themselves, but it took a while. [. . .]

9

RECOGNITION

There are many people who know the facts about the
various projects headed toward space. There are only a
few who interpret, aesthetically or otherwise, our entire
purpose in Space. I have tried to do this quite often.
—*Bradbury to Arthur Schlesinger Jr., April 30, 1962*

NATIONAL INSTITUTE OF ARTS AND LETTERS

Bradbury received word of his National Institute of Arts and Letters honors while he was in Ireland scripting Moby Dick *for John Huston. After touring northern Italy with his family, Bradbury made it to New York by ocean liner with one day to spare for the ceremony. His notification letter was written by one of the many distinguished writers at the ceremony, the Pulitzer Prize–winning novelist John Hersey (1914–1993).*

NATIONAL INSTITUTE OF ARTS AND LETTERS

March 17, 1954

Dear Mr. Bradbury:

It gives me great pleasure to inform you that the National Institute of Arts and Letters has awarded you a Grant of $1,000 in recognition of your creative work in literature. This Grant will be presented to you at our Annual Ceremonial, to be held on Wednesday afternoon, May 26th at three o'clock in the Auditorium of the American Academy of Arts and Letters, 632 West 156th Street, New York City.

    The officers and membership of the Institute will greatly appreciate your attendance at this Ceremonial to receive the award, if it is possible for you to come.

Very sincerely yours,
John Hersey
Chairman of the Committee on
Grants for Literature

P.S. Please keep this in confidence until official notice of it has been given to the press.

———————————————

ARTHUR SCHLESINGER

Two-time Pulitzer Prize–winning historian Arthur Schlesinger Jr. (1917–2007)
was a special assistant to President Kennedy and worked in the White House
between 1961 and 1963. He had read Bradbury's fiction and knew the value of
Bradbury's support for the administration's spaceflight goals. Although some of
the projects that Bradbury cites would be delayed or canceled, Schlesinger and
others did arrange a White House screening of Icarus Montgolfier Wright *for*
members of the White House staff. Bradbury's inscribed books are curated in the
Kennedy Presidential Library.

April 30th, 1962

Mr. Arthur Schlesinger, Jr.
The White House
Washington, D.C.

Dear Arthur: (If I may, please).

You are probably wondering what happened to me after my phone calls
last Thursday. Friday was one of my lost days, traveling all over the
400 square mile Los Angeles territory, lecturing. So, rather than try to
telephone again, I decided on this letter.

Under separate cover, airmail, I'm sending on two complete sets of
all my books. One set is autographed to you. The other is autographed
to the President and Mrs. Kennedy.

I'm sending these for various reasons:

We are moving deeper into the Space Age, a tremendously exciting
time for me, as you can imagine, since I started writing about it when I
was twelve. Now, I hear that there will be a Conference on the Peaceful
Uses of Outer Space, attended by President Kennedy and 1500 of the
top scientists in the field of space travel from all over the world, in
Seattle. A few days later, I'm scheduled to appear as a special Guest at
the Seattle Fair.[1] Our lives move closer together with such events.

Somewhere along the line I may be of some use to the President, or
to you, or to others working with the President. It may be in the field of

writing. Or it might be in some other act I could perform for any one of you.

I'm now finishing a 14 minute film, *Icarus Montgolfier Wright*, based on man's age-old desire to fly. This short has been made with Format Films here, in semi-animation color, and when it is finished I hope to show it to you, and perhaps, the President.[2]

Starting in a few weeks, I will begin to give a series of short talks on *NBC-Monitor-Radio*, coast to coast, dealing with every aspect of the Space Age: music, poetry, painting, architecture, psychology, etc.

My one-act space-age plays will be staged at the Royal Court Theatre in London this summer.[3]

Jean-Louis Barrault, the French actor-mime-director, will open my *The Martian Chronicles* on-stage in Paris this winter, at the Odeon.

François Truffaut, the director of *The 400 Blows*, will film my *Fahrenheit 451* this autumn, in France.

So you see I have thought, written, and now am doing much, in many directions, about the Space Age.

I have marked those stories, particularly, in *The Golden Apples of the Sun* and *The Day It Rained Forever*, which I think might fascinate you and the President.

There are many people who know the facts about the various projects headed toward space. There are only a few who interpret, aesthetically or otherwise, our entire purpose in Space. I have tried to do this quite often.

If the President thinks of any way I might serve him or the Government, with my particular talent, I would be glad to help promote the Space Age as we would all like to see it promoted, as a motion toward peace and survival.

If you wish, you may show this letter to the President.

My cordial best to you,

Ray

Ray Bradbury

10265 Cheviot Drive

Los Angeles 64, Calif.

Schlesinger did indeed give Bradbury's letter and the inscribed set of Bradbury
books to President Kennedy under the following cover memo. These artifacts
are curated in the Kennedy Presidential Library; Bradbury's letter is tucked
into The Illustrated Man. *The other titles are British editions of* The Golden
Apples of the Sun, The October Country, *and* The Day It Rained Forever.
The stories that Bradbury marked for the president in this last volume include
"Icarus Montgolfier Wright," perhaps Bradbury's best-known anticipation of
the Space Age.

THE WHITE HOUSE

WASHINGTON

May 5, 1962

MEMORANDUM FOR THE PRESIDENT

I do not know whether you are familiar with Ray Bradbury. He is the
most interesting writer about the future since H.G. Wells; and his
stories, like those of Wells, combine social satire with fantasy.

In any case, Bradbury has inscribed four volumes of his work to
you. In two volumes—*The Golden Apples of the Sun* and *The Day It Rained*
Forever—he has marked stories that he thought might be of special
interest to you.

I also attach the copy of the letter from Bradbury explaining his
interest in the space age.

Arthur Schlesinger, Jr.

Enclosures (5)[4]

PRESIDENT JOHN F. KENNEDY

THE WHITE HOUSE
WASHINGTON

June 21, 1962

Dear Mr. Bradbury:

I was delighted to receive through Arthur Schlesinger your four
volumes. I am happy to have available so generous a selection of your
writings which will allow me to indulge simultaneously both fantasy and
scientific reality. I have heard from many sources of your talent, and
welcome this chance to experience it at first hand.

   With all good wishes,

Sincerely,
John Kennedy

Mr. Ray Bradbury
10265 Cheviot Drive
Los Angeles 64, California

THE AVIATION/SPACE WRITERS ASSOCIATION

Between 1960 and 1967 Ray Bradbury published three prominent features on the cosmos and the space program in Life *magazine. In preparation for the third, "An Impatient Gulliver Above Our Roofs," Bradbury spent several days in early January 1967 at Houston's Manned Spacecraft Center with a number of the astronauts, dining with them and visiting their homes. "An Impatient Gulliver" was published in the November 24, 1967, issue of* Life, *and subsequently won the 1968 Aviation/Space Writers Association Award and the Robert S. Ball Memorial Award in a NASA ceremony at what was then Cape Kennedy, Florida. But Bradbury, perhaps the most prominent advocate of spaceflight, had not yet overcome his abiding fear of flying. He asked for a stand-in from among those astronauts he had written about in his article. In the end,* Life *magazine arranged to have an oversize picture of Bradbury on his bicycle serve as a stand-in; a* Life *editor subsequently flew out to Los Angeles and delivered the award.*

April 2nd, 1968

Mr. Ralph H. McClarren
Aviation/Space Writers Association

Dear Mr. McClarren:

Thank you for your exhilarating letter of March 27th which came as a complete and wonderful surprise. I am amazed, touched, and grateful. Especially since you offer me not only the Aviation/Space Writers Association 1968 Writers Award in the general magazine category, but also the Robert S. Ball Memorial Award.

I will not be able to attend your Awards Banquet on May 22nd not simply because of a full lecture schedule (which is indeed full to the brim) but because . . . hold on to your helmet . . . I do not fly! I traveled to Houston to meet all those fast people via a very slow train. I take it to visit Cocoa Beach would be a task that would put strain on Jules Verne's hero in *Around the World in 80 Days.*

With trepidation, might I ask one of the following to receive the Awards in my behalf:

John Glenn
Or
Any of the first team of Astronauts.
Or Marshall of *Life* magazine,[5] if he is still located at the *Life* offices in
   Miami.

I suggest the above Astronauts only if they are within easy distance of Cocoa Beach on the night of the Awards. I met most of the Astronauts, briefly, on my visit. I spent part of an evening with John Glenn during that time, a year ago. I do not wish to impose upon their time or good will in any way, but if they *are* in the Vicinity it would be a great and fine thing for me if Mr. Glenn or one of the members of the First team pretended to be Ray Bradbury for one night. Let me know how this strikes you. Failing all this, I am sure that Mr. Smith of *Life* might be available to help out. Again thanks.

Ray Bradbury

PRESIDENT GEORGE H. W. BUSH

More than once, Bradbury's book gifts to the White House crossed political party lines. An early Democrat and supporter of both the Stevenson and Kennedy campaigns, he also supported the space program initiatives of both the Kennedy and Reagan administrations. In 1992 he sent Yestermorrow, *a visionary collection of essays on topics ranging from urban planning to creativity, to President George H. W. Bush during the fall presidential campaign.*

Oct. 4, 1992

Dear Ray,

I love this idea of your "Plaza"—freeing [me] from senseless evenings present.

Thanks for *Yestermorrow*. I shall read it; but that must wait till my deadly debate book[6] begins to gather dust.

Many many thanks
George Bush

PRESIDENT GEORGE W. BUSH

During the early decades of his career, Bradbury held that literary awards were for those who were traditional and intellectually proper, writers who generally preferred the label "Author," with a capital A. His 1962 Academy Award nomination for the animated documentary Icarus Montgolfier Wright *began to break down this attitude; many prestigious recognitions followed, including the National Medal of Arts, presented in a White House ceremony by President George W. Bush and First Lady Laura Bush in November 2004.*

THE WHITE HOUSE

WASHINGTON

December 8, 2004

Mr. Ray Bradbury
10265 Cheviot Drive
Los Angeles, California 90064

Dear Ray:

It was a pleasure to welcome you and your family to the Oval Office
and an honor to present you the National Medal of Arts Award.
Congratulations again on your outstanding achievement.

Laura joins me in sending our best wishes. Thank you for the
inscribed copy of your book, *The Cat's Pajamas*. I appreciate your
thoughtfulness.

Sincerely,
George W. Bush

FIRST LADY LAURA BUSH

During the National Medal of Arts ceremony in 2004, Bradbury had given Laura Bush a copy of his most recent book, the 2003 story collection The Cat's Pajamas. *Two years later, he followed up with a new edition of a book traditionally favored in the classroom.*

THE WHITE HOUSE

August 14, 2006

Mr. Ray Bradbury
10265 Cheviot Drive
Los Angeles, California 90064-4737

Dear Mr. Bradbury,

Dr. Radice[7] passed along the copy of *Dandelion Wine*—my favorite Ray Bradbury book!
    Thank you so much for the book and your warm inscription.

With best wishes,
Laura Bush

THE PULITZER PRIZE BOARD

"I thought that such things as Awards were beyond and away and locked outside me." Bradbury's 1963 observation to his literary agent Don Congdon was proven wrong many times, and never more so than when he received a Pulitzer Prize citation for lifetime achievement in the spring of 2007. He was no longer able to make cross-country trips; the Pulitzer citation was accepted on his behalf by Michael Congdon, who had worked with his father in representing Bradbury for many years.

COLUMBIA UNIVERSITY
IN THE CITY OF NEW YORK
PRESIDENT'S ROOM

April 16, 2007

Mr. Ray Bradbury
c/o William Morrow/HarperCollins
10 E. 53rd Street
New York, New York 10022

Dear Mr. Bradbury,

I am delighted to confirm the Pulitzer Prize Special Citation awarded
to you "for a distinguished, prolific and deeply influential career as an
unmatched author of science fiction and fantasy."

It is also my pleasure on behalf of the Pulitzer Prize Board to invite
you and a personal guest to a luncheon here at Columbia at which we
will present the Prize winners with their Certificates of Award.

The luncheon ceremony, which we intend as a celebration of
achievement, will be held on May 21st at Low Library on the Columbia
campus. You will be receiving a more formal invitation shortly. [...]

I extend my warmest congratulations on an outstanding
achievement, and I hope I shall have the pleasure of greeting you
personally on May 21.

Sincerely,
Lee C. Bollinger

REPUBLIC OF FRANCE

For decades, Bradbury had been recognized in postwar French culture as an influential writer in the surrealist tradition whose supernatural tales and Space Age fantasies echoed the imaginative power and vision of his much-loved Jules Verne. Bradbury's introductions to American editions of Verne's 20,000 Leagues Under the Sea *and other novels were known in France, and his long-time French publisher Denoël arranged many media appearances during Bradbury's frequent working vacations in Paris. His 1978 guest appearances during the 150th anniversary of Jules Verne's birth perhaps served as prelude for his culminating honor from the French government, awarded during mid-December 2007 ceremonies at the official French residence in Los Angeles.*

Ambassade de France
aux Etats–Unis
L'Ambassadeux

Tuesday, December 18, 2007

Dear Ray Bradbury,

My warmest personal congratulations on your decoration.

It was truly my honor and pleasure to decorate someone of your merit as Commandeur in the Order of Arts and Letters. Your writing has brought joy to millions, and for that alone you are more than deserving of this, France's highest distinction. You are a great friend of France, Mr. Bradbury, and for that I thank you.

I send along my best wishes for you and your family and look forward to the opportunity for us to meet again.

Avec toute mon admiration!

Sincerely yours,
Pierre Vimont

10

FRIENDS

The fact is that I don't write pulp, slick, or quality stories.
I don't write stories with labels at all, if I can help it. My
agent and I have a simple agreement, I write "stories."
I write stories the best I know how, at all times.
—*Bradbury to William F. Nolan, January 11, 1951*

FORRY ACKERMAN

Bradbury's enduring friendship with Forrest J Ackerman (1916–2008) began in the fall of 1937 at one of the biweekly meetings of the Los Angeles Chapter of the Science Fiction League, where genre fans and a scattering of professional writers met in the Brown Room at Clifton's Cafeteria on Broadway. Ackerman was already well established in the world of amateur "fanzines," and he immediately put Bradbury to work on the chapter's fanzine Imagination. *At the time, Forry worked at the Academy of Motion Picture Arts and Sciences library and eventually earned an international reputation as a collector and editor documenting the cinema and magazine history of science fiction, fantasy, and horror. A decade into their friendship, Bradbury wrote with news of two early milestones in his rise to mainstream popularity.*

January 2, 1948

Dear 4E:

I want to thank you for your kind thought at New Years, in thinking to send me a six month subscription to the *Fantasy Book*. I shall certainly look for it in my mailbox. [. . .]

News? You'll be glad to hear that I have broken into the slick market, at last, with a science fiction story! I believe this makes me the only other current writer of s.f. to do so.[1] My story, with its locale on Mars, sold to *Maclean's* magazine, the big Canadian publication, published in Toronto, at the very neat sum of 20 cents a word, an exceedingly high raise over the usual 1 or 2 cents a word for the average sf yarn. I'll let you know which issue the yarn appears in.[2]

Also—my play *The Meadow*, has just been selected as one of the *Best American One Act Plays* for 1947–48 and will be included in the Dodd Mead book on same to be published in a few months. *The Meadow* originally won a prize for the atom bomb show *World Security Workshop* a year ago this week.[3]

I hope you and your agency are progressing anon.[4] I shall be to a sf meeting in the near future to gab with you. In the meantime, my thanks to you for your good thought, and all my luck to you in the New Year.

Luff,
Ray

SAM SACKETT

Samuel J. Sackett (1928–2018) was among the first writer/scholars to actively research and map out a biography of Ray Bradbury's life and early career. Shortly after completing graduate work at the University of Redlands, Sackett convinced Bradbury to answer specific questions that began to reach further into his life than he had yet provided for editors and publishers. Sackett did not complete his biographical project, but he did contribute "The Monster Bradbury" to William F. Nolan's Ray Bradbury Review *(1952).*

Ray Bradbury
33 So. Venice Blvd.
Venice, Calif.

July 5, 1949

Dear Mr. Sackett:

Thank you very much for your interest in me; I appreciate it very much.

I am enclosing a copy of the Winter, 1949 issue of *The Fanscient*, which contains about all the information re myself that I can think of, plus a complete listing of all my stories.

I never attended college, so that seems to be out as a source of information. Forrest J. Ackerman, world's leading collector of fantasy and number one fan for many years, is an old friend of mine. You might contact him, at 236½ No. New Hampshire, Los Angeles, Calif., for other information about me. Otherwise, I'm afraid I can't think of any other contacts for you.

Authors who have greatly affected me are John Steinbeck, William Faulkner, Ernest Hemingway, Edgar Allan Poe, Hawthorne, Irving, Thomas Wolfe, Ellen Glasgow, Edith Wharton and Thoreau. I rarely read fantasy fiction any more, believing that the source of originality in any field is found by refreshing one's self in distant meadows and leas. Of the above authors, I believe I would name Faulkner, Steinbeck and Hemingway as my greatest influences, with Poe, Hawthorne and Irving lurking in the background of my childhood as deep and unforgettable influences.

Yes, I would like to see your finished product when you feel like sending it on. If you have any direct questions to ask, please, by all means, make a list of them, mail them to me, and I'll answer them, one by one. Again my thanks to you, and my best wishes.

Cordially,
Ray Bradbury

P.S. Will you please return this copy of *The Fanscient* to me when you have finished with it? Thank you.

R.B.

November 19, 1949

Dear Sam:

Here, I hope, are the answers to your questions:

My great-grandfather's name was Samuel I. Bradbury, who published the *Lake County Patriot* in Waukegan, Illinois after the Civil War, I believe. He was also Mayor of the town. In Chicago, he had a large publishing and job printing office, presumably under the name Bradbury & Sons. (I am relying upon my father's nebulous memory for detail here.)

When my great-grandfather died, my grandfather took over the *Lake County Patriot* and changed its name to the *Lake County Democrat*. My grandfather's name was Samuel Hinkston Bradbury. The *Lake County*

Patriot, later the *Democrat*, was a weekly newspaper; the first, I believe, in that community.

Acting also seemed to run in the family. My great-grandfather Samuel I. is reported to have appeared with a repertory group presenting *Uncle Tom's Cabin*. The trend to acting was carried further by my father's sister, who attended the Art Institute in Chicago, and later by myself. The year of my graduation from L. A. High School here, I wrote and produced a student talent show called the *Roman Review*, which was the first of a series thus called to appear and continue after my graduation. I belonged to the Drama and Poetry Clubs, and appeared in a number of Pageants and plays.

The short story class where I "doubled the output of any writer in the class" was at Los Angeles High School, in 1937. My teacher was Jennet Johnson, a very fine lady, and a good teacher. I am afraid that I sometimes horrified her with my subject matter.

I joined the Wilshire Player's Guild, an actors group started by the young Mormon motion picture actress Laraine Day, in 1939. I was secretary of the group for about a year. When the group dissolved in the summer of 1940, a few of us went to Laraine Day's house for about four nights a week, preparing a very broad satire called *Lame Brains and Daffydills* which we presented for various Mormon groups. Our last performance was in the early spring of 1941. That was the last year I participated in any acting group. From that year on, it was strictly writing.

My father's occupation has been and is trouble-shooter for the Bureau of Power and Light in Los Angeles. My brother Leonard is a high-line man with the same company.

The rehearsals mentioned in *The Damn Thing* for November, 1940, were for the Laraine Day play *Lame Brains and Daffydills*.

The Wilshire Players Guild split up because of, as usual, back-stage politics. I had hoped to transcribe an hour long version of L. Ron Hubbard's *Fear* at that time, and had finished a script of same, when the group failed.

The radio station in Tucson, Arizona was Station KGAR. Year: 1932. It has been defunct for a good number of years. *White's Directory* will probably list it for that year of 1932. I imagine its call letters were given to Kansas City later. I read the comic strips on KGAR on Saturday nights, appeared in plays with bit parts, and was sound effects man for a juvenile radio version of Tailspin Tommy. All at the age of 12.

I don't know if our ancestors came over on the *Lyon* together.[5] When next I'm at my father's I'll check some of his books to see what I find, and let you know.

We now have a little girl, named Susan Marguerite, born on November 5th, at nine-thirty-two in the morning. We are very pleased with her. She does not, however, resemble a Small Assassin.

Incidentally, my mother was once a supervisor in an Envelope Factory in North Chicago. Otherwise, her years have been spent strictly raising children, four of them, three boys and one girl, of which only my brother and I remain.

I hope this terribly disjointed letter will be of some aid to you. I apologize for my rambling method. If I wrote as badly as this all of the time, I am sure I would be the world's most rejected author. Thank you for taking the time to write to me. If there are any further details, please feel free to write again. I'll try to clear them up for you. My very best wishes and thanks.

Cordially,
Ray

WILLIAM F. NOLAN

Bill Nolan was the first writer to attempt a comprehensive accounting of Brad-bury's story publications, re-printings, and work in other media. Even before beginning his own writing career, Nolan began a rich correspondence with Bradbury that often sparked extended reflections on authorial intent. This letter offers perhaps Bradbury's best-defined distinctions between the slick and pulp market, and his abiding intention to avoid any such labeling in his own work.

Jan. 11, 1951.

Dear Bill:

Thanks for your long note of December 21st.

To answer a remark of yours first: ". . . but I thought in your case that you would be killing a vital part of your talent to write only slick." The fact is that I don't write pulp, slick, or quality stories. I don't write stories with labels at all, if I can help it. My agent and I have a simple agreement, I write "stories." I write stories the best I know how, at all times. Then he starts them out at the top of the market list for me. If they sell to *Collier's* or *Harper's*, swell! If not, they go to *Thrilling Wonder* or *Galaxy* or *Startling*. I have only one criterion I try to follow: "Is the work going into this story of such a quality that *Harper's* might possibly consider it?" I have long since realized that *Harper's* is resistant to science fiction, but nevertheless I try to finish all of my work so that its style, at least, is of a quality that I hope might be worthy of *Harper's*. The fact that my work has appeared in the past four years in *Collier's*, *The Post*, *The American Mercury*, etc., is accidental. I do not read *The Post* or *Collier's*, and have not read them for 14 years. I hate and abominate their fiction. But I am not averse to appearing in them if they allow me to write as I wish to write; which is what they have allowed me to do, no interference, no messing around with plots. Therefore, Bill, you see, I am not killing a vital part of my talent by writing only slick. The stories of mine you see in *Collier's*, by another stroke of luck, would have been in *TWS* or *Other Worlds*, if I had submitted them there first. On the day when I start writing "slick" stories with "slick" plotting and a "slick" style, you can turn me around and

kick me out the back door and stuff your Index up my nose.[6] In the great
morass of bad writing appearing in slick magazines today there is only
One way to keep afloat and make a reputation, and that is by being one's
own self, developing an individual imagination and style.

Enough of that. I get pretty wound up when I get going. I could have
said it in a few words like "Don't worry, Bill, no matter where you see
me, I always hope to deserve your attention and time." [...]

More from me later, Bill. Keep me informed on your latest doings.
Thanks for all your hard work on my behalf. I hope always to deserve
your friendship.

Yours,

Ray

---

*Nolan had spent much of 1951 documenting Bradbury's complex record of
publication and media adaptations for a hybrid book-journal titled* The Ray
Bradbury Review (1952). *Bradbury's November 7 update for Nolan included
an accounting of the unusual origins of "Here There Be Tygers," one of his
most intriguing planetary fantasies. Nolan believed that Bradbury's exploration
of death in his supernatural fiction spread into his science fiction as well, but
Bradbury continued to maintain that these themes were restricted to his early
successes in* Weird Tales *and the detective pulps.*

Nov. 7, 1951

Bradbury
10750 Clarkson Rd.
L.A. 64, Cal.

Dear Bill:

Delighted to hear that the work nears its finish; you have really used up
your mind and muscle on this project, God bless you. [...]

Glad you liked "Here There Be Tygers." I did 7 drafts on that story,
by God.[7] Really sweated it down into shape. It is one of the few stories

wherein the original idea was given to me by some one willing person. My agent one afternoon a year ago said, "Ray, why don't you write a story about a planet that is *so* nice that nobody wants to leave it?" It was a rare thing. I liked the idea immediately and went home that afternoon and did a first draft on it.[8] How *many* times I have had story ideas offered me, but never before have I accepted any or used any; that certain *rapport*, that spark, was missing.

Amusing the talk of my death-complex in my stories. It only applies to *Dark Carnival*, my first book. But how can you write a *Weird* tale without death or the fear of death? You can't. Might as well ask Poe to rewrite "Amontillado" or "Usher" and take out the morbidity. The form demands it. But death as a fear or motivating force is 90% absent from my other two books, so why all the palaver by these gents? Thanks again for everything. I look forward to the *Review* with great expectations.

Yours,

Ray

Bill Nolan's quest to document Bradbury's latest publications continued during Bradbury's extended stay in Ireland as screenwriter for Moby Dick. *In his response to Nolan's latest letter, Bradbury described the impact of his first and only Irish autumn and his delightful Dublin encounters with some of his favorite entertainers. His early views on working with John Huston offer no hint of the challenges to come.*

Bradbury
Royal Hibernian Hotel
Dublin, Ireland

October 30, 1953

Dear Bill:

It was good to hear from you after this long time. Thanks for your huge letter full of news.

Glad you liked *Fahrenheit 451*. Your point about Beatty may be well-taken. I'm too close to the book now to be able to decide one way or the other. Anyway, the first reviews have certainly been heartening. Did you see the Orville Prescott review?[9] I'm enclosing a duplicate of this in case you missed it.

Glad you also liked the changes in "The Playground" and "And the Rock Cried Out."[10]

"The Meadow" will be the lead short story in the Dec. *Esquire*. I saw the layout when I was in New York and it looks fine, really fine. Two page spread up front.

I will write Ballantine about the *Fahrenheit* original manuscript. Thanks for reminding me. [. . .]

So far, I've done 55 pages of screenplay on *Moby Dick* which I'm now cutting and rewriting. Huston hasn't seen this, yet, but I'll be showing him the work next week, the first he'll have seen. He's very patient and very kind, and a wonderful story teller on his own hook. We've had some terrific evenings out at his place, good food, fine wine, and much story telling by Huston and Viertel. We went fox-hunting last Tuesday; and it was a beautiful autumn day—my first autumn in more than 19 years. All the leaves on the trees ablaze with autumn. Clear cool wonderful weather, horns blowing, hounds baying, by God, a fine day!

I'm enjoying *Moby Dick* so much; it's a real challenge all the way, and I hope I can do well enough so that Huston won't have to call in any other writer, next spring. The way things shape now, *Moby Dick* will be his next film. At least this is what I hear . . . The Kipling story "The Man Who Would Be King," isn't going well.[11] Huston and Viertel are having script trouble on this, I take it . . . [. . .]

Hurrah for Beaumont. I'll look forward to his debut in *Esq*. Also look forward to his Boucher appearances. Hate to say I told you so, but, if you'll remember, two years ago, I predicted big things on this boy. I still predict them. He's great.

I also predict big things for that story of *yours*; if you'll get to work on it!

Met Burl Ives and had dinner with him and heard him sing at a penthouse party (wonderful!) at a theatre (great!) and at a dinner (swell!) all in one Blue-Tailed Fly 24 hour period![12]

Also saw Laurel and Hardy, in *person*, on the Dublin stage! Wow!

In the Civil Liberties issue of *The Nation*, coming soon, I think they'll reprint my book-burning speech, the Brandeis lecture.[13] Carey McWilliams wrote me about this, anyway. Hope it goes through. Wasn't it a surprise to see "The Garbage Collector" there? I'm darned happy about it. [. . .]

Thanks for everything!

Yours,
Ray

WILMA SHORE

During the late 1940s a writing group formed around Bradbury and other Southern California writers whose work had appeared in Doubleday's Best American Short Stories *annuals. Wilma Shore (1913–2006) was one of the original members, and Bradbury's letter to her alludes to his positive views of her writing. His extended personal observations on his own screenwriting challenges highlight the close nature of the friendship he developed with members of his writing group, most of whom became lifelong friends.*

Feb. 5, 1954

Dear Wilma:

This is no answer at all to the long wonderful letter you wrote weeks and weeks ago; this is merely to let you know I think of you and Lou and all the others. My bureau drawer is stuffed with letters from friends, relatives, and the Screen Writer's Guild wanting to know about dues. I am contemplating starting a small fire in that drawer, which will solve my problems and perhaps salve my guilty conscience . . .

Your letter was charming and wonderfully amusing; I wish you would try your hand more often, in the fiction form, at humor. You seem to have the proper light touch.

I'm sorry about your having to go to New York. In some ways it is a very exciting city and in other ways, as Lou has pointed out, excessively brutal and impolite.[14] If you do go, my good wishes go with you. We'll see you on the way home, next September or October. I'm still working on *Moby*. Finished 162 page first draft in January. Now polishing and cutting. Huston is much like myself, I feel; an "instinctive" intellectual, whatever the hell *that means*! He comes by his logic as hard as I do. Though he is far more logical than myself, he nevertheless comes to many artistic decisions in as difficult a fashion as I have always done. The both of us could use Elliott Grennard at times![15] But we are moving ahead, and the script looks fine. Just this week, for the first time, I saw the other scripts done on *Moby* at earlier dates. One by Charles Grayson and another by Robert Rossen. Rossen's script was well-written but structurally askew. Grayson's wasn't much of anything either way, God bless him; though it was obvious he worked hard. It is a strange experience to know that others have trod the same path ahead of you and that by some good fortune you are the one who hasn't fallen over the cliff into the sea. At least so it seems at this date. Once again I realize that I am one of God's lucky children, I have been protected throughout my life from all the terrible things that hit so many, I have been protected from real poverty, from real sorrow, from war, and from personal failure at my work. All of which means that I haven't developed a turtle-shell and if anything should ever happen to my work or my family I would be left raw and unprotected. You don't get callouses from the sort of life I've been able to lead. The test will come later and I suspect I will not meet it well. What old age and death will do to me should make a very strange study indeed. I will probably be a horrible old son-of-a-bitch, very bitter and carping and completely inhuman because I won't be able to keep all the chips that were so profligately thrown to me when I was young. Well, we'll see. To hell with this *Things to Come* philosophizing.[16] Needless to say part of my luck has been in having all of you as friends in the last four years. Distance lends focus, and if there's a freckle on one of you, I'll be damned if I'll recognize it! I hope this finds all of you writing and beginning to sell again. Love to you all, from

[signed: face with glasses]

WILLIAM F. NOLAN

Less than two weeks after completing his Moby Dick *screenplay in London for John Huston, and finally reunited with his family in Italy, Bradbury sent Bill Nolan his first detailed summary of the arduous working relationship he had forged with both Huston and with Melville's complex novel.*

Bradbury
Hotel Ambasciatori
Rome, Italy

April 28, 1954

Dear Bill,

Thanks so much for your kind and wonderful help in sending on the pages from *Fahrenheit* and the complete manuscript of one of the *Golden Apples* stories for the people at the Institute in New York.[17] They wrote me an enthusiastic letter speaking highly and warmly of your swell and careful selection of just the right sort of material they needed. Bless you.

We'll have much to talk about when I get home; most of it I'll fill in for you then. We'll be home some time in June, tentatively. By then we'll have been gone 8 months, which is long enough to be without roots.

I did over 1500 pages of script to get a 152 page final script of *Moby*. John did little actual writing on it, but much in the way of straightening out my thinking and making me rework page after page, over and over again. Sometimes Huston wrote three or four pages to give me an idea of what he wanted; and then I took over to do a final draft. It is "essence of Melville" which means Melville boiled down, I hope, to his essentials. We have had to rearrange some of his scenes and ideas to give us a step-progression for films, in other words a series of quiet scenes, dramatically loud scenes (you might say) and a series of small climaxes building to a grand finale. It is, in a way, a symphony. Some of Melville's ideas, I have extended out. In the book, the calm scene is briefly mentioned; I have developed it into a mood-dramatic scene, encompassing other elements, which lasts for 14 pages or more. Same with the Typhoon. The entire story begins and ends the same way the book does, with a few minor variations. Starbuck comes forward more in the screen version, as does the Manxman.

   We're now in Rome. A beautiful, beautiful city. We head up for Venice, Florence, and Milan next week; hoping to meet Bernard Berenson, the art-critic, then. Thanks again for your friendly help.

Yours, as ever,
Ray

SAM SACKETT

Sam Sackett, whose early letters to Bradbury elicited more detailed biographical reflections than Bradbury usually offered at midcentury, was now a professor at Ft. Hays State College in Kansas. This January 1958 letter to Sackett referenced one of the first scholarly articles about Bradbury's adaptation of Moby Dick *for the 1956 Warner Brothers film, prompting detailed commentary on how Bradbury decided to remove Fedallah, the mysterious crew captain of Ahab's harpoon boat, from the screenplay and thereby change one of the most famous closing scenes of the original novel.*

January 18, 1958

Dear Sam:

Thanks for your card about *College English* and the article on the film version of *Moby Dick*.[18] I'll look it up. The points you make are excellent . . . nobody ever tries to figure out how difficult it would be to move an item out of one form into another. Alas, if you go to the experts, as you also imply, you don't find agreement anywhere as to what in hell the book is all about. I had to stick out my neck, which is all that any man can do under the circumstances. It's better to stick it out and get your head chopped off than play it safe and come up with vanilla pudding.

I'm proud as hell of my ending for the film, where Ahab, instead of the Parsee, is presented from the deeps upon the return of Moby . . . how much better to see Ahab crucified there and beckoning to his men than to have the Parsee so handled. I never have given a damn for Fedallah. Huston and I discussed him the first day I arrived in Ireland. I said, "Number One, do I kill off Fedallah before I start the script?" "Oh, God, yes," said Huston, "throw him out!" And so I did, and nobody will ever make me feel sorry. He bungles the works. It's a shame Melville didn't get rid of him, too. There's more than enough in the way of mystic symbols and action in the book to carry the message, without Fedallah creeping out.

It's interesting to see that in two versions of *Moby* published, for kids, in the last two years, both have adapted my ending, rather than Melville's. Blasphemy, of course. But egotistically, I warm to the thought that if I don't cut my own niche, someday I may be remembered as a footnote to *Moby*.

> Again thanks for your card,
> Best to you and yours!
> Ray

WILLIAM F. NOLAN

In reacting to the publication of Something Wicked This Way Comes, *more traditional horror writers were unsettled by Bradbury's unconventional way of dealing with humanity's fear of death by laughing it out of existence, and his good friends Bill Nolan and Charles Beaumont were no exceptions. "I just flat don't believe that you can deal with true evil," Nolan maintained, "by laughing it out of existence, by fighting a force of darkness with a smile." In this candid response, between his own successive ellipsis-point pauses, Bradbury defines the bits of magic that he hoped would endure for readers of his first sustained novel.*

July 23rd, 1962

Dear Bill:

Thanks for yours from good old Palm Springs. Mag and I both
understand your love for that place. When we were out there with the
kids 4 weeks ago, it was great being able to walk around half-naked at
night, and go swimming at eleven or midnight under the stars . . . I'd like
to try what you're doing sometime, take my typewriter and sit in there
for ten days and get a big chunk of my new novel going [. . .]

Your remarks on *Something Wicked*, while momentarily depressing,
were accepted with good grace. I've been at bat often over the years.
It is inevitable that on occasion, at long last, I field a few off into the
foul-line or hit some grounders. (Do I sound like Papa?!) I am hoping of
course that your opinion will be the minority opinion . . . how else can I
hope, since I've spent so many years on so many versions of this book?
I am also hoping that even if critics do carp at it, that over the years
people will remember scenes from the book even as people remember
scenes from *Moby Dick* . . . in other words while huge parts of *Moby* bore
people . . . and maybe huge parts of my novel will bore people . . . they
will, on occasion, when together, say, "well, it wasn't his best, but there
were a few scenes there . . . like the fight between the boy, his bows-
and-arrows, and the Dust Witch in the Midnight Balloon, how about
that .?.?. and the scene in the tent with the old old man in the electric
chair . . . and the night scene in the library with the father explaining
what the carnival was all about . . . etc. . . ."

If I can come out with just a bit of that, with a few shreds of praise for
the times I was in focus . . . after all, this is my first real big novel and it is
hard to keep a thing this long always clearly aligned . . . I will be happy. Not
satisfied, of course, for I *did* want more from the book, and it was only after
long years of painstaking rewrite that I finally let the book go off to S. and S.

Finally, I want to thank you again for your honesty with me.
Without it, we wouldn't have a friendship. [. . .]

Your friend,
Ray

LOREN EISELEY

Bradbury always believed that his friend Loren Eiseley (1907–1977) had the most engaging and lucid writing style of any of the prominent midcentury scientific writers. Eiseley's essays explored broad aspects of natural history and the history of science, and these were periodically gathered into popular collections that mirrored Bradbury's ability to pull wide-ranging tales into story collections that also stood the test of time. For Christmas 1973 he sent Eiseley his first collection of verse. The volume opened with "Remembrance," perhaps Bradbury's best poem, and Eiseley's letter of thanks included a glimpse of the darker aspects of nostalgia that populated the memories of his Nebraska childhood.

January 11, 1974

Dear Ray:

Your precious book arrived for Christmas and Mabel and I were delighted to receive it. Your inscription will be forever treasured.

I remember with great pleasure that on the occasion of my previous visit to your home I had the opportunity to read a couple of your poems in manuscript. They have that same lyrical intensity that is so touchingly evident in your short stories.

It would be unseemly and invidious to make choices amidst such treasures but I will tell you that I read "Remembrance" with a kind of preternatural, nostalgic terror, knowing in advance how it would turn out. *My* tree, alas, was chopped down long ago and when, as a stranger, I visited that town and stared across at my old house, looking at what used to be a vacant lot beside it which was now occupied by an apartment house, a stranger on the front porch of my old home spoke to me. I suppose he had merely seen me there gazing rather intently and wanted to be neighborly, perhaps thinking I was a new person in the neighborhood. I spoke the time of day to him, of course, but then turned and went hastily away, filled with inexplicable terror and loneliness. How could I tell that owner, after all of these years, about vanished objects for which I was searching, or that his house was filled with the ghosts of the dead? No, instead I turned and almost ran and I have not returned since. I did not want to tell that man that he had usurped my past, that I, too, was a ghost, and that there was a time before his time. I should not try to explain but this is what the very first pages of your book brought back to me. And then, of course, there is the next poem and the next.

I, too, am one of those who still have my original *Twenty Thousand Leagues Under the Sea* and *Mysterious Island* on my shelves, and *Nemo* is a name with which to conjure. I honestly do not know how they managed to be preserved because most of my possessions, if they still exist, lie scattered and lost in the attics of forgotten lodging houses of the middle west. But Nemo and my toy lion somehow came through, along with a worn old jackknife. My father first told me about *Nemo*, but where and how, on those prairies and their shabby towns far from the sea, he first learned of *Nemo*, I will never know now.

Well, if I go on with this kind of thing, all stirred up by your book, I will only end by weeping out an endless autobiography. I am passably well and in four years will reach the age of mandatory retirement. I do hope before then that we will be able to visit once again under more leisurely circumstances. Tell Maggie I remember her with affection and may life continue to be good to you both. Mabel joins me in these hopes for the future.

Affectionately,
Loren
Loren Eiseley

BRIAN SIBLEY

*British writer Brian Sibley (1949–), well-known for BBC radio documentaries
and literary adaptations, began a long correspondence with Bradbury in the 1970s
and would eventually develop BBC programming on Bradbury and his works.
Sibley's second letter related to his own research on Disney Enterprises, asking
critical questions that prompted Bradbury to champion Disney's vision in his response. Sibley's further correspondence, and his books on other literary mythmak-
ers of our times, led to an enduring long-distance friendship of thirty-eight years.*

8 May 1974

Dear Ray Bradbury:

Thank you for the cuttings—I am very pleased to have read your thoughts
on Disney, particularly since they correspond so exactly with my own!
Your observations in the review of the Finch book are unerringly accurate:
we all of us either love or hate Disney, and hate or love doing so! [. . .]

Do you really believe that Disney's Audio Animatronics are harmless?
Physically maybe (unless the clockwork Lincoln blows a fuse and runs
amok); mentally, spiritually, aesthetically I am *not* so sure. Why do we need
perfection-built, plastic skinned, wind-up Presidents and animals: when we
have actors or the real thing? This ersatz experience thing is what troubles
me most about Disneyland: and then the perfectionism; the shadowy
hinterland where fantasy and reality are indistinguishable. However, if I
ever manage to visit Disneyland, I am sure I would melt completely. . . .

But why, oh why, did he feel the compulsion to build the place to start
with? Arrogance? Assurance of immortality? Financial foresight? Open-
hearted, fun-loving, beneficence? Who knows? Do you know?! [. . .]

Anyway, I look forward to your letter with great interest.

Sincerely yours,
Brian Sibley

[. . .] P.P.S. Do you have a copy of your letter to *Nation*?

June 10, 1974

Dear Brian Sibley:

This will have to be short. Sorry. But I am deep into my screenplay on *Something Wicked This Way Comes* and have no secretary, never have had one . . . so must write all my own letters . . . 200 a week!!!!

Disney was a dreamer and a doer . . . while the rest of us were talking about the future, he built it. The things he taught us at Disneyland about street planning, crowd movement, comfort, humanity, etc., will influence builders, architects, urban planners for the next century. Because of him we will humanize our cities, plan small towns again where we can get in touch with one another again and make democracy work creatively because we will *know* the people we vote for. He was so far ahead of his time it will take us the next fifty years to catch up. You *must* come to Disneyland and eat your words, swallow your doubts. Most of the other architects of the modern world were asses and fools who talked against Big Brother and then built prisons to put us all in . . . our modern environments which stifle and destroy us. Disney the so-called conservative turns out to be Disney the great man of foresight and construction.

Enough. Come here soon. I'll toss you in the Jungle Ride River and ride you on the train into tomorrow, yesterday, and beyond.

Good luck, and stop judging at such a great distance. You are simply not qualified. Disney was full of errors, paradoxes, mistakes. He was also full of life, beauty, insight. Which speaks for all of us, eh? We are all mysteries of light and dark. There are no true conservatives, liberals, etc., in the world. Only people.

Best,
Ray B.

P.S. I can't find that issue of the *Nation*, or the *New Republic*, which ever it was, with my letter in it on Disney.[19] Mainly I said that if Disneyland was good enough for Captain Bligh it was good enough for me. Charles Laughton and his wife took me to Disneyland for my very first visit and our first ride was the Jungle Boat Ride, which Laughton immediately commandeered, jeering at customers going by in other boats! A fantastic romp for me and a hilarious day. What a way to start my association with Disneyland!

R.B.

P.S. Can't resist commenting on your fears of the Disney robots. Why aren't you afraid of books, then? The fact is, of course, that people have been afraid of books, down through history. They are extensions of people, not people themselves. Any machine, any robot, is the sum total of the ways we use it. Why not knock down all robot camera devices and the means for reproducing the stuff that goes into such devices, things called projectors in theatres? A motion picture projector is a non-humanoid robot which repeats truths which we inject into it. Is it inhuman? Yes. Does it project human truths to humanize us more often than not? Yes.

The excuse could be made that we should burn all books because some books are dreadful.

We should mash all cars because some cars get in accidents because of the people driving them.

We should burn down all the theatres in the world because some films are trash, drivel.

So it is finally with the robots you say you fear. Why fear something? Why not create with it? Why not build robot teachers to help out in schools where teaching certain subjects is a bore for *everyone*? Why not have Plato sitting in your Greek Class answering jolly questions about his Republic? I would love to experiment with that. I am not afraid of robots. I am afraid of people, people, people. I want them to remain human. I can help keep them human with the wise and lovely use of books, films, robots, and my own mind, hands, and heart.

I am afraid of Catholics killing Protestants and vice versa.

I am afraid of whites killing blacks and vice versa.

I am afraid of English killing Irish and vice versa.

I am afraid of young killing old and vice versa.

I am afraid of Communists killing Capitalists and vice versa.

But . . . robots? God, I love them. I will use them humanely to teach all of the above. My voice will speak out of them, and it will be a damned nice voice.

Best, R.B.

---

18 June 1974

Dear Ray:

Thank you for your letter, and for leaving *Something Wicked This Way Comes* to write to me. Please make that screenplay beautiful—for me; I loved the book so much that I couldn't bear it being anything else.

Yes, Disney was a paradox, a Chinese puzzle, an insoluble riddle: so are all men; Disney is our archetype, the big-screen projection of us smaller men. [. . .]

I can't agree with all you say about robots (though I love the way you say it) because I think the one flaw in your philosophy is that it is the people you fear who control the robots you trust, and therein lies the danger. Today a harmless clockwork Lincoln amuses American man; tomorrow, a mechanical dictator in the White House, controlled by dark hearts, leads America to destruction. We must know the location of the master-switch that controls simulated men, so that we (the real people) can throw it, if necessary, and cease the functioning of their computerized brain cells.

Oh, but I *am* afraid of books, Ray, otherwise, why would I read them and want to write them? I fear them very greatly—especially yours, and Poe's, and Wells', Huxley's, and Tolkien's, yet I love them dearly for their reconciliation between trust and fear.

Fond regards,
Brian

JOSEPH MUGNAINI

Ray Bradbury's abiding forty-year friendship with the prominent illustrator and artist Joe Mugnaini (1912–1992) also formed one of the most significant working relationships of his career as a writer. He first encountered Mugnaini's work at a 1952 gallery exhibition in Los Angeles, and their collaborations soon opened out into the striking linework illustrations for Bradbury's The Golden Apples of the Sun, *the iconic burning man cover and associated art for* Fahrenheit 451, *jacket art and interior illustrations for Bradbury's* The October Country, *and the Academy Award–nominated 1962 animated short film* Icarus Montgolfier Wright.*

Bradbury's assessment of Mugnaini's influence on his career, often spoken but rarely written, surfaced in this 1983 letter, written shortly after a chance encounter with his friend at the famous Harris Ranch restaurant and hotel complex in California's Central Valley region.

Dear Joe:

Seeing you so unexpectedly at the Harris Ranch the other day made me realize all over again how much I love and respect you. Ours has been a phenomenal friendship, and I am deeply in debt to you for the ways you have enriched my life. Driving away from our encounter I thought again and again of how wonderful a coincidence it was, the night Mag and I saw your first etching in a window in a benefit gallery in Beverly Hills more than 31 years ago.

And, of course, the great thing is you have not stayed the same, you have grown and grown over the years, with your fabulous work. And, of course, you and I are on the same search for the same truths, whatever in hell they may be, most of it damned mysterious, eh?

I love you, Joe, and am glad our paths crossed, which caused me to sit down this weekend to tell you about our friendship, all over again.

Please, please live to be 90 or 95, yes? I'll be damned if I'll write books if you're not around to illustrate them! You *hear*?!

Bless you,
Ray
October 22, 1983

TOM COTTER

"The President of the Union of Soviet Socialist Republics and Mrs. Gorbachev request the pleasure of the company of Mr. Ray Bradbury at luncheon on Thursday, May 31, 1990, at 1:00 p.m." Bradbury was one of only two American writers invited to the Soviet Embassy for this event, along with many distinguished guests from the world of international politics, the current American political scene, and Hollywood. The following day, he wrote to Tom Cotter, his principal location producer for the Ray Bradbury Theater *television series, and told him how he discovered the reason for his invitation.*

June 1st, 1990

Tom Cotter
& Assorted Cohorts
Alberta Filmworks:

Dear Tom:

[. . .] My luncheon with the Gorbachevs and multitudinous intellectuals and actors and performing dogs was a smashing success. Gorby only mentioned two writers during his luncheon speech, Asimov and myself! When I was introduced to Raisa she turned, grabbed her husband's elbow and cried, "Mikail, this is the man our daughter loves!" "Yes!" he replied. "It's true. She thinks you are the greatest writer in the world!" Later, at lunch, I found the spelling of the daughter's name, wrote a note on my calling card to her, and had a waiter take it over to Mrs. G. When she saw it, she jumped to her feet and stared around to find me. I waved, She waved back and blew a kiss. I tossed a kiss right back to her! I think, dear Tom, I have made a friend. [. . .]

Best to everyone,
Ray

EDDIE ALBERT

Veteran actor Eddie Albert (1906–2005), twice nominated for the Academy Award, was also a successful television actor and Bradbury friend. Albert starred in the Ray Bradbury Theater *adaptation of "A Touch of Petulance," broadcast on October 12, 1990; Bradbury's comments in this letter are based on his advanced screening of the episode in his role as writer and executive producer of the series.*

July 9, 1990

Dear Eddie,

Delighted to have your letter. I am sending this by FAX so it will reach you in a few days rather than the 10 days it often takes for airmail from France.

Your performance in "A Touch of Petulance" is a beaut. I laugh when I recall that, a few months ago, you asked to have lunch with me to get an idea of how to play your part. Without me, you are brilliant! As is the young man who played opposite you. What a team! I will write to your friend, Mr. Krasno, and see what can be done about my Soviet rubles when I return to L.A. in Sept. It is too early in my new relationship to some Soviet folks to know whether funds can be transferred or otherwise used. I don't want to rush. I would prefer to be invited over next year. When I am there, *then* I could nudge them on the money owed for 38 years of their printing my books without my permission. Sept 6th *Ice Cream*, the musical, with music by Jose Feliciano, opens at the Pasadena Playhouse. You will be invited. Again, congratulations on your great performance in "Petulance" . . . even better than *Three Men on a Horse*! (This elephant never forgets. I was in L.A. High that year!) Fond wishes,

Ray

LEWIS FRUMKES

Writer, educator, and journalist Lewis Burke Frumkes (1939–) is best known for his books on writing and his long-running New York radio show featuring interviews with a broad range of writers. Bradbury and many of his literary contemporaries have been interviewed for this show, resulting in the influential compilation Advice for Young Writers. *In 1993, Frumkes sent Bradbury these reflections on a conversation with award-winning Canadian author Margaret Atwood.*

December 1, 1993

Ray,

I spent some time with Margaret Atwood the other day. She's a highly intelligent woman and a wonderful writer, Canadian, *Cat's Eye*, *The Handmaid's Tale*, and her current best-seller, *The Robber Bride*. We talked about many things, including her latest villain, Zenia, whom she described as a shapeshifter, and then suddenly she asked me, "You know the greatest tale ever told about a shapeshifter, don't you? It was that wonderful story in Ray Bradbury's *The Martian Chronicles* with the Martian who could change into family members. Wow! Was that spooky. I still get the chills thinking about it." And so do I, Ray.

So I thought I'd relate that little exchange, and use it as an opportunity to see how you are—and to say what a terrific human being I think you are, not to mention a writer, and to wish you and your wife a merry Xmas, and a happy new year.

Best,
Lewis

JOHN TIBBETTS

Bradbury's Hollywood memories were sometimes stimulated through his correspondence with John C. Tibbetts (1946–), who conducted Bradbury interviews on a wide range of subjects. Tibbetts, a portrait artist, pianist, and emeritus professor of film studies at the University of Kansas, once triggered Bradbury's long-buried personal memories of the seminal silent film comedian Buster Keaton.

September 30, 2004

Dear John:

Thank you for your essay on laughter.[20] It's a beautiful piece of work and I'm honored to be mentioned along with Buster Keaton and G.K. Chesterton. I'm sure that the audience reacted well to your reading your essay to them. It's a fine job, John.

I don't think I ever told you that Buster Keaton was one of my customers when I sold newspapers on the corner of Olympic and Norton, here in L.A., when I was nineteen. He used to come to the corner at least once a month. I don't know if he lived in the area or had friends he was visiting, but I sold him newspapers over a period of two or three years and occasionally had a chance to talk to him. This was years before he was rediscovered, of course. In 1939 he was still an unknown quantity from the past. So it warms my heart to think that I knew him on a somewhat personal level when I was so very young.

In any event, your essay is beautiful. Thank you for sending it to me.

I send you much love,
Ray

JOHN GODLEY, 3RD BARON KILBRACKEN

Bradbury first met the Anglo-Irish journalist John Godley, the 3rd Baron Kilbracken (1920–2006), in October 1953, shortly after arriving in Ireland to write the screenplay for John Huston's film adaptation of Moby Dick. *Lord Kil-*

*bracken helped Bradbury cope with the cold Irish winter and the challenges of
working for the demanding John Huston, but Kilbracken himself was unexpectedly drawn into the world of the Hollywood expatriate Huston, who eventually
hired him to modify Bradbury's finished script during the shooting phase of film
production. The shared challenge of working for Huston only strengthened the
bond of friendship between Bradbury and Kilbracken, and in 1986 Bradbury
told his friend of a recent encounter with Huston.*

[ca. early January 1986]

Dear John:

How wonderful to hear of that joyous gift, your four year old son!
What pleasures are ahead for you in the ten years before he begins to
turn into a young man. Even then, if you are fortunate, the gift will
remain. I can't say, for I am surrounded by four daughters and three
grand-daughters! We will be in London in late April, staying at Brown's.
Wouldn't it be nice if we all met at that time? I hope you will be in
London, then. We are coming over for about 8 days to promote my new
novel *Death Is a Lonely Business*, which is out here and selling well, to
nice reviews.

I saw John Huston in a restaurant two weeks ago, the first time I
had seen him in some 20 years. The old feelings of love plus hate rose
up in me. Mainly love, I imagine, for he changed our lives all to the good
by giving me my first job at screenwriting. After that, I never had to beg
for jobs.

I've just finished a half hour film for my own TV series. We have
filmed "Banshee," which you helped out on,[21] in Toronto, with Peter
O'Toole playing Huston. It has turned out well. I am half tempted to call
Huston and ask him to a screening to see how he would like himself,
played by O'Toole.

That's it for now. A long full wonderous life to Sean.

I am working on a long book of my Irish essays, plays, stories,
poems, titled *Green*. At the proper time I will ask your permission to
quote from that wonderous letter you wrote me, years back, reacting to
my Irish stories.

Meanwhile, please God, London, April and us. Yours with fond
memories,

                                                                                Ray

---

By 1991 Bradbury had decided to merge Green, *the unpublished Irish story collection he had mentioned to Lord Kilbracken, into his long-deferred novelization
of his seven-month 1953–1954 sojourn in Ireland. As he prepared liner notes for
the newly transformed book, Bradbury reached out to Kilbracken to recall their
shared memories of those days; he also attached a letter written by Kilbracken
a quarter century earlier that had convinced Bradbury that his Irish stories,
essentially humorous and at times annoyingly stereotypical, also captured "certain profound truths" of the Irish spirit.*

                                                                [ca. September 1991]

Dear John:

It's been a long while, perhaps five years, perhaps six, since last we
exchanged letters, and a long long while, many many years, in which
our children have grown and shared friends have died, but at last I have
finished, after 37 years work, my book of Irish stories, which have turned
into a kind of novel, tentatively titled *Green*[22] for lack of something
more imaginative. The book will contain all my Irish tales, most of
which you know from my having sent them on to you at one time or
another, plus short remembrances of Huston stashed here and there in
the welter of fancies. The book will be published by Knopf next April
or May, and some of it is funny and some of it is sad, with the sadness
of rain and time and the falling away of lives. I hear that the Royal
Hibernian Hotel was torn down a few years ago, and I could feel the
timbers go in my heart.

Now, back in 1965 you wrote me the most beautiful letter I have
ever received about my work, about my Irish tales, and about me. I
enclose a copy. I have kept it all these years as a treasure. What I am
asking now is this, if I send you a proof of the book and you still liked

what you found in it, would you allow me to use a portion of that remarkable letter in the jacket copy for the book? Everything would depend, of course, on your appreciation or lack thereof of something on which you had several changing opinions. With the added factor that I have not kept up the friendship and now come asking a kind favor. I can only call upon memory and the fact that you and Deacon[23] helped save our lives in that long winter in Dublin. Maggie has often spoken kindly on our shared weeks and months, our dinners and lunches and our visit to Killegar.[24] I remember sadly your long wait for Huston, sadist that he was, to make up his mind about you and Ishmael, and the terrible despair in your voice when you telephoned me on your return from America and called to find out the final verdict and it was left to me (why not Huston, for God's sake?) to tell you you would not play the film's lead. My heart died with yours, hearing your voice, smothered, on the phone.

So there you have it. Please re-read your letter and decide if you wish to see the *Green* proofs. And even if you accept to read them, there would be no obligation. If you decided not to allow us to quote your letter, I would accept that with good grace.

[...] There's not much else to say except, no matter what your various decisions, your 1965 will always remain very close and dear to my heart. I hope all is well with you and your family. Fond good wishes from Maggie and,

Ray

KILBRACKEN TO BRADBURY [ATTACHED LETTER]

October 23rd 1965

Dear Ray:

I have a special tray for unanswerable letters. Now, having returned from a vastly interesting trip to Mozambique and the Congo, having

written my pieces and processed my pictures, having answered all my
answerable letters and put the farm in order, I have at last turned to
this tray; and *your* letter, your letter dated New Years Day 1965, is the
last letter left in it. When I've finished writing to you, my unanswerable-
letter tray will be empty. Why is yours the last of the last?

You sent me some plays of yours. You had indeed sent them to
me before, but I didn't think of them as plays when you asked me if I'd
received them (still do not) and so now I have two copies. You also sent
me a copy of your story "The Beggar on the Dublin Bridge," which is
still clipped to your letter in my unanswerable tray because I keep the
tray extremely well organized. When I wrote to you, I would have to
tell you what I thought of these "Irish" tales and, because I admire your
work very greatly and like you as much as I respect it, this would have to
be a somewhat detailed critique. For reasons which will appear, I have
not been able to face writing this (and even now, driven by no special
impetus beyond the sight of your letter lying lonely, find it far from
easy).

I have read your stories several times. I hated them. I thought:
"Here is a good friend, here is Ray Bradbury, a famous writer, who came
to my country (yet *is* it my country?); here is a big, rich, soft American
who had never before left the comfortable pseudo-cocoon of American
pseudo-civilization, who came here and spent a certain number of
months here and yet, despite that intuition and sensitivity and power
of observation with which I credited him beyond anything, failed to
acquire the smallest understanding of what Ireland and the Irish are
really like, failed to reach beyond the most superficial level, failed to
appreciate to the smallest possible degree the values and the wit and
the intelligence and the humanity which exist here: but was principally
impressed by what he took to be abject poverty and squalor, which may
indeed (does indeed) contrast rather strongly with the standards, on
an absolutely material level, of the Great American Society, as it exists
in fact or maybe only in the imagination of prosperous Americans,
yet is infinitely higher than in a hundred other countries unknown to
him, and is in any case outweighed by other less material, non-material
characteristics."

That is what I thought when first I read your stories. (It didn't matter that you wrote "Meynooth" and "Kilashandra" for Killeshandra and Maynooth.) And that is why, you'll realize, I found it very hard indeed to answer your unanswerable letter. And it went into the unanswerable tray. And then during the summer, home between Honduras and Florida, the house full of children, boats on the lake, picnics in the Pottle Woods, I chanced one day to pick up your book again,[25] then to re-read your story in the *Post*, and now I found, rather to my astonishment, that a degree of ambivalence was entering my feelings towards them. And, since the stories themselves had not changed, this can have been due only to a change of some kind in myself, and I began to wonder what it was.

I came to realise that the ambivalence I had detected was not in fact an ambivalence towards your stories but an ambivalence in my own feelings towards Ireland, arising from rather complex subjective reasons: partially my own position as an Anglo-Irishman, my English childhood, my childhood Protestantism, my non-Catholicism, my English accent, my long absences, and partially the kind of defensiveness which not merely causes sensitivity to criticism, but is actively *looking* for (because expecting) criticism of a country that, though beautiful, blessed and above all human, *is* backward, *is* poor, *is*, I dare say, very often squalid. And since such defensiveness for his country is very frequently visible even in an American (who himself may criticise the KKK, policy in Vietnam, Jackie Kennedy's dress-sense or what have you, but just let a damned Limey try it), how much more likely is it to occur in God's Own Country, even to one who particularly despises it when he espies it in others. And there is a further danger beyond the resentment of criticism even though the criticism be justified, even though, indeed, there be in fact no criticism at all: it is the resentment that a damned outsider, after a mere few months in a great and ancient country, should discover, recognise and set down in brilliant language certain profound truths about it which the reader himself, if he had even recognized them, had never fully admitted, or, if he had admitted them, would never have been able to express so admirably.

I had come about this far in my reconsideration of Bradbury when I was dispatched to Sebastian, Florida, where the Real Eight Corporation is salvaging Spanish gold and silver—doubloons and pieces of eight worth several million dollars—from the wrecks of two galleons which foundered on an offshore reef in a July 1715 hurricane. No sooner had I returned than I departed for Mozambique, where no previous reporter had been allowed to enter the battle area in the North, alongside Lake Malawi, where the Portuguese colonialists are engaged in guerrilla warfare with the Frelimo (a kind of Mozambiqui IRA) on quite a considerable scale. And so it has not been until today, what with one thing and another, that I have been able to write and tell you about my feelings toward *The Anthem Sprinters*; and at the same time, incidentally but relevantly, about my feelings for Ireland and my feelings for myself.

Congratulations on a wonderful piece of writing. If I write that I find it almost unbelievable that a visiting writer, in the course of such a relatively short stay, which he spent largely in the cushioned background of the Royal Hibernian Hotel or in Hustonian glimmer at Kilcock, should have acquired such a deep and true feeling and understanding of this country, you may possibly think (for you too have the defensiveness, the insecurity, which led *me* to wrong inferences, to wrong judgments) that I write with sarcasm. I do not. I mean it very sincerely; and it's true.

Ever yours,
John

I send this as written, straight out of the typewriter, with no first rough draft.

11

FAMILY

It was a good life for us kids, in Waukegan. I have always looked back on it with affection and gladness that we could have lived as near to nature as we did, having the ravine there, in the town, to play in every day, and having the lake and the country so close, if we wanted it.

—*Bradbury to Leo and Esther Bradbury, August 3, 1957*

LEO AND ESTHER BRADBURY

Bradbury's three-month 1945 journey across vast areas of Mexico had the purpose of collecting indigenous masks for the Los Angeles County Museum, but this adventure would have a lasting impact on his writing. His Halloween midnight journey by canoe across Lake Pátzcuaro to celebrate the Day of the Dead, and his subterranean encounter with the Mummies of Guanajuato two weeks later, radiated out into some of his best stories and books, including "The Next in Line" and The Halloween Tree. *Bradbury touched on these events in the following three letters to his parents, written and posted from central Mexico. The first is a postcard written after visiting the Pyramid of the Sun at Teotihuacán during the eighteen days that he stayed in Mexico City, in the same lodgings where John Steinbeck was also accommodated during the filming of his novel* The Pearl. *Bradbury often adapted a "gee-whiz" tone when writing to his parents as a young man, and he would never fully abandon it as he grew older.*

[mid-October 1945]

Hi People:

This is one of the pyramids I visited yesterday. They've been here for many centuries. The old Aztecs used to have sacrifices and dances on them. Nice, huh? Hope you are all well. I am fine.

Love,
Shorty.

John Steinbeck, the writer, is staying here with me! Ya-hoo!

———————————————

On October 29, Bradbury and his traveling companion Grant Beach departed Mexico City and headed into the Tarascan Indian culture before turning north, where they would eventually encounter the Mummies of Guanajuato.

November 3rd, 1945

Dear Folks:

This is written in Patzcuaro, Michoacan, on the shores of lovely Lake
Patzcuaro. Two nights ago, on the Day of the Dead (the Mexican
equivalent of Halloween) we took a small motor boat across the lake at
midnight with three French women, who turned out to be the French
Ambassador's wife and daughter and friend, to visit the graveyard on the
island of Janitzio during the rites there; the people of the town came to
the graveyard bearing huge masses of flowers and candles were lighted
on each tomb and garlands of orchids strewn over them, and there was
singing and wailing and a great carrying on in and out of the church
and churchyard. The fog came up and it was cold going back across
the lake, and very atmospheric and mysterious. We struck up a lively
acquaintance with the French Ambassador's wife and daughter and
they invited us to visit them next time we come to Mexico. Mexico is a
great country, you never know who you'll bump into next. We are both
well and are now heading for Paricutin Volcano, will probably be there
tomorrow, and then on up to Guadalajara and Guanajuato. The trip
continues to be stimulating and new. Hope everything is okay in L.A.

Hope you are all well and enjoying yourselves. Don't know if I told
you, but Margaret Sullavan's husband Leland Hayward[1] contacted me
in Mexico City and wants to be my agent. I'm sure you know Maggie
Sullavan from her many pictures. It has been very flattering. But I'm not
going to tie up with anyone for a while yet. Well, enough. Love to you all
from me all.

Cherro.
Shorty

[November 16, 1945]

Dear Folks:

This is Nov. 16th—Sunday—in El Mante—and tomorrow night we'll
be in Lenares—followed by Monterrey and—two days later—Laredo,
Texas—the weather is warm here—bananas taste like strawberries—
we're about 380 miles from the U.S. on the Laredo Highway—we saw
the catacombs in Guanajuato—BRRRR,—105 corpses standing up
against the walls of a dungeon—100 years old—very lovely—other
details later—much love to you all—be good.

Shorty

MARGUERITE McCLURE BRADBURY

*In the late spring of 1951, Bradbury set out on his third trip to New York in three
years to work with Don Congdon and some of his editors. After arriving in New
York, Bradbury wrote this reflective "love letter" to Maggie, who was caring for
eighteen-month-old Susan and their second daughter, Ramona, who was born
just before her husband began his long rail journey east. Over time, Bradbury
would sometimes reflect in private about the way that Maggie had brought love
and light into his life when they met in the spring of 1946; this letter includes
perhaps his earliest expression of that awakening.*

Wednesday May 6, 1951

Dear Sweet Marguerite:

You know, I don't call you Marguerite often enough, and I should, for if
ever a name was pretty enough and good enough and nice enough for a
lovely lady, Marguerite is just the name for you.

I guess I'm going to embarrass you this morning by writing you a
love letter. Being away gives me so much chance to think of what you
mean to me and what we have meant to each other and I feel continually

and humbly grateful for the good fortune that brought us together. I guess I am terribly hammy and literate even in my most private thoughts, but last night it rained during the night here and I lay in my hotel room thinking that you were the fine rain after the long draught, you have been the five good years after the five bad, the five years of plenty after the five years of famine. And I went on in that way in my mind, and the best part of all was that all of it was true. I considered the happiness and rest you have given me and I hope I have given you, and I thought of wonderful Susan and the swell work you have done with her, and I was filled with gratitude and happiness.

It is good to be away so that I can bring myself to put these things on paper to you, for it is important that people who are as close as we can sometimes stand off and repeat aloud what we know in our hearts.

As I said, this was going to be a love letter, and nothing else. I love you, dear mama-bun, and if the rest of our life together is only half what our first five years have been it will be very wonderful indeed.

Yours,
Ray

LEO AND ESTHER BRADBURY

Three weeks after agreeing to write the Moby Dick *screenplay for John Huston and Warner Brothers, Bradbury, his wife, his two very young daughters, and a governess found themselves bound east from Los Angeles by rail and ocean liner to Europe. Much of this letter to his parents concerns the process of arranging how Leo and Esther Bradbury would deal with his obligations and live in his house during what would become nearly nine months away from home.*

Sunday September 20, 1953

Dear Mom and Dad:

Here we are, the fourth day at sea, and a rough day it is, with enough good big waves to make you swallow a dose of Mothersill's seasick remedy.[2] We are all coming through fine, however, and the ocean is incredibly beautiful to see, even with waves running like foothills all about.[3]

I meant to tell you before I left that under no circumstances is anyone who comes to the house to be allowed to look into my file. I don't anticipate anyone coming to do such a thing, but on the off-chance that anyone should ask to look through my filing cabinet, the best thing for you to say is 'No' with a capital N. I suggest you say that you haven't the key and that even if you did have it you wouldn't let the file be opened.

I have so many hundreds of good unpublished stories in the files that the whole collection, in face-value alone, must be worth many thousands of dollars. Therefore, in case any unscrupulous soul should come to you and tell you that I have a story of his in the file, it is simply untrue and you are to ignore this sort of talk, eh?, and communicate with me if such a circumstance does arrive. Thanks.

Any books or magazines that arrive should, of course, be held there for us, thanks. Any manuscripts that come in manila envelopes should be held there, if they come by mail. All other small mail can be sent on to me in Europe after we are located. I'll send you my address as soon as possible.

We think about you and talk about you a great deal, and hope you are both well and fully settled into your new housekeeping situation. It was certainly swell of both of you to help us out at this time.

Ballantine Books will probably be sending on extra copies of my new book *Fahrenheit 451*, which I hope you'll open and read. The extra copies can be stacked in the nursery. [. . .]

Time to buzz off. More from me when we land. Wish you were here.

Love from us all.
Ray

Bradbury's waterborne journey to Ireland, by way of Le Havre, Paris, London, and Holyhead, opened out into a whole new world of experience and history. It was less of a shock for Maggie, who had studied history and literature in college, but Bradbury's experiences emerged with a touch of wonder in his first letter home from Dublin.

October 7, 1953

Dear Mom and Dad:

Hope this finds you all well and happy and things running good for you.

We're finally in Dublin, after three days in London, where we visited the Tower of London, saw the Crown Jewels, witnessed the changing of the Guard at Buckingham Palace, the Trooping of the Colors at St. James Palace, and the Change of the Horse Guard at still a third royal house.

We went over to Madame Tussaud's Wax Museum and saw the famous wax work figures there from various eras in history, and then on Monday night this week we left for Ireland. Ireland is every bit as beautiful as you saw it in *The Quiet Man*, as lovely as ten thousand miles of billiard table felt and green moss, and high trees, and a soft light over everything. The drive from Dublin out to Huston's place in the country is one of the most enchanting in my memory. I wouldn't mind staying here until December one bit.

We met the director William Wyler and he is a very nice man indeed. Last night I had dinner with Mrs. Walter Huston, a very charming woman, very much like her son.[4]

My letters are spaced out terribly, I realize, but we've been pulling up stakes so often, it's been difficult to settle down and write, and now that work has begun on the script, I'll be up to my gills. I hope to write at least once a week anyway.

We are all well and fine, the girls love traveling and Regina Ferguson, our governess, has turned out splendidly, a cheerful, boisterous, and alert companion for us all. One big happy family.

Time to buzz off. Love you both so very much and think of you every day. Mag sends her love. You can write me now care of this address: American Express, Dublin, Ireland.

That's all the address you need.

> More from me soon,
> Yours,
> Love
> Ray

The long winter in Dublin was intensified by growing tensions in Bradbury's working relationship with John Huston over the Moby Dick *script. In early February 1954 he had sent his family on to Taormina in Sicily to ease the impact on them, and he soon followed Huston to London to finish revisions. In this long-delayed letter to his parents, Bradbury notes how he has warmed to the casting of Gregory Peck as Ahab (he had initially wanted Sir Laurence Olivier), and offers his first known reaction to meeting Lord Bertrand Russell on April 8.*

Sunday, April 11, 1954

Dear Mom and Dad:

Time gets along so swiftly, I hardly realized it's been such a time since I wrote you; one day passes into another and I do more pages on *Moby Dick* and we come closer to the finish, but, nevertheless, the work goes on and on and we seem never to let up. Gregory Peck is in town and I watched them fit him for his ivory-leg that he wears in the film, the other day. You can't imagine a nicer man; he is so well thought of by everyone.

We went down to Limehouse the other night to have a Chinese dinner; it seemed so strange to be in a district that I had heard about and read about, from childhood, in the Fu Manchu and Sherlock Holmes stories.

I've had countless other offers to write films in Paris, in London, and Hollywood, the last few weeks. It is wonderful to be so much wanted everywhere.

I went out to visit Bertrand Russell the other night, England's most brilliant living philosopher and probably one of the greatest minds of our age and of many ages.[5] He had read my book *Fahrenheit 451* and we had a fine discussion about it and about that s.o.b. Senator McCarthy and about the world situation in general. I know very well, of course, that it is idiotic to think I could keep up with Lord Russell in a conversation, I'm a pygmy alongside his mind, but it was nice for me, nevertheless.

You can see, I manage to keep busy, but it is not easy being alone in London. I just talked to Maggie on the phone and the latest news was that Ramona had swallowed another snail. I suggested the best thing is to give her a little oyster sauce immediately after; thus making her a real French gourmet.

I hope to leave here some time in the next week or so, but again cannot predict how things will go. I'll try to write again, in a week. In the meantime, I hope this finds you both chipper, perky, and sassy as all hell.

All my love to both of you, and my best to the neighbors on all sides.

Your ornery offspring,
Ray

Ray Bradbury wrote fairly regularly to his parents during his nine months in Ireland, England, and Europe, but two of the last letters written stand out for the detail with which he described the family's final days in Italy and their first days back in New York en route home to Los Angeles. Bradbury returned with a new awareness of the art and history of the Western world, and he received major recognitions for his achievement with Fahrenheit 451. *Following his return, Bradbury tended to write more reflective, nostalgia-based stories and fewer of the edgy or dark tales that had established his reputation in earlier times.*

May 15, 1954

Dear Folks:

Just a note on the afternoon of our departure from Venice, Italy, heading north for Paris. We've had a wonderful and exciting time here, meeting

Bernard Berenson, the art-historian again, and seeing some of the really great art-works of the Renaissance. Venice is everything we expected it might be. So beautiful, so very beautiful.

This trip has been an opening-up of our lives for us; we have seen so much and learned so many new things about the world and about ourselves and about living. We'll look back on this time as our own private Renaissance, I'm certain. We've learned to come to personal terms with the wonderful paintings we've seen, and all through meeting Mr. Berenson and reading his books. He is an incredible man, who will celebrate his ninetieth birthday next month; can you imagine!?

Our plans remain about the same as stated before; arriving New York May 25th. Will phone you from there.

God bless you, yes, we accept your invitation for a dinner when we come home. How could we resist? Could you make a gigantic double batch of your delicious Swedish meatballs, your wonderful potato salad, and some baked beans? That strikes us as the most incredible sort of dinner we could enjoy! Topped off by—apricot pie! Would that be possible? If you're not feeling up to it, please tell me when I call from New York. But if it is possible, Lord how wonderful it would be! Thanks for asking!

I'll write again from Paris before we leave there. Hoping this finds you all well and happy. Love from us all to you. We're glad to know Nurrie will be available when we return.[6] Please give her our love, also.

Yours, as ever,

Ray

June 1st, 1954

Dear Folks:

So much has happened since we arrived in New York I hardly know what to tell you about first. Most important of all, I must apologize again for the delay in calling you—it came about for many reasons, mainly those of time-difference between New York and Los Angeles. When I was in the hotel it was the wrong hour to call you, or if I was out of the hotel, it was the right hour. Our day became hectic as soon as we arrived. The first night we were here, I received the Benjamin Franklin Award for the Best Story published in the United States during 1953. The next day I received an Award from the Institute of Arts and Letters for "contributing to American literature." All of which was immensely exciting and amazing. On top of this, we were invited to about three dozen parties and faced up to meeting half a hundred editors and writers in the coming days. The *New York Times* wants to do an article on me and wants me to write one for them. Also, I've sold stories to *Charm*, *Cosmopolitan* and *The Saturday Evening Post*.[7] On top of this, William Wyler, the film director of *The Best Years of Our Lives*, *The Heiress*, and *Roman Holiday*, asked me, three days ago, to write a film for him.[8] This offer, with the others, I've turned down. Right now we only want to get home.

Tentatively, we'll be leaving on the 8th or 9th, the time is still indefinite, since our train reservations are not made at this writing. We're having difficulty clearing space on the trains. I'll telephone you again before we leave to let you know the details. Then, please, you might relay the news on to "Nurrie."

Lord, it'll be good to see all your loving faces again. We've missed you so very much, believe me, we've missed you both with all our hearts. The girls, Mag, and I, send all our love.

Yours, as ever,

Ray

Barbizon-Plaza Hotel

New York City

Hollywood would once again create an opportunity for Bradbury and his growing family to visit England, France, and Italy. He would never return to Ireland, but his collaboration with director Sir Carol Reed in London on adapting his story "And the Rock Cried Out" for film would provide the means to visit friends and, with Maggie, further explore the museums, galleries, and architecture of

Renaissance and medieval Europe. These adventures were punctuated by new experiences with theater, and letters to his parents and his aunt Neva offered glimpses of all these discoveries.

Kensington Palace Hotel
De Vere Gardens
London, W.8

June 27, 1957

Dear Mom & Dad:

You can address us, from now on, at the address above, where we will stay for the rest of the summer. Thank God, at the last moment, when it looked as if we would have to keep moving from hotel to hotel, Lady Reed telephoned the manager of the Kensington Palace Hotel and played upon his sympathies for us, so we now have two fine large rooms and two fabulous bathrooms to knock about in. The last place we stayed in, you had to go up a flight of stairs to the toilet, late at night. It was a really bad setup, considering Bettina.[9] Now, we are all happy.

Ray Harryhausen arrived in town yesterday! It was swell seeing him. We took him out to supper and then showed him around Piccadilly Circus and took him over to see Big Ben, the Houses of Parliament, and to walk along the Thames embankment late at night; a wonderful evening. Ray is on his way to Barcelona to work on a fantasy film there for Columbia.[10] He is such a good sweet fellow. You can imagine how happy we were to be with him. [. . .]

The weather there sounds terrific! The weather here, the first few days, was exceptionally hot, also. 95 degrees, which is *really* hot in London, with humidity and all. Thank God I brought my summer suit! Now, the days are cooler and there have been a few nice rains.

Maggie went up to Stratford-on-Avon the other day to see Shakespeare's grave and his wife's house, and to visit the Earl of Warrick's Estate. Polly and the girls are off to visit Windsor Castle today. Polly is wonderful;[11] she really loves the children and enjoys taking them around to see things.

Mag and I are having a ball, visiting the theatres, seeing lots of good plays, evenings. The script goes very well. I am already on page 72, which is fine. I enjoy working for Carol Reed so much. I wish you could meet his wife some day. A very beautiful, very kind woman.

Enough for now. I'll write again next week. Until then, thanks again for your constant, loving help. Love to you both, from Mag, the kids, and your wily son.

Ray

AUNT NEVA BRADBURY

Bradbury's aunt Neva, a fashion designer and artist, had inspired his early reading, and he would often discuss events with her and her companion, Anne Anthony. Bradbury and his family spent the summer of 1957 in London while he worked with Sir Carol Reed to expand his post-colonial nuclear war story "And the Rock Cried Out" into a feature film. The project turned into one of Bradbury's best director-writer relationships, but it was overshadowed by Stanley Kramer's production of On the Beach, *and the film was never made.*

Bradbury
Kensington Palace Hotel
DeVere Gardens,
London, W8, England.

July 23, 1957

Dear Neva:

Hope this finds you and Anne prosperous, happy, and healthy, and busy with all your many things to do! I wish you could be here with us to see many of the things we are seeing. Some day, by God! you *will* come to Europe, I know!

I have been working for almost six weeks now on the screenplay of "And the Rock Cried Out." I am on page 175 of the screenplay today.

Sir Carol Reed, my director, is fantastically happy with my work, so far. I hope to finish the first draft, of about 200 pages, by the end of the coming week, send it off to Beverly Hills, where it will be read by Burt Lancaster, Harold Hecht and their partner James Hill, who will decide then whether the film will finally be shot at all. If they okay the project, I will cut the script down to size . . . about 140 pages in the final version, I imagine. Then, Mag and the kids, Polly, our nurse, and I will head for Italy where we hope to stay for a few weeks or perhaps months, before coming home. We have heard from our friend Bernard Berenson, the art historian, in Florence, and he wants to see us there, if we can make it.

We went to see Sir Laurence Olivier and Vivian Leigh in *Titus Andronicus* the other night at the Stoll Theatre here. Afterwards, we had supper with one of the leading ladies, Maxine Audley, who played Tamora, the Queen of the Goths in it, and were introduced backstage to Sir Laurence and Lady Olivier. What a shock to meet a quiet, beautifully mannered man in a pair of soft-grey horn-rims and a correct suit, half an hour after seeing him play Titus, whose sons are slain right and left and whose daughter is raped and maimed, her tongue cut off, her hands cut off . . . ! A thrill for both Mag and myself. [. . .]

Love to you both!

Yrs,
Ray

LEO AND ESTHER BRADBURY

Bradbury's dozen-year struggle with his Illinois novel finally yielded Dandelion Wine, *comprising the more nostalgic tales taken from the original novel and bridged into a well-integrated novelization of memories compressed into a single unforgettable season—summer 1928. The book came to him in Europe, fresh from the printers, and he immediately requested copies for his parents back in Los Angeles. This letter offered a prelude to the experience of reading about their own lives reimagined in their son's new book. It was a timely gift, for his father would enter his final illness just as Bradbury and his family returned home.*

Kensington Palace Hotel
DeVere Gardens,
London, W8, England.

                                                        August 3rd, 1957

Dear Mom & Dad:

Glad you liked my story in *Harper's*.[12] It has been one of my favorites. I certainly appreciated your sending on a copy of the magazine. Yes, please *do* send those two copies of *Harper's* to Joe Mugnaini. His address is: 4226 Canyon Crest Road, Altadena, Calif.

I have written to Doubleday in New York and sometime in the next week you should receive in the mail a copy of *Dandelion Wine* which has finally come from the printers. It is a beautiful book. They have done a fine job all around. When you get your copy, take off the dust-jacket for a moment and look at the nice yellow linen binding they used to help carry out the idea of the wine and the summer. Simple but effective. And the book reads well, after all this time, for me. I hope you both enjoy it and find overtones of yourself and our earlier life in it. It is a work of real love, evoking many of the memories of those summers which seemed perfect to me, regardless of how they may have seemed to the adults around me, such a long time ago now. I wish Grandmother could have lived to have read this and seen herself in book form.

And as for you, Mom and Dad, how does it feel, winding up on

paper, yourselves? Early on in the book, Dad, you'll find a report of one
of our berrying expeditions, which I think you read in the *Reporter* a few
months ago, and then of course, there is the section about ice-cream,
Mom, and our walking down to the ravine one night to call for Skip
when I was seven or eight, a night you may have long since forgotten,
but which I recall vividly still.

It was a good life for us kids, in Waukegan. I have always looked
back on it with affection and gladness that we could have lived as near
to nature as we did, having the ravine there, in the town, to play in every
day, and having the lake and the country so close, if we wanted it.

Dad, how I'd love to take a stroll with you again, down to the old
bath-house in summer and lie on the beach again the way you and I and
Skip did then. I can smell the smoke and the cinders now, as we went
down across the rr-tracks toward the boathouse!

All goes beautifully here. I have finished the first-draft of my script
and it is 210 pages long!!! Next week will be my eighth week, my final
week of work, then a ninth week of waiting for a final verdict, and we
hope to plow off for Italy. I'll keep you posted in plenty of time, as to
our final departure. The time has flown here. We are all very well and
happy and think of you often and sincerely wish you could be here.

Love to you both from your loving son,
Ray

After finishing up his draft screenplay for Sir Carol Reed in mid-August, Brad-bury and his family departed London and headed for Italy and a final visit with Bernard Berenson, now nearly 95 years old; he would pass away in the late summer of 1959, corresponding into his last year of life. Bradbury wrote a final letter to his parents from Paris, where his friends and publishers held a series of personal and literary events. They sailed from Le Havre a few days later and arrived in New York, where Bradbury received word that his father had suffered a stroke; he would pass away a few weeks after his son arrived home in Los Angeles. The following letter home preceded the unforeseen.

Paris, Sept. 10th, 1957

Dear Folks:

Just a quick one, from Paris, where we landed two days ago. Weather here is rainy and very cool, but it is a fascinating city nevertheless. The girls and I had lunch up in the Eiffel Tower yesterday. Today we went to the church of the Sacre Coeur (to say a prayer for Dad, natch!)[13] and tomorrow we go to the Louvre. Tonight we go out with Monsieur and Madame Garreau-Dombasle—you remember, he was ambassador to Mexico twelve years ago when I met her at Lake Patzcuaro on the Night of the Day of the Dead? And also tomorrow we go out to Versailles with Madame and her daughter Françion from whom Bettina takes her second name. I haven't seen Françion since October 1945, when she was 16!!!

Tonight the reporters from a Swiss newspaper are coming to interview me, and late tomorrow my publisher in Paris, Denoel, is throwing a cocktail party to which are invited many critics and writers. They are publishing my *October Country* next month. Over in England, also in Oct., *Dandelion Wine* will appear a month later than its American publication. The first reports from NYC on *Wine* are excellent!!! I have been compared favorably, in the *Saturday Review*, with Mark Twain. What a wonderful thing, even if it is not true in any way. I *am* flattered.

I'll write you again, or telephone you, probably, from New York. Our plans are unchanged. We land in NY on Thursday Sept. 17th. You'll hear from me by phone either that day or Wednesday the 18th.

I hope your plans for Tucson are proceeding. It sounds like an exciting change for you both. And—when we hit L.A. late in the month, how are chances for an apricot pie? With dried apricots, if necessary!

More, from New York. It'll be good to hear your voices!

Love!
Ray

12

REFLECTIONS

I find great refreshment in the sea, it is so irrevocably
old and it says to me, little man, what are your
problems? Fifty years from now where will you be?
—*Bradbury, August 18, 1947*

Bradbury's poem "Remembrance" describes a note written as a young boy and buried deep in the bole of a tree, to be remembered and discovered by the man he would become. From time to time in his life, he would type out such notes, expressing a moment, or a series of moments, pulled out of time's passing experiences and recaptured as a letter written for his own eyes. These are a few memories of a mind that reflected.

Just a month before his marriage to Marguerite McClure and only four days shy of his twenty-seventh birthday, Bradbury was still sharing a room with his brother Skip in his parent's home on Venice Boulevard. His writing environment centered on the detached garage, where his walled-off typing space looked west onto the adjacent power company substation and the brightly lit machinery that hummed away well into the night. About six long city blocks farther west was the Pacific Ocean, and this combination of man-made electricity and the far greater energies of the sea were triggers for his own creativity. Bradbury's resulting self-reflective note offered the kind of creative renewal that he would need from time to time throughout his career.

Monday afternoon at three o'clock—August 18th, 1947.
Mother's birthday. Her round button gold earrings.

I have had days of unaccountable depression in which I sat in my studio and looked out along the burnt meadow to where the ice factory makes its hushing, cool sound of constantly pouring water, and then over to the Doll Factory in whose windows I have never glanced, and I have torn up page after page of bad stuff written during the morning. Then I lock up my typewriter, fling my leg over my brother's bicycle and ride, clicking gently, for the thing has a free-wheeling mechanism on it, all down to the sea. I find great refreshment in the sea, it is so irrevocably old and it says to me, little man, what are your problems? Fifty years from now where will you be? And I have been here forever, passing between sun and earth in passionate exchanges and gentle redistributions. Naturally, in California, the sea is certain to be of a more quiet aspect, for there are eight months here when we see no cloud in the sky. We may have vapors and mornings of mist that hang over and occlude vast territories of sky, but these whisper down only futile little moistenings upon sidewalk and snail, rose bush and bus-stop. On many evenings when the wind is right you can smell the sea pouring over Los Angeles in invisible waves, subtle and vanishing. But there is no thunder, no downpour, no lightning. There is always the summer season, with certain days which take onto themselves, for an hour or so, the sound and the feel of autumn, some mock autumn which the next day is denied by a sudden hot summer again. And so you cannot expect too much of our sea here on our shore; it will not be as violent, it will comb in curves and foamings, it will rear and crash, but it is, after all, a California sea. It is enough, however, for me.

Not all of these self-reflective notes offered renewal; many of them carried cautionary messages, as does this reminder of the darkness that sometimes comes from within the human soul itself.

The more one sees of self-destruction, the more one tries to stand against it. We are surrounded, often, by the names and deeds of people in our recent past, and present, who ran a car off a road, stuck a head in an oven, sipped poison, cut throat, or blew out the last candle in their head with a gun.

I think of Carson McCullers' husband, Reeves, with his head in an oven. I remember Sam Cobean who died in his car.[1] Jackson Pollack the same. Hemingway and his shotgun. James Whale found floating in his pool.[2] My dentist, Dr. Block, who held a party for thirty and at midnight shot his wife and himself. I think of my little Mexican actress in *Juan Diaz*,[3] who danced late one night with friends, and who that afternoon had sent a suicide note that arrived after her self-imposed death. Vanished sad people, all. So soon its over anyway. They rushed to meet darkness. I do not want to rush. With gun, or over-eating, or over-drinking, or over-action at parties, I wish to hold back, continue work and, God Willing, stay sane to the natural end. We need much inner strength for this. We doubt we have it. Yet somehow we do continue. These others terrify us with their pell-mell excursioning into the grave. Perhaps they give us strength by scaring us.

R.B. August 4, 1966

Bradbury came from a close-knit and loving family where truthfulness and sim-plicity were constants of their lives together. For Bradbury, his brother Skip, and his parents, there were also remembrances of the brother and sister who did not survive infancy. When his mother died in November 1966, Ray Bradbury suddenly realized that for all of the shared love, he never really knew his mother at all.

The boy who truly loved his mother is buried deep under all the years when that love was tested and somehow failed because mother withdrew, neither understanding her husband or her sons. Poor lost girl, who was she? We know so little of each other, but I know even less of her. I will send a ten year old boy to the graveyard to put flowers on her grave. I will return a 46 year old man, bewildered at the fact of buried love dug up and for a moment exhibited in the cold December light.

R.B. December 1966

In the winter of 1967 Bradbury had been deeply affected by the premature pass-ing of Charles Beaumont, one of the first significant writers he had mentored. Though not a Catholic, Bradbury kept Beaumont's funeral missal for the rest of his life. Just four years later, in the spring of 1971, he was shocked once again by the passing of Beaumont's wife, Helen, leaving four children. Bradbury went to the service in North Hollywood, departing afterward with the heartfelt but un-founded misapprehension that her body would remain unattended. A few days later, he wrote a note to himself reflecting on the way that we say goodbye to those we love. He also sent her oldest child, future writer Christopher Beaumont, a letter and a donation with the simple inscription, "Flowers fade; Bills don't."

The thing that bothered me Sunday night at the church in Woodland
Hills was all of us going out after the Bible reading and leaving Helen
Beaumont's body in her coffin there alone by candlelight all night. I felt
someone should stay with her. You don't get over the feeling of a patient
in a hospital right away, I guess. But somehow the church seemed like
an empty and lonely place to be. Death is lonely enough. We succeed, in
some of our rituals, by making it seem lonelier than need be. Would it
have been better back at the funeral home? In some ways, yes. There are
other bodies there for company. Stupid, silly thought. They know not
each other. What we want is comfort for ourselves. There it is, cliché on
cliché.

R.B. May 20, 1971

Bradbury was fairly compensated for the film rights to The Illustrated
Man, *and he was able to see close friends Rod Steiger and Claire Bloom featured in the 1969 Warner Brothers film adaptation. But he had no hand in
the script, or in the decisions about which stories from* The Illustrated Man
*would be featured, and only on rare occasions was he able to catch glimpses
of the making of this film. It took four years for this remembrance to take
its final form.*

Fascinating suddenly to remember that on the night of the cast party
for *Illustrated Man* when it was all over and various groups went off for
smaller celebrations here or there, neither the actors, the producer, or
the director of the film invited the Writer, Ray Bradbury, to join them.
The film, now over, finished, done, was an act of God, all to itself.
The Writer? Who was *he*?

R.B. Jan. 1972

---

*Ray Bradbury enjoyed writing verse, and he knew better than to consider him-
self a serious poet. Poetry offered an early morning warmup for the story ideas
that would well up from his subconscious mind without bidding and provided*

an alternative to fiction as a way to express memories of the past and contem-
plate ideas of the future. This note was written sometime in 1973, as his first
collection of poetry was nearing publication.

You write poetry for thirty years or so not because anyone wants you
to; they don't want you. The world is full of poet grandmothers and
poet waitresses. Everyone writes poetry. There seem days when poets
brim out of God's ears. You can't escape them. You would like to. And
suddenly you find yourself doing the same damn thing. People run when
they see you approach. They suspect you of the same trick your barber
pulled on you once, getting you half-cut in the chair, tied in by a sheet,
and then getting out his songs to sing to you. Your fixed smile damaged
your jaw muscles for a month after. What do you say to a man armed
with a scissors or a razor? Bravo, of course. But you never forgive him.
And you never have your hair cut again. At least by him.

[undated, ca. 1973]

Bradbury's long friendship with American novelist and short story writer Jes-
samyn West (1902–1984) demonstrated a shared passion for the quiet reflec-
tions of Midwestern youth coming of age in simpler times. He captured this vivid
image of her fictional world on the morning after the ninth anniversary of her
passing.

Jessamyn West's *The Friendly Persuasion* is like early morning freshly
laid hens eggs, warm milk cooling in the coolshed at noon, straw for
nests, calico in a woven basket, silver laid on an empty table, polished
by kitchen light, waiting for folks, harvests, seedings, thanksgiving
every day at supper, thanks and amens, lives lived from one far end to
the other, everything used, not to excess, but used, everything fitting,
with, on occasion, the sweet burden of washing the newly dead for not
prolonged burials and then back to the seeds and harvests.

The Friendly Persuasion is an American Ecclesiastes. Its growth and flowering are here, but its roots, of course, were long in other places across the seas where plain people made bed coverlets like charts and maps of their lives, cut in shapes and colors like the shapes and colors of days. To everything there is a time, they said, and proved it without pride or arrogance.

R.B.

Wednesday morning, 10:30 a.m. to 10:45 a.m.

February 24, 1993

Acknowledgments

Ray Bradbury often lamented the fact that he never kept a diary—with the exception of very brief and occasional entries on loose-leaf pages after graduating from high school, and sporadic notes on the tiny pages of a daily calendar or on the covers of working file folders, he never had the time to document what was happening in his life. "Oh, God—you know, what I hate about myself, I've never kept a diary," he once told me. "All these years have gone by, all these thousands of days I was so lucky, I met so many people, but there's no record. And it's *terrible* that I didn't spend two minutes at the end of every night and put down that I met some of these people."

Over the years I would often remind him that his correspondence was essentially a half cousin to a diary, with the added advantage of showing how others responded to his words and ideas. In October 2006 I broached the idea of publishing portions of his correspondence, and his reaction was unequivocal: "Oh sure, oh yeah, because it's the story of my *life*."

I had already copied significant letters from his incoming correspondence, and with those markers as guides I had also reached out to many institutional and private archives in search of his outgoing letters. This combined harvest informed my chapters of the coauthored *Ray Bradbury: The Life of Fiction* (2004); these and many more letters provided the same underpinning for my further books on his life and career, *Becoming Ray Bradbury* (2011), *Ray Bradbury Unbound* (2014), and *Bradbury Beyond Apollo* (2020). I'm deeply grateful to the people and institutions that provided access and permissions over the years for the letters I've now gathered and edited for *Remembrance: Selected Correspondence of Ray Bradbury*.

These acknowledgments include those who assisted with the earlier books, as well as new sources for letters recovered in more recent years as *Remembrance* began to take shape. That process began in the summer of 2018, when Michael Congdon, the Ray Bradbury estate's literary agent and head of Don Congdon Associates, asked me to transform my 2006 promise into reality. Michael encouraged the evolution of *Remembrance* through years of competing obligations leading up to Ray Bradbury's 2020 centennial year; in addition to granting permissions to publish the selected Bradbury letters, Michael and DCA's Cristina Concepcion have provided support and advice all along the way.

Letters are ephemeral things, often subject to loss or destruction over time, and I owe my deepest debt of gratitude to the remarkable preservation efforts of Donn Albright, professor emeritus at the Pratt Institute in New York. Donn was Ray Bradbury's good friend and principal bibliographer for decades; he owns and preserves most of the incoming correspondence through the 1960s and has allowed me unrestricted access to the correspondence files in his possession. After Ray Bradbury's passing, Donn and the Bradbury family gifted the remaining years of incoming correspondence and papers to Indiana University's Center for Ray Bradbury Studies during my years as director.

"If you want to learn about my work and life," Bradbury told me in the late 1980s, "you must learn from Donn Albright. He knows me better than I know myself." The letters he has preserved, and his deep knowledge of Ray's life and career, equipped me to follow the trail to find many of the outgoing Bradbury letters that form the other half of his correspondence. I'm grateful as well to Donn's wife, Michelle Nahum Albright, who helped to document Donn's personal Bradbury collection. Their daughter, Elizabeth Nahum Albright, Ray Bradbury's goddaughter, provided photographic documentation for many of my research trips to the Bradbury home.

Bradbury's six decades of correspondence with his literary agents, Michael Congdon and the late Don Congdon, form a foundational part of the correspondence record. These archives are preserved on deposit in Columbia University's Butler Library. I am grateful for access since 2005 to the papers of Don Congdon Associates (1983–) and the papers of the Harold Matson Agency, where Don Congdon represented Bradbury from 1947 until forming his own agency in 1983. Bradbury's letters to *Ellery Queen's Mystery Magazine* founding editor Frederick Danay are also held at the Butler. I was supported in my work at Columbia by Butler librarian Jennifer B. Lee and Bernard Crystal, curator of manuscripts at the time of my 2005 research visit, and to Tara C. Craig and Jason Marchi, who coordinated my access to the Matson deposit with Ben Camardi.

Bradbury's letters to his mentors Leigh Brackett Hamilton, Edmond Hamilton, and Jack Williamson are preserved in the Jack Williamson Science Fiction Library at Eastern New Mexico University. My proxy access to these letters was coordinated in the early 2000s by collection archivist Gene Bundy for Betty Williamson, niece of the late Jack Williamson. Bradbury's letters to Arkham House founding publisher August Derleth are preserved by the Wisconsin Historical Society in Madison; archives reference assistant Alexis Ernst-Treutel and Kimberly O'Brien, my proxy researcher, provided research copies from this significant collection.

The Syracuse University Special Collections Research Center holds Bradbury letters to Frederik Pohl Jr., Forrest J Ackerman, and the poet Robert Hillyer. Librarian Carolyn Davis provided copies of the Bradbury letters, as well as copies of letters held in the Mercury Press archive written to *Magazine of Fantasy and Science Fiction* founding editors Anthony Boucher and Mick McComas and their successors. Research copies of other Bradbury letters to Boucher (a pseudonym for William Anthony Parker White) and a portion of Bradbury's correspondence with his Doubleday editor Walter Bradbury (no relation) were provided by Indiana University's Lilly Library in Bloomington.

The Alfred A. Knopf publishing deposit at the University of Texas (Austin) includes Bradbury letters spanning his twenty-five-year history as a Knopf author, and the Ransom Humanities Center staff provided research copies of this correspondence in the early 2000s. I'm grateful to the Ransom Center staff and to my proxy researcher, Dr. Albert Lewis, for essential on-site support.

In 2005 I had the great good fortune of finding Ray Bradbury's significant body of letters to the prominent Renaissance Italian art historian and critic Bernard Berenson safely archived at Berenson's Villa I Tatti estate and library near Florence, home to Harvard University's Center for Italian Renaissance Studies. Dr. Michael Rock, the Nicky Mariano Librarian of Biblioteca Berenson, and Dr. Fiorella Superbi were instrumental in providing photocopies of the Bradbury letters, and I was able (with Ray Bradbury's permission) to reciprocate with copies of the Berenson half of the correspondence.

In more recent years, I was fortunate to work with Elspeth Healey, special collections librarian of the Kenneth Spencer Research Library at the University of Kansas, Lawrence, in tracking down Bradbury's letters to Theodore Sturgeon and Donald Wollheim. Donn Albright provided photocopies of Bradbury's letters to early science fiction writer and Bradbury collaborator Henry Hasse, made many years ago from the originals then held by Hasse. Christopher Bond, son of the prolific Golden Age science fiction writer Nelson Bond, provided copies of Bradbury's letters to his father.

Bradbury's long-lasting correspondence with the late Anglo-Irish peer John Godley, the 3rd Baron Kilbracken, is also represented in *Remembrance.* I'm grateful to Lord Kilbracken's younger son, Sean Godley, and his mother, Lady Sue Kilbracken, who verified the existence of Bradbury's half of the correspondence. Sean and his elder brother Christopher, the present Lord Kilbracken, kindly gave permission to draw on this correspondence in *Remembrance.*

Alexandra Bradbury, who worked closely with her father in all his professional endeavors for three decades, proved invaluable in recovering computer files of letters from the intangible world of emails and fax transmissions. Many other late-life letter exchanges were preserved in the correspondence and papers gifted to Indiana University's Center for Ray Bradbury Studies by Donn Albright and the Bradbury family in 2013, which included all incoming letters (hardcopy and transmission) remaining with Bradbury from the 1970s forward, as well as significant earlier letters subsequently harvested from his files and working papers as the gift was processed.

Bradbury's filing system was reactive and hard to follow in the extreme, and many letters never made it into his filing cabinets at all prior to the gift transfer. The Bradbury Center's staff volunteer archivist Nancy Orem has created a work-in-progress spreadsheet for 14,000 letters and their attachments, an achievement that has greatly aided the evaluation of letter candidates for inclusion in this volume. She was assisted by lead staff volunteer Debi Eller and Museum Studies graduate interns Katie Watson and Alisha Nichole Beard.

Remembrance includes letters to Ray Bradbury from a range of correspondents, gathered principally from the two main sources—the originals held in Donn Albright's personal collection and the originals curated by the Center for Ray Bradbury Studies. Letters to and from Bradbury curated in other archives are so noted in the Calendar of Letters. The Permissions List identifies the sources of licenses granted for the many individuals whose letters are represented in this volume.

Calendar of Letters Included in This Volume

Letter descriptions include the terms TL (typed letter), TLS (typed letter, signed), ALS (autograph letter signed), and the correction terms "holograph" (corrected by hand) and "overstrike" (corrected by typeover). Sources for the letters published in this volume are abbreviated in the individual calendar entries; these repositories include:

Albright: Donn Albright (private collection originals; photocopies curated in the Bradbury Center)

Boston: Graham Greene Papers, MS.1995.003, Box 12, Folder 48, John J. Burns Library, Boston College

Bradbury Center: The Ray Bradbury Center, Indiana University School of Liberal Arts

Cinématheque: The Truffaut Collection, Cinématheque Française, Paris

Columbia: Don Congdon Associates deposit and Frederic Dannay collection, University Rare Book and Manuscript Library (Butler Library), Columbia University

ENMU: Jack Williamson Science Fiction Library (Brackett-Hamilton Collection), Golden Library Special Collections, Eastern New Mexico University

Georgetown: Ray Bradbury Letters (Nelson Bond), GTM-141117, Georgetown University Manuscripts Repository, Booth Family Center for Special Collections

Harvard (I Tatti): Berenson correspondence, Harvard University Center for Italian Renaissance Studies, Villa I Tatti, Florence, Tuscany, Italy

Harvard: Gore Vidal Papers, Harvard Houghton Library, MS AM 2350, Carton 28, folder Bot– through Brad–.

Herrick: The John Huston Papers, folder 371, Margaret Herrick Library (AMPAS), Los Angeles

Kennedy: John F. Kennedy Presidential Library and Museum, White House Central Name File, Box 290, Bradbury. White House Central Subject Files, Box 275, GI 2-8/B, Literature, Books-Poetry (Executive), Schlesinger

Killegar: Kilbracken Estate, Carrigallen, Co. Leitrim, Republic of Ireland (private collection)

Kirk: The Russell Kirk Center for Cultural Renewal, Mecosta, Michigan

Illinois: Carl Sandburg Connamara Accession, Correspondence Series Box 1-002-216, Rare Book & Manuscript Library, University of Illinois

Indiana: Bradbury II MSS and William Anthony Parker White MSS, The Lilly Library, Indiana University, Bloomington

Kansas: Sturgeon Collection, Letters 1947 (MS303, Box 10, folders 8, 12, 16); Wollheim Collection, Correspondence, MS 250, Box 4, Folder 2, Spencer Research Library Special Collections, Kansas University

Marchi: Jason Marchi (private collection)

Miller: Gregory Miller (private collection)

Mugnaini: Mugnaini-Robinson Family Trust collection

Sibley: Brian Sibley (private collection)

Syracuse: Ackerman, Hillyer, Mercury Press, and Pohl collections, Special Collections Research Center, Syracuse University

Texas: Alfred A. Knopf Collection, the Harry Ransom Center, University of Texas, Austin

UCLA: Gerald Heard Papers, 1054 Series 9: Correspondence, Box 29 folder 1, UCLA Special Collections, Young Library

Wisconsin: August Derleth Collection, Wisconsin Historical Society, Madison

ACKERMAN, FORREST J

Bradbury to Ackerman, January 2, 1948. TLS, 1 p., with overstrike and holograph corrections. Syracuse.

ALBERT, EDDIE

Bradbury to Albert, July 9, 1990. TLS, 1 p., original fax. Bradbury Center.

ALLEN, LEWIS

Bradbury to Allen (re: Truffaut), March 27, 1964. TLS, 1 p.; Columbia (Congdon).

ARONICA, LOU

Bradbury to Aronica, July 7, 1996. TLS, 1 p., fax original. Bradbury Center.

BACH, RICHARD

Bach to Bradbury, February 4, 1962. TLS, 3 pp.; first page has "R.B. 3/14/62" response notation in Bradbury's hand. Albright.

BALDWIN, FAITH

Baldwin to Bradbury, October 30, 1962. AMS, 2 pp., on personal letterhead. Albright.

BEAUMONT, CHARLES

Bradbury to Beaumont, October 21, 1953. TLS, 2 pp., on Royal Hibernian Hotel stationery, Dublin. Bradbury's photocopy; Bradbury Center.

Beaumont to Bradbury, October 30, 1953. TLS, 2 pp. Albright.

Bradbury to Beaumont, December 4, 1953. TLS, 1 p., on Royal Hibernian Hotel stationery, Dublin. Bradbury's photocopy; Bradbury Center.

Bradbury to Beaumont, [ca. September 28, 1954]. TLS, 1 p., n.d. (dated by content). Holograph postscript comment. Bradbury's photocopy; Bradbury Center.

Bradbury to Beaumont, September 29, 1954. TLS, 1 p., with overstrike revisions and holograph date. Bradbury's photocopy; Bradbury Center.

Bradbury to Beaumont, October 21, 1954. TLS, 1 p., with holograph date and overstrike revisions. Bradbury's photocopy; Bradbury Center.

Beaumont to Bradbury, February 11, 1955. TLS, 1 p., with holograph postscript continuing to verso. Albright Collection.

Beaumont to Bradbury, March 6, 1955. TLS, 1 p.; Albright.

Bradbury to Beaumont, March 11, 1955. TLS, 2 pp., with holograph date. Bradbury's photocopy; Bradbury Center.

Bradbury to Beaumont, August 30, 1955. TLS, 1 p., holograph date. Bradbury's photocopy; Bradbury Center.

Beaumont to Bradbury, October 18, 1959. TLS, 1 p., on home address letterhead (12808 Collins Street North Hollywood, California). Albright.

Beaumont to Bradbury, October 3, 1962. TLS, 1 p.; Albright.

BERENSON, BERNARD

Bradbury to Bernard Berenson, December 12, 1954. TLS, 3 pp.; Harvard (I Tatti).

Bradbury to Bernard Berenson, August 4, 1955. TLS, 3 pp.; Harvard (I Tatti).

Bradbury to Bernard Berenson, March 23, 1956. TLS, 7 pp.; Harvard (I Tatti).

Bradbury to Bernard Berenson, February 28, 1958. TLS, 4 pp., on Clarkson Road home letterhead. Harvard (I Tatti).

Berenson to Bradbury, March 6, 1958. TLS, 1 p., Villa I Tatti address heading. Typed by Nicki Mariano; closing and signature ("B.B.") in Berenson's hand. Bradbury Center.

BEVINGTON, HELEN

Bevington to Bradbury, February 24, 1986. TLS, 2 pp., on home address (Durham, NC) letterhead. Bradbury Center.

Bradbury to Bevington, March 21, 1986. TLS, 2 pp., with holograph revisions. Illustrated Man (Mugnaini lithograph) decorated stationery. Bradbury photocopy. Bradbury Center.

BOND, NELSON S.

Bradbury to Bond, February 15, 1949. TLS, 1 p., with home address above date (33 South Venice Blvd. Venice, Calif.). Georgetown, "Ray Bradbury Letters," GTM-141117.

Bradbury to Bond, April 2, 1950. TLS, 1 p., with holograph revisions and home address above date (33 South Venice Blvd. Venice, Calif.). Georgetown.

BOUCHER, ANTHONY (WILLIAM ANTHONY PARKER WHITE)

Bradbury to Boucher, January 10, 1952. TLS, 3 pp., with holograph corrections. Lilly.

Bradbury to Boucher and Mick McComas, August 7, 1952. TLS, 1 p.; Syracuse.

Bradbury to Boucher [late March 1955]. TLS, 2 pp., with holograph corrections. Lilly.

Bradbury to Boucher, August 7, 1958. TLS, 2 pp., on home address (Clarkson Road) letterhead with holograph and overstrike corrections. Lilly.

BRACKETT, LEIGH (SEE ALSO HAMILTON, EDMOND AND LEIGH BRACKETT HAMILTON)

Brackett to Bradbury, August 31, 1944, TPCS, n.d. (dated by postmark). Albright.

Brackett to Bradbury [ca. September 1944] ALS, 1 p., in Brackett's hand. Albright.

Brackett to Bradbury (Hamilton to Bradbury postscript, November 15, 1951). ENMU.

BRADBURY, LEO AND ESTHER

Bradbury, R. to Bradbury, L. and E. [mid-October 1945]. TPC, with typed signature beside a self-doodle. Pyramid of the Sun, Teotihuacán, Mexico; postmarked Cuernavaca, October 20, 1945. Albright.

Bradbury, R. to Bradbury, L. and E., November 3, 1945. TL with typed signature, 1 p., on hotel stationery (Posada de Don Vasco, Pátzcuaro, Michoacan, Mexico). Albright.

Bradbury, R. to Bradbury, L. and E. [November 16, 1945]. Posted airmail from Monterrey, Mexico, November 21, 1945. Bradbury Center.

Bradbury, R. to Bradbury, L. and E., September 20, 1953. TLS, 1 p., with holograph and overstrike revisions. Composed at sea aboard SS *United States*. Albright.

Bradbury, R. to Bradbury, L. and E., October 7, 1953. TLS, 2 pp., with overstrike revisions on Royal Hibernian Hotel (Dublin) stationery. Signature includes a self-caricature. Albright.

Bradbury, R. to Bradbury, L. and E., April 11, 1954. TLS, 1 p., with holograph and overstrike revisions. Bradbury Center.

Bradbury, R. to Bradbury, L. and E., May 15, 1954. TLS, 1 p., with overstrike revisions and holograph date. Albright.

Bradbury, R. to Bradbury, L. and E., June 1, 1954. TLS, 1 p., with overstrike revisions. Albright.

Bradbury, R. to Bradbury, L. and E., June 27, 1957. TLS, 2 pp., with self-doodle face by signature on Kensington Palace Hotel stationery (DeVere Gardens, London). Albright.

Bradbury, R. to Bradbury, L. and E., August 3, 1957. TLS, 1 p., with overstrike revisions. Albright.

Bradbury, R. to Bradbury, L. and E., September 10, 1957. TLS, 1 p., hotel stationery (Excelsior Hotel, Florence). Albright.

BRADBURY (EDITORIAL)

Bradbury to the Republican Party, *Daily Variety*, November 10, 1952

BRADBURY, MARGUERITE [McCLURE]

Bradbury, R. to Bradbury, M., May 6, 1951. TLS, 1 p., with overstrike corrections. Albright.

BRADBURY, NEVA

Bradbury, R. to Bradbury, Neva, July 23, 1957. TLS, 1 p., with overstrike and holograph revisions on Kensington Palace Hotel stationery (DeVere Gardens, London). Albright.

BRADBURY, WALTER I.

Bradbury, R. to Bradbury, W. I. [ca. December 10, 1949]. TLS, 3 pp., n.d. (dated by content). Lilly.

Bradbury, W. I. to Bradbury, R., December 14, 1949. TLS, 1 p., on Doubleday letterhead. Albright.

Bradbury, R. to Bradbury, W. I., July 22, 1950. TLS, 3 pp., with holograph corrections. Lilly.

Bradbury, W. I. to Bradbury, R., March 10, 1952. TLS, 1 p., on Doubleday letterhead. Albright.

Bradbury, R. to Bradbury, W. I., March 13, 1952. TLS, 4 pp., with holograph corrections. Albright. A fair-copy signed draft; final version (unlocated), dated March 15, 1952, acknowledged in a letter from W. I. Bradbury (March 17, 1952).

BREHL, JENNIFER

Bradbury to Brehl, September 21, 1997. TLS, 1 p., on Bradbury letterhead. Bradbury Center.

Bradbury to Brehl, April 28, 1998. Bradbury Center.

Bradbury to Brehl, September 7, 1999. TLS, 1 p., on Bradbury letterhead (Mugnaini *Halloween Tree* jacket). Fax original, Bradbury Center.

Brehl to Bradbury, October 1, 2000. TLS, 2 pp., with fax heading. Received fax printout, Bradbury Center.

Brehl to Bradbury, September 1, 2005. TL with typed signature, 1 p., received fax printout, Bradbury Center.

BURROUGHS, EDGAR RICE

Bradbury to Burroughs, n.d. [November 1937]. TL, 1 p.; typed signature. Albright.

Burroughs to Bradbury, Nov 15, 1937. TLS, 1 p., on corporate letterhead (Edgar Rice Burroughs, Inc. | Tarzana, California). Albright.

Burroughs to Bradbury, November 22, 1937. TLS, 1 p., on corporate letterhead. Albright.

BUSH, GEORGE H. W.

From President G. H. W. Bush to Bradbury, October 4, 1992, ALS, 1 p., handwritten on White House presidential stationery (notepad). Bradbury Center.

BUSH, GEORGE W.

From President G. W. Bush to Bradbury, December 8, 2004. TLS, 1 p., on White House embossed-seal presidential stationery. Bradbury Center.

BUSH, LAURA

From First Lady L. Bush to Bradbury, August 14, 2006. TLS, 1 p., on White House stationery. Bradbury Center.

CHAON, DAN

Bradbury to Chaon, April 30–May 1, 1982. TLS, 2 pp., with overstrike and holograph corrections. Bradbury Center (photocopy from Dan Chaon).

Chaon to Bradbury, August 29, 1982. TLS, 3 pp., on yellow bond paper. Bradbury Center

CHONIN, TENNY

Bradbury to Chonin, February 23, 2007. Email (tr. Alexandra Bradbury), 4 pp. Bradbury Center.

CLARKE, SIR ARTHUR C.

Clarke to Bradbury, May 24, 1968. AMS, 1 p., on Brown Palace Hotel stationery (Denver), address crossed out. Albright.

Clarke to Bradbury, August 11, 1992. TLS, 1 p., on Clarke's home office stationery (Colombo, Sri Lanka). Bradbury Center.

CLAYTON, JACK, AND JEANIE SIMS

Bradbury to Clayton and Sims, August 31, 1981. TLS, 3 pp., with overstrike and holograph corrections on letterhead. Bradbury Center.

CONGDON, DON

Congdon to Bradbury, August 27, 1945. TLS, 1 p., on short form Simon & Schuster letterhead. Original unlocated; Bradbury Center (photocopy from Michael Congdon).

Bradbury to Congdon, December 30, 1948. TLS, 2 pp. (Bradbury's carbon). Albright.

Congdon to Bradbury, October 7, 1949. TLS, 2 pp., on Matson Agency letterhead; holograph postscript. Albright.

Congdon to Bradbury, January 12, 1951. TLS, 2 pp., on Matson Agency letterhead; holograph revisions. Albright Collection.

Congdon to Bradbury, August 6, 1952. TLS, 1 p., on Matson Agency letterhead; holograph postscript. Bradbury's notational "X" and holograph "Answered R.B. August 10th" on recto; verso, also in Bradbury's hand: "At Midnight in the Month of June"; "The Warm Cannon-ball That Rolled to Our Porch One Day." Albright.

Congdon to Bradbury, July 24, 1953. TLS, 2 pp., on Matson Agency letterhead, with typed postscript; holograph revisions. Albright.

Bradbury to Congdon, July 30, 1953. TLS, 4 pp., with overstrike and holograph corrections and revisions; "Bradbury" typed above date. Columbia.

Congdon to Bradbury, August 18, 1953. TLS, 4 pp., on Matson Agency letterhead; holograph postscript (not included). Albright.

Bradbury to Congdon, March 31, 1955. TLS, 2 pp., with holograph and overstrike revisions. Matson Agency routing stamp. Columbia.

Bradbury to Congdon, April 8, 1955. TLS, 1 p., with holograph date and closing. Matson Agency routing stamp. Columbia.

Congdon to Bradbury, April 12, 1955. TLS, 2 pp., on Matson Agency letterhead; with holograph postscript and revision. Albright.

Bradbury to Congdon, April 18, 1955. TLS, 2 pp., with overstrike revision. Matson Agency routing stamp. Columbia.

Bradbury to Congdon, May 5, 1955. TLS, 1 p., with holograph date. Matson Agency routing stamp. Columbia.

Bradbury to Congdon, October 4, 1957. TLS, 1 p., with holograph corrections, Bradbury home letterhead (Clarkson Road); "Thanks for Italian painting" below letterhead, in Congdon's hand. Matson Agency routing stamp. Columbia.

Bradbury to Congdon, October 14, 1957. TLS, 1 p., with holograph corrections and postscript, Bradbury home letterhead (Clarkson Road). Matson Agency routing stamp. Columbia.

Congdon to Bradbury, November 6, 1957. TLS, 2 pp., with holograph revision on Matson Agency letterhead. Albright.

Bradbury to Congdon (re: Kuttner), February 7, 1958. TLS, 3 pp., with holograph and overstrike corrections and Matson Agency routing stamp; marked "Air Special" in Bradbury's hand. Columbia.

Bradbury to Congdon, April 16, 1958. TLS, 2 pp., with holograph and overstrike revisions. Matson Agency routing stamp. Columbia.

Bradbury to Congdon, October 24, 1958. TLS, 2 pp., with holograph and overstrike revisions, on Hecht-Hill-Lancaster film production letterhead; Matson Agency routing stamp. Columbia.

Bradbury to Congdon, December 24, 1958. TLS, 2 pp., with holograph and overstrike revisions, on Hecht-Hill-Lancaster film production letterhead. Columbia.

Bradbury to Congdon, May 30, 1959. TLS, 1 p., with typed address heading (Cheviot Drive); Matson Agency routing stamp. Columbia.

Bradbury to Congdon, n.d. [received June 19, 1959]. TLS, 1 p., with holograph correction; Matson Agency routing stamp. Columbia.

Bradbury to Congdon, June 25, 1959. TLS, 2 pp., with holograph date; Matson Agency routing stamp. Columbia.

Bradbury to Congdon, July 18, 1960. TLS, 1 p., on MGM studio letterhead. Matson Agency routing stamp. Columbia.

Bradbury to Congdon, July 24, 1960. TLS, 2 pp., with Matson Agency routing stamp. Columbia.

Bradbury to Congdon, July 29, 1960. TLS, 1 p., on MGM studio letterhead, with overstrike revisions. Matson Agency routing stamp, with brief annotation ("orig to Seldes 8/1") referring to the attached letter formalizing his recent break with editor Tim Seldes and Doubleday. Columbia.

Bradbury to Congdon, August 22, 1960. TLS, 1 p., with holograph revision. Matson Agency routing stamp. Columbia.

Congdon to Bradbury, August 24, 1960. TL initialed memo, 5 pp., with holograph postscript ("Take from this what's useful, of course."). Columbia.

Bradbury to Congdon, August 27, 1960. TLS, 1 p., with typed Cheviot Drive address heading. Matson Agency routing stamp. Columbia.

Bradbury to Congdon, September 14, 1960. TLS, 1 p., with overstrike corrections. Columbia.

Bradbury to Congdon, November 3, 1960. TLS, 1 p., with a holograph correction. Matson Agency routing stamp. Columbia.

Bradbury to Congdon, January 20, 1961. TLS, 1 p., with holograph corrections. Matson Agency routing stamp. Columbia.

Bradbury to Congdon, April 14, 1961. TLS, 1 p., on MGM studio letterhead, with holograph and overstrike revisions. Matson Agency routing stamp. Columbia.

Bradbury to Congdon, September 4, 1961. TLS, 1 p., with Matson Agency routing stamp. Columbia.

Bradbury to Congdon, August 6, 1962. TLS, 1 p., with Matson Agency routing stamp. Columbia.

Bradbury to Congdon (re: Truffaut and Davidson), August 19, 1962. TLS, 2 pp., with a holograph revision. Columbia.

Bradbury to Congdon, November 20, 1962. TLS, 1 p., with holograph revisions. Matson Agency routing stamp. Columbia.

Bradbury to Congdon, December 19, 1962. TLS, 1 p., with a holograph revision. Matson Agency routing stamp. Columbia.

Bradbury to Congdon, December 1, 1963. TLS, 2 pp., with overstrike revisions; Cheviot Drive home address letterhead. Matson Agency routing stamp on p. 2. Columbia.

Bradbury to Congdon, March 24, 1964. TLS, 1 p., with holograph revisions. Matson Agency routing stamp. Columbia.

Bradbury to Congdon, August 20, 1964. TLS, 1 p., with holograph date. Matson Agency routing stamp. Columbia.

Bradbury to Congdon, November 23, 1964. TLS, 1 p., with a holograph revision, on Jack L. Warner's Studio stationery. Matson Agency routing stamp. Columbia.

Bradbury to Congdon, February 15, 1965. TLS, 1 p., Matson Agency routing stamp. Columbia.

Bradbury to Congdon, May 5, 1965. TLS, 1 p., with holograph revisions. Matson Agency routing stamp. Columbia.

Congdon to Bradbury (re: Truffaut), August 4, 1965. TLS, 2 pp., on Matson Agency letterhead. Albright.

Bradbury to Congdon, December 27, 1965. TLS, 2 pp., with holograph date; holograph and overstrike revisions. Matson Agency routing stamp. Columbia.

Bradbury to Congdon, September 20, 1966. TLS, 1 p., with overstrike revisions. Matson Agency routing stamp. Columbia.

Bradbury to Congdon, March 21, 1975, TLS, 1 p., with overstrike revisions by Bradbury and notes by Congdon. Matson Agency routing stamp. Columbia.

Bradbury to Congdon, April 10, 1992. TLS, 1 p., on Bradbury letterhead. Bradbury Center.

Bradbury to Congdon, September 18, 1996. TLS, 1 p., fax original. Bradbury Center.

COTTER, TOM

Bradbury to Cotter, June 1, 1990. TLS, 1 p., with a holograph correction on Bradbury letterhead. Bradbury original (fax). Bradbury Center.

DANNAY, FREDERIC

Bradbury to Dannay, August 10, 1952. TLS, 1 p. Columbia.

DARABONT, FRANK

Bradbury to Darabont, January 16, 2007. Fax email (tr. Alexandra Bradbury), transmitted January 19, 2007. Bradbury Center.

DAVIDSON, AVRAM

Davidson to Bradbury, August 13, 1962. TLS, 2 pp., on *Fantasy & Science Fiction* stationery (recycled cover stock). Albright.
Bradbury to Davidson, August 16, 1962. TLS, 1 p.; Bradbury carbon. Albright.
Bradbury to Davidson, November 9, 1962. TLS, 1 p.; Bradbury carbon. Albright.

DAVIS, RUTH ALBEN

Bradbury to Davis, July 6, 1995. TLS, 1 p., with doodle of a gargoyle embracing the text. Photocopy in the Bradbury Center, made from Davis's fax transmission of the original in October 2004.

DERLETH, AUGUST

Bradbury to Derleth, January 13, 1949. TLS, 1 p., with holograph revisions. Wisconsin.
Bradbury to Derleth, May 18, 1950. TLS, 3 pp., with holograph date. Wisconsin.
Bradbury to Derleth, May 28, 1950. TLS, 1 p., with overstrike revisions. Wisconsin.
Bradbury to Derleth, January 15, 1963. Wisconsin.

EDGLEY, LESLIE

Bradbury to Edgley, December 30, 1952. Albright.

EISELEY, LOREN

Eiseley to Bradbury, January 11, 1974. TLS, 1 p., with holograph corrections and revisions. Marchi.

FELLINI, FEDERICO

Fellini to Bradbury, January 26, 1978. TLS, 1 p., in English on Fellini (name only) letterhead. Albright.
Bradbury to Fellini [February 1978]. TLS, 1 p.; transcribed from Bradbury's unsigned carbon, Bradbury Center.
Fellini to Bradbury, March 3, 1978. TLS, 1 p., in English on Fellini (name only) letterhead. Albright.

Fellini to Bradbury, December 28, 1980. TLS, 2 pp., in English on letterhead with address. Bradbury Center.

FRUMKES, LEWIS

Frumkes to Bradbury, December 1, 1993. TLS, 1 p., on personal letterhead (Grace Terrace, New York). Bradbury Center.

GODLEY, JOHN (SEE KILBRACKEN, LORD JOHN)

GOTTLIEB, ROBERT A.

Bradbury to Gottlieb, January 7, 1962. TL, 1 p. (Bradbury's carbon). Albright.

Gottlieb to Bradbury, May 14, 1962. TLS, 1 p., on Simon & Schuster letterhead, with Bradbury holograph notation "R.B. | 6/4/62." Albright.

Bradbury to Gottlieb, June 3, 1962. TL, 2 pp. (Bradbury's carbon with faint signature impression). Albright.

Gottlieb to Bradbury, October 30, 1962. TLS, 2 pp., on Simon & Schuster letterhead, with Bradbury's notational cross-through superimposed. Albright.

Bradbury to Gottlieb, October 31, 1962. TL, 3 pp. (Bradbury's carbon with faint signature impression). Albright.

GREENE, GRAHAM

Bradbury to Greene, April 18, 1979. TLS, 1 p., with holograph corrections, on Bradbury letterhead. Boston.

Greene to Bradbury, May 2, 1979. TLS, 1 p., on personal letterhead (Antibes). The Bradbury Center.

Bradbury to Greene, June 22, 1979. TLS, 1 p., on Bradbury letterhead. Boston.

Greene to Bradbury, December 15, 1984. TLS, 1 p., on personal letterhead (Antibes). The Bradbury Center.

Bradbury to Greene, January 11, 1985. TLS, 1 p., on Bradbury letterhead. Boston.

Greene to Bradbury, January 22, 1985. TLS, 1 p., on personal letterhead (Antibes). The Bradbury Center.

Bradbury to Greene, February 6, 1985. TLS 2 pp., with holograph revision on Bradbury letterhead (Mugnaini's *Illustrated Man* line art). Boston.

HAMILTON, EDMOND, AND LEIGH BRACKETT
HAMILTON (SEE ALSO LEIGH BRACKETT)

Bradbury to Hamilton, October 7, 1943. TLS, 2 pp., with overstrike revisions and self-doodle by signature. ENMU.

Hamilton to Bradbury, December 31, 1944. TL, opening page only; subsequent page(s) unlocated. Addressed from 1611 Pennsylvania Avenue, New Castle, Penna. Albright.

Bradbury to Hamilton, [September 1945]. TLS, 1 p., with overstrike revisions and a self-doodle by signature. ENMU.

Bradbury to Hamilton and Brackett [ca. 1949]. TLS, 1 p., on half sheet with overstrike revisions. ENMU.

Bradbury to Hamilton and Brackett, January 13, 1950. TLS, 1 p., with overstrike revisions; 33 South Venice Blvd address at top and self-doodle by signature. ENMU.

Bradbury to Hamilton, October 8, 1950. TLS, 1 p., with holograph and overstrike revisions and Clarkson Road address at top. ENMU.

Bradbury to Hamilton and Brackett, March 30, 1951. TLS, 2 pp., with holograph date. ENMU.

Bradbury to Hamilton and Brackett, June 25, 1951. TLS, 2 pp., with overstrike revisions and Clarkson Road address at top. ENMU.

Bradbury to Hamilton and Brackett [ca. early November 1951]. TLS, 2 pp. (single leaf recto-verso), with holograph revisions and holograph Clarkson Road address heading. ENMU.

Hamilton to Bradbury, November 15, 1951. TLS, 2 pp., with postscript TLS by Brackett on the second page; personal address typed above date ("RD 2, | Kinsman, Ohio"). Albright.

Bradbury to Hamilton, August 23, 1953. TLS, 1 p., with holograph date. ENMU.

Hamilton to Bradbury, September 14, 1953. TLS, 1 p., with home address (RD2, Kinsman, Ohio) above date. Albright.

HASSE, HENRY

Bradbury to Hasse, August 2 [1942]. TLS, 2 pp., with human figure doodle through the first page; Hasse's penciled date of receipt (August 6 '42) in top margin. Photocopy (Albright) made in the 1970s from the original (subsequently returned to Hasse; unlocated).

Bradbury to Hasse, December 1942. TLS, 2 pp., 670 Venice Blvd. address typed above salutation. Actual composition is January–February 1943. Photocopy (Albright).

HEARD, [H.] [FITZ]GERALD

Heard to Bradbury, November 4, 1950. TLS, 1 p., with overstrike corrections. Albright.

Heard to Bradbury, January 18, 1951. AMS, 1 p., with holograph correction. Albright.

Bradbury to Heard, August 2, 1951. TLS, 1 p., with AMS correction. UCLA.

Heard to Bradbury, August 5, 1951. TLS, 1 p., with overstrike and holograph corrections. Albright.

HEINLEIN, ROBERT A.

Heinlein to Bradbury, August 9, 1940. TLS, 1 p., with overstrike corrections. Albright.

HILLYER, ROBERT

Bradbury to Hillyer, September 10, 1959. TLS, 1 p. Syracuse (carbon, Albright).

Hillyer to Bradbury, September 29, 1959. AMS, 2 pp., on personal letterhead. Albright.

Hillyer to Bradbury, December 28, 1959. AMS, 2 pp., on personal letterhead. Albright.

Bradbury to Hillyer, January 9, 1960. TLS, 1 p., with overstrike and holograph correction. Syracuse.

Hillyer to Bradbury, April 1, 1961. TLS, 2 pp., with overstrike and holograph corrections. Albright.

Bradbury to Hillyer, May 17, 1961. TLS, 1 p. Syracuse (carbon, Albright).

HOURIGAN, KATHY

Bradbury to Hourigan, May 15, 1997. Fax original, Bradbury Center.

Bradbury to Hourigan, March 28, 2007. Fax original, Bradbury Center.

HUSTON, JOHN

Huston to Bradbury [ca. late February 1951]. AMS, 2 pp., on letterhead (Claridge's | Brook Street, W1). Bradbury Center.

Huston to Bradbury, February 1, 1953. TLS, 1 p., on Huston's production company stationery (Romulus Films, Ltd, 27 Soho Square, London W.1). Bradbury Center.

Bradbury to Huston, March 23, 1953. TLS, 1 p., Bradbury's Clarkson Road address typed above date, with blue ink holograph "BRADBURY" in Bradbury's hand above address. Herrick.

Bradbury to Huston, June 18, 1954. TLS, 1 p., signed in blue ink on lightweight blue paper with overstrike and holograph revisions and filing mark ("cc Kohner"), Bradbury's Clarkson Road address typed below date. Herrick.

Bradbury to Huston, July 12, 1954, 3 pp., on lightweight blue paper with overstrike and holograph revisions and filing mark ("cc Kohner"), Bradbury's Clarkson Road address typed above date. Herrick.

KAY, ROGER

Bradbury to Kay, May 15, 1961. TLS, 1p., Bradbury's unsigned carbon. Albright.

KENNEDY, JOHN F.

President Kennedy to Bradbury, June 21, 1962. TLS, 1 p., on White House stationery. Bradbury family (original); Kennedy (carbon).

Bradbury to President Kennedy, September 1, 1962. Cable. Kennedy.

KILBRACKEN, LORD JOHN (JOHN GODLEY)

Godley to Bradbury, October 23, 1965. TLS, 4 pp., with holograph revisions on estate letterhead (Killegar, Cavan, Ireland). Albright.

Bradbury to Godley, n.d. [early January 1986]. Killegar.

Bradbury to Godley [ca. September 1991]. Killegar.

KING, STEPHEN

King to Bradbury, November 8, 1979. TLS, 1 p. Bradbury Center.

Bradbury to King, ca. November–December 1979. Transcribed from *Danse Macabre* (1981), pp. 326–28.

KIRK, RUSSELL

Kirk to Bradbury, July 8, 1967. TLS, 3 pp., carbon. Kirk.

Kirk to Bradbury, September 12, 1967 TLS, 3 pp., carbon. Kirk.

Bradbury to Kirk, September 16, 1967. TLS, 1 p. Kirk. Extracts in Kirk, *Enemies of the Permanent Things* (New Rochelle, NY: Arlington House, 1969), pp. 118, 120.

KUTTNER, HENRY

Kuttner to Bradbury, December 21, 1944, TLS, 2 pp., with overstrike corrections and typed address heading (Hastings-on-Hudson, N.Y.) and mouse caricature below signature. Albright.

Bradbury to Kuttner (draft), December 25, 1944, TLS, 4 pp., with overstrike corrections and holograph revisions and closing caricature; a draft of the posted letter. Albright.

Kuttner to Bradbury, March 5, 1945. TLS, 2 pp., with holograph and overstrike corrections. Albright.

Kuttner to Bradbury, January 15, 1946. TLS, 1 p., with overstrike corrections. Albright.

Bradbury to Congdon (re: Kuttner), February 7, 1958. See entry under Congdon, Don.

MANESS, DAVID

Bradbury to Maness [ca. March 1969]. TLS, 1 p., Bradbury's unsigned carbon. Albright.

MATHESON, RICHARD

Matheson to Bradbury, September 8, 1950. TLS, 1 p. Albright.

Bradbury to Matheson, September 12, 1950. TLS, 1 p. fax to Bradbury (7/5/2005). Bradbury Center.

Matheson to Bradbury, January 13, 1951. TLS, 1 p. Albright.

Bradbury to Matheson, January 22, 1951. TLS, 2 pp., with overstrike and holograph corrections. Fax to Bradbury (7/5/2005). Bradbury Center.

Matheson to Bradbury, January 28, 1951. TLS, 2 pp. Albright.

Matheson to Bradbury, May 17, 1996. TLS, 1 p., with holograph corrections. Bradbury Center.

MAUGHAM, W. SOMERSET

Maugham to Bradbury, April 9, 1959. TLS, 1 p. Albright.

McCLARREN, RALPH H.

Bradbury to McClarren, April 2, 1968. TLS, 1 p., Bradbury's unsigned carbon. Albright.

McKIMMEY, JAMES

Bradbury to McKimmey, October 24, 1963. TL, 2 pp. (Bradbury carbon). Lilly (White MSS).

MILLER, GREGORY

Miller to Bradbury, May 10, 2004 (email). Miller.

Bradbury to Miller, May 11, 2004 (email). Miller.

MUGNAINI, JOSEPH

Bradbury to Mugnaini, July. 28, 1980. TLS, 2 pp., with three holograph drawings and captions (see volume illustrations). Mugnaini.

Bradbury to Mugnaini, October 22, 1983. TLS, 1 p., with holograph correction, on Disney studio letterhead (*Something Wicked This Way Comes*). Mugnaini.

NATIONAL INSTITUTE OF ARTS AND LETTERS

John Hersey to Bradbury, March 17, 1954. TLS, 1 p., on Institute letterhead. Bradbury Center.

NICHOLAS, NANCY

Nicholas to Bradbury, August 25, 1971. TL, 4 pp. Bradbury Center.

Bradbury to Nicholas, September 15, 1971. TLS with overstrike corrections, 1 p., on home address letterhead. Texas.

Nicholas to Bradbury, November 10, 1971. TL, 1 p. Bradbury Center.

Bradbury to Nicholas, December 3, 1971. TLS, 1 p., with holograph revision, on home address letterhead. Texas.

Bradbury to Nicholas, January 19, 1972. TLS, 1 p., with holograph revision, on home address letterhead. Texas.

Bradbury to Nicholas [June 18, 1973]. TLS (partial signature), 1 p., on home address letterhead. Texas.

Bradbury to Nicholas, February 15, 1975. TLS, 1 p., with overstrike correction, on home address letterhead. Texas.

Nicholas to Bradbury, February 26, 1980, 1 p. Texas.

NIN, ANAÏS

Nin to Bradbury, November 30, 1964. AMS, 1 p., on Trans World Airways airmail letterhead. Albright.

NOLAN, WILLIAM F.

Bradbury to Nolan, January 11, 1951. TLS, 3 pp., with overstrike corrections and holograph date. Albright (photocopy).

Bradbury to Nolan, November 7, 1951. TLS, 1 p., with typed address heading (Clarkson Road). Albright (photocopy).

Bradbury to Nolan, November 10, 1952. TLS with holograph date and holograph correction. Albright (photocopy).

Bradbury to Nolan, October 30, 1953. TLS, 2 pp. (recto-verso), with annotations by Nolan to Donn Albright. Albright (photocopy).

Bradbury to Nolan, April 28, 1954. TLS, 1 p., with typed address heading (Hotel Ambasciatori | Rome, Italy) and holograph corrections. Albright (photocopy).

Bradbury to Nolan, July 23, 1962. TLS, 2 pp., with holograph corrections. Albright (photocopy).

POHL, FREDERIK, JR.

Bradbury to Pohl [August 1939]. TLS, 1 p., with holograph cartoon face by Bradbury (top right corner). Syracuse.

Pohl to Bradbury, August 19, 1939. TLS, 1 p., on his author's agent letterhead (280 St. John's Place, Brooklyn, NY). Syracuse.

Bradbury to Pohl [ca. January 1941]. TLS on memo stock, 1 p., with curatorial identifiers in brackets. Syracuse.

Bradbury to Pohl, November 11, 1954. TLS, 1 p., with holograph date. Syracuse.

Pohl to Bradbury, October 25, 1962. TLS, 1 p., on Galaxy Publishing Corporation letterhead. Vertical line by Bradbury acknowledging receipt. Albright.

Bradbury to Pohl, Halloween [October 31], 1962. TLS, 1 p. Syracuse.

PULITZER PRIZE BOARD

From Lee C. Bollinger to Bradbury, April 16, 2007. TLS, 1 p., on Columbia University (President's Room) stationery. Bradbury Center.

RHYMER, PAUL

Bradbury to Rhymer, December 1, 1949. TLS, 2 pp., Bradbury's carbon. Albright.

ROBERTS, JOSEPH

Bradbury to Roberts, February 11, 1963. TLS, 1 p. carbon. Albright.

RUSSELL, BERTRAND

Russell to Ruth Simon (Hart-Davis publishers), March 13, 1954. TLS, 1 p., on Russell's Richmond letterhead (forwarded to Bradbury). Bradbury Center.

SACKETT, SAM

Bradbury to Sackett, July 5, 1949. TLS, 1 p. transcription. Miller.

Bradbury to Sackett, November 19, 1949. TLS, 2 pp. transcription. Albright.

Bradbury to Sackett, January 18, 1958. TLS, 1 p., with holograph revisions, transcription. Miller.

SANDBURG, CARL

Sandburg to Bradbury, March 21, 1961. TLS, 1 p., to John Huston (unsigned carbon), with signed holograph note to Bradbury below the text. Bradbury Center.

Bradbury to Sandburg, March 26, 1961. TLS, 1 p., on armillary image (top left) stationery, Cheviot Hills address across lower margin. Illinois.

Sandburg to Bradbury, April 4, 1961. TLS, 1 p., on George Stevens Productions stationery. Bradbury Center.

SCHLESINGER, ARTHUR, JR.

Bradbury to Schlesinger, April 30, 1962. TLS, 2 pp. Kennedy.

Schlesinger to Kennedy, May 5, 1962. TLS, 1 p. Kennedy.

SCHWARTZ, JULIUS

Schwartz to Bradbury, September 8, 1945. TL, typed signature, 1 p. Albright.

Schwartz to Bradbury, March 25, 1946. TLS, 1 p., with holograph and overstrike corrections. Albright.

SHORE, WILMA

Bradbury to Shore, February 5, 1954. TLS, 2 pp., with caricature signature and holograph and overstrike corrections on Royal Hibernian Hotel stationery (Dublin). Bradbury Center (gifted by Dinah Stevenson, 2018).

SIBLEY, BRIAN

Sibley to Bradbury, May 8, 1974. AMS, 2 pp., in Sibley's hand with holograph heading address (Chislehurst, Kent, UK). Bradbury Center.

Bradbury to Sibley, June 10, 1974. TLS, 2 pp., on *Leviathan '99* performance stationery. Bradbury Center scan courtesy of Brian Sibley.

Sibley to Bradbury, June 18, 1974. TLS, 1 p., with typed address heading (Chislehurst, Kent, UK). Bradbury Center.

STEIGER, ROD, AND CLAIRE BLOOM

Bradbury to Bloom and Steiger [summer 1968]. TLS, 1 p., Bradbury's unsigned carbon. Albright.

STEINBECK, THOMAS

Steinbeck to Bradbury, June 27, 2003. TLS, 6 pp. Bradbury Center.

STURGEON, THEODORE

Sturgeon to Bradbury, October 22, 1946, TLS, 1 p., Sturgeon's agency letterhead (151 Eighth Avenue, New York). Albright.

Bradbury to Sturgeon, October 30, 1946, TLS, 2 pp. Kansas.

Bradbury to Sturgeon, February 3, 1947. TLS, 2 pp., with holograph and overstrike revisions. Kansas.

Sturgeon to Bradbury, February 18, 1947. TLS, 8 pp., with overstrike and holograph corrections. Albright.

Bradbury to Sturgeon, March 18, 1947. TLS, 2 pp., with holograph revisions and character doodles down the left margin of the first page. Kansas.

Sturgeon to Bradbury, March 18 [1947]. TLS, 2 pp., with overstrike and holograph corrections. Albright.

Bradbury to Sturgeon, February 22, 1948. TLS, 1 p., with overstrike revisions and holograph date. Kansas.

Sturgeon to Bradbury, March 5, 1948. TLS, 2 pp., with overstrike and holograph revisions. Albright.

THOMAS, THOMAS THURSTON

Thomas to Bradbury, April 8, 1965. TLS, 2 pp. Albright.

Bradbury to Thomas, May 5, 1965. TLS, 2 pp. carbon, with overstrike corrections. Albright.

TIBBETTS, JOHN

Bradbury to Tibbetts, September 30, 2004. TLS, 1 p., on Bradbury letterhead (Moundshroud by Mugnaini). Bradbury Center scan (courtesy Tibbetts).

TRUFFAUT, FRANÇOIS

Truffaut to Bradbury, April 27, 1962. TLS, 3 pp., in French with final paragraph and closing in holograph. On Les Films Du Carrosse letterhead. Albright.

Bradbury to Truffaut, May 3, 1962. TLS, 1 p., signed in light blue ink, Bradbury's name and home address typed across the lower margin. Cinématheque.

Truffaut to Bradbury, May 29, 1962. TLS, 2 pp., in French on Les Films Du Carrosse letterhead. Albright.

Bradbury to Truffaut, June 11, 1962. TLS, 1 p., signed in blue ink. Cinématheque.

Bradbury to Truffaut, August 12, 1962. TLS, 1p., Bradbury's name and home address typed across the lower margin, original unlocated, Bradbury's carbon, the Bradbury Center.

Bradbury to Truffaut, August 31, 1962. TLS, 2 pp., with holograph and overstrike correction; Bradbury name and home address stamped in red centered in the top margin. Cinématheque.

Truffaut to Bradbury, September 24, 1962. TLS, 2 pp., in French on Les Films Du Carrosse letterhead. Albright.

Truffaut to Bradbury, November 15, 1965. TLS, 1 p., in French with holograph corrections on personal letterhead. Albright.

Bradbury to Truffaut, November 19, 1965. TLS, 1 p., typed on the inner page of a Hallmark card, signed in orange ink "Ray" above typed "Bradbury" in lower right margin, dated (lower left margin) in orange ink. Cinématheque.

Truffaut to Bradbury, January 16, 1966. TLS, 1 p., on personal letterhead; envelope (postmarked London 17 January 1966) with return address (M.C.A. studio offices, London), translated into English by Helen Scott, signed by Truffaut. Albright.

Bradbury to Truffaut, January 24, 1966. TLS, 1 p., signed in blue ink with date typed below signature, letterhead has Bradbury name and Cheviot Hills address centered between horizontal lines. Cinématheque.

Bradbury to Truffaut, February 27, 1966. TLS, 1 p., signed in blue ink with date typed below signature, holograph emphasis added in salutation, letterhead has Bradbury name and Cheviot Hills address centered between horizontal lines. Cinématheque.

Bradbury to Truffaut, July 20, 1966. TLS, 1 p., with overstrike corrections on gold bordered paper. Cinématheque.

Bradbury to Truffaut, August 31, 1966. TLS, 2 pp., with holograph and overstrike corrections, signed in blue ink, European-style numeral 1 in circle at top left of first page. Cinématheque; Bradbury's carbon, Bradbury Center.

Bradbury to Truffaut, September 18, 1966. TLS, 2 pp., with holograph corrections, signed in blue ink, numeral 3 in circle at top left of first page. Cinématheque.

Bradbury to Truffaut, January 10, 1967. TLS, 1p., on Cheviot Hills home letterhead. Cinématheque.

Truffaut to Bradbury, February 6, 1967. TL. 2 pp., transcribed by Helen Scott for Truffaut. Albright.

URIS, LEON

Bradbury to Uris, May 10, 2001, TLS, 1 p. fax original. Bradbury Center.

VIDAL, GORE

Vidal to Bradbury [ca. July 1. 1951]. TLS, 2 pp., with Bradbury's holograph annotation at top of p. 1 "Answered July 5, 1951—R.B." Albright.

Bradbury to Vidal [July 5, 1951]. TLS, 1 p., with postscript typed at top of page. Harvard.

Bradbury to Vidal, July 31, 1951. TLS, 1 p., with typed Clarkson Road address. Harvard.

VIMONT, PIERRE

From Ambassador Vimont to Bradbury, December 18, 2007. TLS, 1 p., with holograph closing, on letterhead of the Ambassador of France to the United States. Bradbury Center.

WEST, JESSAMYN

West to Mr. Johnson (Doubleday), March 23, 1953. TL (carbon) with "copy" typed at top, sent to Bradbury by West. Bradbury Center.

WILHITE, TOM

Bradbury to Wilhite [July 1982]. TL (carbon), 1 p. Bradbury Center.

WILLIAMSON, JACK

Bradbury to Williamson, April 23, 1941. TLS, 3 pp., with overstrike revisions and a penciled cartoon figure in left margin of each page. ENMU.

WOLLHEIM, DONALD

Bradbury to Wollheim, July 1941. TLS, 1 p. Kansas.

Bradbury to Wollheim, August 18, 1941. TLS, 2 pp., with holograph date and revisions. Kansas.

Bradbury to Wollheim, March 31, 1950. TLS, 1 p. Kansas.

Permissions

Bach, Richard. Letter by Richard Bach to Ray Bradbury is reprinted by permission of Richard Bach.

Baldwin, Faith. Letter by Faith Baldwin to Ray Bradbury is reprinted by permission of Harold Ober Associates. Copyright © 1962 by Faith Baldwin.

Beaumont, Charles. Letters by Charles Beaumont to Ray Bradbury are reprinted by permission of Don Congdon Associates, Inc., on behalf of Christopher Beaumont.

Berenson, Bernard. Letter by Bernard Berenson to Ray Bradbury is reprinted by permission of Biblioteca Berenson, I Tatti – The Harvard University Center for Italian Renaissance Studies, courtesy of the President and Fellows of Harvard College.

Bevington, Helen. Letter by Helen Bevington to Ray Bradbury is reprinted with the permission of Steve Bevington, Sarah Bevington, and Kate Bevington.

Brackett, Leigh. Letter and postscript letter from Leigh Brackett to Ray Bradbury are reprinted with the permission of Robert Douglass, care of Spectrum Literary Agency, Inc.

Bradbury, Ray. Letters by Ray Bradbury and personal photographs are reprinted courtesy of Ray Bradbury Literary Works, LLC.

Bradbury, Walter I. Letters by Walter Bradbury to Ray Bradbury are reprinted with the permission of Dennis E. Bradbury.

Brehl, Jennifer. Letters by Jennifer Brehl to Ray Bradbury are reprinted with the permission of Jennifer Brehl.

Burroughs, Edgar Rice. Letters by Edgar Rice Burroughs to Ray Bradbury are reprinted by permission of Edgar Rice Burroughs, Inc.

Chaon, Dan. Letter by Dan Chaon to Ray Bradbury is reprinted with permission by Dan Chaon.

Clarke, Sir Arthur C. Letters by Sir Arthur C. Clarke to Ray Bradbury are reprinted by permission of David Higham Associates, Ltd.

Congdon, Don. Don Congdon's letters to Ray Bradbury are reprinted by permission of Michael Congdon.

Davidson, Avram. Letter by Avram Davidson to Ray Bradbury is reprinted by permission of Seth Davis.

Eiseley, Loren. Letter by Loren Eiseley to Ray Bradbury is reprinted by permission of the Trustees of the University of Pennsylvania.

Fellini, Federico. Letters by Federico Fellini to Ray Bradbury are reprinted by permission of Francesca Fabbri Fellini on behalf of the Federico Fellini Estate.

Frumkes, Lewis. Letter by Lewis Frumkes to Ray Bradbury is reprinted by permission of Lewis Frumkes.

Gottlieb, Robert A. Letters by Robert Gottlieb to Ray Bradbury are reprinted by permission of Robert A. Gottlieb.

Greene, Graham. Letters by Graham Greene to Ray Bradbury are reprinted by permission of David Higham Associates, Ltd.

Hamilton, Edmond. Letters by Edmond Hamilton to Ray Bradbury are reprinted by permission of Robert Douglass, care of Spectrum Literary Agency, Inc.

Heard, [H.] [Fitz]Gerald. Letters by Gerald Heard to Ray Bradbury © 2023 the Barrie Family Trust; reprinted by permission of Harold Ober Associates and John Roger Barrie, literary executor of Gerald Heard. Photograph of Gerald Heard, circa 1955, photograph by Jay Michael Barrie, appears courtesy of the Barrie Family Trust.

Heinlein, Robert A. Letter by Robert Heinlein to Ray Bradbury is reprinted by permission of the Robert A. and Virginia Heinlein Prize Trust.

Hillyer, Robert. Letters by Robert Hillyer to Ray Bradbury reprinted by permission of Francesca Hillyer Combs.

Huston, John. Letters by John Huston to Ray Bradbury are reprinted by permission of the Estate of John Huston, care of Susan J. Ollweiler, Jess S. Morgan, and Company, Inc.

Interlandi, Frank. *Below Olympus* editorial cartoon by Frank Interlandi is reprinted by permission of Mia Interlandi-Ferreira, © 1976 by the *Los Angeles Times*.

Kilbracken, John (Godley), 3rd Baron Kilbracken. Letter by John Godley Kilbracken to Ray Bradbury is reprinted by permission of Kilbracken of Killegar, 4th Baron Kilbracken.

King, Stephen. Letter by Stephen King to Ray Bradbury is reprinted by permission of Stephen King, care of Darhansoff and Verrill Literary Agents.

Kirk, Russell. Letters by Russell Kirk to Ray Bradbury are reprinted by permission of Russell Kirk Legacy, LLC, care of Annette Y. Kirk, cofounder and past president of the Russell Kirk Center for Cultural Renewal.

Kuttner, Henry. Letters by Henry Kuttner to Ray Bradbury are reprinted with the permission of Don Congdon Associates, Inc., on behalf of Carole Ann Rodriguez.

Lewis, C. S. Quotation from a letter by C. S. Lewis to Nathan Comfort Starr, appearing as epigraph to this volume, is from C. S. Lewis, *Selected Letters*, vol. III © copyright 2006 C. S. Lewis Pte Ltd. Extract used by permission.

Matheson, Richard. Letters by Richard Matheson to Ray Bradbury are reprinted by permission of Don Congdon Associates, Inc., on behalf of RXR, Inc.

Maugham, W. Somerset. Letter by W. Somerset Maugham to Ray Bradbury is reprinted by permission of United Agents LLP (www.unitedagents.co.uk) on behalf of the Royal Literary Fund (Copyright © the Royal Literary Fund) and Paradigm Talent Agency.

Miller, Gregory. Letter by Gregory Miller to Ray Bradbury is reprinted by permission of Gregory Miller.

Nicholas, Nancy. Letters by Nancy Nicholas to Ray Bradbury are reprinted by permission of Nancy Nicholas.

Nin, Anaïs. Letter by Anaïs Nin is reprinted by permission of Anaïs Nin Trust, care of Tree L. Wright, literary agent.

Pohl, Frederik, Jr. Letters by Frederik Pohl Jr. to Ray Bradbury are reprinted by permission of Frederik Pohl IV, manager of FrederikPohlsGateway, LLC.

Russell, Bertrand. Letter by Bertrand Russell forwarded to Ray Bradbury is reprinted by permission of the Bertrand Russell Archives, McMaster University Library.

Sandburg, Carl. Letters from Carl Sandburg to Ray Bradbury copyright © 2022. Printed by arrangement with John Steichen and Paula Steichen Polega, care of the Barbara Hogenson Agency. All rights reserved.

Schwartz, Julius. Letters by Julius Schwartz to Ray Bradbury are reprinted by permission of the Julius Schwartz Estate, care of Andrea D. Hopkins (executor).

Sibley, Brian. Letters by Brian Sibley to Ray Bradbury are reprinted by permission of Brian Sibley.

Steinbeck, Thomas M. Letter by Thomas M. Steinbeck to Ray Bradbury is reprinted by permission of Gail Knight Steinbeck.

Sturgeon, Theodore. Letters by Theodore Sturgeon to Ray Bradbury are reprinted by permission of Noël Sturgeon, trustee, Theodore Sturgeon Literary Trust.

Thomas, Thomas Thurston. Letter by Thomas T. Thomas to Ray Bradbury is reprinted by permission of Thomas T. Thomas.

Truffaut, François. François Truffaut's letters to Ray Bradbury are reprinted with the permission of Don Congdon Associates, Inc., on behalf of Laura Truffaut Wong, Eva Truffaut, and Josephine Truffaut.

Vidal, Gore. Letter by Gore Vidal to Ray Bradbury is reprinted by permission of President and Fellows of Harvard College.

West, Jessamyn. Letter by Jessamyn West forwarded to Ray Bradbury is reprinted by permission of the Jessamyn West Estate.

Notes

C. S. LEWIS EPIGRAPH

1. From Walter Hooper, ed., *C. S. Lewis, Collected Letters*, vol. 3 (New York: Harper-One, 2007), 287–88. *The Silver Locusts* is a British variant title for *The Martian Chronicles*.

1: MENTORS AND INFLUENCERS

1. Dr. David H. Keller (1880–1966), a psychiatrist who turned to science fiction in midlife, published "Revolt of the Pedestrians" (1926), a story that influenced Bradbury's path toward *Fahrenheit 451*.

2. Mark S. Reinsberg (1923–1981) was a Chicago area fan-reviewer who also published in the genre pulps. Reinsberg chaired the committee organizing ChiCon I, the 1940 Chicago World Con. Bradbury did not attend.

3. *FuFa* was used by writers and fans in reference to Bradbury's fanzine *Futuria Fantasia* (four issues, summer 1939 to September 1940); the final issue included Robert A. Heinlein's story "Heil!," as by Lyle Monroe (revised and reprinted under Heinlein's byline in *Expanded Universe* [1980] as "Successful Operation").

4. E. E. "Doc" Smith (1890–1965), author of the popular Lensman series, was often featured in *Astounding*.

5. Bradbury didn't find success in the detective pulps until 1944; "On the Nose" was never published. The publisher of *Flynn's Detective Fiction*, the Frank Munsey Company, sold it to Popular Publications in 1942, and Bradbury would place a story in the August 1944 issue (he remained unsuccessful with Popular's *Black Mask*). He would publish seventeen science fiction stories in *Thrilling Wonder* and one with a crime-story premise ("Doodad") in Street and Smith's *Astounding*.

6. Bradbury's initial pulp magazine rejections included most of the well-edited but chronically underfunded second-tier pulp titles: F. Orlin Tremaine's short-lived *Comet* (1940–1941); Donald A. Wollheim's *Cosmic Stories* and *Stirring Science Stories* (1940–1942); Frederik Pohl's *Astonishing Stories* (1940–1943) and the longer-lived *Super Science Stories* (1940–1943, 1949–1951); and Charles D. Hornig's tenure with *Science Fiction* (1939–1941) and *Future Fiction* (1939–1941). The titles that Bradbury mentions were never published and for the most part remain unlocated; he even-

tually published eight stories in *Astonishing Stories* and *Super Science Stories* before and during his transition to the first-tier pulps and the major-market magazines.

7. Bradbury's Los Angeles newspaper stand at the corner of Olympic and Norton was closed for a time due to road construction; the temporary loss of income was a factor in his decision not to attend the third Science Fiction Convention in Denver that summer.

8. By 1942 Hasse had married and moved from the West Coast to Washington, D.C.

9. Malcolm Reiss, editor-in-chief of Fiction House, publishers of *Planet Stories* and other genre pulp magazines.

10. "The Candle," *Weird Tales* (November 1942).

11. *Astounding Science Fiction* (July 1942). "Junior" was shorthand for *Astounding*'s editor, John W. Campbell Jr.

12. Julius Schwartz, Bradbury's New York pulp market agent, also represented Hasse until 1943. "The Piper" (February 1943) and "Promotion to Satellite" (Fall 1943), in *Thrilling Wonder Stories*; "Gabriel's Horn" (with Hasse), in *Captain Future* (Spring 1943).

13. "Chrysalis" was rejected by *Astounding* and shortened to story length for *Amazing Stories* (July 1946).

14. Bradbury attended Perdue's writing group for a few months, in addition to his periodic appearances at the Mañana Society meetings at Robert Heinlein's Laurel Canyon home.

15. Genre writers Ross Rocklin (published as Rocklynne) and Charles R. Tanner.

16. Although he ushered some symphony evenings at the Hollywood Bowl and eventually for ballet at the Philharmonic Auditorium, there is no evidence that he ushered at the Biltmore.

17. Their mutual Seattle friend Hannes Bok (Wayne Woodard) had stayed for a time in Los Angeles and provided art for Bradbury's *Futuria Fantasia* (1939–1940). Bradbury later helped Bok get established as an award-wining pulp magazine illustrator.

18. Context (opening sentence and sales information) indicates actual composition in late January or February 1943.

19. Helen Finn knew Bradbury from what was, by this time, the Los Angeles Science Fantasy Society (LASFS).

20. Fiction House subeditor Wilbur S. Peacock edited *Planet Stories* for Malcolm Reiss through 1945.

21. "The Candle" (November 1942), "The Wind" (March 1943), and "The Crowd" (May 1943).

22. Popular Publications' editor-in-chief Alden Norton bought "Subterfuge" for *Astonishing Stories* (April 1943). "Promotion to Satellite" (*Thrilling Wonder Stories*, Fall 1943) was his third sale to Standard Magazines' editor-in-chief Leo Margulies.

23. "Gabriel's Horn," *Captain Future* (Spring 1943); Campbell soon bought two Bradbury submissions for the September 1943 *Astounding*: the "Liar's Tale" column short-short "And Watch the Fountains" and "Doodad," the only full-length Brad-

bury tale that Campbell ever published in the magazine. Palmer purchased "I, Rocket" for *Amazing* (May 1944).

24. Bradbury was medically disqualified for military service (4-F) due to poor eyesight; the others were LASFS friends Paul Freehafer, who had a heart condition, Bruce Yerke, and Arthur Louis Joquel II, known as "the twoth."

25. Hasse published two collaborations in *Planet Stories* with Albert DePina: "Star of Panadur" (March 1943) and "Alcatraz of the Starways" (May 1943).

26. A similar 1949 or 1950 incident with another friend occurred late at night along Wilshire Boulevard. This incident, and perhaps the Hasse walking memory, became a flashpoint for his 1951 story "The Pedestrian."

27. The last two Bradbury-Hasse collaborations, "City of Intangibles" and "The Emotionalists," remained unpublished.

28. At the request of *Astounding*'s John Campbell, Kuttner provided a long-distance critique of Bradbury's "Chrysalis." From 1942 until the fall of 1944, Leigh Brackett critiqued a wide range of Bradbury stories during more or less weekly Sunday afternoon meetings at Santa Monica Beach.

29. Anthony Boucher's space mystery included actual science fiction writers and fans as characters (NY: Duell, Sloane and Pearce, 1942, as by "H. H. Holmes").

30. Bok, *The Sorcerer's Ship* (*Unknown Worlds*, December 1942).

31. Alden Norton purchased "King of the Gray Spaces" for *Famous Fantastic Mysteries* (December 1943) on March 24, 1943, but it was accepted earlier. This was Bradbury's third sale to Popular's magazines, following "Subterfuge" (sold October 1942) and "And Then—The Silence" (sold January 1943).

32. Catherine Moore, *Judgment Night*, *Astounding* (August–September 1943); Albert DePina, "Keeper of the Deathless Sleep," *Planet Stories* (Winter 1944). *Planet*'s Wilbur Peacock bought the DePina tale.

33. Fantasy and science fiction author L. Sprague De Camp sent a critique of Kuttner's novel *A Million Years to Conquer* (*Startling Stories*, November 1940) through a card to Leo Margulies, editor-in-chief at *Startling*'s parent syndicate, Standard Magazines.

34. Raymond Chandler, "The Simple Art of Murder," *The Atlantic Monthly* (December 1944); Virgil Partch, *It's Hot in Here* (McBride, 1944).

35. Henri Rousseau (1844–1910), a self-taught post-impressionist French painter who influenced twentieth-century avant-garde artists; his painting *The Sleeping Gypsy* (1897, Museum of Modern Art) is one of his best-known works. Kuttner compares him to the German-born Dadaist/Surrealist artist Max Ernst (1891–1976).

36. *Farewell, My Lovely* (1944) was the preview release title for the RKO Studio film adaptation of Raymond Chandler's novel *Murder, My Sweet* (1940); the title of the actual novel was substituted for nationwide release in early 1945. *The Man in Half Moon Street* (Paramount, 1945) was adapted to screen from the Barré Lyndon stage play.

37. Although Kuttner used the diminutive "Kat" in reference to C. L. Moore, Bradbury consistently used "Cat" from the actual spelling of "Catherine" during this period.

38. Bradbury's comments on C. L. Moore's "No Woman Born," and his thoughts on the ballet indicate that such a story was emerging in his own mind. In the months following this letter, he wrote "The Dancer," a 554-word unpublished vignette of a paralyzed girl who uses phonograph music to imagine herself to be an accomplished ballerina. A longer Bradbury story about a similar dancer/actress, "One Woman Show" (composed 1952), would eventually be published in *One More for the Road* (2002).

39. *The Mad Tristan* premiered at the International Theatre, New York, December 15, 1944, performed by the Ballet International.

40. "Gaseous vertebrate," a somewhat pejorative term for anthropomorphic and omnipresent God, probably came to Bradbury in variation from H. L. Mencken: "a vertebrate without substance, having neither weight, extent, nor mass . . ." (*The American Mercury*, March 1930). Within a year Bradbury would publish in *The American Mercury*, a magazine that Mencken had founded.

41. Henry Kuttner, "Before I Wake," *Famous Fantastic Mysteries* (March 1945).

42. Sterling North, "Strictly Personal: Back to Witchcraft," *Saturday Review of Literature* (December 2, 1944): 20–21.

43. New York Governor Thomas Dewey, *The Case Against the New Deal* (Harper, 1940).

44. During 1944 Bradbury was taking Bates Method exercises and rest periods to improve his eyesight.

45. The Will Jenkins major trade anthology (edited under his principal pseudonym, Murray Leinster) appeared seven years later as *Great Stories of Science Fiction* (New York: Random House, 1951). Kuttner and Moore were represented, but not Bradbury.

46. Bradbury's unlocated winter 1945 letter described some of his brief cross-border travels into Mexico during the summer of 1944. Kuttner and Moore deferred their own Mexican travel plans due to illness.

47. [Wilber Scott] Peacock bought Brackett's "Red Sea of Venus" novella concept for *Planet Stories* in 1944. Bradbury wrote the second half of the novella after Brackett went to work as part of the screenwriting team for *The Big Sleep*; the novella was submitted as *Lorelei of the Red Mist* in March 1945 (*Planet Stories*, Summer 1946).

48. Bradbury's earliest working title (ca. 1944) for what would become *Dark Carnival* (1947).

49. Before publishing *The Great Fog and Other Weird Tales* (1944), Gerald Heard had published his first two "Mycroft Holmes" murder mystery novels, *A Taste for Honey* (1941) and *Reply Paid* (1942).

50. The D'Orsay literary agency in Los Angeles was run by Kuttner's uncle, author Laurence Thalmore, under his pen name, Laurence R. D'Orsay.

51. A reference to the Mexico travel recommendations in Bradbury's previous letter.

52. Both Bradbury and Kuttner took fiction classes at Los Angeles High School taught by Stanford University graduate Jennet Johnson.

53. "Pendulum," *Super Science Stories* (November 1941), with Henry Hasse, was based on Bradbury's earlier fanzine version.

54. Ian Ballantine published many Kuttner-Moore paperback collections and novels in the 1950s, but it would be Doubleday, where Walter Bradbury had edited all of Ray Bradbury's trade volumes to that point, that would publish *The Best of Henry Kuttner* (1975) with a Bradbury introduction.

55. The *Atlantic Monthly* rejection may have been one of the three major market stories he was circulating on his own at that time: "Interval in Sunlight," "Powerhouse," or "The Great Fire."

56. Bradbury's only known West Indies story from this period is "The Cricket Cage," an unpublished 5,000-word tale written in February 1945 that focuses on crime and drugs rather than cult magic.

57. A play on Henry Kuttner's humorous tale in *Super Science Stories* (May 1943), "Reader, I Hate You!"

58. Henry Kuttner's pseudonym Lewis Padgett (see Kuttner to Bradbury, March 5, 1945).

59. "The Meadow," *World Security Workshop* (ABC), broadcast January 2, 1947.

60. Bradbury visited Arkham House publisher August Derleth at his Sauk City, Wisconsin, home in September 1946, en route to New York.

61. "Powerhouse" (*Charm*, March 1948) would place third in the *O. Henry Prize Stories 1948* anthology (1949).

62. Possibly "Touch and Go," "Pillar of Fire," or an early circulating version of "The Illustrated Man."

63. "The Children's Hour" was one of the two stories sent on to *Collier's*; it was returned and subsequently appeared in *Planet Stories* under the revised title "Zero Hour."

64. Writer's cant for "typewriter."

65. A reference to the top-tier pulp status of *Astounding Science Fiction* mentioned in Bradbury's February 3 letter to Sturgeon.

66. Shorthand for *Astounding*'s editor, John W. Campbell Jr.

67. Satevepost (*The Saturday Evening Post*). Malcolm R. Jameson (1891–1945), who published stories in Campbell's *Astounding* and *Unknown*.

68. Part of the Columbia Masterworks series of 12-inch 78-rpm two-disk albums; set *X-216* was Bach's Passacaglia and Fugue in C Minor, arranged and conducted by Leopold Stokowski (All-American Orchestra); from the Hopper Columbia Discography.

69. Sturgeon's eight-page letter (February 18, 1947) included four pages of plans to renovate a tenement flat on New York's Lower East Side.

70. Pseudonym of science fiction writer Philip Klass (1920–2010), a good friend of Sturgeon's.

71. A play on the 1944 hit recording "Is You Is or Is You Ain't (Ma' Baby)," charted by both Bing Crosby (with the Andrews Sisters) and by Louis Jordan.

72. Georges Rouault (1871–1958), a French painter known for his use of contrastive colors. See also Bradbury's "Prologue" to *The Illustrated Man* (1951).

73. The Columbia Masterworks album with the Stokowski recording of Bach (see Sturgeon, February 18, 1947).

74. Paul L. Payne (1921–1992) edited *Planet Stories* (1946–1950) during Bradbury's best years with that magazine.

75. Heinlein, "The Green Hills of Earth," *Saturday Evening Post* (February 8, 1947).

76. Bradbury, "Zero Hour," *Planet Stories* (Fall 1947); subsequently collected in *The Illustrated Man* (1951).

77. The fifth of nine symphonic suites composed by the Brazilian composer Heitor Villa-Lobos between 1938 and 1945 (Columbia Masterworks 71670-D), with baroque elements in the tradition of Johan Sebastian Bach—a Sturgeon favorite.

78. Singer Mary Mair (ca. 1925–unknown) was married to Sturgeon from 1949 to 1951.

79. Alexander L. C. Wilder (1907–1980), privately taught American composer of popular hits and innovative classical compositions; author of the influential *American Popular Song: The Great Innovators, 1900–1950*.

80. Russian Symbolist composer Alexander Scriabin (1871–1915); Italian composer Gaetano Pugnani (1731–1798).

81. Hamilton had a command of seminal works across the humanities on one hand, but he was also the primary author of the Captain Future series, tales of an orphaned genius and man of action who secretly continues the scientific advances of his parents.

82. Bradbury's 4-F medical disqualification from military service; his alternate service involved writing periodic blood drive broadcasts for radio.

83. Edward L. Bodin was a writer and agent who represented L. Ron Hubbard for a time. Bradbury found him through an article in *Writer* and engaged him briefly to circulate his stories among the major market magazines. Bodin handled at least four Bradbury stories in 1944, but he did not sell any.

84. "Eat, Drink, and Be Wary," *Astounding* (July 1942); "And Watch the Fountains," *Astounding* (September 1943).

85. Bradbury's father worked for the BPL and rented his home from the company.

86. Prior to her screenwriting assignment on the Warner Brothers adaptation of *The Big Sleep*, Brackett had scripted *The Vampire's Ghost* for Republic.

87. Bradbury, "The Poems," *Weird Tales* (January 1945).

88. Richard Hughes's *A High Wind in Jamaica*, also published as *Innocent Voyage*, would have an impact on some of the stories novelized in *Dandelion Wine* (1957), most notably "Season of Disbelief" (1950).

89. As a non-driving passenger in his friend Grant Beach's car, Bradbury's main stops became Monterrey, Zimapan, Mexico City, a day trip to Veracruz, a southern trip through Taxco to Acapulco, and finally Pátzcuaro, the newly formed Paricutín volcano, Guadalajara, and Guanajuato. There was no time to reach the Yucatán.

90. Bradbury took his typewriter and wrote some short mood pieces and sketches during the trip. On the way home, Bradbury left Beach in Laredo and continued on by bus; Beach subsequently threw Bradbury's typewriter in a river.

91. Hamilton returned to Los Angeles in the fall of 1945 and married Leigh Brackett in early January 1946.

92. "The Big Black and White Game," *American Mercury* (August 1945); "Invisible

Boy," *Mademoiselle* (November 1945); and "One Timeless Spring," *Collier's* (April 13, 1946).

93. "Cold Front Coming," *Blue Book* (June 1945). Williamson had enlisted and spent much of World War II as a meteorologist, drawing on that training in this short story.

94. "Lost Elysium," *Weird Tales* (November 1945) was Hamilton's second and final Brian Cullan story.

95. A tongue-in-cheek comment; Bradbury was now a top contributor to *Weird Tales*, having placed stories in all six of the 1944 bimonthly issues and in five of the six 1945 issues.

96. Bradbury's May 1950 *Martian Chronicles* promotional trip to New York (by rail) did not allow time to visit Brackett and Hamilton in rural Kinsman, Ohio.

97. Susan Marguerite Bradbury, their first child, born November 5, 1949.

98. "The World the Children Made" (variant title for "The Veldt"), *Saturday Evening Post* (September 23, 1950).

99. "The Citadel of Lost Ages," *Thrilling Wonder Stories* (December 1950).

100. *Shadow Over Mars*, *Startling Stories* (Fall 1944); as a stand-alone novel, World Distributors (1951). The unpublished novel may have been *The Long Tomorrow* (1955), considered one of Brackett's best novel-length works.

101. A probable reference to "Red Sea of Venus," the original working title of their collaborative novella, *Lorelei of the Red Mist* (1946).

102. "The Pumpernickel," *Collier's* (May 19, 1951) and "The Beast from 20,000 Fathoms," *Saturday Evening Post* (June 23, 1951, variant title "The Fog Horn"); "Zero Hour" was adapted for NBC Television's *Lights Out* program, but the July 23, 1951, broadcast record has not been verified.

103. The Doubleday story collection would eventually shake out as *The Golden Apples of the Sun* (1953). Stories from Bradbury's Illinois novel would be broken out into *Dandelion Wine* (1957); the remaining structure was finally published as *Farewell Summer* (2006).

104. Bradbury's design survives (Bradbury Center); it served as the basis for the actual first edition Stanley Butchkis jacket.

105. The Bantam anthology would finally be published in 1952 as *Timeless Stories for Today and Tomorrow*.

106. From September 1953 through mid-April 1954, Bradbury would work with John Huston in Ireland and London to write the screenplay for the 1956 Warner Brothers production of *Moby Dick*.

107. Mr. Gumpox and his horse were characters on Paul Rhymer's long-running NBC Radio program *Vic and Sade*.

108. Maggie's father, Lonal McClure, was one-quarter Cherokee; Maggie's mother was of multicultural Austro-Hungarian heritage.

109. The two Doubleday contracts were for the Illinois novel and *The Golden Apples of the Sun*. The three Bantam paperback contracts may have included his multi-author anthology, *Timeless Stories for Today and Tomorrow* (1952).

110. Julius Schwartz was his genre pulp agent from 1941 to 1947.

111. *City at World's End* (New York: Frederick Fell, 1951).

112. Henry Kuttner, *Man Drowning* (New York: Harper, 1952); Jack Williamson, *Dragon's Island* (New York: Simon & Schuster, 1951).

113. One of the "Mars Is Heaven!" offers came from Robert L. Lippert Sr., but it's not clear which one.

114. The Venus project remains a mystery, but Brackett declined to continue his work. The following year Bradbury developed an unproduced adaptation of Jack Vance's "Hard Luck Diggings" for Twentieth Century Fox.

115. CBS producer John Haggott already had a television adaptation of "The Man" airing as the December 23, 1951, episode of *Out There*, and he wanted five more Bradbury scripts for the 1952 season. These never materialized.

116. "These Things Happen," *McCall's* (May 1951); "The April Witch," *The Saturday Evening Post* (April 5, 1952). His sale of the controversial "And the Rock Cried Out" to *Mademoiselle* fell through; after publication as "The Millionth Murder," *Manhunt* (September 1953), it would be collected in the first edition of *Fahrenheit 451* (1953) under the original title.

117. Hamilton, *The Star Kings* (New York: Frederick Fell, 1949). The first British edition (London: Museum Press, ca. 1950) was also marketed in Australia.

118. An allusion to Eugene O'Neill's dramatic comedy, *Ah, Wilderness* (1933).

119. "The Dwarf," *Fantastic* (January–February 1954); collected in *The October Country* (New York: Ballantine, 1955).

120. L. Sprague De Camp, *Science-Fiction Handbook* (New York: Heritage House, 1953).

121. Edmond Hamilton, "The Unforgiven," *Startling Stories* (October 1953).

122. Edmond Hamilton, "What's It Like Out There?," *Thrilling Wonder Stories* (December 1952).

123. Hamilton refers to either "Runaway," *Startling Stories* (Spring 1954), or "The Tweener," *Magazine of Fantasy & Science Fiction* (February 1955).

124. Nelson Bond, "The First Thousand Words," *Writer's Digest* (November 1940).

125. Nelson Bond, "The Bookshop," *Blue Book Magazine* (October 1941).

126. From the late 1940s through the 1960s, British *Argosy* reprinted more than seventy Bradbury stories, often with variant titles.

127. "Mars Is Heaven!," *Planet Stories* (Fall 1948) was reprinted in *Esquire* (December 1950) and *Argosy* (U.K., April 1950) as "Circumstantial Evidence," and in the *Esquire*-owned *Coronet* (June 1950) as "They Landed on Mars." Radio adaptations were broadcast on *Escape* (CBS, June 2, 1950) and *Dimension X* (NBC, July 7, 1950).

128. Bond's "Conqueror's Isle" (*Blue Book Magazine*, June 1946) was reprinted in August Derleth's anthology *The Other Side of the Moon* (Pellegrini & Cudahy, 1949), along with Bradbury's "Pillar of Fire" and "The Earth Men."

129. Hemingway's *Across the River and Through the Trees*, serialized in *Cosmopolitan* (February–June 1950).

130. "The Enemy in the Wheat," *New Rave* (August 1994); collected in *One More for the Road* (2002).

131. *The Remarkable Exploits of Lancelot Biggs: Spaceman* (Doubleday, 1950).
132. Bradbury was unable to expand "Frost and Fire," originally "The Creatures That Time Forgot," *Amazing Stories* (Fall 1946); *The Illustrated Man* became the second book in his Doubleday contract.
133. *The Thirty-First of February* (New York: Gnome Press, 1949).

2: MIDCENTURY MENTORS

1. Antonina Vallentin, *H. G. Wells: Prophet of Our Day* (New York: John Day Co., 1950). Heard's review TS, possibly with references to Bradbury, Gerald Heard Papers at UCLA (LSC 1054).
2. American journalist and historical novelist Scott O'Dell (1898–1989).
3. Max Eastman, *Enjoyment of Poetry* (New York: Scribner's, 1913).
4. British poet Christopher Fry (1907–2005), best known for stage plays written in blank verse.
5. Heard, "The Collector," *Magazine of Fantasy & Science Fiction* (August 1951).
6. Bradbury, "The Beast from 20,000 Fathoms," *Saturday Evening Post* (June 23, 1951).
7. The full text of Heard's *Martian Chronicles* endorsement is preserved in the Gerald Heard Papers at UCLA (LSC 1054).
8. Published as a chapbook, "The Shop of Mechanical Insects" (Burton, MI: Subterranean Press, 2009).
9. "The Day It Rained Forever," *Harper's* (July 1957), was Bradbury's fourth and final Best American Short Stories selection (collected in *A Medicine for Melancholy*, 1959).
10. Nicky Mariano, Berenson's long-time secretary, companion, and librarian.
11. *Happy Anniversary 2116* (1956), an operetta, was never produced for Laughton and his wife, Elsa Lanchester, for whom it was primarily written. It was staged and subsequently filmed as *Merry Christmas, 2116* (2009).
12. Bradbury saw the *Laocoön*, a largely restored Greek sculpture in the Vatican, shortly before meeting Berenson in April 1954. The *Laocoön* shows a sea serpent killing the high priest Laocoön of Troy and his sons, who have warned the Trojans to beware of the giant wooden horse left by the Greek warriors as they seemingly depart from their ten-year siege of Troy. Bradbury had also recently seen the death of Laocoön reenacted in London for a performance of the opera *The Trojans* (*Les Troyens*) by Hector Berlioz.
13. *A Medicine for Melancholy* (1959) and *Something Wicked This Way Comes* (1962), respectively.
14. *The Relic and other Poems* (New York: Knopf, 1957).
15. An allusion to Bradbury's "The Day It Rained Forever," collected in *A Medicine for Melancholy*.
16. "Forever Voyage," *Saturday Evening Post* (January 9, 1960). Collected by Bradbury in *The Machineries of Joy* (1964) as "And the Sailor, Home from the Sea."
17. Bradbury was included in the brochure as a member of the writing staff for the

August 1961 Bread Loaf Writers' Conference, but he withdrew in June when his screenwriting obligations to MGM were extended by the studio.

18. Novelist and poet Theodore Morrison was director of the Bread Loaf Writers' Conference from 1932 to 1955; Pulitzer Prize–winning historian and literary critic Bernard DeVoto (1897–1955), who read and enjoyed Bradbury's *The Golden Apples of the Sun* in the spring of 1953.

19. Bradbury had seen the Russian prima ballerina Aleksandra Danilova perform on tour in the 1940s; his fourth daughter Alexandra was named after her.

20. The poet John Ciardi, who had invited Bradbury to the 1961 Bread Loaf Writers' Conference, and poet Oscar Williams corresponded with Bradbury.

3: EMERGING WRITERS

1. Beaumont's first collection, *The Hunger and Other Stories* (New York: Putnam, 1957).

2. *Esquire*'s editor-in-chief Frederic Birmingham eventually rejected Beaumont's "The Crooked Man"; it was first published in *Playboy* (August 1955).

3. Beaumont completed *Run from the Hunter* with Jon Tomerlin (New York: Gold Medal, 1957), under the joint pseudonym Keith Grantland. *The Intruder* (New York: Dell, 1959), was Beaumont's only other published novel. The science fiction novel was apparently never completed. The Doubleday contract may refer to an agreement for his first story collection, *The Hunger and Other Stories*, which eventually went to Putnam's instead.

4. Bradbury, "Day After Tomorrow: Why Science Fiction?," *The Nation* (May 2, 1953).

5. Bradbury, "Introduction," *Without Sorcery*, Theodore Sturgeon (Philadelphia: Prime Press, 1948).

6. "Open House," *Esquire* (February 1955) as "The Murderers."

7. "Miss Gentilbelle," first published in *The Hunger and Other Stories* (1957).

8. Bradbury's long relationships with the editors of *Collier's* and *Mademoiselle* yielded no results on behalf of Beaumont; both "Fair Lady" and "Tears of the Madonna" were first published in *The Hunger and Other Stories*.

9. "Point of Honor," *Manhunt* (November 1955).

10. Bradbury's Illinois novel *Summer Morning, Summer Night* had been under contract with Doubleday since 1951. Certain story-chapters became *Dandelion Wine* (1957); the overarching frame became *Farewell Summer* (2006).

11. Their mutual friend, Forrest J Ackerman.

12. Beaumont and Chad Oliver, "The Guests of Chance," *Infinity Science Fiction* (June 1956).

13. L. Sprague de Camp and Fletcher Pratt, *Tales From Gavagan's Bar* (New York: Twayne, 1953).

14. Beaumont, "The Vanishing American," *Magazine of Fantasy and Science Fiction* (August 1955).

15. Beaumont's "The Magic Man" was first published in his third story collection, *Night Ride and Other Journeys* (New York: Bantam, 1960). Bradbury's ten-draft

story was "The Sound of Summer Running" (first published as "Summer in the Air"), *Saturday Evening Post* (February 18, 1956), sold on March 7, 1955.

16. Joan Harrison produced the early *Alfred Hitchcock Presents* episodes based on Bradbury stories. "Special Delivery" aired November 29, 1959.

17. Beaumont began *Where No Man Walks*, his first attempt at a novel, in early 1957; he may have taken it up again in 1962, when he mentioned it to Bradbury in this letter. It remained unfinished at his death in 1967.

18. Bradbury's *Icarus Montgolfier Wright*, an animated short film version of Bradbury's 1956 short story, had a limited release as a short feature in theaters. Beaumont may be referring to a private screening.

19. "A Few Notes on the *Martian Chronicles*," *Rhodomagnetic Digest* (June 1950), was Bradbury's May 22nd address at the Invisible Little Man Award dinner in San Francisco.

20. Matheson, "Third from the Sun," *Galaxy* (October 1950). Bradbury, "Sometime Before Dawn," *The Cat's Pajamas* (New York: HarperCollins, 2004).

21. "Born of Man and Woman," in the Boucher and McComas–edited *Magazine of Fantasy & Science Fiction* (Summer 1950).

22. Bradbury, "The Last Night of the World," *Esquire* (February 1951).

23. Two years after writing to Matheson, Bradbury would begin doubling the length of "The Fireman" to create *Fahrenheit 451*.

24. "Where's your next *Weird* yarn—and don't forget *horror*, not arty or child stuff." Julius Schwartz to Bradbury, October 12, 1944 (Albright Collection). Schwartz was Bradbury's wartime agent in the genre pulp market.

25. A reference to Hernán Cortéz's comrade-in-arms Bernal Díaz del Castillo, who authored *The True History of the Conquest of Mexico* (1632).

26. Horace Gold, founder of *Galaxy Science Fiction* and editor from 1949 until 1962.

27. Matheson, "Through Channels," *Magazine of Fantasy & Science Fiction* (April 1951).

28. Journalist and writer Charles Fort (1874–1932), chronicler of unexplainable things in *The Book of the Damned* (1919) and other works that influenced science fiction writers.

29. The Santa Fe Railroad's Super Chief passenger liner, connecting Chicago with Los Angeles, was also one of Bradbury's favorite trains. This route's only long tunnel crosses the Raton Pass on the Colorado–New Mexico border.

30. Hemingway's *Across the River and into the Trees* (1950) was not well-received by critics.

31. Bradbury, "The Long Years" story-chapter of *The Martian Chronicles*.

32. Matheson's son, writer Richard Christian Matheson.

33. *Stranger to the Ground* (New York: Harper & Row, 1963).

34. The special screening of Gene Kelly's *Invitation to the Dance* occurred in 1955; Kelly's attempt at marketing the evolving *Dark Carnival* script continued for several years.

35. As "The Electric Grandmother," Bradbury's "I Sing the Body Electric!" was adapted for broadcast on *NBC Peacock Theatre*, January 17, 1982.

36. This observation on writers and college first appeared in Bradbury's Christmas 1944 letter to Henry Kuttner, but was moderated as he began to speak frequently at college events.

37. *They Have Not Seen the Stars: The Collected Poetry of Ray Bradbury* (Lancaster, PA: Stealth, 2002), and *A Chapbook for Burnt-Out Priests, Rabbis, and Ministers* (Forest Hill, MD: Cemetery Dance, 2001).

4: LITERARY CONTEMPORARIES

1. Bradbury's "April 2005: Usher II" in *The Martian Chronicles* contains allusions to various Oz characters. Vidal's "thirty-odd" refers to the original nineteen Oz volumes by L. Frank Baum and follow-on volumes by Ruth Plumley Thompson and Jack Snow.

2. Marguerita (Rita) Smith, sister of novelist Carson McCullers and fiction editor at *Mademoiselle*; Christopher Isherwood, the expatriate British Modernist writer, was an early reviewer and enthusiast for *The Martian Chronicles*.

3. Christopher Isherwood, *The World in the Evening* (London: Methuen, 1954).

4. The sprawling novelized story cycle *Summer Morning, Summer Night*, part of which was published by Doubleday as *Dandelion Wine* (1957) under this contract.

5. "The Beast from 20,000 Fathoms," *Saturday Evening Post* (June 23, 1951), illustrated by James Bingham.

6. The first chapter of Truman Capote's short novel, *The Grass Harp* (Random House, October 1951), appeared in the July 1951 issue of *Harper's Bazaar*. Bradbury thought highly of *A Curtain of Green* (Doubleday, 1941), Eudora Welty's first story collection, but found her subsequent collections diminished in power.

7. Vidal, *A Search for the King* (New York: E. P. Dutton, 1950).

8. Bradbury, "The April Witch," *Saturday Evening Post* (April 5, 1952).

9. Bradbury's best-known telling of his "I'm alive" moment is "Illumination" (*Reporter*, May 16, 1957), subsequently revised for *Dandelion Wine* (1957).

10. In his story "Farewell Summer" (*The Stories of Ray Bradbury*, 1980), he reversed this death-ship metaphor in a dream where he leaves his childhood home and sails away from life, looking back at the living friends and family who wave from the shore. This tale became the title chapter of his long-deferred Illinois novel, *Farewell Summer* (2006).

11. *Death Is a Lonely Business* became the title of the first of Bradbury's three late-life detective novels (1985).

12. *Picasso Summer* (Warner Brothers / Seven Arts, 1972) was based on Bradbury's short story "In a Season of Calm Weather," *Playboy* (January 1957); collected in *A Medicine for Melancholy* (1959). A dramatic reading adaptation of *Dandelion Wine* (set to music) opened for a short run at New York's Lincoln Center in April 1967.

13. "From the Academy: Count Dracula and Mr. Ray Bradbury," *National Review* (April 4, 1967): 365; later revised for *Enemies of the Permanent Things* (1969).

14. Kirk is alluding to Bradbury's radio play version of "The Meadow" (ABC's *World Security Workshop*, 1947).

15. Kirk's previous letter (July 8, 1967) appears in section 8, "War and Intolerance."

16. Bradbury's picture book *Switch on the Night* (New York: Pantheon, 1955) was inspired by his desire to teach his daughters not to fear the dark.

17. "Foreword," in Neil McAleer's *Arthur C. Clarke: The Authorized Biography* (Chicago: Contemporary Books, 1992).

18. In his foreword, Bradbury recalled an early 1980s experience in a Los Angeles computer store, where Clarke showed him the first "lap computer" that Bradbury had ever seen.

19. Isaac Asimov, longtime friend of both Bradbury and Clarke, passed away in April 1992.

20. The independent film production consortium of Harold Hecht, James Hill, and actor Burt Lancaster, where Bradbury worked on contract at times between 1957 and 1959.

21. Bradbury knew Conrad, a senior editor at *Horizon* in 1979 and 1980, through Conrad's father (Barnaby Conrad II), founding director of the annual Santa Barbara Writers Conference, where Bradbury spoke for many years.

22. Reed died suddenly of a heart attack on April 25, 1976, at his London home.

23. Bradbury, who knew Cukor through Katharine Hepburn, had counseled Cukor not to make *The Blue Bird* (1976), a film burdened with the objective of being a symbol of goodwill between the U.S. and the USSR. Earlier, Cukor had directed the film adaptation of Greene's 1969 novel *Travels with My Aunt* (MGM, 1972).

24. Greene's three-act stage play *The Potting Shed*, first produced on Broadway (1957) and in London (1958).

25. *Fahrenheit 451* was adapted for opera by David Mettee (composer) and Georgia Holof (lyrics).

26. The favored Irish story was probably "The Great Collision of Monday Last" (1958) or "A Wild Night in Galway" (1959); "The Terrible Conflagration Up at the Place" was not published until 1969.

5: FILMMAKERS

1. Bradbury's gift to Huston consisted of *Dark Carnival*, *The Martian Chronicles*, *The Illustrated Man*, and the February 1951 issue of *Galaxy Science Fiction* magazine containing "The Fireman," the novella-precursor to *Fahrenheit 451*.

2. Huston's 1952 film *Moulin Rouge*, which was nominated for seven Academy Awards, won two.

3. Lorraine "Lorry" Sherwood, Huston's secretary.

4. Peter Viertel worked with Huston on *The African Queen* (1951) and novelized that experience in *White Hunter, Black Heart*. He became Bradbury's friend during the pre-production phase of *Moby Dick*.

5. Hollywood agent Paul Kohner represented John Huston.

6. Montgomery Clift had turned down the narrative center portrayed by Ishmael; the role went to Richard Basehart.

7. Huston had moved his pre-production team from Ireland to his London offices

for the final script work in March 1954; Bradbury departed London in mid-April to reunite with his family in Sicily for an Italian vacation prior to returning to Los Angeles.

8. During the composition of *Moby Dick*, Melville spoke deeply of metaphysical things in conversations at Pittsfield, Massachusetts, but these words were spoken to Hawthorne later, at the American Consulate in Liverpool, during Melville's visit: "Melville, as he always does, began to reason of Providence and futurity, and of everything that lies beyond human ken, and informed me that he had 'pretty much made up his mind to be annihilated.'" (Hawthorne, *The English Notebooks*).

9. Herman Melville, "Hawthorne and His Mosses," *The Literary World* (August 17 and 24, 1850).

10. Melville, "Hawthorne and His Mosses." The actual reading is: "Through the mouths of the dark characters of Hamlet, Timon, Lear, and Iago, he craftily says, or sometimes insinuates the things, which we feel to be so terrifically true, that it were all but madness for any good man, in his own proper character, to utter, or even hint of them."

11. Bradbury's revisions to the chartroom scene between Ahab and Starbuck were made on July 14, 1954. All of Bradbury's light revisions arrived too late for use during the filming of *Moby Dick*.

12. Huston's wife Enrica (Ricki) Soma Huston, traveling secretary Lorry Sherwood, and Huston's London-based secretary Jeanie Sims.

13. In his subsequent May 17, 1962, letter to Truffaut, Congdon would explain that retained story rights would only apply to the original idea to make a film of short stories; Truffaut would be able to secure television broadcast rights for his version of *Fahrenheit 451*.

14. Truffaut, *Le Cinéma selon Alfred Hitchcock* (Paris: Éditions Robert Laffont; variant title *Hitchcock/Truffaut*).

15. An implicit allusion to Paris, long known in Western culture as the City of Light.

16. Bradbury toured Truffaut through the sprawling upscale Piggly Wiggly Continental Market in Encino.

17. Truffaut may be describing Bradbury's editorial letter and his article, "How to Keep and Feed a Muse," both printed in the July 1961 issue of *The Writer*.

18. Adaptations of Bradbury's "The Jar" (broadcast February 14, 1964) and "The Life Work of Juan Diaz" (October 26, 1964) aired during the final season of *The Alfred Hitchcock Hour*.

19. Simon & Schuster now had the *Fahrenheit 451* hardbound rights from the lapsed Ballantine original and brought out a new hardbound edition in 1967. Ballantine brought out a new issue of the mass-market paperback with a still photograph from the film featured on the front wrapper.

20. The resulting article was the award-winning "An Impatient Gulliver Above Our Roofs," *Life* (November 24, 1967). The Apollo launchpad tragedy in Florida occurred just days after Bradbury's return from his Manned Spacecraft Center interviews in Houston.

21. Esther Moberg Bradbury died on November 12, 1966, in Los Angeles, after the New York premier of *Fahrenheit 451* on November 2 and before the official release in the United States of November 14.

22. His associate Helen Scott translated Truffaut's outgoing letters to Bradbury.

23. Truffaut's telegram declining *Something Wicked This Way Comes* is dated January 18, 1967 (Albright Collection). The short story omnibus film was never made.

24. Bradbury's Swedish publisher met Truffaut at the Cannes Film Festival and asked if he could include a reprint of the director's *Fahrenheit 451* diary notes in the Swedish book edition.

25. Doubleday's hesitation over *Something Wicked This Way Comes*, along with long-standing issues over limited advertising commitments, led Bradbury and Congdon to Simon & Schuster.

26. Spender, the archaeologist of the fourth expedition ("—And the Moon Be Still as Bright"), represented Bradbury's antipathy toward exploitation, genocide, and rampant consumerism in *The Martian Chronicles*.

27. A compromise was reached and Bradbury returned to work at MGM through the spring of 1961, but *The Martian Chronicles* film was never produced.

28. John O'Hara's novel *Butterfield 8* (1935) was successfully produced and released by MGM, winning a 1960 Academy Award for Elizabeth Taylor, who, like Bradbury and others, had considered the story disagreeable.

29. Producer Julian Blaustein had sponsored Bradbury's *Martian Chronicles* contract with MGM, but his pre-production work in Europe for his next film, *The Four Horsemen of the Apocalypse*, left almost no time to guide Bradbury's work at all.

30. Bradbury's voice track allowed composer Miklós Rózsa to synchronize the orchestra track with the edited film. Bradbury's voice would be replaced by that of Orson Welles before release; neither received screen credit.

31. The score was composed by award-winning Hollywood composer Jerry Goldsmith; that year he also scored Bradbury's *Christus Apollo* verse in cantata form.

32. Presumably director Jack Smight and writer/co-producer Howard B. Kreitsek.

33. The final running time was slightly cut from 109 minutes to 103 minutes for the March 1969 release.

34. The eldest Bradbury daughter, Susan, attended studies in London and Oxford during the summer of 1968. Steiger and Bloom returned to England to make their final film together, Peter Hall's *Three into Two Won't Go*.

35. Fellini's Swiss publisher was Diogenes Verlag, the same Zurich-based house that published Bradbury's Swiss editions.

36. Bradbury's Christmas broadside poem for 1980 was "And Yet the Burning Bush Has Voice," *Questar* no. 9 (October 1980); collected in *The Haunted Computer and the Android Pope* (New York: Knopf, 1981).

37. Fellini's next film would be *And the Ship Sails On* (released 1983).

38. Fellini's wife, the actress Giulietta Masina, who starred in such Fellini films as *La Strada* (1954), *Nights of Cabiria* (1957), and *Juliet of the Spirits* (1965).

39. Bradbury was part of Laraine Day's amateur Wilshire Players group in 1940–41.

40. Disney's early July 1982 screening of *Something Wicked This Way Comes* led to selective reshooting during the fall and winter. Bradbury's viewpoint was valued during reshooting, but he did not play a significant role; the major changes were largely determined by the vice president for production at Disney, Tom Wilhite.

41. Marty Sklar brought Bradbury in to work with and inspire the Imagineer teams that fulfilled Walt Disney's dream for Disney World and eventually Euro Disney. Even though he did not directly oversee the film, Roy E. Disney was influential in acquiring Bradbury's film adaptation of *The Wonderful Ice Cream Suit*, released to home video in 1998.

6: EDITORS AND PUBLISHERS

1. Julius Schwartz was now Bradbury's New York agent; he and established genre writer Edmond Hamilton had driven west to Los Angeles following the Science Fiction Worldcon in Denver earlier that summer.

2. Wollheim, "The Haters," *Unknown Fantasy Fiction* (November 1940). Campbell edited both *Unknown* and *Astounding*.

3. Robert A. Heinlein and LASFS member Bruce Yerke had attended the World Science Fiction Convention in Denver.

4. The Anglicized spelling "Grey" only appeared in the August 1944 *Super Science Stories* Canadian reprint and the 1953 EC Comics adaptation.

5. Don Congdon was Bradbury's agent with the Harold Matson Agency.

6. *Collier's*, "The Window" (August 5, 1950) and "Season of Disbelief" (November 25, 1950); *Saturday Evening Post*, "The World the Children Made" ("The Veldt," September 23, 1950); *Esquire*, "The Great Hallucination" ("The Earth Men," November 1950), "Mars Is Heaven!" ("The Third Expedition," December 1950), and "The Immortality of Horror" ("Carnival of Madness," "Usher II," November 1951); *Coronet*, "They Landed on Mars" ("Mars Is Heaven!" condensed, June 1950). The network radio shows referenced are "The Crowd" (*Suspense*, September 21, 1950), *The Martian Chronicles* (NBC *Dimension X*, August 18, 1950), and "—And the Moon Be Still as Bright" (NBC *Dimension X*, September 29, 1950).

7. During the New York World Science Fiction Convention, Bradbury met Robert O. Erisman, editor of *Marvel Science Stories*, on July 7, 1939, in the magazine's Manhattan publishing offices, accompanied by Forry Ackerman, Wollheim, and perhaps others. Frank R. Paul painted the cover art for the November 1938 issue.

8. Hamilton, "Fessenden's Worlds," *Weird Tales* (April 1937); Donald Wandrei, "Colossus," *Astounding* (January 1934).

9. Dr. David Keller, "The Revolt of the Pedestrians," *Amazing Stories* (February 1928) was an influence on Bradbury's anti-authoritarian "The Pedestrian," *Reporter* (August 7, 1951).

10. Alpheus Hyatt Verrill, "The World of the Giant Ants" (*Amazing Stories Quarterly*, Fall 1928).

11. Bradbury's handwritten outline of *The Space War* survives, but no story-chapter drafts are known.

12. First published as "The Mad Wizards of Mars," *Maclean's* (Canada, September 15, 1949). The new title was Bradbury's, but some of his internal revisions were suggested by Derleth for the version in *Beyond Time and Space*.
13. Derleth, "Fine Writing in Science Fiction Tale," *Chicago Sunday Tribune*, May 21, 1950.
14. John Dos Passos (1896–1970), author of the U.S.A. trilogy, often grouped with the more prominent Lost Generation writers John Steinbeck and Ernest Hemingway, and James T. Farrell (1904–1979), author of the Studs Lonigan trilogy of novels.
15. Fletcher Pratt, "Beyond Stars, Atoms, and Hell," *Saturday Review of Literature* (June 17, 1950); Anthony Boucher, "Probable Future of Man Told in a Warm Style," *Chicago Sun & Times Book Week* (June 4, 1950).
16. William Anthony Parker White (1911–1968), a founding editor of *The Magazine of Fantasy & Science Fiction*, used several pen names, but was best known as Anthony Boucher. Bradbury had been in San Francisco to receive the Invisible Little Man Award from the Bay Area's science fiction fan club, which included novelist and historian Fletcher Pratt (1897–1956).
17. *Leviathan '99* became a radio play (BBC, 1968) and a stage play (most notably produced at the Samuel Goldwyn Theater, 1972) before it was finally published as a novella in *Now and Forever* (New York: HarperCollins, 2007).
18. "El Dia De Muerte" (*Touchstone*, Fall 1947) was actually reprinted in *Gamma 2* (1963) as "Sombra Y Sol" and collected by Bradbury under the original title in *The Machineries of Joy* (1964).
19. "They All Had Grandfathers," concerning a re-created town from the Old West on Mars, was cut prior to galley composition at press. Bradbury restored "The Fathers" (as "The Fire Balloons") to the first British edition (published as *The Silver Locusts*); it subsequently appeared in American editions of *The Illustrated Man* and in some later American editions of *The Martian Chronicles*. Two bridge passages, "The Disease" and "The Wheel," were deleted and never restored by Bradbury in any of his trade editions.
20. Ray Bradbury ultimately retained "The Off Season" in all editions. In addition to its focus on criticizing the conspicuous consumerism that seemed, at least to Bradbury, as all too likely in the future colonization of Mars, "The Off Season" also relates the explosion of Earth in atomic war as framed in the bridges that precede ("The Luggage Store") and follow ("The Watchers") the actual story.
21. Walt Bradbury worked very closely with Don Congdon in the publication of Ray Bradbury's Doubleday titles.
22. A single-page handwritten outline survives, dated November 24, 1949 (Albright Collection); *The Illustrated Man* (1951) bled off some of the stories intended for the novel, and it remained undeveloped.
23. This planned expansion of his short novella "The Creatures That Time Forgot" (*Planet Stories*, Fall 1946) never materialized, although he would later lightly revise the story and retitle it "Frost and Fire" (collected in *R Is for Rocket*, 1962). His second Doubleday book would be the science fiction story collection *The Illustrated Man* (1951).

24. Given Bradbury's late-life commentary for the 2001 Gauntlet edition of *Dark Carnival*, it is likely that the four problematic stories in Bradbury's mind included three very short sketch-like pieces he included in the first edition of 1947: the disturbing tales "The Maiden" and "Interim," and the enigmatic story "The Night Sets."

25. "Christopher Isherwood Reviews *The Martian Chronicles*," *Tomorrow* (October 1950). He would later compose "Migration to Mars," a different but equally favorable review for *The Silver Locusts* (the British edition of the *Chronicles*) in the (London) *Observer* (September 16, 1951).

26. Literary critic and commentator Clifton Fadiman (1904–1999) subsequently wrote the introduction to the 1957 Doubleday reissue of *The Martian Chronicles*. Joseph Hamilton Basso (1904–1964) was a prominent magazine editor and novelist.

27. Arkham House cofounder August Derleth was known for his prolific output of fiction, nonfiction, and book reviews.

28. The sketch of the boy in new tennis shoes became "Summer in the Air," *Saturday Evening Post* (February 18, 1956). It is untitled in *Dandelion Wine*.

29. "The Happiness Machine," *Saturday Evening Post* (September 14, 1957), "Dandelion Wine," *Gourmet* (June 1953), and "Illumination," *The Reporter* (May 16, 1957) would all be extracted from *Summer Morning, Summer Night* to form story-chapters of *Dandelion Wine*.

30. "The Beautiful Child" (variant titles "The Murderer" and "The Murder") was never published (Albright Collection).

31. The problem Bradbury addressed in these three stories was postwar censorship of supernatural fiction, and thereby the potential decline of freedom of the imagination; all three were, in various ways, precursors to *Fahrenheit 451*.

32. The science fiction writer and fan group in the Berkeley area was known as the Elves', Gnomes', and Little Men's Science Fiction Chowder and Marching Society. Central figures in the "Little Men" included Boucher and Mick McComas. Boucher's wife was Phyllis.

33. Bradbury lived with his parents in a subdivided rental home on S. St. Andrews Place during those years, about ten blocks west of Rosedale Cemetery, which anchored the northeast corner of the intersection of Washington Street and Normandie Boulevard. The "Free Dirt" sign that both Beaumont and Bradbury saw was somewhere along the large Rosedale frontage near this intersection.

34. A popular idiomatic distortion of a quotation attributed to Confederate Civil War general Nathan Bedford Forrest.

35. The first "complete" edition of the *Chronicles*, including "The Fire Balloons" (from *The Illustrated Man*) and "The Wilderness" (from *The Golden Apples of the Sun*) was the 1964 Time trade paperback special edition.

36. Before publishing this story, Bradbury adapted it for *The Twilight Zone* as "I Sing the Body Electric!" (broadcast May 18, 1962).

37. From the *Rubáiyát of Omar Khayyám*, quatrain LI, FitzGerald translation (1859).

38. On May 13, 1962, Bradbury and Rod Serling participated in a science fiction panel discussion held at the Seattle World's Fair.

39. Bradbury read and corrected galleys for *Something Wicked This Way Comes* during the last week of April 1962. In an April 21 letter, Bradbury asked that the title page lettering be redesigned to resemble the eerie whirlwind lettering of Gray Foy's dust jacket art.

40. A phrase resurrected from Bradbury's amateur anecdote "Mathematical Minus" (*Imagination* 1:10, July 1938), a parody of John Russell Fern's "Mathematica" and "Mathematica Plus," where Bradbury notes "Mr. Darwin wrote: The bones of the head are frontal, backal, sidal, topal, and bottomal."

41. The prominent French theater talent Jean-Louis Barrault's production was finally ready to open in the spring of 1968, but student activists used his Orpheum Theater as a headquarters during the student riots; the *Martian Chronicles* set was heavily damaged, and the Orpheum was permanently closed by the French government.

42. Lillian de la Torre, "Nightmare Unlimited," *New York Times Book Review* (November 4, 1962).

43. [unsigned], "Books Briefly Noted," *New Yorker* vol. 38 (October 27, 1962).

44. Orville Prescott, "Books of the Times," *New York Times* (September 19, 1962): 37.

45. Robert Bloch recommended *The Circus of Dr. Lao* to Bradbury in 1947; Bradbury's expressed distaste for it suggests that he had some familiarity with the contents around that time. For the most part, after 1944, Bradbury only read science fiction and fantasy published by mentors or good friends.

46. After the Ninth Circuit Court of Appeals 1961 decision in favor of Bradbury, CBS gave notice to file with the US Supreme Court. When Bradbury and his lawyers announced that they would also file, CBS settled in August 1961.

47. Pulitzer Prize–winning historian Arthur Schlesinger was the cultural advisor to President Kennedy and a fan of Bradbury's fiction; George Stevens Jr., another fan, was film and television director for the US Information Agency. The White House screening of *Icarus* occurred on Monday, October 30; the Cuban Missile Crisis prevented Kennedy from attending.

48. Thank God.

49. Bradbury, "Cry the Cosmos," *Life* magazine (September 14, 1962).

50. Bradbury did not share Nolan's enthusiasm; "Time Intervening" was dropped from the contents.

51. Published as "Bright Phoenix"; the evolving draft titles (1947–1950) had been "Tiger, Tiger" and "Burning Bright," both from the first line of William Blake's "The Tiger." Bradbury's famous Book People first surface in this story.

52. Joseph Mugnaini painted a collage of Bradbury's literary creations for the May 1963 special issue cover.

53. Bradbury, "To the Chicago Abyss," *Magazine of Fantasy & Science Fiction* (May 1963); collected by Bradbury in *The Machineries of Joy* (1964).

54. Bradbury, "The Vacation," *Playboy* (December 1963).

55. The W. C. Fields anecdote became lecture and essay material, but not a published poem.

56. Bradbury, "The Whole Town's Sleeping," *McCall's* (September 1950), subsequently revised and bridged (untitled) into *Dandelion Wine* (1957).

57. Bradbury accepted the second of these scanning suggestions for "Remembrance."

58. The musical *Dandelion Wine* opened as scheduled in early March on the Cal State Fullerton campus. Bradbury's stage production of *Leviathan '99* was delayed until late November 1972.

59. To open the volume, Nicholas used the early *Dark Carnival* (1947) versions of "The Night" and six tales later revised for *The October Country* (1955).

60. Brackett collaborated with William Faulkner and Jules Furthman on the screenplay of *The Big Sleep* (Warner Brothers, 1946), featuring Bogart and Bacall.

61. Ten Bradbury stories were rejected by *The New Yorker* even before the 1947 sale of "I See You Never." His only other *New Yorker* sale was his nostalgic science fiction essay "Take Me Home," published on June 4, 2012—the day before Bradbury passed away.

62. Bradbury began work on *Somewhere a Band Is Playing* in the late 1950s.

63. *One More for the Road* (New York: Avon, [April] 2002); *Let's All Kill Constance!* (New York: Avon, [December] 2002).

64. Neither of these Bradbury scripts were ever produced.

65. Bradbury, "Cities on the Moon," *Playboy* (January 2000).

66. Revised from "West of October," first published in Bradbury's collection *The Toynbee Convector* (1988); originally composed as "Trip to Cranamockett," 1946.

67. Bradbury settled on Peter, William, Philip, and Jack.

7: AGENTS

1. Philadelphia fan Milton A. Rothman (1919–2001). Asimov, like Pohl, had started out as part of the Futurian fan and writer group in New York.

2. This Queens-based faction of New York fans was opposed to the Futurians and blocked most of the membership from participation in the 1939 first WorldCon.

3. During 1939 and 1940, Bradbury published four issues of the fanzine *Futuria Fantasia*. The art of Hannes Bok, and the pro authors who contributed material, helped make it one of the better fanzines of the period. The Brooklyn-based Futurian group of fans included writers and editors John B. Michel, Robert A. W. Lowndes, Isaac Asimov, Donald A. Wollheim, Doris Baumgardt (writing as Leslie Perri), Frederik Pohl Jr., and, for a time, Damon Knight.

4. Bradbury's bus journey home included a visit to San Francisco's Golden Gate International Exposition.

5. Schwartz sold "Pendulum" on July 18, 1941, to *Super Science Stories* (November 1941).

6. By February 1940 Pohl was editor of *Super Science Stories* and *Astonishing Stories*.

7. Possibly "The Hunt," "Levers," or "Shut the Door—It's Coming Through the Window" (all unlocated). Pohl apparently rejected these, and "Pendulum."

8. "One Timeless Spring," *Collier's* (April 13, 1946); "Invisible Boy," *Mademoiselle* (November 1945).

9. Schwartz made "The Piper" sale in December 1941 to *Thrilling Wonder Stories* (February 1943).

10. Bradbury's Arkham House contract for *Dark Carnival* (1947) gave August Derleth 50 percent on subsequent reprint sales for the individual stories.

11. As editors with All-American Comics, Schwartz and Mort Weisinger convinced several science fiction and fantasy writers they had known or represented in the genre pulps to write stories for various comic book serial superheroes. These friends included Otto Binder, Manley Wade Wellman, Henry Kuttner, and Alfred Bester. Bradbury declined the offer.

12. Williamson, "Cold Front Coming," *Blue Book* (June 1945).

13. Francis T. Laney was a contemporary of Bradbury's in the Los Angeles chapter of the Science Fiction League, later the Science Fantasy Society.

14. Bradbury's "The Watchers," *Weird Tales* (May 1945) was anthologized in *Rue Morgue No. 1* (1946).

15. After *Astounding*'s John W. Campbell had turned down "Rocket Summer," a story about a fabricated first lunar expedition, Malcolm Reiss of Fiction House bought it for *Planet Stories* (Spring 1947).

16. "The Irritated People," *Thrilling Wonder Stories* (December 1947), a satirical tale using weaponized broadcasts of irritating mass media shows to attack an enemy.

17. Bradbury's outline for "Riabouchinska" was adapted for radio and broadcast on *Suspense* (CBS), November 13, 1947; the better-known story version, "And So Died Riabouchinska," was eventually published in *The Saint Detective Magazine* (June–July 1953). "The Baby" was sold, as "The Small Assassin," to *Dime Mystery* (November 1946).

18. The postwar British science fiction magazine *New Worlds* (1946–1959) was edited by Ted Carnell.

19. Campbell rejected "The Children's Hour." It was published in *Planet Stories* (Fall 1947) as "Zero Hour."

20. Editor Mike Tilden, a good friend of Schwartz, had bought a number of Bradbury stories for *Dime Mystery* and other Popular Publications detective pulps, but Bradbury was beginning to pull away from the genre.

21. Although Harper's failed to pick up on Bradbury's idea for multi-author Martian anthologies, in a few short years Bradbury would be able to select and edit *Timeless Stories for Today and Tomorrow* (Bantam, 1952), featuring previously published science fiction and fantasy stories by mainstream authors who rarely wrote in these areas. These included such authors from his initial concept as John Steinbeck and Walter van Tilburg Clark.

22. Bradbury's earlier cross-country bus and rail trip placed him in New York from June 8 to 19, 1949, where he and Congdon made a two-book deal with Doubleday's Walter Bradbury.

23. "Interval in Sunlight" was finally published in *Esquire* (March 1954).

24. A package of the stories that would become *The Golden Apples of the Sun* (New York: Doubleday, 1953).

25. Edgar Allan Poe, "The Sleeper" (1831).

26. Henry James, "The Art of Fiction" (1884), and elsewhere.

27. Bradbury, "Touch and Go," *Detective Book* (Winter 1948); reprinted *Ellery Queen Mystery Magazine* (January 1953) (collected by Bradbury as "The Fruit at the Bottom of the Bowl," in *The Golden Apples of the Sun*).

28. Spanish philosopher José Ortega y Gasset (1883–1955); British historian Arnold Toynbee (1889–1975).

29. "The Day After Tomorrow: Why Science Fiction?" *The Nation* (May 2, 1953).

30. Ian Ballantine's editor-in-chief Stanley Kauffmann, who worked directly with Bradbury on proof corrections of *Fahrenheit 451* in Los Angeles during August 1953.

31. Ballantine Books publisher Ian Ballantine and editor Stanley Kauffmann, who published both *Fahrenheit 451* (1953) and *The October Country* (1955) under combined hardbound and paperback contracts.

32. For many years Don Congdon negotiated Bradbury's British editions with the A. D. Peters Agency in London. With A. D. Peters's assertion that Bradbury would be "the ideal choice to do the screenplay," *1984*'s producer, Peter Rathvon, gave Bradbury serious consideration until Bradbury himself declined.

33. Despite ongoing negotiations with Bradbury's Hollywood agent, Ben Benjamin, the need to defer to autumn led Oscar-winning director William Wyler to select Michael Wilson to script *The Friendly Persuasion*. Bradbury's voluntary hiatus from screenwriting lasted another two years.

34. Bradbury, "Marvels and Miracles—Pass It On!," *New York Times Magazine* (March 20, 1955).

35. Published as "Tread Lightly to the Music," *Cavalier* (October 1962). Collected as "Getting Through Sunday Somehow," *Long After Midnight* (New York: Knopf, 1976).

36. Published as "Summer in the Air," *Saturday Evening Post* (February 18, 1956).

37. The J. Walter Thompson Advertising Agency developed the *Kraft Television Theatre* for NBC, where the program ran from 1947 to 1958.

38. Robert Alan Aurthur wrote for both CBS Television's *Studio One* and NBC's *Goodyear Television Playhouse*; a deal for *Fahrenheit 451* failed to materialize, but Aurthur's subsequent script for "A Sound of Different Drummers" (CBS, *Project 90*) led to Bradbury's *Fahrenheit 451* lawsuit, which was settled after a US Court of Appeals decision in Bradbury's favor.

39. Bradbury and his film agent Ben Benjamin were actively marketing *Report from Space*, a television series of selected *Martian Chronicles* story-chapters. Kirk Douglas and his Bryna productions showed great interest, but it was never produced. Stuart Scheftel, grandson of Macy's cofounder Isador Straus, may have also considered the *Martian Chronicles* television venture; Bradbury met Scheftel and his wife, acclaimed actress Geraldine Fitzgerald, during a transatlantic voyage earlier that summer.

40. "Lime Vanilla Ice" was first published as "The Swan," *Cosmopolitan* (September 1954); this story and "The Magical Kitchen," *Everywoman's* (February 1954), as "Dinner at Dawn," became untitled chapters of *Dandelion Wine* (1957).

41. Bradbury used the pressure of the October 1957 launch of *Sputnik* to lobby Doubleday for a new hardbound edition of *The Martian Chronicles*. Doubleday declined to re-set type for a new edition, but the 1958 reissue had a new dust jacket and a preface by Clifton Fadiman.

42. Science fiction editors Ted Dikty and Everett Bleiler, who had included a Bradbury story in their best science fiction anthology of 1949.

43. For years, Reed attempted to secure backing for *And the Rock Cried Out*, but neither this script, nor Bradbury's script for *The Dreamers*, was ever produced.

44. During the fall and winter of 1953–54, Bradbury and his family took lodgings at the Royal Hibernian Hotel in Dublin. Several times a week he commuted out to Courtown House, the manor leased by John Huston west of Dublin near Kilcock, to review his work with Huston on the *Moby Dick* script.

45. Ingo Preminger, agent-brother of film producer Otto Preminger.

46. Paul Wellman's *Jericho's Daughters* (1956) and Edna Ferber's Alaskan novel *Ice Palace* (1958) were both heavily promoted mainstream novels published by Doubleday.

47. Hollywood agent Ben Benjamin.

48. Acting on a suggestion by Jack Guss, a longtime member of Bradbury's informal writers group, he combined the characters of Mr. Ellis, the eccentric but wise library custodian, and Charles Halloway, Will's father, in the third draft of the novel.

49. In mid-June 1961 Bradbury sent a letter to John Ciardi withdrawing from the Bread Loaf writing faculty due to extended commitments at MGM.

50. "The Anthem Sprinters" short story was published as "The Queen's Own Evaders," *Playboy* (June 1963).

51. *Elmer Gantry* won three Academy Awards, including Best Screenplay for Brooks. By early summer 1961, MGM had decided against developing the *Martian Chronicles* project beyond Bradbury's submitted screen treatment.

52. Bradbury was scripting Stanley Ellin's "The Faith of Aaron Menefee" for *Alfred Hitchcock Presents* (aired January 30, 1962).

53. The University of Southern California, where Esther McCoy, his good friend and a prominent historian of architecture, lectured.

54. The off-Broadway run of the three one-acts at the Orpheum, delayed until October 1965, would be canceled after the first weekend due to bad reviews and other factors beyond Bradbury's control.

55. Congdon's gift to Bradbury may have been *The Complete Work of Michelangelo* (NY: Reynal, 1965).

56. The prominent Hollywood filmmaking team of producer Alan Pakula and director Robert Mulligan.

57. Bradbury, *Pillar of Fire and Other Plays* (New York: Bantam, 1975).

58. In spite of these conversations, the Marceau stage adaptations were never developed.

59. Canadian-based Atlantis was the lead consortium partner, along with USA Network (all but HBO's season 1) and the partnership of actor-producer Larry Wilcox and Martin Leeds. Associate producer and show runner Tom Cotter was on location in New Zealand.

60. Published and recorded prior to its inclusion in the 1940 MGM film *Lady Be Good*; composed by Jerome Kern with lyrics by Oscar Hammerstein II.

61. NBC Radio's *Shell Chateau*, hosted by Al Jolson in 1935 and 1936, included appearances by operetta, musical, and film composer Sigmund Romberg, whose work had helped to establish Jolson's recording career. During one broadcast, Jolson playfully stepped down into the audience and tried to put on Bradbury's roller skates.

8: WAR AND INTOLERANCE

1. Bradbury's "The Big Black and White Game," a story exploring racial intolerance as seen from a young boy's perspective, was published in the August 1945 issue of *The American Mercury*. The 1950 sale of *The American Mercury* led to a deeply conservative shift in the magazine's editorial position, prompting Bradbury to turn away from that market.

2. "The World the Children Made," *Saturday Evening Post* (September 23, 1950); collected as "The Veldt" in *The Illustrated Man* (1951).

3. "The Flying Machine," based on a legend of ancient Chinese imperial tyranny in suppressing the invention of a flying machine and killing the inventor, was first published in *The Golden Apples of the Sun* (1953).

4. Two members of Bradbury's writing group, founder Dolph Sharp and Wilma Shore, had been members of *California Quarterly*'s editorial board.

5. Bradbury eventually relented and allowed publication of "Death in Mexico" in *California Quarterly* 3:2 (1954).

6. "Christmas on Mars" was sold to *Esquire* in the early 1950s, but it was never published.

7. Bradbury sent "The Strawberry Window" to publisher Ian Ballantine for the Ballantine Books paperback anthology, *Star Science Fiction Stories 3* (1954).

8. Portions of the Illinois novel became the novelized story cycle *Dandelion Wine*.

9. The Committee for a SANE Nuclear Policy, founded 1957. After merging with the Nuclear Weapons Freeze Campaign (1987), the organization became Peace Action (1993).

10. Bradbury refers to the long-range Jupiter missiles and their nuclear warheads, placed on American installations in 1959 and removed as a result of the Cuban Missile Crisis negotiations.

11. The noted portrait photographer and artist Yusuf Karsh, who in later life would photograph Ray Bradbury.

12. The New York World's Fair, where Bradbury's narration would form a major part of the United States Pavilion experience.

13. SRA's reading comprehension card sets were widely used in schools; the SRA book in question is unknown.

14. Kirk refers to the April 1967 reading performances of the *Dandelion Wine* musical at Lincoln Center in New York.

15. The Kirk Center for Cultural Renewal is in the village of Mecosta, Michigan; Ferris State is located in Big Rapids, the Mecosta County seat.

16. Scholastic Book Services sent the text of the letter to Bradbury; it was from an elementary school in Allendale, Michigan, and read in part: "To me this was a disgrace to send a book like this to fourth graders. I showed it to other teachers in my building and they wouldn't have it in their rooms. I burned it."

9: RECOGNITION

1. Events at the Century 21 Exposition in Seattle (April to October, 1962) included a May 13 science fiction panel featuring Bradbury and Rod Serling. As it turned out, the president was represented at the National Conference on Space by Vice President Johnson.

2. The White House screening of *Icarus Montgolfier Wright* occurred on October 25, 1962, for many staff members; President Kennedy, involved in the final negotiations of the Cuban Missile Crisis, was unavailable.

3. The Royal Court Theatre project eventually failed to materialize.

4. The books and letters are featured in https://jfk.blogs.archives.gov/2017/08/22/the-most-interesting-writer-about-the-future/ by Stacey Flores Chandler.

5. Marshall Smith, onetime sports editor at *Life* magazine.

6. The 1992 presidential candidate debates took place on October 11, 15, and 19, shortly after President George H. W. Bush's note to Bradbury.

7. Art historian Dr. Anne-Imelda M. Radice.

10: FRIENDS

1. Bradbury refers to Robert A. Heinlein, who had found major market success with *Scribner's* magazine.

2. "The Long Years," *Maclean's* (September 15, 1948), was revised for *The Martian Chronicles* (1950).

3. "The Meadow," ABC Radio *World Security Workshop*, January 2, 1947; *The Best One-Act Plays of 1947–48* (New York: Dodd, Mead, 1948).

4. Ackerman occasionally agented stories in foreign markets, including a few of Bradbury's in the 1940s Mexican pulps.

5. The family of Mary Perkins sailed from Bristol, England, aboard the *Lyon* in 1631; her future husband, Thomas Bradbury, arrived in Massachusetts several years later.

6. Nolan's index of Bradbury published stories and reprintings appeared in his privately published *Ray Bradbury Review* (1952).

7. Two versions of "Here There Be Tygers" reached print; the final version appeared first, in the anthology *New Tales of Space and Time* (New York: Holt, 1951). An earlier version was subsequently published in *Amazing Stories* (April–May 1953).

8. Milo Frank, one of Bradbury's film agents at the Famous Artists Agency in Los Angeles, provided the question that sparked the idea for "Here There Be Tygers."

9. Orville Prescott, *New York Times* (October 21, 1953); Prescott coined the often-repeated but controversial declaration that Bradbury was "the uncrowned king of the science-fiction writers."

10. In America (but not in Great Britain), the *Fahrenheit 451* first edition included both of these stories.

11. Peter Viertel and Huston were not able to complete this script; *The Man Who Would Be King* was finally produced under Huston's direction in 1975, with a Gladys Hill script.

12. Folk singer and actor Burl Ives's 1948 hit "Blue Tail Fly" (with the Andrews Sisters).

13. "No Man Is an Island" (1953) was privately printed by the Los Angeles chapter of Brandeis University's National Women's Committee and did not appear in *The Nation*.

14. Shore's husband, television and film writer and producer Lou Solomon.

15. Writer, music journalist, and composer Elliott Grennard, for a time part of the Los Angeles writing group.

16. H. G. Wells, *The Shape of Things to Come* (1933, filmed as *Things to Come* [1936]), epitomized Bradbury's fears and hopes for the future.

17. The National Institute of Arts and Letters was preparing a grant citation for Bradbury's achievements in literature.

18. Milton R. Stern, "The Whale and the Minnow: *Moby Dick* and the Movies," *College English* 17:8 (May 1956). Stern criticized Bradbury's decision to resequence certain scenes to generate "a fast-paced narrative."

19. Bradbury, "Not Child Enough," the *Nation* (June 28, 1958). His reference to *Mutiny on the Bounty*'s Captain Bligh alludes to Charles Laughton's famous portrayal of Bligh in the 1935 film.

20. Tibbetts, "The Happiness Machine," a paper delivered at the Buster Keaton Festival, Iola, Kansas, September 2004.

21. "Banshee" first aired February 22, 1986, on the HBO cable TV channel. Kilbracken had read an early version of the script and provided advice on the mythology of the Banshee in a letter to Bradbury dated February 7, 1983.

22. *Green Shadows, White Whale* (NY: Knopf, 1992).

23. Godley's good friend Derek "Deacon" Lindsay, author of the bestselling 1958 novel *The Rack* (published as by A. E. Ellis). Lindsay befriended Bradbury in both Dublin and London.

24. On November 8, 1953, Bradbury and his family arrived for a weekend visit to Lord Kilbracken's Irish estate, Killegar. Bradbury's youngest daughter and her governess saw Killegar's ghost lady in the guest quarters.

25. Bradbury, *The Anthem Sprinters and Other Antics* (New York: Dial, 1963), containing four Irish plays.

11: FAMILY

1. Leland Hayward (1902–1971) was in the final years of his marriage to film and stage star Margaret Sullavan (1909–1960).

2. A Canadian remedy for seasickness and other motion-triggered illness, manufactured in Quebec during the 1930s and 1940s.

3. As Bradbury finished his first full read-through of *Moby Dick* in preparation for his screenwriting assignment with John Huston, the SS *United States* encountered the most powerful hurricane that the ship had ever logged at sea.

4. Mrs. Walter Huston was probably his fourth wife, Ninetta (Nan) Sunderland Huston (1898–1973). John Huston's mother, Rhea Gore Huston, had died in 1938.

5. Bradbury's evening with Lord and Lady Russell occurred on April 8, 1954. In preparation, he read two slim volumes of science fiction stories that Russell had published the year before. However, Russell was more interested in learning how Bradbury had been able to work with the demanding John Huston in adapting *Moby Dick* to film.

6. Nurrie was a nanny, sitter, and occasional cook for the Bradbury children during the 1950s.

7. "The Wonderful Death of Dudley Stone," *Charm* (July 1954); "The Swan," *Cosmopolitan* (September 1954); "They Knew What They Wanted," *Saturday Evening Post* (June 26, 1954).

8. Bradbury declined Wyler's offer to adapt Jessamyn West's *The Friendly Persuasion*.

9. The Bradburys' third daughter Bettina was only two years old that summer.

10. The Technicolor production of *The 7th Voyage of Sinbad*, with special effects by Harryhausen, who would soon move to England permanently.

11. Before leaving Los Angeles, the Bradburys had hired Polly Jesse as a governess for their three daughters throughout the trip.

12. "The Day It Rained Forever," *Harper's* (July 1957).

13. Leo Bradbury had been hospitalized for two weeks with appendicitis and undetected peritonitis, a complication that may have contributed to his subsequent stroke.

12: REFLECTIONS

1. Bradbury met novelist Carson McCullers and *New Yorker* cartoonist Sam Cobean during his September 1946 trip to New York. In 1953, Reeves McCullers committed suicide in Paris, apparently by means of a sleeping pill overdose.

2. British stage and Hollywood film director James Whale, who constructed a miniature stage plan for the futuristic light operetta Bradbury had created for their mutual friends, Charles Laughton and Elsa Lanchester, "Happy Anniversary 2116."

3. The very popular Mexican actress Pina Pellicer starred in the *Alfred Hitchcock Hour* NBC television adaptation of Bradbury's Mexican story, "The Life Work of Juan Diaz," broadcast October 26, 1964. Pellicer committed suicide just several months later on December 4, 1964.

Index

Page numbers in **boldface** refer to letters between Bradbury and the subject. From page 469 on, page numbers refer to notes.